D0732414

HOW THE US CREATES
"SH*THOLE" COUNTRIES

HOW THE US CREATES "SH*THOLE" COUNTRIES

edited by
Cynthia McKinney

CLARITY PRESS, INC

© 2018 Cynthia McKinney

ISBN: 978-0-9998747-1-4

EBOOK ISBN: 978-0-9998747-2-1

In-house editor: Diana G. Collier

Cover: R. Jordan P. Santos

Names: McKinney, Cynthia, 1955- editor.

Title: How the US creates "sh*thole" countries / [edited] by Cynthia McKinney.

Description: Atlanta, GA. : Clarity Press, Inc., 2018. | Includes
      bibliographical references and index.

Identifiers: LCCN 2018032527 (print) | LCCN 2018034208 (ebook) | ISBN
      9780999874721 | ISBN 9780999874714 (alk. paper)

Subjects: LCSH: Developing countries--Foreign relations--United States--21st
      century. | United States--Foreign relations--Developing countries--21st
      century. | United States--Emigration and immigration--Government policy. |
      United States--Politics and government--2017- | Imperialism.

Classification: LCC D888.U6 (ebook) | LCC D888.U6 M35 2018 (print) | DDC
      327.7301724--dc23

LC record available at https://lccn.loc.gov/2018032527

Clarity Press, Inc.
2625 Piedmont Rd. NE, Ste. 56
Atlanta, GA. 30324 , USA
http://www.claritypress.com

TABLE OF CONTENTS

| FOREWORD |

A PEACE MOVMENT WHOSE TIME IS NOW

Senator Mike Gravel

I am a peace activist. And when given the option, every time my vote will be for peace. That's why in 1971, after serving in our country's military, I used the power of my position as a United States Senator from Alaska to block renewal of the draft, filibustering—alone—against legislation to renew it. My filibuster lasted five months, eventually resulting in the end of the military draft in the U.S.

At the time, the U.S. was involved in a war in Vietnam—not to support the liberation of the Vietnamese people from colonialism, but to extend their servitude to America instead of to France. Despite my service in the military—and perhaps because of it—I knew in my heart that the U.S. needed to be on the side of self-determination. Just as our Founding Fathers in the U.S. chose their right of self-determination—so too, should other countries around the world, including Vietnam, be able to do. Subjugating and oppressing the people of Vietnam, in my opinion, is not what the U.S. military should be used to do.

It was this kind of thinking that led me to do, in the U.S. Senate, something I've also become well-known for: releasing all 4,100 pages of the Pentagon Papers to the U.S. public by inserting each and every page into the Congressional Record. Every Member of Congress can release official documents to the public during the course of official business. I used this prerogative to release the Pentagon Papers because the people of the U.S. had and have the right to know how their tax dollars are being used. The people of the U.S. have a right to know what their military is doing in far off lands. And the Pentagon Papers, first disclosed by whistleblower Daniel Ellsberg, told us more than we wanted to know about the crimes that our country committed in the prosecution of the Vietnam War. "The only thing worse than soldiers dying in vain is more soldiers dying in vain." And our soldiers were dying in vain in Vietnam. Just like in Iraq. And everywhere else our soldiers are deployed, like in Niger, that don't make them safe and make all of us more unsafe. What on heaven's earth is our country's military doing in Niger right now?

Back in 1971, I was not afraid to take a stand for peace—alone. But, this time, I am not alone. This book demonstrates that something new is happening in our country when known activists and professors from the populist left to the populist right and everything in between are able to come together and provide invaluable research about the effects of U.S. wars around the world—both on us and on our victims. This book represents a departure in that from left to right and everything in-between, we now take a stand against war—together. We are ready to emerge from the fabricated and sometimes real ideological silos constructed for us to state categorically our opposition to the current U.S. wars around the world. So, Cynthia and these Contributors seized this important political moment to concretize how pervasive anti-war sentiment is throughout U.S. public opinion.

I am proud of the anti-war legacy that I left in the U.S. Congress. I only wonder where is the Mike Gravel of today in that body?

I have since begun to question the very nature of the U.S. political system that allows policies to be made that clearly do not represents the wishes or the outcomes desired by the electorate. Can we really believe that, if U.S. citizens only knew, they would agree to their government debasing and ruining defenseless third world countries for the enrichment of a few corporations, many of whom pay minimal or no taxes in the US and don't manufacture their products here?

China is moving its citizens out of poverty while U.S. citizens fall deeply into poverty. China is building roads and bridges and railways while the U.S. policy makers take our tax dollars and blow them up! There is something terribly wrong with a system that creates war as its energy and industrial policy, immigration as its labor policy, and debt as its investment policy. Somehow, the U.S. political system has inserted a banker between the student and his or her professor; an insurance bureaucrat between the doctor and his or her patient. The U.S. is seriously on the wrong track, and we need revolutionary political thought to come to grips with what we are presently doing in order to begin thinking about how to put us back on the right track.

It has been fifty years since Dr. Martin Luther King, Jr., a national leader who had focused, just like me, on the abomination that the Vietnam War made the U.S. become, said that the U.S. needed a revolution in values. Perhaps this book is the opening salvo in a heightened public consciousness that seeks to outweigh all of the other real and fabricated divisions that divide us. One thing is for sure, as long as we are divided, the War Party will win.

That the contributors in this book have been able to come together has been no easy feat. Let me repeat: bringing the Contributors together in this book was not an easy feat. But, I believe finding ways to reconcile the disparate political views of the American people is a necessary feat if We the People are ever going to defeat the U.S. Deep State War Party. I believe this book might just be the revolution of understanding and values that we need at this time and that Dr. King so eloquently stated as he articulated a pro-peace, anti-war politics.

Get ready to have some of your cherished ideas challenged by some of the Contributors. I found its reading to be very much like a roller coaster ride: sometimes fast, sometimes curvy, sometimes wild, sometimes even lifting me out of my seat, sometimes quiet—never boring, and always exciting for what might come next. This book begins the conversation that we need to have as a country—inside the United States—about what our values really are, and who our policies really benefit and hurt. Consider this: despite the purported right-left split, I enjoyed reading the works selected and edited by former Congresswoman and 2008 Green Party nominee, Cynthia McKinney—while I was running in that same year for the Libertarian nomination for President. There is so much that we can find to agree on.

I hope you won't just stop at reading these chapters. My hope is that you will also be motivated to join the values revolution that this book represents and work in your community to make peace a reality: within you, first and foremost, and then by reaching out to others who are not like you, but who share your concern for your community, state, and eventually for our country and our world.

Finally, I cannot let this moment with you pass without sharing my thoughts on another one of our transformational leaders slain just weeks after Dr. Martin Luther King, Jr. I'm referring to Bobby Kennedy who was surely on his way to the U.S. Presidency. In one of his many acts of braveness, he ventured to apartheid South Africa and, speaking to the privileged Whites in that country, said the following:

> Each time a man stands up for an ideal, or acts to improve the lot of others, or strikes out against injustice, he sends forth a tiny ripple of hope, and crossing each other from a million different centers of energy and daring those ripples build a current which can sweep down the mightiest walls of oppression and resistance.

Let the ripples of the values revolution begin! I hope that this book will become like a rock in the water, creating ripples for justice and peace during the Donald Trump Presidency. Join with us and let's improve America—together!

| INTRODUCTION |

A DEEPER LOOK AT TRUMP'S EPITHET, "SH*THOLE" COUNTRY

Cynthia McKinney

I wish I could take full credit for the idea of doing a book on President Trump's unfortunate characterization of some countries as "shithole" countries (verified recently by fired ex-White House staffer, Omarosa Manigault). The idea was brought to me by a Facebook friend and I immediately saw the brilliance of the idea! Although, at the time, the President tried to walk back the revelation that he used such language to describe certain countries, he couldn't help himself and during the visit of Nigeria's President at the White House, he doubled down on the characterization saying that certain countries were "tough" places to live. It was only recently that Omarosa confirmed that yes, the President had described certain countries as "sh*thole" countries.

The media had a field day with the at-that-time "alleged" remarks. Steve Dempsey of the Bay Area News Group compiled a slideshow of cartoons from national news outlets that lambasted the President. *The Mercury News* online ran the slide show that included hilarious[1] cartoons by Rick McKee at the Augusta Chronicle and Bob Englehart with Cagle Cartoons, and others. Mark Schuller, writing in the *Huffington Post*, noted:

Haiti has been targeted for its decisive role in challenging what Southern planters—including eight U.S. Presidents—called a 'peculiar institution.' The Haitian Revolution was the first time slaves were able to permanently end slavery and forge an independent nation. It also was a tipping point in U.S. history, leading to the 1803 Louisiana Purchase, paving the way for U.S. "Manifest Destiny" stretching from sea to shining sea and eventual dominance. Chicago, the country's third largest city, was founded by a Haitian, Jean Baptiste Point du Sable, who Haitian historian Marc Rosier called an 'agent' of the Haitian government to pursue a pro-freedom international policy.[2]

Jen Kirby went further and in an online media outlet *Vox* interview with a Stanford University history professor the word "eugenics" was used as a descriptor for what Trump's characterization actually represented. Stanford Professor Ana Minian said in the interview: "What he [Trump] said was basically a form of eugenics — in which he's saying, 'This is the population we want: people from places like Norway.' White people. We don't want people from African countries or from Haiti. That's what's really symbolic here." Minian makes it clear that in the US immigration debate, "legality" became a proxy for race without talking overtly about it.

Ryan Teague Beckwith and Maya Rhodan of *Time Magazine* added their two cents' worth to the discussion of the President's choice of words by choosing to discuss the immigration laws that occasioned Trump's telling words.[4] They began their discussion this way: "President Donald Trump's 'sh*thole countries' comments ricocheted around the world, spurring criticism from U.S. allies, rebuttals from Americans with roots in those countries and condemnation from some in his own party."

Reaction was swift from around the world, including from those countries so characterized by the President. Zambia even humorously featured Trump's words in a tourism advertisement and appeal. My Facebook friend thought that the President's words should occasion a deeper look at what these so-called "sh*thole" countries were, how they were created, and why they continue to exist. And that is exactly what the contributors in this book do. Sort of like the proverbial turtle sitting on the fence post—you know these countries didn't get the way they are without some help. And it is precisely that help, from the US, its allies, its multinational corporations, its military, and United Nations peacekeeping operations in Haiti and Democratic Republic of Congo which it also controls, on which this book focuses. Thus, the US relationship to conditions in those countries is clear from US military occupation of Haiti, financing of death squads in El Salvador, and support for dictators in all of them, indeed all over the African Continent. Therefore, for our purposes, a "sh*thole" country is a country whose residents' present quality of living conditions can be tied to historical or current US foreign and military policies that have negatively impacted the ability of that state to deliver quality of life policies to its residents. In this regard, for too many US residents, the Unites States, itself, can also be characterized as a "sh*thole" country, resulting from its deliberate choice to fund the war machine and corporate policies that produce negative consequences for the countries and territories, in some cases colonies, that are profiled here. The United States as itself a "sh*thole" country could be explored in much depth in future efforts.

The characterization of certain countries as "sh*thole" countries has captured the imagination of the global community, whether the localities and individuals concerned are for or against US President Donald J.Trump. This book seizes this unique moment, when attention of people inside and outside of the US is focused on the President's alleged words, to explain the structure of international politics, the conditions inside certain countries, specific US policies that created or maintain those conditions, and the consequences of those policies on US residents themselves. Policies, unfortunately, that US residents pay for, but about which they know very little. This book seizes this moment to dismantle with evidence and facts an official narrative justifying US wars against the world, destroying whole countries in the process.

How the US Creates Sh*thole Countries, then, should be construed as a shot across the bow at the US war party. The authors come from all walks of life, every angle of the political spectrum: some of them held high positions in government, including at the United Nations; some of them taught or teach at prestigious universities; some of them are in forced exile because of their political beliefs and the exercise of their Constitutional rights; some of them have spent time in prison because they acted on their beliefs; one of them sacrificed the limbs on his body because of his beliefs. All of them act on conscience. And every one of them is a hero. This book presents new analyses of old narratives that wither under scientific scrutiny and calls for a new, innovative vision for US policy created by courageous leadership, like that shown everyday by the contributors to this book.

ENDNOTES

1   Steve Dempsey, "Cartoons: Donald Trump and his 'Shithole countries' Comment," *The Mercury News* January 16, 2018 located at https://www.mercurynews.com/2018/01/16/cartoons-donald-trumps-shithole-countries-comment/ accessed June 5, 2018.

2   Mark Schuller, "What is a 'shithole country,' and why is Trump obsessed with Haiti?" *Huffington Post*, January 13, 2018 located at https://www.huffingtonpost.com/entry/what-is-a-shithole-country-and-why-is-trumpobsessed_us_5a5a6837e4b01ccdd48b5ce5 accessed on June 5, 2018.

3   Jen Kirby, "'What he said was basically a form of eugenics': a professor on Trump's 'shithole countries' remarks: A historian helps explain how the president's rhetoric reaches back to the time of racial immigration quotas," Vox, January 12, 2018 located at https://www.vox.com/2018/1/12/16882498/trump-shithole-countries-immigration-quotas-eugenics accessed on June 5, 2018.

4   Ryan Teague Beckwith and Maya Rhodan, "Here's the Plan Trump Was Attacking When He Said 'Shithole Countries,'" *Time Magazine*, January 12, 2018 located at http://time.com/5101057/donald-trump-shithole-countries-tps-daca/ accessed one 5, 2018.

TOWARD AN UNDERSTANDING OF U.S. FOREIGN POLICY

2017, A YEAR OF OVERT IMPERIALISM —AND 2018?

Alberto Rabilotta

The agitated year 2017 left us with decadent imperialism making a pathetic strip-tease—the National Security Strategy[1]—in order to reveal itself without embellishment and to generate fear. This augurs for 2018 being increasingly chaotic and dangerous, though full of possibilities for societies and countries that are defending themselves, or should do so, from the destructive policies of neoliberal totalitarianism.

Shortly before Christmas and evoking a "political realism" worthy of the Cold War, President Donald Trump revealed his National Security Strategy (NSS) designed to retrieve the supremacy of the "unipolar world order" and to continue to subjugate the greater part of the world. And (half-jokingly) he made it clear that from now on the traditional imperialist stick is fully real and could even become nuclear, while the carrot will continue to be completely virtual.

Dimitri Peskov, spokesman of the Kremlin, declared that: *"Looking through [the strategy], particularly those parts concerning our country, one can see the imperial nature of the document, as well as persistent unwillingness to abandon the idea of a unipolar world and accept a multipolar world";* while the Secretary of the Russian Security Council, Nikolay Patrushev, noted that behind the images of "aggressive

States", as Washington describes them, are the real economic interests and the same expansionist positions that were present during the Cold War and that have not changed for decades (*Tass*, 26-12-2017).

For their part, the official Chinese news agency *Xinhua*, pointed out that to speak of the "Chinese threat" has for a long time now been a strategy which confused ideologists have resorted to so as to attract attention; but that these affirmations are clearly out of date and reflect a zero sum game outlook and a Cold War mentality (*Xinhua*, 28-12-2017).

One positive outcome is that no one can now be—or claim to be—incredulous, since the NSS definitively throws the pretenses of the "birthplace of democracy" into the garbage-bin of history. This is the country that sowed military dictatorships with the goal of "defending democracy and the State of liberal law" from the "communist threat" represented by the Soviet Union. That created the "Alliance for Progress" to prevent the example of the Cuban Revolution from demonstrating the way to reclaim national and popular sovereignty to the peoples of the Caribbean and Latin America. And of course, it invented the perverse disguise of "humanitarian intervention" in order to dismember and destroy nations, following the breakup of the Soviet Union: a historic event to which Washington actively contributed, and which enabled them to establish a unipolar international order, in an attempt to make Russia become just one more vassal; moreover an almost totally disarmed one, as evidenced by recently revealed official documents.[2]

The grand imperialist project was (I put this in the past tense because it is no longer advancing and even many who support it recognize it is dying): to create an "international order" dominated by Washington to subject the whole world to their utopian "neoliberal globalization." Basically this was nothing more than demanding the application and respect of US laws—to consecrate definitively their extraterritorial reach that Washington had always claimed—in order for the signatory countries of free trade agreements to surrender their national and popular sovereignty. They were also required to disarm their societies in the face of the increased power of "self-regulating markets": that brutal force of globalized capital, concentrated in the hands of transnational companies and Wall Street, with the Pentagon playing the role of gendarme.

A recent book by Fritz R. Glunk[3] outlines the "socially destructive course" of a system dominated by transnational interests at the service of capital, in which the state "no longer makes the decisions, it just mediates" and the resulting legal realm is "independent of democratic rights as we know them and without state participation (or even its legitimacy)."

Academic analyst Carlos Fazio[4] cites US professor Robert Bunker, of the Strategic Studies Institute of the US Army War College, according to whom the "winners of globalization"—represented by multinational corporations and the transnational capitalist class—are seeking to withdraw from the regulatory, taxation and even the political authority of states. Meanwhile, they use their coercive instruments—the armed, police and espionage forces, as well as the Executive, Legislative and Judicial powers— to transform and instrumentalize them in their favour.

Now that it is decadent and with ever fewer allies (and some of them, such as Israel and Saudi Arabia, so uncontrollable and thuggish that it would be better not to have them as such), imperialism speaks in its own name to regroup and unite the internal forces (because their society is frankly fractured) and the external forces (which are not abundant, as the voting in the General Assembly of the UN indicates). To this end, the NSS states that this offensive will reestablish a

> strategy that sets a positive strategic direction for the United States that will restore America's advantages in the world and build upon our country's great strengths. (…) We will rebuild America's military strength to ensure it remains second to none. (…) We will ensure the balance of power remains in America's favor in key regions of the world: the Indo-Pacific, Europe, and the Middle East.

And if the Latin American hemisphere does not appear among the "key regions of the world", maybe this is because Washington thinks that it is able to maintain the rightward push and the subjugation that it has achieved through "soft *Coups d'État"*, such as the juridical-media conspiracy in Brazil, electoral fraud, as in Honduras, or—as has already occurred in some countries and clearly in Mexico—putting an end to the liberal State of law that sustained the "bourgeois democracy", and establishing the State of permanent exception alongside the totalitarianism of neoliberal globalization.

What is the Reason for the Blunt Speaking by the NSS?

The NSS explains it thus: the objective is to restore *"America's advantages in the world and build upon our country's great strengths"*, or in clear terms, put an end to the threat to this unipolar and neoliberal "order", represented by the defined enemy: *"Revisionist powers, such as China and Russia, that use technology, propaganda, and coercion to shape a world antithetical to our interests and values"*.

After these "revisionist powers" that clearly constitute the much-needed principal enemy, the NSS identifies as threats *"regional dictators that spread terror, threaten their neighbors, and pursue weapons of mass destruction."*

In order to clear up any doubts and to put the hypocrisy of Washington in its place, it is worth recalling that the "regional dictators" (Iran and North Korea) are forged by the US with its fusillade of sanctions, attempts at regime change and disregard of laws and international treaties (as in Iran) and threats of mass destruction, even with nuclear power, as in North Korea. In the case of Iran, a country that respects international laws—which is not the case of Israel, for example—it would be sufficient to recognize, instead of repudiating, the international treaty that put an end to the Iranian nuclear program with potential to develop an atomic weapon, which the other signatories—Great Britain, Germany, France, Russia and China, and the agency that controls its application—the UN International Atomic Energy Agency—all consider that Teheran is respecting.

In the tragic and dangerous case of North Korea, it would be enough for Washington to put an end to its policy in the Korean peninsula, unchanged since 1950 when it divided the peninsula and launched a war against the communists, destroying the infrastructure and the economy of that country, and causing millions of deaths. That would mean withdrawing its forces and military bases from South Korea—that also serve to control the seas and skies of the Far East—ceasing threats and application of sanctions, and accepting a fair process of negotiation that would allow the denuclearizing of Pyongyang and leaving the Koreans of North and South to decide the future of the peninsula.

Next, the NSS names as a threat the *"Jihadist terrorists that foment hatred to incite violence against innocents in the name of a wicked ideology, and transnational criminal organizations that spill drugs and violence into our communities"*.

Here the hypocrisy reaches its pinnacle. The intellectual author of the creation of these jihadists, Zbig. Brzezinski himself (National Security Counsellor from 1977 to 1981 and known ideologue of the strategies of subversion) recognized that the jihadists and other terrorists were created by Washington and its allies, as from the 1970s, in order to bog down and destroy the USSR in Afghanistan. Since then they have served and continue to serve—as in Syria—to destabilize and thus control or destroy countries of the Middle East and Central Asia. These jihadists of the Islamic State, that the US is now removing from Syria to prevent them from destroying the Syrian army, will in the future be utilized by Washington in other countries, perhaps against Iran.

On the drug traffickers, official documents, already made public, confirm that the CIA created drug trafficking to finance counterrevolutionary operations in Indochina and later in Central America. At the internal level, drugs—and in particular the "crack" of the 1980s—enabled the US government to profoundly damage the social structure of Afro-American communities,[5] and to fill the prisons with young Afro-Americans and Latinos. For decades, the violence and corruption associated with drug trafficking has served the Pentagon to destabilize many Latin American societies and thus introduce a policy of militarization of the struggle against violence, as a step towards the installation of US military bases or posts, so as to reinforce the military-political control of the region, and that serves to justify, as recently in Mexico, the adoption of a permanent State of exception.[6]

Both the jihadists and the drug traffickers are a potential threat to societies throughout the world. In the former case, there is already a successful experience of how to fight against them and defeat them through military assistance agreements, political and diplomatic collaboration, respecting national sovereignty of the country under attack by terrorists, as is the case of Syria, where the success was not due to the US and their "international coalition", but to the collaboration of Russia, Iran and Turkey with the Syrian government and army, and to the solid process of negotiations among the parties in conflict so as to create the bases of a social pacification, and of a political exit created by the Syrians themselves.

On the other hand, it is known that the struggle against violence and corruption that comes with drug trafficking should not be considered exclusively as a matter for the police—and even less the military—but as a complex social, political and economic problem. The struggle against drug addiction and to reduce illegal drug trafficking can take on different forms, but the worst of these has been that of the United States, where it caused severe damage in Afro-American communities and has only served to fill (privatized) prisons with millions of youths[7] who are utilized practically as slave labour by private enterprises. They are thus doubly alienated and it will be difficult for them someday to become responsible citizens.

The Struggle of Chaos Against Stability, or of Big Capital Against Society

Yet the most significant and important part of the NSS strategy concerns what it describes as Russia and China "revisionists": What is it that Russia and China are "revising"? What they are "revising"—or rather "refusing"—is the unipolar order and neoliberal globalization that has enabled the US to dominate the world, launch wars, encircle Russia militarily, apply commercial, financial and economic sanctions in order to deindustrialize and undermine the societies of many countries, and disregard with complete impunity international laws and agreements, thus weakening international institutions, and the UN in particular, in order to continue to sow chaos throughout the world.

The "mortal" sin of Russia has been that President Vladimir Putin began more or less a decade ago to challenge the neoliberal order so as to defend society from the destructive effects of policies implanted by the globalization of the Yeltsin era. In other words, Putin began the task—as he himself pointed out—of *reconstructing and consolidating* society and the economy that had suffered an unprecedented destruction in times of peace after the *coup d'état* of Boris Yeltsin which dismantled the Soviet Union and ransacked state enterprises and the wealth of the country, condemning millions of Russians to unemployment and destitution. In concrete terms, because he recalls the history of Russia, Putin has returned to the policy of defending national sovereignty and of "state intervention" in economic and social affairs, not excluding sectorial or branch planning.

In the case of the People's Republic of China, the "mortal" sin is promoting the policy of maintaining a Socialist State directed by the Communist Party that preserves national sovereignty and conserves the power of final decision-making with the objective of ensuring social stability—a fundamental pillar, since the revolution, to confront the enormous challenge of raising the living standards of the most numerous national population on the planet—and framing in these terms the economic opening where state enterprises along with private and mixed national and foreign companies participate. It goes without saying that these policies reflect cultures, political experience and ways of being and organizing that are very ancient, because fortunately the Chinese do not forget their history.

"Really existing" imperialism and capitalism cannot ignore the challenge implied by the fact that Russia and China have united forces to create development policies and economic growth at a regional level—within "the silk road" and bilaterally—and that a growing number of countries have joined or are in the process of joining this important regional dynamic. In any case, and to confirm this reality (and perhaps give a response to the NSS), 2017 ended with the Chinese President, Xi Jinping, stating that he is *willing to join with his homologue of Russia, Vladimir Putin, to consolidate mutual political and strategic confidence and to expand the integral pragmatic cooperation between the two countries* (*Xinhua 31-12-2017*).

This not only further weakens neoliberal globalization, but strengthens the national economies involved, as well as the multilateral and regional process. It explains why both nations have created, through this cooperation, a "zone of stability" and of predictability regarding international relations and trade, economic and monetary relations. This in turn strengthens the struggle for a multipolar system based on mutual respect among nations, in contrast to the unpredictable policy of chaos and destabilization of the US and some of its allies. This in practice will contribute to preventing the US from recreating a unipolar world.

Since few new things occur in history, it is worth recalling a premonitory text of Karl Polanyi, that dates from 1945,[8] entitled "Universal Capitalism or Regional Planning?", in which he warned that the US would by definition continue being the "home" of a liberal capitalism sufficiently powerful to promote for itself the utopia of restoring a liberalism such as that of the 19th century, "a universality that engages those who believe in it to reconquer the globe". In contrast to this utopian project, Polanyi pointed out, was the promising regional planning of a regional dimension of the USSR.

The "regional planning" of the *"zone of stability"* will be constructed through the logic of "pragmatic cooperation" in the project shared by Russia and China. This already includes several countries and is sufficiently attractive to have led to the establishment—at the end of last December and at the level of Ministers of Foreign Relations—of the "Pakistan, Afghanistan and China dialogue,"[9] which, in addition to seeking peace for Afghanistan under the motto "peace process directed by Afghanistan and property of Afghanistan," opens the way to incorporate Afghanistan and Pakistan into the "silk road" project. It goes beyond saying that if this Russian-Chinese initiative develops as foreseen, incorporating Iran, Syria and other countries of the Middle East and Central Asia, it will be, as Brzezinski would have said, the final defeat of the ambition of global supremacy of Washington.

Meanwhile, any neutral observer can see that the role of Russia in Syria to combat the jihadists—thanks to the persistent and efficient diplomacy of Moscow, with respect to Syrian sovereignty and regional multilateralism. Moreover, the harmful influence of the powers of the empire—the USA, England and France—is vanishing in thin air in the face of the "security and respect for commitments" that Russia irradiates, an additional aspect of great political importance of the "zone of stability".

This is why the policies of Russia and of China do not go unnoticed in countries that, being part of the Middle Eastern conflict— and feeling they are in the losing camp—have strengthened relationships with Moscow and Peking (Turkey) or are seeking to strengthen them (Saudi Arabia, Afghanistan, Pakistan and some countries of the Persian Gulf, and also of Africa).

This struggle between "imperialist chaos and revisionist stability", following the reasoning of the NSS, constitutes the most relevant aspect of present international politics and will have a direct influence on national social struggles insofar as chaos represents the destructive force of globalized capitalism, and stability an opportunity to organize the social forces to reconstruct societies on the basis of respect for national and popular sovereignty, in which society controls the economy, and not the contrary as with neoliberalism.

On the international plane, this "zone of stability" and of predictability could be the beginning of the construction of a multilateral order that respects the legitimate interests of countries, be they small, medium or large. Its influence in the Eurasian continent is unquestionable, and is now taking its first steps in Latin America—as we see in the support that Russia and China are providing for a besieged Venezuela, for Cuba under sanctions and for other countries—and in Africa.

ENDNOTES

1. The NSS text: https://www.whitehouse.gov/wp-content/uploads/2017/12/NSS-Final-12-18-20 17-0905.pdf
2. https://www.strategic-culture.org/news/2017/12/19/how-us-swindled-russia-early-1990s.html; Debt against nuclear disarmament: https://www.theguardian.comworld/2017/dec/29/john-major-soviet-debt-return-disarmament.
3. F. Glunk. "Shadow Powers: How transnational networks determine the rules of our world":https://sputniknews.com/analysis/201712291060412241-shadow-powers-international-networks-democracy/;https://www.elpais.cr/2017/12/29/como-amenazan-las-fuerzas-sombrias-a-las-democracias-occidentales/
4. Carlos Fazio. La insurgencia plutocrática y la LSI http://www.jornada.unam.mx/2017/12/31/opinion/016a2pol See also, Robert Bunker, Op-Ed: Not Your Grandfather's Insurgency–Criminal, Spiritual, and Plutocratic, *Strategic Studies Institute, February 20, 2014.*
5. http://www.finalcall.com/artman/publish/National_News_2/article_101888.shtml; http://theinfluence.org/how-ronald-reagans-drug-war-fueled-americans-addiction-to-racist-ideas/
6. Carlos Fazio, La Insurgencia Plutocrática y la LSI.
7. Of the 6.8 million people in the prisons of the US in 2014, 34% (2.3 million) were Afro-Americans, and 20% Latinos, in both cases mainly youths and people imprisoned for drug consumption. http://www.naacp.org/criminal-justice-fact-sheet/
8. Karl Polanyi, Universal Capitalism or Regional Planning? Published in January 1945 in *The London Quarterly of World Affairs.* In French it is included in the book Essais de Karl Polanyi, Editions du Seuil, pages 485 to 493.
9. About this meeting and its scope: http://spanish.xinhuanet.com/2017-12/27/c_136854838.htm; http://www.atimes.com/article/beijing-complicates-washingtons-afghan-strategy/; https://sputniknews.com/middleeast/201712261060326683-afghanistan-taliban-peace-talks/; https://sputniknews.com/middleeast/201712271060356882-china-afghanistan-terror-fight/

TRUMP'S 'NEO-NEOCON' DEEP STATE

Wayne Madsen

Donald Trump represents Version 2.0 of the same neoconservative crowd that dominated the George W. Bush administration. The cabal of pro-corporation, xenophobic, and nationalistic right-wingers, which includes such outliers as the alt-right—a less-threatening title than white nationalist, neo-Nazi, or Ku Klux Klan—are now in the driver's seat in Washington. Trump is nothing more than a corporate trademark or logo for what can be called the "neo-neocon" movement, which is led by individuals who have long been embedded in the US intelligence community, law enforcement, media, and military.

Many of the neo-neocons in the Trump administration entered the political scene by infiltrating supposed "populist" groups like the Republican Tea Party and other right-wing movements. Among these are Secretary of State Mike Pompeo and Trump's former chief campaign advisers and strategists Steve Bannon and Corey Lewandowski. Others are long-time players in neocon politics, who have operated under the umbrella of Christian evangelical, Zionist, and neo-confederate organizations. These include National Security Adviser John Bolton, Bolton's National Security Council chief of staff Fred Fleitz, and National Security Council official John Hannah. The one common denominator between all these neo-neocon players is that their ultimate financing comes from dubious corporations, hedge funds, and international criminal syndicates, including what the Federal Bureau of Investigation refers to as the "Eurasian Mafia." These corporations and syndicates have been the source of revenue for the massive electoral psychological operations campaigns conducted by Cambridge Analytica; Cambridge's parent company, Strategic Communication Laboratories (SCL); Karl Rove's Deep Root Analytics; Trump 2020 campaign manager Brad Parscale's Giles-Parscale of San Antonio, Texas; and such chapeau companies as Facebook and Twitter. All of these neo-neocon deep state operations are now being exposed thanks to the investigations being conducted by Department of Justice Special Counsel Robert Mueller's team and the Democratic minority staff of the House Intelligence Committee.

Perhaps no Trump administration official represents the neo-neocon deep state more than the president's director of the Central Intelligence Agency, Gina Haspel. Very little is publicly known about Haspel, a long-time CIA clandestine operations officer, who joined the agency in 1985. Haspel is known in the CIA as "Bloody Gina," a reference to her involvement in developing and carrying out the CIA's "enhanced interrogation" program of torturing extraordinarily-renditioned detainees in such gulags as Guantanamo Bay, Cuba and a secret "black site" in Thailand code-named "Cat's Eye." Haspel served as Cat's Eye's chief of base (COB) before serving as the CIA's chief of station twice in London, where she developed a close relationship with current British Prime Minister, Theresa May, the former Home Secretary, who was then in charge of the domestic Security Service (MI-5). Haspel and May share the same birthday, October 1, 1956. Haspel also enjoyed close working links with the British Secret Intelligence Service (MI-6).

After Trump's first choice to head the CIA, former Kansas Republican Representative Mike Pompeo, a member of the Kansas Tea Party, took over the reins at Langley, he appointed Haspel to be his deputy director. In 2013, CIA director John Brennan, another architect of the CIA's kidnapping and torture program, named Haspel as the CIA's director of the National Clandestine Service. Although Brennan has been an ardent critic of Trump, he has no problem with Haspel being named as the CIA's first female director. Haspel and Brennan are merely two sides of the same neo-neocon deep state coin. In 2005, Haspel actually violated federal court orders when she ordered a dozen court-subpoena videotapes—depicting torture sessions, including waterboarding, at the

Cat's Eye site in Thailand—to be destroyed. Haspel ordered the tapes be removed from a classified safe at the CIA station at the US embassy in Bangkok and destroyed.

Nevertheless, House Intelligence Committee chairman Devin Nunes, one of many neo-neocon deep state operatives serving in Congress, said of Haspel's nomination to be CIA director, "Gina has worked closely with the House Intelligence Committee and has impressed us with her dedication, forthrightness, and her deep commitment to the intelligence community. She is undoubtedly the right person for the job." Nunes hails from a family that originally emigrated to California from the Azores. Nunes was born in California in 1973. In 1974, wealthy Azorean-American families like the Nunes's were relied upon by the CIA to support the Azores independence movement, which was an attempt by Langley to pry the islands, host of an important US military base, away from a new post-fascist government of socialists and communists that took power in Portugal.

Donald Trump has praised the CIA's enhanced interrogation program and has stated he wants the level of torture increased. Such policies are welcomed by the neo-neocon deep state. CIA torture programs, although eschewed by such presidents as Gerald Ford, Jimmy Carter, Ronald Reagan, and Bill Clinton, were restored by George W. Bush and abandoned by Barack Obama. Under Trump, these policies have been resurrected and supplemented by new methods, some of which were developed over decades and were originally based on research conducted by the Nazis and Japanese in World War II and later by the CIA's MK-ULTRA and MK-NAOMI projects in test programs conducted in veterans hospitals, mental clinics, the Special Operations Division (SOD) at Fort Detrick in Frederick, Maryland, and South Vietnamese prisoner-of-war camps. Haspel also served as the CIA's chief of station in New York, a facility that mainly targets the United Nations. While in New York, Haspel worked closely with the Israeli Mossad station, which operates under the official cover of the Israeli Consulate-General. Although little is known about Haspel's religious preference, the name Haspel is a common Ashkenazic Jewish Yiddish and German surname, which means "reel," as in that used in weaving.

Haspel has also worked as a CIA clandestine services agent in Turkey, Singapore, Ethiopia, and Central Asia. Haspel is seen as working closely, for the past year, with her former boss, Pompeo. Pompeo's political campaign was funded by the right-wing Koch Brothers and Mitt

Romney's Bain Capital—major financiers of the neo-neocon deep state. Trump's son-in-law Jared Kushner, is a virtual White House "enforcer" for the neo-neocons who support Israel at all costs. The neo-neocon deep state is supplemented by the US ambassador to the UN, Nikki Haley, Treasury Secretary Steve Mnuchin, Interior Secretary Ryan Zinke, and Environmental Protection Agency Administrator Scott Pruitt (since replaced, but what about Andrew Wheeler?), the latter rumored to be a Trump favorite to replace Attorney General Jeff Sessions.

The neo-neocon deep state has its sights set on Special Counsel Mueller, just as it targeted FBI director James Comey and his deputy, Andrew McCabe. These neo-neocons are led by war-hawk Bolton as National Security Adviser. Previously, Bolton was the only unconfirmed ambassador to have ever served as US ambassador to the UN. In a Sept. 3, 2017, Fox News interview, Bolton declared that the only option left to address the North Korean nuclear challenge is "to end the regime in North Korea" and strike first. His early action included nearly sinking a projected Trump-Kim Jong Un June 2018 Summit, having previously torpedoed relations with North Korea under George Bush.

Trump and Africa

What was lost on the corporate media's coverage of the sudden firing by Donald Trump of Secretary of State Rex Tillerson was that it was carried out while Tillerson was on an official trip to Africa to smooth over fractured relations stemming from Trump's referral to African countries as "shitholes" and his statement that Nigerians live in "huts." In fact, Tillerson was forced to cut short his trip while in Nigeria, where he was expected to apologize to Nigerian leaders for Trump's past racist statements.

Tillerson's visit to Africa had other priorities, in addition to apologizing for Trump's racist bluster. He warned the leaders of Ethiopia, Djibouti, Kenya, Chad, and Nigeria to be wary of expanding Chinese economic and military influence on the continent. African leaders, including those at the African Union headquarters in Addis Ababa, Ethiopia, basically told Tillerson that Africa's relationships with China or any other country was none of Washington's business.

While Tillerson was in N'Djamena, Chad, he had to explain to government leaders why Chad, a US ally in military operations against jihadist rebel groups, was included on Trump's US travel ban list.

Tillerson's trip was punctuated by his "taking ill" while in Kenya. We now know that Tillerson's "illness" was caused by a phone call from White House chief of staff John Kelly warning the Secretary of State that Trump was preparing to fire him via Twitter. The firing actually occurred while Tillerson was in the Nigerian capital of Abuja for what were to be two days of talks with President Muhammadu Buhari and his government.

That Trump fired Tillerson while he was on an official visit to Nigeria was not lost on the country where Trump suggested people live in "huts." Undersecretary of State for Public Diplomacy Steve Goldstein crafted a hasty announcement on Tillerson's early departure from Nigeria: "Due to demands in the Secretary's schedule, he is returning to the U.S. one day early, after concluding official meetings in Chad and Nigeria." Goldstein was fired by Trump shortly after Tillerson was sacked.

The Chinese news agency Xinhua weighed in on Trump's firing of Tillerson in the middle of the secretary of state's African tour, stating in a report: "Africa has been marginalized in the Trump administration's foreign policy, and the situation will likely remain so during his time in office." In fact, the Chinese are correct. After more than a year in office, Trump has not nominated an assistant secretary of state for Africa nor has he filled several vacant ambassadorships on the continent, including an ambassador to South Africa.

Trump's firing of Tillerson while in Africa enabled China to score the biggest propaganda coup imaginable, thanks to Trump's ability to damage, beyond repair, American foreign relations. The task of further unraveling US relations with the rest of the world will now be handed to Pompeo, who shares, in every way, Trump's record of racist dog-whistles and ignorant statements.

But what about Pompeo, Tillerson's replacement? Trump's pick to replace Tillerson, the former CEO of Exxon Mobil, is former Central Intelligence Agency director Mike Pompeo, previously a Republican congressman who, in a social media message, once referred to his Indian-American Democratic election opponent in Kansas as a "turban-topper." Kansas State Representative Ray Goyle's campaign responded, saying Pompeo's message went "beyond the rules of engagement in politics." Pompeo, a Kansas Tea Party activist who was funded by the billionaire Koch brothers, blamed the tweet on a campaign staffer.

Pompeo is also associated with the racist anti-Muslim group "ACT for America." One of Pompeo's first actions as Secretary of State was to haul out of retirement David Satterfield and appoint him acting Assistant Secretary of State for Near East Affairs. In 2005, Satterfield was identified by the FBI as an interlocutor in an Israeli espionage operation involving two American Israel Public Affairs Committee (AIPAC) officials and a Defense Intelligence Agency employee.

Trump and the Middle East

It was Israeli influence over his son in law, Jared Kushner, that helped lead to Trump's ill-advised decision to move the US embassy from Tel Aviv to Jerusalem. US intelligence sources also believe that Kushner, Friedman, and Greenblatt are funneling US intelligence to Las Vegas casino tycoon Sheldon Adelson, a chief financier of Trump's political campaign coffers and a close ally of Israel's scandal-plagued Netanyahu. Friedman represents another leaky-sieve ambassador to Israel for sensitive US intelligence being illegally handed over to the Israelis. Martin Indyk, Bill Clinton's ambassador to Israel, lost his security clearance after it was discovered he was transmitting classified information, including cryptographic material, to the Israeli government. It was the first and only time a US ambassador ever lost a security clearance.

Kushner has been a dream-come-true for Israel. Trump has carried out numerous Israeli wishes, including de-certification of the P5+1 Joint Comprehensive Plan of Action (JCPOA) with Iran over its nuclear power program, supporting Saudi actions against Qatar and Yemen, cutting off direct US aid to the Palestinian Authority and to the United Nations Relief and Works Agency (UNWRA), which assists Palestinian refugees, continuation of support to Israeli-backed jihadist rebel groups battling Syrian President Bashar al Assad, support for pro-Israeli Egyptian President Abdel Fattah al-Sisi's economic blockade of the Hamas government of Gaza, and freezing security assistance to Pakistan.

But there was more than just Kushner promoting Israeli interests inside the Trump campaign.

The discovery of an illegal $2.5 million money transfer from the United Arab Emirates via a murky Canadian company and Elliott Broidy, a Jewish Republican fundraiser convicted in 2009 for pension fraud, points to high-level Israeli intelligence penetration of the 2016 Donald Trump presidential campaign. The UAE financial transfer to Trump campaign coffers also involved the mysterious George Nader, a Lebanese-American lobbyist for the government of the UAE and its crown prince and *de facto* leader, Mohammed bin Zayed al Nahayan. The revelation of a joint UAE-Israeli intelligence operation to funnel illegal contributions to the Trump campaign also highlights the close relationship between Israeli intelligence and the intelligence service of the UAE, as well as that of the UAE's close ally, Saudi Arabia.

The current status of Nader, who agreed to become a witness for Department of Justice Special Counsel Robert Mueller, is not known. There are reports that he fled to the UAE. Nader was convicted in a Czech Republic court in 2003 of 10 counts of sexually abusing minors. In 1985, US authorities charged Nader with importing sexually explicit materials, including magazines and pictures that depicted "nude boys" and other materials showing boys "engaged in a variety of sexual acts." Nevertheless, Nader was the key conduit between the UAE and Broidy, a key leader of the strongly pro-Israel Republican Jewish Coalition and a backer of the neocon Hudson Institute and Foundation for the Defense of Democracies (FDD).

One of the founders of the FDD is former Senator and 2000 Democratic presidential candidate Joe Lieberman, who also happens to be a law partner of the Kasowitz, Benson, Torres and Friedman law firm, led by one of Trump's attorneys, Marc Kasowitz. The UAE contributions to Trump also reportedly played a major role in Trump taking the side of the UAE and Saudi Arabia in their diplomatic and economic conflict with Qatar. It is known that Israel, the UAE, and Saudi Arabia conspired to have House Foreign Affairs Committee chairman Ed Royce (R-CA) and key Trump administration officials brand Qatar as a terrorist-supporting state because of the presence in the Qatari capital of Doha of a large Iranian embassy, as well as diplomatic offices of Hamas, Lebanese Hezbollah, and the Afghan Taliban. In July 2017, After Royce introduced legislation branding Qatar a supporter of terrorism, Broidy funneled $5,400 to Royce's re-election campaign. Royce has since announced he would not seek re-election, an indication that the FBI told him they were pursuing an investigation that could lead to an indictment for campaign finance fraud.

Trump son-in-law Jared Kushner, his brother Joshua Kushner, and their father, Charles Kushner—convicted in 2005 on 18 federal counts of making illegal campaign contributions, tax evasion, and witness tampering—attempted in April 2017 to shake down the Finance Minister of Qatar, Ali Sharif Al Emadi during a meeting in New York. The Kushners insisted that El Emadi invest a half billion dollars in the "financially stressed," i.e., bankrupt, Kushner building at 666 Fifth Avenue in Manhattan. Joshua Kushner was also looking for Qatari investment in his and Jared's high-tech venture capital firm, Thrive Capital.

Broidy, who is married to a former senior executive of 21st Century Fox, which was, before its sale to Disney, a sister company of Fox News, was involved in a major pension fraud case in New York in 2009. Broidy pleaded guilty to a single federal count of attempting to provide "excessive gratuities" to former New York State Comptroller Alan Hevesi. These included luxury trips to Israel. In 2011, Hevesi, a Democrat, was convicted on corruption charges and served 20 months in federal prison.

Broidy also served as the Republican National Committee's Deputy Finance Committee chairman. He worked under casino mogul Steve Wynn, born Stephen Weinberg, who resigned earlier this year after being hit with a number of sexual assault charges. In 2012, Wynn blamed the failure to secure funding for a major Israeli-owned casino-hotel complex in Las Vegas, led by Israeli business tycoons Yitzhak Tshuva and Nochi Dankner, on President Barack Obama's "anti-business policies." Tshuva and Dankner bought the Vegas land for their proposed complex from Phil Ruffin, a Vegas real estate partner of Donald Trump.

Broidy was also involved in a shakedown of the government of Malaysia. Broidy reportedly assured Malaysia's then-Prime Minister Najib Razak that he could get the U.S. Justice Department to drop a probe of the Malaysian state investment fund 1MDB, which had siphoned off a $1 billion bribe of Saudi investment money to Razak and helped pave the way for a 2017 visit by Razak to Washington and a meeting with Trump at the White House. Broidy stood to make $75 million from the deal with Malaysia and Razak.

Broidy also arranged for the attendance of two Romanian Social Democratic Party politicians, both embroiled in scandal, to Trump's January 2017 inaugural in Washington. Liviu Dragnea, head of the Social Democratic Party and speaker of the lower house of the Romanian Parliament, and then-Prime Minister Sorin Grindeanu, were introduced by Broidy to Trump at a pre-inaugural banquet. In 2012, Dragnea was convicted in Romania for rigging votes in a national referendum to impeach the then-president. When he met Trump in 2017, Dragnea was due to go on trial for skimming $23 million from European Union contracts for the benefit of an organized criminal syndicate. Grindeanu was removed from office after his meeting with Trump. Grindeanu wanted to decriminalize the theft of state funds under $50,000. The Romanian criminal syndicate, which is linked to Israel, ensured that Dragnea backed moving the Romanian embassy in Tel Aviv to Jerusalem, the same extortion applied by Israeli mafia elements on Trump and the presidents of the Czech Republic, Guatemala, Honduras, and Paraguay.

In 2015, Broidy acquired a Fredericksburg, Virginia-based intelligence contractor, Circinus LLC. Circinus's active contract with the Army's Intelligence and National Security Command (INSCOM) that provided Broidy's Israeli intelligence colleagues an entree into the US intelligence infrastructure that was unmatched until Jared Kushner began demanding Top Secret/Special Compartmented Information (SCI) files on National Security Agency intercepts of key Saudi and Emirati government officials and businessmen. This intercept information was then provided to Saudi Crown Prince Mohammed bin Salman and UAE Crown Prince Mohammed bin Zayed for the arrest of several Saudi princes and Saudi and Emirati officials known to be in favor of withdrawing Gulf forces from Yemen, establishing closer relations with Iran, and freezing relations with Israel. INSCOM provides signals intelligence (SIGINT) feeds from Army ground and mobile stations to NSA intercept databases.

Broidy has ensured that Circinus gained a higher profile in Washington. In July 2017, Circinus began to be represented by the lobbying firm Fidelis Government Relations. Circinus has seen an increase in US intelligence contracts, as well as a $200 million sweetheart contract with Romania's state defense manufacturer, Romarm. One of Fidelis's two principals is Bill Smith, former chief of staff to Vice President Mike Pence. This connection represents the discovery of a first major link between Pence and the Israeli-Saudi-Emirati illegal campaign operations surrounding Trump and the Kushners.

The exposure of the Broidy connection to the UAE and previously-reported links of Blackwater mercenary firm founder Erik Prince to UAE influence operations within the Trump campaign have laid bare the close military and intelligence alliance that currently exists between Israel, the UAE, and Saudi Arabia. With pro-Israeli neocon John Bolton taking over the National Security Council, Israeli intelligence penetration of the White House will be complete. In many respects, the presence of neocons and "Kosher Nostra" criminal elements spells doom for the rule of law in the United States and makes America a vassal state of a global criminal enterprise.

THE END OF WASHINGTON'S "WARS ON THE CHEAP"

The Saker

With the Neocon coup against Trump now completed (at least in its main objective, the neutralization of Trump; the subsidiary objective, impeaching Trump and removing him from office, remains something for the future) the world has to deal, yet again, with a very dangerous situation: while the AngloZionist Empire is on a rapid decline, the Neocons are back in power in the United States, and they will do anything and everything in their power to stop and reverse this trend. It is painfully obvious from their rhetoric, as well as from their past actions, that the only "solution" the Neocons see is to trigger some kind of war. So the pressing question now becomes this: "Who will the Empire strike next?" Will it be the DPRK or Syria? Iran or Venezuela? In the Ukraine, maybe? Or do the Neocons seek war with Russia or China?

As all modern theories of deterrence imply a "rational actor" and not a crazy lunatic on a suicidal rampage, we will assume that there is a semblance of rational thinking left in Washington DC and that even if the Neocons decide to launch some clearly crazy operation, somebody in the top levels of power will find the courage prevent this, just like Admiral Fallon did it with his "not on my watch!"[1] which possibly prevented a US attack on Iran in 2007. So, assuming a modicum of rationality is still involved, where could the Empire strike next?

The Empire's Ideal Scenario

Here's the template for typical Empire action: find some weak country, subvert it, accuse it of human right violations, slap economic sanctions, trigger riots and intervene militarily in "defense" of "democracy", "freedom" and "self-determination" (or some other combo of equally pious and meaningless concepts). But that is only the "political recipe". What I want to look into is what I call "the American way of war", that is, the way US commanders like to fight.

During the Cold War, most of the US force planning, procurement, doctrine and training was focused on fighting a large conventional war against the Soviet Union and it was clearly understood that this conventional war could escalate into a nuclear war. Setting aside the nuclear aspect for a while (it is not relevant to our discussion), I would characterize the conventional dimension of such a war as "heavy": centered on large formations (divisions, brigades), involving a lot of armor and artillery. This kind of warfare would involve immense logistical efforts on both sides and that, in turn, would involve deep-strikes on second echelon forces, supply dumps, strategic axes of communications (roads, railways, bridges, etc.) and a defense in depth in key sectors. The battlefield would be huge, hundreds of kilometers on both sides of the FEBA (Forward Edge of Battle Area, or "front line"). On all levels, tactical, operational and strategic, defenses would be prepared in two, possibly three, echelons. To give you an idea of the distances involved, the Soviet 2nd strategic echelon in Europe was deployed in the Ukraine! (This is why the Ukraine inherited huge ammo dumps from the Soviet Union, and why there never was a shortage of weapons on any side for the conduct of the Ukrainian civil war.) With the collapse of the Soviet Empire, this entire threat to the West disappeared almost overnight. While the Gulf War provided the US armed forces and NATO one last, but big, opportunity to deploy their heavy weaponry (against an enemy which had absolutely no chance to prevail), soon thereafter it seemed pretty clear to US strategists that "heavy war" was over and that armored brigades might not be the most useful war-fighting tool in the US arsenal going forward.

This is when US strategists, mostly from Special Operation Forces, developed what I like to call "war on the cheap". It works something like this: first, get the CIA to fund, arm and train some local insurgents (if needed, bring some from abroad); next embed US Special

Forces with these local insurgents and provide them with FACs (forward air controllers, frontline soldiers specially trained to direct close-support fixed and rotary wing aircraft to strike at enemy forces in direct contact with US forces and their "friendlies"); finally, deploy enough aircraft in and around the combat zone (on aircraft carriers, in neighboring countries or even on seized local airstrips) to support combat operations day and night. The key notion is simple: provide the friendly insurgents with an overwhelming advantage in firepower. We have all seen this on YouTube: US and "coalition" forces advance until they get into a firefight and, unless they rapidly prevail, they call in an airstrike which results into a huge BOOM!!! followed by cheering Americans and friendlies, and the total disappearance of the attacked. Repeat that enough times, and you get an easy, cheap and rapid victory over a completely outgunned enemy. This basic approach can be enhanced by various "supplements" such as providing the insurgents with better gear (antitank weapons, night vision, communications, etc.) and bringing in some US or allied forces, including mercenaries, to take care of the really tough targets.

While many in the US armed forces were deeply skeptical of this new approach, the dominance of the Special Forces types and the at least temporary success of this "war on the cheap" in Afghanistan made it immensely popular with US politicians and propagandists. Best of all, this type of warfare resulted in very few American casualties and even provided them with a high degree of "plausible deniability" should something go wrong. Of course, the various three-letter spooks loved it too.

What so many failed to realize in the early euphoria about US invincibility was that this "war on the cheap" made three very risky assumptions:

First and foremost, it relied on *a deeply demoralized enemy* who felt that, like in the series "Star Trek", resistance to the Borg (aka the USA) was futile because even if the actual US forces deployed were limited in size and capabilities, the Americans would, no doubt, bring in more and more forces if needed, until the opposition was crushed.

Second, this type of warfare assumes that the US can get *air superiority over the entire battlefield*. Americans do not like to provide close air support when their aircraft can be shot down by enemy aircraft or missiles.

Third, this type of warfare requires the *presence of local insurgents* who can be used as "boots on the ground" to actually occupy and control territory.

We will now see that all three of these assumptions are not necessarily true or, more explicitly, that the AngloZionists have run out of countries in which these assumptions still apply. Let's take them one by one.

Hezbollah, Lebanon 2006

While this war did not officially involve the USA, it did involve Israel, which is more or less the same, at least for this particular discussion. While it is true that superior Hezbollah tactics and preparation of the battlefield did play an important role, and while it is undeniable that Russian anti-tank weapons gave Hezbollah the capability to attack and destroy even the most advanced Israeli tanks, the single most important development of this war was that, for the first time in the Middle-East, a rather small and comparatively weak Arab force showed no fear whatsoever when confronted with the putatively "invincible Tsahal". The British reporter Robert Fisk was the first person to detect this immense change and its tremendous implications:

> You heard Sharon, before he suffered his massive stroke, he used this phrase in the Knesset, you know, "The Palestinians must feel pain." This was during one of the intifadas. The idea that if you continue to beat and beat and beat the Arabs, they will submit, that eventually they'll go on their knees and give you what you want. And this is totally, utterly self-delusional, because it doesn't apply anymore. It used to apply 30 years ago, when I first arrived in the Middle East. If the Israelis crossed the Lebanese border, the Palestinians jumped in their cars and drove to Beirut and went to the cinema. Now when the Israelis cross the Lebanese border, the Hezbollah jump in their cars in Beirut and race to the south to join battle with them. But the key thing now is that Arabs are not afraid any more. Their leaders are afraid, the Mubaraks of this world, the president of Egypt, King Abdullah II of Jordan. They're afraid. They shake and tremble in their golden mosques, because they were supported by us. But the people are no longer afraid.[2]

This is absolutely huge and what the "Divir
the Party of God first achieved in 2006 is now be.
Syria, Afghanistan, Yemen, Iraq and elsewhere. The fear oɪ ˎ
superpower" is finally gone, replaced by a burning desire to settle ɑ.
infinite list of scores with the AngloZionists and their occupation forces.

Hezbollah also proved another very important thing: the
winning strategy when faced against a superior enemy is not to try to
protect yourself against his attacks, but to deny him a lucrative target. Put
simply: "a cammo tent is better than a bunker" or, if you prefer "if they
can spot you, they can kill you". The more academic way to put it would
be this: *"Don't contest your enemy's superiority—make it irrelevant"*.

Looking back it is quite obvious that one of the most formidable
weapons in the AngloZionist arsenal was not the nuclear bomb or
the aircraft carrier, but its propaganda machine which for decades
successfully convinced millions of people around the globe that the US
was invincible: the US had the best weapons, the best trained soldiers,
the most advanced tactics, etc. Turns out this is total nonsense—the
US military in the real world was nothing like its propaganda-world
counterpart: when is the last time the US actually won a war against an
adversary capable of meaningful resistance? The Pacific in WWII?

I chose the example of Hezbollah in 2006 to illustrate the
collapse of the "scared into surrender" paradigm, but the better, and
earlier, example to illustrate the "don't contest your enemy's superiority—
make it irrelevant" paradigm would be Kosovo in 1998-1999 when a
huge operation involving the entire NATO air forces lasted for 78 days
(the Israeli aggression against Lebanon lasted only 33 days) resulting in
exactly nothing: a few destroyed APCs, a few old aircraft destroyed on the
ground, and a Serbian Army Corps which was unscathed, which Milosevic
had ordered to withdraw for personal, political reasons. The Serbs were
the first to prove this "target denial" strategy as viable even against an
adversary with advanced intelligence and reconnaissance capabilities.

The Russian Task Force, Syria 2015

The Russian operation in Syria was not a case of "the Russians
are coming" or "the war is over". The reality is that the Russians sent in
a very small force and that this force did not so much defeat Daesh as
it changed the fundamental character of the political context of the war:
simply put—by going in, the Russians not only made it much harder

politically for the Americans to intervene, they also denied them the ability to successfully use their favorite "war on the cheap" paradigm against the Syrians.

When the Russians first deployed their task force to Syria they did not bring with them anywhere near the kind of capabilities required to deny the Americans the use of Syrian air space, were the full panoply of US and NATO air power to be brought against them. Even after the shooting down of the Russian SU-24 by the Turks, the Russians only deployed sufficient air-defenses and air superiority fighters to protect *themselves* from a similar attack by the Turks. Even as I write these words, if the USAF or USN decided to take control of the Syrian airspace they could undoubtedly do it simply because, in purely numerical terms, the Russians still do not have enough air defenses or, even less so, combat aircraft (a constantly changing mix of Su-27SM3, MiG-29SMT, Su-30M, Su-35S and Su-34, only a minority of which are composed of aircraft capable of air-to-air engagements), to deny the Syrian airspace to the Americans. While such a US attack would come at a very real cost for the Americans, both militarily and politically, the tiny Russian air contingent of 33 combat aircraft (and an unknown number of S-300/S-400/S-1 Pantsir batteries cannot possibly defeat the combined airpower of CENTCOM and NATO.

Rather, the problem for the Americans is formed by a matrix of risks which, of course, includes Russian military capabilities, but also includes the political risks of establishing a no-fly zone over Syria. Not only would such a move be another major escalation in the already totally illegal US intervention in this war, but it would require a sustained effort to suppress the Syrian (and, potentially, Russian) air defenses and that is something the White House is not willing to do right now, especially when it remains completely unclear what such a risky operation would achieve. As a result, the American strike here and there, just like the Israelis do, but in reality these efforts are pretty much useless.

But now the Russians are turning the tables on the Americans and providing *the Syrian forces* with FACs (Forward Air Control) and close air support, especially in key areas. The Russians have also deployed artillery controllers and heavy artillery systems, including multiple-rocket launchers and heavy flamethrowers, which are all giving the firepower advantage to the government forces. Paradoxically, it is the Russians who are now fighting a "war on the cheap" while denying this option to the Americans and their allies.

"Good" Terrorists, aka the Free Syrian Army, Syria 2017

The main weakness of the Free Syrian Army is that it does not really exist, at least not on the ground. While there are plenty of FSA Syrian exiles in Turkey and elsewhere, there are also plenty of Daesh/ al-Qaeda types who try hard to look like an FSA to suit the likes of John McCain, and there are a few scattered armed groups here and there in Syria who would like to be "the FSA". But in reality this was always an abstraction, a purely political concept, as the Pentagon was forced to admit to Congress, reporting the fruit of its extensive training as resulting in "four or five" actual fighters.[3] Nonetheless, this virtual FSA provides many useful things to the Americans: a narrative for the propaganda machine, a political ideal to try to unify the world against Assad and the Syrian government, a pious pretext to send in the CIA, and a small fig leaf to conceal the fact that Uncle Sam was in bed with al-Qaeda and Daesh. But what the FSA could never provide was "boots on the ground". All the other players had them: Daesh and al-Qaeda for sure, but also the Syrians, the Iranians and Hezbollah and, of course, the Turks and the Kurds. But since the Takfiris were officially the enemy of the USA, the US was limited in the scope and nature of the support given to them. The Syrians, the Iranians and Hezbollah had been demonized and so it was impossible to work with them as these had long been billed as the elements that "had to go". That left the Turks, who had terrible relations with the USA, especially after the US-backed coup against Erdogan, and the Kurds who were not too eager to fight and die deep inside Syria and whose every move was observed with a great deal of hostility by Ankara. Besides, the Kurds had little reason to trust American policy taking into account Kurdish interests.[4] As the war progressed the terrible reality finally hit the Americans: they had no "boots on the ground" to support, or with whom to embed their Special Ops.

The best illustration of this reality is the latest American debacle in the al-Tanf region near the Jordanian border. The Americans, backed by the Jordanians, quietly invaded this mostly empty part of the Syrian desert with the hope of cutting off the lines of communications between the Syrians and the Iraqis. Instead, the Syrians cut the Americans off by reaching the border first, thereby making the American presence simply useless. It appears that the Americans have now given up, at least temporarily, on al-Tanf, and that US forces will be withdrawn and redeployed elsewhere in Syria.

So Who Is Next—Venezuela?

A quick look back in history shows us that the Americans have always had problems with their local "allies" (i.e. puppets). Some were pretty good (South Koreans), others much less so (the Contras against Nicaragua), but all in all, each US use of local forces comes with an inherent risk: as in Afghanistan, the locals often have their own, sometimes very different, agenda and they soon come to realize that if they depend on the Americans, the Americans also depend on them. Add to this the well-known fact that Americans are not exactly known for their "multi-cultural sensitivity and expertise" (few of them even know the local language!) and you will see why US intelligence usually becomes aware of this problem by the time it is far too late to fix it (no amount of fancy technology can be substituted for solid, expert human intelligence). The reality is that Americans are typically clueless about the environment in which they operate. The US debacles in Syria, Libya, or the Ukraine, for that matter, provide excellent illustrations of this.

Now that we have identified some of the doctrinal and operational weaknesses of the US "war on the cheap" approach, let's apply them to a list of potential target countries:

Assumption	Demoralized enemy	Air superiority	Boots on the ground
North Korea	?	Yes	No
Syria	No	No	No
Iran	No	Yes	No
Venezuela	?	Yes	Yes?
Russia	No	No	No

Note: "Demoralized enemy" and "air superiority" are my best guesstimates; "boots on the ground" refers to an indigenous and combat capable force already inside the country capable of seizing and holding ground, and not just some small insurgent group or a political opposition, or a force brought in from outside.

If my estimates are correct, then the only candidate for a

successful US intervention would be Venezuela. However, what is missing here is the time factor: a US intervention, to be successful, would require a realistic exit strategy (the US is already overextended and the very last thing the Empire needs would be getting bogged down in another useless and unwinnable war à *la* Afghanistan.] Also, while I gave the Venezuelan opposition a tentative "yes" for its ability to bring "boots on the ground" into play (especially if backed by Colombia), I am not at all sure that the pro-American forces in Venezuela have anywhere near the capabilities of the regular armed forces (which, I believe, would oppose a US invasion) or the various Leftist guerrilla groups who tolerated the Chavez-Maduro rule but who have kept their weapons "just in case". Furthermore, there is the issue of terrain. While Caracas might be easy to seize in an optimistic scenario, the rest of the country would be difficult and dangerous to try to operate in. Finally, there is the issue of staying power: while Americans like quick victories, Latin American guerrillas have already proven many times over that they can fight for decades. For all these reasons, while I don't see the USA as capable of imposing a new regime in power and imposing their control over that country, I do think that the USA is capable of intervening in Venezuela and messing it up beyond all recognition, i.e. of creating yet another sh*thole country. Yet this is where the future of US interventions may lie: not in colonialism (the US has never been a "colonial" country for the simple reason that it has neither interest nor much by way of capacity in the many skills that would be required to manage one) nor even in client regimes (as abandoned in Iraq), but simply in complete and utter ruination of the rebellious state.

Conclusion: Afghanistan 2001-2017

Afghanistan is often called the "graveyard of Empires". I am not so sure that Afghanistan will ever become the graveyard of the AngloZionist Empire per se, but I do think that Afghanistan will become the graveyard of the "war on the cheap" doctrine, which is paradoxical since Afghanistan was also the place where this doctrine was first applied with what initially appeared to be a tremendous success. We all remember the US Special Forces, often on horseback, directing B-52 airstrikes against rapidly retreating Afghan government forces. Sixteen years later, the Afghan war has dramatically changed and US forces are constantly fighting a war in which 90% of the casualties come from IEDs, where all the efforts at some kind of political settlement have miserably failed and where both victory and withdrawal appear as completely impossible. The fact that now the US propaganda machine has accused Russia of "arming the Taliban" is a powerful illustration of how desperate the AngloZionists are. Eventually, of course, the Americans will have to leave, totally defeated, but for the time being all they are willing to admit is that they are "not winning".

The US dilemma is simple: while the Cold War is long over, and so is the Post Cold War, and a complete reform of the US armed forces is clearly long overdue, this is as yet also politically impossible. Right now the state of the US armed forces is the bizarre result of the Cold War, the subsequent "war on the cheap" years, and failed military interventions. In theory, the US should begin by deciding on a new national security strategy, then develop a military strategy in support of this national security strategy, followed by the development of a military doctrine which itself would then produce a force modernization plan which would affect all aspects of military reform from training to force planning to deployment. It took the Russians over a decade to do this, including a lot of false starts and mistakes, and it will take the Americans at least as long, or even more. Right now even the decision to embark on such a far reaching reform seems to be years away. For the time being, garden variety propaganda ("we're number one, second to none!!") and deep denial seem to be the order of the day. Just as in Russia, it will probably take a truly catastrophic embarrassment (like the first Russian war in Chechnya) to force the US military establishment to look reality in the eye and to actually act on it. But until that happens, the ability of US forces to impose their domination on those countries which refuse to surrender to various threats and sanctions will continue to degrade.

So is Venezuela next? I hope not. In fact, I think not. But if it is, it will be one hell of a mess with much destroyed and precious little achieved. The AngloZionists have been punching above their real weight for decades now and the world is beginning to realize this. Prevailing against Iran or the DPRK is clearly beyond the actual US military capabilities. Attacking Russia or China would be suicidal. Which leaves the Ukraine. But even if the US might send some weapons to the junta in Kiev and organize some training camps in the western Ukraine that would be about the extent of it. None of that will make any real difference.

The era of significant "wars on the cheap" is over and the world is becoming a very different place than it used to be. The USA will have to adapt to this reality, at least if it wants to retain some level of credibility, but right now it does not appear that anybody in Washington DC—except Ron Paul—is willing to admit this. As a result, the era of major US military interventions might well be coming to an end, even if there will always be some Grenada or Panama size country to "triumphantly" beat up, if needed. There are plenty of options for this in Africa, and here, many such efforts are already underway, but mainly low-key and via surrogates. This new reality immediately raises the issue of what will back the US Dollar in the future since in this, US military power has played a significant role.

ENDNOTES

1   See https://thinkprogress.org/centcom-commander-fallon-attack-on-iran-will-not-happen-on-my-watch-921d57aeb703/

2   Robert Fisk, Reports From Lebanon On the Intensifying Israeli Attack, Qana, Tony Blair and the Possibility of a Ceasefire, Democracy Now, August 1, 2006. https://www.democracynow.org/2006/8/1/robert_fisk_reports_from_lebanon_on

3   "US has trained only 'four or five' Syrian fighters against Isis, top general testifies" *The Guardian*, 6 September 2015. https://www.theguardian.com/us-news/2015/sep/16/us-military-syrian-isis-fighters

4   https://www.brookings.edu/blog/markaz/2017/11/02/masoud-barzani-and-the-roots-of-kurdish-distrust-of-the-united-states/

WESTERN WARS AND IMPERIAL EXPLOITATION UPROOT MILLIONS

James Petras

Imperial Wars and Mass Immigration

The US invasions and wars in Afghanistan and Iraq uprooted several million people, destroying their lives, families, livelihood, housing and communities and undermining their security. As a result, most victims faced the choice of resistance or flight. Millions chose to flee to the West since the NATO countries would not bomb their residence in the US or Europe. Others who fled to neighboring countries in the Middle East or Latin America were persecuted, or resided in countries too poor to offer them employment or opportunities for a livelihood. Some Afghans fled to Pakistan or the Middle East but discovered that these regions were also subject to armed attacks from the West. Iraqis were devastated by the western sanctions, invasion and occupation and fled to Europe and to a lesser degree the US, the Gulf states and Iran.

Libya prior to the US-EU invasion was a 'receiver' country accepting and employing millions of Africans, providing them with citizenship and a decent livelihood. After the US-EU air and sea attack and arming and financing of terrorist gangs, hundreds of thousands of Sub-Sahara immigrants were forced to flee to Europe. Most crossed the Mediterranean Sea to the west via Italy, Spain, and headed toward the affluent European countries which had savaged their lives in Libya.

The US-EU financed and armed client terrorist armies which assault the Syrian government and forced millions of Syrians to flee across the border to Lebanon, Turkey and beyond to Europe, causing the so-called "immigration crises" and the rise of rightwing anti-immigrant parties. This led to divisions within the established social democratic and conservative parties, as sectors of the working class turned anti-immigrant. Europe is reaping the consequences of its alliance with US militarized imperialism whereby the US uproots millions of people and the EU spends billions of euros to cover the cost of immigrants fleeing the western wars. Most of the immigrants' welfare payments fall far short of the losses incurred in their homeland. Their jobs homes, schools, and civic associations in the EU and US are far less valuable and accommodating then what they possessed in their original communities.

Economic Imperialism and Immigration: Latin America

US wars, military intervention and economic exploitation have forced millions of Latin Americans to immigrate to the US. Nicaragua, El Salvador, Guatemala and Honduras engaged in popular struggle for socio-economic justice and political democracy between 1960-2000. On the verge of victory over the landed oligarchs and multinational corporations, Washington blocked popular insurgents by spending billions of dollars, arming, training, advising the military and paramilitary forces. Land reform was aborted; trade unionists were forced into exile and thousands of peasants fled the marauding terror campaigns.

The US-backed oligarchic regimes forced millions of displaced and uprooted poor, unemployed and landless workers to flee to the US.

US supported coups and dictators resulted in 50,000 deaths in Nicaragua, 80,000 in El Salvador and 200,000 in Guatemala. President Obama and Hillary Clinton supported a military coup in Honduras which overthrew Liberal President Zelaya— which led to the killing and wounding of thousands of peasant activists and human rights workers, and the return of death squads, resulting in a new wave of immigrants to the US. The US promoted free trade agreement (NAFTA) drove hundreds of thousands of Mexican farmers into bankruptcy and into low wage maquiladoras; others were recruited by drug cartels; but the largest group was forced to immigrate across the Rio Grande.

The US "Plan Colombia" launched by President Clinton established seven US military bases in Colombia and provided 1 billion dollars in military aid between 2001-2010. Plan Colombia doubled the size of the military. The US backed President Alvaro Uribe, resulting in the assassination of over 200,000 peasants, trade union activists and human rights workers by Uribe-directed narco-death squads. Over two million farmers fled the countryside and immigrated to the cities or across the border. US business secured hundreds of thousands of Latin American low wage agricultural and factory workers, toiling almost all without health insurance or benefits—though they paid taxes.Immigration doubled profits, undermined collective bargaining and lowered US wages. Unscrupulous US 'entrepreneurs' recruited immigrants into drugs, prostitution, the arms trade and money laundering. Politicians exploited the immigration issue for political gain—blaming the immigrants for the decline of working class living standards and distracting attention from the real cause: wars, invasions, death squads and economic pillage.

Conclusion

Having destroyed the lives of working people overseas and overthrown progressive leaders like Libyan President Gadhafi and Honduran President Zelaya, millions were forced to become immigrants. Iraq, Afghanistan, Syria, Colombia, Mexico witnessed the flight of millions of immigrants—all victims of US and EU wars. Washington and Brussels blamed the victims and accused the immigrants of illegality and criminal conduct. The West debates expulsion, arrest and jail instead of reparations for crimes against humanity and violations of international law. To restrain immigration the first step is to end imperial wars, withdraw troops, and to cease financing paramilitary and client terrorists. Secondly, the West should establish a long term multi-billion-dollar fund for reconstruction and recovery of the economies, markets and infrastructure they bombed. The demise of the peace movement allowed the US and EU to launch and prolong serial wars which led to massive immigration—the so-called refugee crises and the flight to Europe. There is a direct connection between the conversion of the liberal and social democrats to war-parties and the forced flight of immigrants to the EU.

The decline of the trade unions and worse, their loss of militancy, has led to the loss of solidarity with people living in the midst of imperial wars. Many workers in the imperialist countries have directed their ire to those 'below'—the immigrants—rather than to the imperialists who directed the wars which created the immigration problem.

Immigration, war, the demise of the peace and workers movements and left parties has led to the rise of the militarists and neo-liberals who have taken power throughout the West. Their anti-immigrant politics, however, has provoked new contradictions within regimes, between business elites and among popular movements in the EU and the US. The elite and popular struggles can go in at least two directions—toward fascism or radical social democracy.

SOME VICTIMS TO REMEMBER (AND HOW THEY GOT THAT WAY)

HAITI

WHAT IS A "SH*THOLE COUNTRY" AND WHY IS TRUMP OBSESSED WITH HAITI?

Mark Schuller

On Thursday, the day before the eighth anniversary of the earthquake in Haiti that killed at least 230,000 people, President Trump called Haiti—as well as a single, undifferentiated "Africa"—"shithole countries."

Of course, the president's first impulse was to deny the statement, just as he had denied the statement made public through an anonymous source to the New York Times that "all Haitians have AIDS."[1]

Triggering the conversation is his administration's denial of Temporary Protected Status (TPS)[2] for 58,000 people from Haiti currently living in the US, some for as much as thirty years.[3]

His comments speak to the callous attitude of an individual that feels no accountability, who thinks he can rewrite history as is convenient. Senator Durbin (D-IL) confirmed that indeed 45 had spoken these "hate filled words"[4] many times in a conversation about immigration policy, which Trump has been actively sabotaging despite an apparent deal with Senator Jeff Flake (R-AZ) for his "yes" vote on Trump's tax plan.[5]

It would be unfortunate if the media were to exceptionalize Trump's comments as the latest gaffe from an individual too accustomed to bullying people on Twitter, recently claiming that his "nuclear button" is bigger than North Korea's. The comments are also indicative of an unchallenged white supremacy that has unfortunately been allowed to fester in our society. It is more useful to see this as an open expression of often hidden feelings, unresolved cultural aftershocks of the institution of plantation slavery that our nation has to deal with head on and with courage and honesty.

As Haitian literature professor Regine Jean-Charles has written, she was not surprised by the comments, as "evidence of a brand of racism that has always been present in US society, which since the 2016 campaign has been fanned into virulent flame."[6]

What is behind Trump—and white America's—obsession with Haiti?

Haiti has been targeted for its decisive role in challenging what Southern planters—including eight US Presidents—called a "peculiar institution." The Haitian Revolution was the first time slaves were able to permanently end slavery and forge an independent nation. It also was a tipping point in US history, leading to the 1803 Louisiana Purchase, paving the way for US "Manifest Destiny" stretching from sea to shining sea and eventual dominance. Chicago, the country's third largest city, was founded by a Haitian, Jean Baptiste Point du Sable, who Haitian historian Marc Rosier called an "agent" of the Haitian government to pursue a pro-freedom international policy.[7]

Haiti's contribution to US "greatness" has long been unacknowledged. The pivotal Haitian Revolution was literally "unthinkable," as Haitian anthropologist Michel-Rolph Trouillot argued.[8] The demonization of Haiti was so strong, its inspiration to slaves so dangerous, that Congress imposed a gag order in 1824, preventing the word *Haiti* from being uttered in Congress, a year after the imperialist Monroe Doctrine.

White supremacy was not defeated in the Appomattox Court House in 1865, nor by the 13th Amendment that allowed for a back-door legalization of slavery, nor in the 1954 *Brown v. Board of Education* Supreme Court ruling, nor in the 1965 Voting Rights Act following "Bloody Sunday" in Selma, nor in the 2008 election of the first African American President.

Through it all, as Haitian anthropologist Gina Athena Ulysse analyzed, Haiti has served as the "bête noir" in a deliberate smear campaign against the descendants of the people who said no to white supremacy.[9]

These narratives of Haiti continued throughout the initial response to the 2010 earthquake, from the likes of televangelist Pat Robertson and *The New York Times'* David Brooks. As *New Yorker* contributing writer Doreen St. Felix pointed out, this obsession with Haiti has to do with white society's rejection of black self-determination.[10]

These discourses have definite and powerful material consequences.

France, which in 2001 declared slavery a "crime against humanity," extorted 150 million francs from Haiti as a condition of recognition of Haitian independence, plunging Haiti into a 120-year debt that consumed up to 80% of Haiti's tax base. Socialist president Jacques Chirac scoffed at Haitian president Jean-Bertrand Aristide's demand for reparations before being the first to call for his resignation in 2004.

Calling Haiti "ungovernable" provided justification for US intervention: The United States invaded Haiti twenty-six times from 1849 to 1915, when US Marines landed and occupied the country for nineteen years. During the US Occupation, the Marines set up the modern army, opened up land for foreign ownership, solidified class and racial inequality, laying the groundwork for the 1957-1971 Duvalier dictatorship.

Incorrectly blaming Haiti for its role in the AIDS epidemic killed the tourist industry, which, along with the deliberate destruction of Haiti's pig population, sent the economy in a nosedive. Neoliberal capitalist interests seized the opportunity to take advantage of the massive rural exodus to build sweatshops, exploiting people's misery by offering the lowest wages in the world. With poverty wages, and a crippling foreign debt that according to the IMF's own recordkeeping went to the paramilitary *tonton makout,* Port-au-Prince's shantytowns had no services and no government oversight. These foreign interventions were the main killer in the 2010 earthquake.

Fearing Haitians as "looters" or the other familiar racist scribes, and calling Haiti a "failed state," led to the invisiblity of Haitian people's heroic first response, and also to the complete exclusion of Haitian state and non-state actors in rebuilding their own country and providing aid. Bill Clinton co-chaired the Interim Haiti Reconstruction Commission, making decisions about aid, and humanitarian aid was coordinated in a UN Logistics Base, where Haitian people were excluded by foreign soldiers responsible for the cholera epidemic that killed almost 10,000 people or by the English language of the meetings. Nongovernmental organizations reproduced a top-down, hierarchical structure that excluded people living in the camps from decisions. These humanitarian aftershocks led to, among other consequences, the breakup of Haitian families and increasing violence against women.[11]

Calling the world's beacon of freedom a "shithole" sullies not only Haiti's ten million residents on the island and three million in the US, but is an affront to human freedom and equality.[12]

As award-winning Haitian author Edwidge Danticat argued, "today we mourn. Tomorrow we fight."[13]

ENDNOTES

1   https://www.nytimes.com/2017/12/23/us/politics/trump-immigration.html

2   http://www.cnn.com/2017/11/20/politics/dhs-temporary-protected-status-haiti/index.html

3   https://www.huffingtonpost.com/entry/you-live-under-fear-50000-haitian-people-at-risk_us_58ff6f7ce4b047ce3ee27c5c

4   https://www.commondreams.org/news/2018/01/12/calling-out-trump-denial-durbin-confirms-president-said-those-hate-filled-words

5   https://www.azcentral.com/story/opinion/op-ed/laurieroberts/2017/12/01/jeff-flake-sells-out-middle-class-daca/914102001/

6   https://www.americamagazine.org/politics-society/2018/01/12/i-am-part-haitian-diaspora-heres-why-i-wasnt-surprised-trumps-comments

7   https://play.google.com/store/books/details?id=ih7gDAAAQBAJ&source=productsearch&utm_source=HA_Desktop_US&utm_medium=SEM&utm_campaign=PLA&pcampaignid=MKTAD0930BO1&gclid=EAIaIQobChMIxqKpjdbV2AIVA4ezCh0xVwWbEAYYAiABEgKNLvD_BwE&gclsrc=aw.ds&dclid=CNLojJLW1dgCFYweHwodJ_kNVg

8   http://www.beacon.org/Silencing-the-Past-P1109.aspx

9   http://www.upne.com/0819575449.html

10 https://www.newyorker.com/news/news-desk/trumps-fixation-on-haiti-and-the-abiding-fear-of-black-self-determination/amp?__twitter_impression=true

11 https://www.rutgersuniversitypress.org/humanitarian-aftershocks-in-haiti/9780813574233

12 http://lenouvelliste.com/article/181706/le-gouvernement-haitien-condamne-les-propos-de-trump-convoque-le-charge-daffaires-americain-selon-paul-altidor

13 http://www.miamiherald.com/opinion/op-ed/article194492199.html

AFGHANISTAN

WHY ARE WE IN AFGHANISTAN?

Paul Craig Roberts

It is long past time for someone in the shithole known as Washington to tell us why Americans have been killing and dying in Afghanistan for 17 years. Is it to steal the country's minerals? Is it to control the location of pipelines? Is it to keep American taxpayers' money flowing to the US military/security complex? Is it to finance the CIA's black operations with drug profits? Or is it to prove that the neoconservatives' dream of US world hegemony is a chimera?

Here are some questions for you from a voice you never have heard, originally published here: https://alemarah-english.com/?p=25640

Letter of the Islamic Emirate to the American People!

To the American people, officials of independent non-governmental organizations and the peace loving Congressmen!

With the hope that you will read this letter prudently and will evaluate the future of American forces and your profit and loss inside Afghanistan in light of the prevailing realities alluded to in the following lines!

The American people!

You realize that your political leadership launched a military invasion of our country 17 years ago. This invasion was not only contrary to the legal and national norms of our own sovereign country but also a violation of all international rules and regulations, but still the following three main points were put forward by your authorities to justify this illegitimate invasion:

- Establishing security by eliminating the so called terrorists inside Afghanistan.
- Restoring law and order by establishing a legal government.
- Eradicating narcotics.

However let us analyze how successful your war-monger leaders were in achieving the above three slogans in this illegitimate war?

Increased Insecurity and Fighting

In 2001 when your ex-president George W. Bush ordered the invasion of Afghanistan, his justification for that felonious act was the elimination the Islamic Emirate (Taliban) and Al-Qaeda.

But despite continuing this bloody war for seventeen years and accepting huge casualties and financial losses, your current president Donald Trump—to continue the illegal 17 year old war in Afghanistan—acknowledged increased insecurity and emergence of multiple groups instead of the single unified Islamic Emirate (Taliban).

This was stated by Trump while declaring his new war strategy for Afghanistan and South Asia on 23rd August 2017 and seventeen years later, again ordered the perpetuation of the same illegitimate occupation and war against the Afghan people. Since your authorities admit the presence of multiple warring factions inside Afghanistan, it verifies our claim that by invading Afghanistan and overthrowing a unified responsible government of Taliban, the Americans have merely paved the way for anarchy in the country.

No matter what title or justification is presented by your undiscerning authorities for the war in Afghanistan, the reality is that tens of thousands of helpless Afghans including women and children were martyred by your forces, hundreds of thousands were injured and thousands more were incarcerated in Guantanamo, Bagram and various other secret jails and treated in such a humiliating way that has not only brought shame upon humanity but is also a violation of all claims of American culture and civilization.

In this lopsided war and as confirmed by your own military authorities, 3546 American and foreign soldiers have been killed, more than 20,000 American forces injured and tens of thousands more are suffering mentally but in reality the amount of your casualties is several times higher and is deliberately being concealed by your leaders. Similarly this war has cost you trillions of dollars thus making it one of the bloodiest, longest and costliest war in the contemporary history of your country.

Chaos and the most Corrupt Regime

Even though it is not the duty of America to draft laws and suggest systems for other countries but nevertheless, the second excuse of George W. Bush for the invasion of Afghanistan was to establish a supposed legitimate government. But despite seventeen years of war costing thousands of American and coalition lives and billions of dollars, such a system has taken root in Afghanistan which has achieved the following administrative, legal, military and political records:

- Number one internationally in administrative and financial corruption.
- Number one internationally in violating human rights.
- Number one internationally in usurping of land and embezzling international aid.
- Number one internationally in violence against women, etc. etc.

The latest example of the corrupt regime formed in the wake of American invasion is the presence of a two-headed system which is unparalleled in the established laws of forming a government throughout the world.

Production and expansion of narcotics

The third justification of George W. Bush to invade Afghanistan was the prevention and eradication of narcotics. Let us examine the amount and levels of production and expansion of the narcotic trade in Afghanistan after seventeen year war effort.

According to the data provided by UNODC (United Nations Office on Drugs and Crimes)—prior to the American invasion—poppy was cultivated only on 185 hectors land of Afghanistan and only in areas controlled by anti-Taliban forces whereas the level of heroin addiction among Afghans was next to nil. But following the American invasion of Afghanistan, poppy cultivation skyrocketed from 185 hectors to 328,000 hectors while under the shadow of seventeen year occupation, the number of drug addicts has reached 3 million people.

On 21st December 2017, the UNODC (United Nations Office on Drugs and Crimes) reported that drug production increased by 87% and poppy cultivation increased by 63% during the year 2017, thus mounting the total production of narcotics to 9000 metric tons.

The American People!

You proclaim to be a developed and civilized nation of the world. Since the imposed government in Afghanistan is established by you therefore we leave it to your judgment to decide— according to your logic and conscience—whether the present system and its pertinent changes, insecurity, chaos and 87% increase in narcotics are reforms or crimes against humanity. Your authorities proclaim that tens of billions of dollars have been spent on various reconstruction projects in Afghanistan. Of course this is the same money which is collected from you as taxes and revenues, but here it has been distributed among thieves and murderers. Do you agree that the hard earned money of your labor should be wasted on such a corrupt system where in only one criminal case, $900 million were stolen from Kabul Bank by corrupt officials?

Do you consider it the rule of law in American culture and lexicon where the first deputy of a government is a person involved in the felonious act of sexual assault on a 70-year-old man besides hundreds of other crimes against humanity?

Is this the civilization, modernity and rule of law proclaimed by you in the world?

Were your 3546 forces killed in Afghanistan to establish and empower such a system?

Can your scholars, intellectuals and unbiased analysts produce an answer to our questions?

You must understand that our people are living, watching and closely analyzing all these calamities and that is why the regime working under the shadow of your military support and the corrupt elements assembled therein are not looked upon as a legitimate government rather they are considered a band of usurpers, looters, mafia warlords and drug-dealers while at the same time, the resistance against them is considered their legal, moral and national obligation. The people working alongside you to impose this system are committing treason against our nation and national interests. On the other hand, the people who waging armed resistance against your corrupt regime are the defenders of their homeland, national interests, sovereignty as well as their dignity and they are revered by the Afghan masses as their heroes. That the American media is propagating against the Afghan resistance and labelling them as foreign terrorists instead of Afghan freedom fighters, all of this is baseless propaganda aimed at concealing their own humiliating defeat. To repudiate this propaganda, we only want to say that had there been any chance of success in Afghanistan with foreign support, the American invaders and their coalition forces would definitely have succeeded due to enjoying the political and military support of a powerful country like the United States of America as well as the support of a well-equipped military alliance like NATO.

The People of America!

We would like to summarize our message to you in the following words:

The Afghans who are fighting your forces and any other invader today, this is their legal, religious and national obligation. However mighty and well-equipped your forces might be, even if supported by the entire world, this resistance will be sustained by the Afghan people due to their religious, legal and national obligation. This resistance is considered by Afghan masses as a sacred responsibility of defending their creed and country. To relinquish this sacred obligation is considered by them as abandoning Islam and all human values and this disgrace is never acceptable for any valiant Muslim Afghan individual.

Afghans have continued to burn for the last four decades in the fire of imposed wars. They are longing for peace and a just system but they will never tire from their just cause of defending their creed, country and nation against the invading forces of your war-mongering government because they have rendered all the previous and present historic sacrifices to safeguard their religious values and national sovereignty. If they make a deal on their sovereignty now, it would be unforgettable infidelity with their proud history and ancestors.

Afghanistan is a country which has maintained its independence throughout its several thousand year history. Even in the 19th and 20th century when most Muslim countries were occupied by the then European imperial powers, Afghanistan was the only country in the region to preserve its independence and despite an eighty year imperialistic endeavor, the British failed make them accept occupation. It is the same inherent zeal and historic succession in the hearts and minds of Afghan masses which presently inspires this empty-handed nation to continue protracted resistance against your occupying forces. This is not exaggeration rather irrefutable reality that today the valiant Afghan self-sacrificial attackers are competing among themselves to carry out martyrdom seeking attacks against your invading forces.

This national religious resistance of the Afghans is not a futile war, rather it is progressing everyday as various parts of the country are liberated. At this moment the head of SIGAR (Special Inspector General for Afghanistan Reconstruction) acknowledged that sixty percent of Afghan territory is under the control of Taliban (Islamic Emirate).

In 2001 during the American invasion of Afghanistan, a number of world countries came under the influence of misleading propaganda by your officials and supported the warring strategy of the then president George W. Bush. But today we see that your government has lost that international support as a number of your coalition partners have withdrawn their forces from our country by discerning the prevailing realities and they are currently seeking a political solution. The international community at large is now backing our justified resistance against the illegitimate American occupation. If your government is still insisting on perpetuating the war in Afghanistan by conjuring excuses, it will further undermine American prestige in the world.

The People of America!

In the American society where the main source of power is the masses and the authorities are elected by public votes, the Islamic Emirate of Afghanistan—as representatives of the will of Afghan nation—asks the American people and the peace loving Congressmen to put pressure on your authorities and demand an end to the occupation of Afghanistan because stubbornly seeking the protraction of this war and existence of a corrupt and ineffective regime here in Kabul will have dreadful consequences for the region and particularly for the stability of America herself. The Afghan masses feel pity for the whole American nation because they are being sacrificed and are losing respect through the world with each passing day solely due the war-mongering policies of a few war-mongering officials.

Your intellectuals, peace loving Congressmen and independent chiefs of civil organizations should question your authorities as to why the American people are so insecure and detested at home and abroad despite their international prestige.

For how long will your modern country and your children continue to be sacrificed for the war-mongering policies of a few war-mongering officials?

And what eventual benefit will these warring policies bring for your country?

The American People!

Your president and his military and political officials following his war policies still speak the language of war in Afghanistan. They intentionally release fake statistics for the sake of their vested interests and misguide you and the world by throwing dust in your eyes. The reality is that in contemporary world, the use of force and arms has been replaced by peaceful dialogue and wars cannot be won with lies.

Only in past September—in accordance with Trump's new strategy—American forces used all their new powers and carried out 751 air strikes. You should ask your Generals that despite using such force, have you retaken even a single inch of land from the Taliban or have they become even more powerful.

If you do not understand the inexperienced policies of president Trump and his war-monger advisors, then look no further than his irrational decision of shifting the American embassy to from Tel Aviv to Jerusalem which brought America in opposition with 128 countries of the world.

Truly it is humiliating for a civilized people like you to be confronted with such a decisive international majority. It was only due of the pursuit of policies of force which pitted majority of the world countries against America, and your authorities are still insistent upon that ridiculous policy!!

The Islamic Emirate had asked America from the very beginning to solve her issues with the Islamic Emirate through talk and dialogue. The use of force has adverse consequences, and you might have now discerned the bitter consequences of American aggression against Afghanistan. If the policy of using force is exercised for a hundred more years and a hundred new strategies are adopted, the outcome of all of these will be the same as you have observed over the last six months following the initiation of Trump's new strategy.

According we still believe that it is not too late for the American people to understand that the Islamic Emirate—as representative of its people—can solve its problems with every side through healthy politics and dialogue. Needless use of force only complicates the issues by creating new dimensions which gradually move out of the realm of control. The Islamic Emirate is a regional power with deep roots which cannot be subdued by sheer force. The chances of dialogue however are not exhausted. The American people must understand that the Islamic Emirate understands its responsibility and can play a constructive role in finding a peaceful solution for issues but this can never mean that we are exhausted or our will has been sapped. It is our policy that logic should be given a chance before the use of force. Whatever can be achieved by logic, should not be relinquished due to the use of force. It is the moral obligation of the Islamic Emirate of Afghanistan to inform you, the American masses, about these realities.

We must state that the Islamic Emirate of Afghanistan undertakes legitimate efforts for the independence of our homeland. Having a sovereign country free from any foreign occupation is our natural and human right. Seeking freedom of our homeland and establishing an Islamic system conforming to the creed of our people can never be called terrorism by any law of the world. It is worth mentioning that we have no agenda of playing any destructive role in any other country and we have practically proven over the past seventeen years that we have not interfered in any other country. Likewise we will not allow anyone else to use Afghan territory against any other country. War is imposed on us, it is not our choice. Our preference is to solve the Afghan issue through peaceful dialogues. America must end her occupation and must accept all our legitimate rights including the right to form a government consistent with the beliefs of our people. After gaining independence, we would like to have positive and constructive relations with all countries of the world including our neighboring countries. We welcome their assistance and support in the reconstruction and rehabilitation of our country. We want to play a beneficial role in regional and world peace and stability, provide high standard education and employment opportunities for our people and guarantee all human and legal rights of every child, woman and man, secure our youth from drugs and all other moral indecencies, provided job opportunities to every individual such that they not leave their homeland or seek refuge abroad.

In brief, insisting on prolonging the war in Afghanistan and maintaining American troop presence is neither beneficial for America nor for anyone else, rather it endangers the stability of the entire world. This is irrefutable reality which is only rejected by your arrogant authorities. If you want peaceful dialogue with the Afghans specifically and with the world generally, then make your president and the war-mongering congressmen and Pentagon officials understand this reality and compel them to adopt a rational policy towards Afghanistan!

This will be the most constructive step for the stability of your people, the Afghans as well as the whole world.

Our only obligation is to convey (the message) to you!

The Islamic Emirate of Afghanistan
28/05/1439 Hijri Lunar
25/11/1396 Hijri Solar
14/02/2018 Gregorian
https://alemarah-english.com/?p=25640

PHILIPPINES

US IMPERIALISM PLAGUES THE PHILIPPINES

Jose Maria Sison

US imperialism has imposed itself on the Filipino people and violated their national sovereignty and thwarted their aspirations for democracy, social justice and development since 1898 by military, political, economic and cultural means.

In this connection, I wish to discuss first how monopoly capitalism or modern imperialism arose as the final stage in the development of capitalism and how the era of imperialism began. Monopoly capitalism is parasitic, decaying and moribund, opening more widely than before the possibility of socialism. In being imperialist, it is emphatically violent and aggressive in repressing revolution and in acquiring economic and political territory abroad.

As early as the middle of the 19th century, from 1848 to 1868, England demonstrated at least two major characteristics of imperialism: its possession of vast colonies and its industrial monopoly by means of which it could draw monopoly profits or superprofits. It was the first among the capitalist countries in which free competition capitalism developed into monopoly capitalism as the dominant force in the economy.

However, it was not until the last three decades of the 19th century that several other countries—the US, France, Germany, Italy, Japan and Russia—would see the development of free competition capitalism to monopoly capitalism. Together with England, they manifested the five features of imperialism. The fifth feature, which is the completed division of the world by the capitalist powers, directly set the stage for imperialist wars:

1. the dominance of capitalist monopolies in the economy;

2. the merger of industrial and bank capital and the emergence of the finance oligarchy;

3. the greater importance of the export of surplus capital than the export of surplus commodities as the means to obtain superprofits;

4. the alliances and counter-alliances of cartels, syndicates and trusts on an international scale;

5. the completion of the division of the world by the great capitalist powers, covering underdeveloped or less developed countries or areas as economic territories (sources of cheap raw materials and cheap labor, captive markets and fields of investment) and as political territories (colonies, semi-colonies, protectorates, dependent countries and spheres of influence).

For a monopoly capitalist power, a certain country or area abroad becomes a more reliable economic territory when it is also a political territory acquired through military intervention or aggression. The newcomers in the colonial game like the US had to engage in acts of aggression in their emergence as imperialists. In comparison to the Western imperialist powers, Russia and Japan had developed monopoly capitalism to a lesser extent but again, aggressive use of military power enabled them to acquire territories from which to extract monopoly profits.

Then as now, the capitalist powers try to amicably divide the world market among themselves, until their economic competition and political rivalry breaks out into wars. The completion of the division of the world among the capitalist powers towards the end of the 19th century laid the ground for the violent struggle among them for the redivision of the world. Latecomers in the colonial game upset the balance of forces and pushed the outbreak of wars.

Thus, the era of modern imperialism was inaugurated by wars and took final shape in the period of 1898 to 1914. The Spanish-American War (1898), the Anglo-Boer War (1899–1902), the Russo-Japanese War (1904–05) and the economic crisis in Europe in 1900 were the chief historical landmarks in the new era. Lenin categorically stated that the era of imperialism did not begin earlier than 1898 to 1900 and that neither Marx nor Engels lived long enough to see it.

I. The Perpetuated US Aggression

The US fully assumed the character of an imperialist power, on the basis of monopoly capitalism, when it deliberately provoked the Spanish-American War of 1898 in order to seize the colonies of Spain: Cuba, Puerto Rico and the Philippines. In connection with said war, the US pretended to make friends with the Aguinaldo junta in Hong Kong and actually brought Aguinaldo back to the Philippines on an American cutter to proclaim Philippine independence (under the "protection" of the US) and to resume the national war of independence against Spain.

The Filipino people succeeded in liberating themselves nationwide and were about to seize Intramuros, the walled citadel of the Spanish colonizers. But the US interfered with the deployment of Filipino troops for this purpose and maneuvered to prepare for the landing of more US troops. Behind the back of their supposed Filipino allies, the US arranged a mock battle with the Spanish side on August 13, 1898 to justify the Spanish surrender to the US. This was done on the day after Spain and the US had signed an armistice agreement ending the Spanish-American War.

The US and Spain then forged the Treaty of Paris of December 10, 1898 in which Spain sold the Philippines to the US for the amount of US$20 million. On December 21, 1898 US President McKinley issued the Proclamation of Benevolent Assimilation to manifest the US plan to colonize the Philippines. The US started to unleash its war of aggression against the Filipino people on February 4, 1899. This has come to be known as the Filipino-American War. The US used superior military force and extreme barbarity by more than 126,000 troops to conquer the nation of 7,000,000 people. It ruthlessly carried out massacres, torture of captives, concentration camp internment of the population, scorched earth tactics and food blockades. It killed more than 700,000 or 10 per cent of the Filipino people from 1899 to 1902, directly through its brutal operations and indirectly through consequent famines and epidemics. Then it proceeded to similarly kill a further 800,000 Filipinos up to 1916.

In order to keep the Philippines as a colony, the US established military bases at various strategic points. It organized the so-called

Philippine Scouts as puppet troops and subsequently converted them into the Philippine Constabulary. As a result of relentless demands of the Filipino people for national independence, the US decided as early as 1935 to make the Philippines a semi-colony in 1946 after a ten-year transition period under the so-called Commonwealth government.

The National Defense Act of 1936 was this government's first legislative act, making the puppet constabulary the First Regular Army under the direct supervision of the US Army's Philippine Department. Commonwealth president Quezon made General Douglas MacArthur the field marshal of the puppet army, which the US had formed, indoctrinated, equipped and trained. On the eve of World War II, the US placed this puppet army within the framework of the US Army Forces in the Far East (USAFFE).

When World War II broke out in 1941, the Japanese fascists defeated the US army in Bataan and occupied the Philippines up to 1945. To recover the Philippines as a colony, the US coordinated with the USAFFE guerrillas. Before granting nominal independence to the Philippines in 1946, the US imposed on the puppet Filipino leaders the Treaty of General Relations, which ensured the continuance of US military bases and the property rights of US citizens and corporations. This treaty even required in advance that the diplomatic relations of the Philippines would be subject to approval by the US.

After the Philippines became a semi-colony, the US perpetuated its successful aggression and continued to control the Philippine state militarily. It obtained a military assistance agreement to make the Philippine armed services dependent on US planning, training, intelligence and equipment; and a military bases agreement for US military forces to stay in the Philippines for another 99 years. It also bound the Philippines to a mutual defense pact and a US-controlled regional security pact, the South East Asia Treaty Organization (SEATO).

Because of its military power over the Philippines, the US has been able to dominate the Philippine economy and politics and intervene at will in Philippine affairs since 1946. It manipulated the outcome of presidential elections in favor of the candidate most compliant with and servile to US interests in the Philippines and in the region. It instigated the Marcos fascist dictatorship in 1972 in a futile attempt to suppress the revolutionary mass movement that had emerged and developed since 1961 because of the wanton extraction of superprofits by US corporations, bureaucratic corruption and the exhaustion of the land frontier.

The Filipino people were outraged that the fascist regime could persist for so long—from 1972 to 1986—because of US military and economic assistance to it. They were also incensed by the direct and indirect consequences of US planes, ships and troops operating in and around the US bases. Thus, after the downfall of Marcos, the framers of the 1987 constitution enjoyed overwhelming popular support and took courage in adopting provisions that banned foreign military bases, troops, facilities and nuclear weapons from the Philippines. This ban was indeed the fruit of the people's revolutionary struggle against the fallen US-instigated dictatorship.

The military bases agreement with the US was terminated in 1991 by the Philippine Senate, with the open and strong support of the national democratic movement. But since then, the US has resorted to all sorts of maneuvers to circumvent the constitutional ban on foreign military bases. by invoking the US-RP mutual defense pact. It has used the Balikatan joint US-Philippine military exercises and interoperability training as pretext for the forward stations and rotational presence of US troops in the Philippines.

The US has been able to obtain a Visiting Forces Agreement starting 1999 and a Mutual Logistics Support Agreement starting 2002 to allow the entry and stationing of US military forces anywhere in the Philippines for any duration of time. It has used the September 11, 2001 events and the so-called US global war on terror to justify US military presence and intervention in the Philippines. It has also expanded the pretexts for such intervention. These include humanitarian aid, medical missions, civic actions, disaster-related aid for rescue, relief and rehabilitation, and so on.

The latest US pretext for further entrenching itself militarily in the Philippines is its strategic pivot to the Asia-Pacific region which purports to protect the country from Chinese aggression in view of the overreaching claims of China over 90 per cent of the South China Sea, encroaching on 90 per cent of the exclusive economic zone (EEZ) and 100 per cent of the extended continental shelf (ECS) of the Philippines. Thus, with the servile collaboration of the Benigno Aquino regime, the US has been able to obtain the so-called 2014 Enhanced Defense Cooperation Agreement (EDCA).

This agreement allows the US to establish military bases in an indefinite number of so-called Agreed Areas, fortified at Philippine expense, while paying no rent, enjoying perimeter security from puppet troops free of charge, barring Philippine authorities from any knowledge of activities inside the US military enclaves or bases. It also allows US air planes and ships to come and go, barring the Philippine authorities from knowing whether such vessels carry nuclear, chemical, bacteriological and/or other weapons of mass destruction. Moreover, the agreement requires the AFP to provide or facilitate access by US forces to any place whatsoever in Philippine territory that the US decides.

Despite the treason and obsequiousness of the Aquino regime in acceding to EDCA, US President Obama in his 2014 visit to Manila clearly declared that the US is neutral over the Philippine-China maritime dispute in the West Philippine Sea and that US policy is not to counter or contain China. In fact, the US has a dual policy of cooperation and contention with China and makes its decisions according to US national interest. At any rate, the US has far more interest in relations with China than in those with the Philippines, leading to the possibility that the US and China could agree to jointly explore and exploit the oil, gas and other natural resources in the EEZ and ECS of the Philippines.

President Trump has been expanding the US war machine in the Philippines under the pretext of war against ISIS and counterinsurgent operations. The 2018 US Operation Pacific Eagle-Philippines ensures continual increase in US troop deployment to the Philippines, US military weapons including planes and drones, and US funds and training for special units of the Armed Forces of the Philippines and the Philippine National Police. As such, current Philippine power-hungry dictator Rodrigo Duterte is getting explicit support and funding from Trump

In the face of the perpetuated aggression of US imperialism in the Philippines, the Filipino people and their revolutionary forces have adopted the line of people's democratic revolution through protracted people's war. They are waging a civil war against the semi-colonial political system. At the same time, they condemn the escalating military intervention of the US in favor of the puppet regime. They are therefore prepared to wage a war of national liberation should the US unleash a full-scale war of aggression. They are not afraid of such a possibility but rather they prepare against it. They consider it an opportunity to realize justice for the heroes martyred by US imperialism and for the suffering of millions of people as a consequence of the direct and indirect rule of US imperialism.

II. Continuing Economic Plunder

The US had a strategic motive and objective for seizing and making the Philippines its colony. This was connected with the expressed desire of the US to expand the international market for its manufactures, to turn the Pacific Ocean into an "American lake" for the purpose and to have a base for launching efforts to get a share of China in the frenzy of the capitalist powers to establish spheres of influence.

The US floated bonds in Wall Street to finance its war of aggression in the Philippines. Ultimately, it made the Filipino people pay for their own military conquest through taxation. But the biggest gain for US imperialism came from the extraction of superprofits from the colonial exchange of US manufactures and Philippine raw materials as well as from the direct and indirect US investments in the Philippines. In the process, the US imperialists turned the Philippine economy from feudal to semi-feudal.

US imperialism did not have to eliminate feudalism. It merely superimposed the imperialist mode of exploitation to change the total complexion of the social economy to semi-feudal. In an attempt to appease the people's hatred of the landed estates owned by the foreign religious orders, the US colonial government expropriated some of them for redistribution to the peasants. But the peasants could not afford to complete the payments for the redistribution. The land eventually fell into the hands of the landlord class.

The US colonial government lifted the feudal restrictions on the physical movement of peasants. This enabled peasants to open land in frontier areas or to seek jobs in urban areas, public works and mines. Bureaucrats and landlords enticed peasants to make their homesteads in frontier areas but ultimately they claimed and registered the land as their own. Merchant usurers also followed the peasants into frontier areas and eventually became landlords.

The US colonial rule differed significantly from that of the Spanish by taking superprofits from a far greater flow of manufactured imports and raw material exports, from the chronic need of the Philippines to take loans to cover its trade deficits, from new schemes of overconsumption and from the far greater inflow of direct foreign investments. The US opened the mines, expanded the plantations for raw-material export production and established a few factories manufacturing consumer products from locally available raw materials. The roads, bridges, ports and other means of transport and communications were improved for the growing domestic and foreign trade. The system of public and private schools was developed to produce professionals and technicians for the expanded bureaucracy and business enterprises.

In the semi-feudal economy and society, the joint class rule of the big compradors and landlords (one per cent of the population) arose and replaced the singular dominance of the landlord class in the feudal period of previous centuries. The intermediate social strata of middle bourgeois and urban petty bourgeoisie expanded and would ultimately come to 1 and 8 per cent, respectively. From a few percentage points of the population, the working class grew to 15 per cent of it. The peasantry descended from a feudal high of about 90 per cent to its current semi-feudal level of about 75 per cent.

The US economic domination of the Philippines was interrupted by the Japanese invasion and occupation during World War II. Japan's imperialist character and war of aggression prevented it from making credible its slogan of "Greater East Asia co-prosperity." The Japanese aggressors wrought havoc and destruction on the lives, communities and properties of Filipinos. In the course of recapturing the Philippines, especially in its haste to oust the Japanese through massive bombardment, the US added to and aggravated the destruction of lives and properties. US war damage payments were made mainly to the US corporations for reestablishing US economic domination of the Philippines.

The US not only retained the property rights of US corporations and citizens through the Treaty of General Relations before the grant of nominal independence to the Philippines in 1946 but also imposed on the supposedly independent Philippine state the so-called Parity Amendment in the Philippine Constitution. This amendment allowed US corporations and citizens to have the same rights as Filipinos in owning public utilities and exploiting natural resources. Furthermore, through the Laurel-Langley Agreement, the US extracted from the Philippines the privilege of owning and operating all kinds of businesses without restriction.

A civil war broke out in the Philippines between the reactionary forces of foreign and feudal domination and the revolutionary forces of national liberation and democracy in 1948. The demand for national industrialization and land reform became so strong that the reactionary authorities had to fake land reform in the form of land resettlement programs and token expropriation of landed estates as well as to feign national industrialization in the form of import-substitution manufacturing which was in fact reassembly and repackaging operations dependent on licensing, financing, technical and marketing agreements with US corporations.

The Philippine economy went from bad to worse when the Marcos regime went on a spending and borrowing spree to build infrastructure and conspicuous tourist facilities and opted for the so-called export-oriented manufacturing in export-processing zones and for the export of labor in the absence of real industrial development for generating local employment. Export-oriented manufacturing is a far worse kind of pseudo-industrialization than the import-substitution manufacturing. It overprices the imported components and underprices the exported semi-manufactures to the benefit of the corporations involved. Workers are mostly categorized as casuals, apprentices or learners. They are paid substandard wages and are deprived of job security. Their trade union and other democratic rights are curtailed.

To this day, export-oriented manufacturing is misrepresented as industrial development. It has been greatly set back by the Asian financial crisis of 1997 and the global financial meltdown of 2007-08. The reassembly and export of semi-conductors and other products have plunged. What has become glossier than export-oriented manufacturing is the bubble in office and residential towers and upscale tourist enclaves, which is now about to pop because of the growing flight of portfolio investments.

All regimes since the time of the puppet president Ramos have gone into a mad frenzy of opening the entire country to foreign mining companies that ruin agriculture and the environment, preempt future industrialization and take mineral ores out of the country without paying the commensurate taxes.

Philippine economic policy has always been dictated by US imperialism. In the time of Marcos, the World Bank was active in pushing a Keynesian policy of undertaking public works to promote raw-material production and the colonial exchange of raw material exports and manufactured imports and thereby diverting resources and foreign loans from what should be a line of national industrialization. The first Aquino regime drew the Philippines further away from national industrialization by following the US-dictated policy of neoliberalism and carrying out trade liberalization at the expense of local industry and even agriculture. The Ramos regime followed up the anti-industrialization policy by channeling huge resources and foreign loans to upscale private construction and tourist facilities.

Altogether the post-Marcos regimes have been bound to exporting raw materials and labor and have been trapped within the framework of the imperialist policy of neoliberal globalization under the so-called Washington Consensus of the IMF, the World Bank (especially its private investment arm IFC) and the WTO (including its GATT predecessor). The US has used these multilateral agencies to push the liberalization of trade and investments, privatization of public assets, deregulation of social and environmental protections and the denationalization of underdeveloped economies such as the Philippines. Like their imperialist masters, the puppet regimes in the Philippines have clung to the neoliberal policy because it suits their greed; they believe that they can always shift the burden of crisis to the people and they still await a more powerful revolutionary mass movement to challenge them.

Under the general auspices of the WTO and the proliferation of bilateral and multilateral free trade agreements with the US and other imperialist powers, the Philippines is prevented from upholding economic sovereignty, conserving its national patrimony for the benefit of the Filipino people and/or undertaking national industrialization and land reform. The Asia-Pacific Economic Cooperation, the Trans Pacific Partnership Agreement and ASEAN Economic Community are frameworks for binding the Philippines to the imperialist system of plunder and particularly to its neoliberal policy of unbridled monopoly capitalist greed.

In the face of the continuing plunder of the Philippines by US imperialism, enjoying the collaboration of the local exploiting classes of big compradors and landlords, the Filipino people and their revolutionary forces are committed to fighting for national liberation and democracy, realizing social justice, conserving their national patrimony and carrying out a program of development through national industrialization and land reform. They can end the underdevelopment of the Philippines only by destroying the exploitative system of big compradors and landlords subservient to US imperialism and thereby releasing the patriotic and progressive forces to undertake genuine development and achieve social justice.

III. The Creation and Formation of the Puppet Leadership Class

Even while it carried out its war of aggression against the Filipino people, the US sought to entice leaders of the Philippine revolutionary government to surrender. This caused a split within the Aguinaldo Cabinet, between the revolutionary members like Apolinario Mabini and Antonio Luna and the capitulationists like Pardo de Tavera, Paterno and Buencamino. But the revolutionary mass movement was too strong to be derailed by the capitulationists, who were ridiculed as asimilistas and Sajonistas.

The US aggressors carried out a brutal war of conquest to serve the interests of US monopoly capitalism. But hypocritically they declared that they came to the Philippines to "civilize" and "Christianize" the people, after more than three centuries of Spanish colonial rule and Roman Catholic proselytization. They also claimed to have no interest in possessing the Philippines but rather simply in teaching democracy and self-government to the Filipinos, despite the success of the Filipinos in exercising democracy by building a revolutionary government and army and defeating Spanish colonialism.

They touted Jeffersonian democracy to embellish the image of modern imperialism. With this, they were confident of being able to co-opt the bourgeois liberals leading the Philippine revolution. The Filipino bourgeois liberals derived their political enlightenment from the study of bourgeois liberalism in Europe. They did not arise as the offshoot of a manufacturing bourgeoisie as in Europe. In fact, they were the children of landlords, colonial bureaucrats and merchants.

The US calculated that it could rely on a growing number of political collaborators by developing the semi-feudal economy of the big compradors and landlords, using both the Philippine educational system and the pensionado system of sending native scholars to US universities to promote a pro-US colonial mentality and by expanding the bureaucracy and businesses to accommodate those produced by the schools.

After his capture in 1901, President Aguinaldo was threatened with death and coaxed by his US captors to issue a Peace Manifesto calling on the revolutionary forces to surrender. The leaders who turned against the revolution were given positions at various levels of the US colonial government and were encouraged to form in 1901 the Partido Federal to serve the colonial regime and to help it to discourage and suppress the revolutionary resistance of the people.

Those who continued to wage revolutionary resistance were subjected to a series of draconian laws and were made to suffer torture and death by hanging and other means. Several years after the formal end of the Filipino-American War, the US issued in 1907 the Flag Law prohibiting the Filipino people from even displaying the Philippine flag. The Filipino people continued to be subjected to massacres, arbitrary detention and torture, food blockades and internment in concentration camps.

When the US calculated that it had sufficiently broken the armed revolutionary movement and had trained a sufficiently large corps of puppet politicians and professionals, it allowed the Nacionalista Party to exist and call for immediate, absolute and complete national independence. The Nacionalista Party was a reformist party, committed to demanding national independence only by legal and peaceful means and sending missions to Washington to plead for an eventual grant of independence.

Consequent to the inspiration of the victorious Great October Revolution in 1917 and the dire colonial and social conditions, the modern trade union movement which started in 1902 became relatively stronger and the basis for the establishment of the Communist Party of the Philippine Islands in 1930. The US immediately tried to suppress this party by trumping up charges of sedition against the leaders. When the Great Depression worsened social conditions in the Philippines in the 1930s and the danger of fascism was running high, the rise of the broad anti-fascist Popular Front paved the way for the release of communist leaders from prisons and internal exile.

By 1935 the US was ready to establish the Commonwealth government as a transition to a semi-colonial status for the Philippines. It approved the Philippine Constitution as framed by Filipino politicians and promised the grant of national independence by 1946. The Japanese imperialists and fascists invaded and occupied the Philippines from 1941 to 1945 and pretended to be even more generous than US imperialism by swiftly granting nominal independence to a puppet Philippine republic. In the course of the inter-imperialist war, the Communist Party was able to build a people's army against Japan (Hukbalahap), local organs of political power and a powerful mass movement that confiscated land from the landlords.

During World War II, the US kept a Commonwealth government in exile in Washington and directed from Australia the Filipino guerrilla forces, which swore loyalty to the US Army Forces in the Far East. It was able to recover the Philippines in 1945 and grant national independence in 1946 to a group of Filipino puppets headed by Manuel Roxas who had broken away from the Nacionalista Party and formed the Liberal Party. Thus, the Philippines became a semi-colony run by puppets who served US imperialism and the local exploiting classes of big compradors and landlords.

The US and the local exploiting classes provoked the revolutionary resistance of the people by making impositions on them in violation of national independence and the national patrimony, by nullifying land reform and other social gains made by the anti-Japan revolutionary movement and by carrying out brutal campaigns of military suppression. The backbone of the armed revolutionary movement was broken in the early 1950s. But it succeeded in calling attention to the dire semi-colonial and semi-feudal conditions and the need for a democratic revolution led by the working class.

It seemed as if the phony democracy of the big comprador-landlord oligarchs could go on forever as a game of musical chairs between the Nacionalista and Liberal parties, with each party trying to replace the other in periodic elections that they monopolized. The two parties were a duopoly patterned after that of the Republican and Democratic parties in US. But the chronic crisis of Philippine society kept on worsening, exposing the inability of every regime to solve the crisis, pointing to the need for a revolution but also tempting a president like Marcos to carry out a counterrevolution.

The Communist Party of the Philippines was reestablished in 1968 as the advanced detachment of the working class under the guidance of Marxism-Leninism-Mao Zedong Thought (or Maoism). It rectified the errors and shortcomings of the previous revolutionary movement. It put forward the general line of people's democratic revolution through protracted people's war. It considered the peasantry as the main force of the revolution in combination with the proletariat. The basic worker-peasant alliance linked itself with the urban petty bourgeoisie as a revolutionary force and further with the middle bourgeoisie against the joint class dictatorship of the big compradors and landlords.

Upon the instigation of the US, Marcos launched a fascist dictatorship under the pretext of "saving the republic and building a new society" in 1972. He sought to destroy the armed revolutionary movements of the Filipino and Moro people. He succeeded only to inflame the resistance of the broad masses of the people. Eventually, the people totally discredited, isolated and overthrew the fascist regime. Even Marcos' US imperialist master turned against him when it became indubitably clear that he was more of a liability than an asset. Fearing that the revolutionary forces could grow strong enough to overthrow the entire ruling system, the US and the local exploiting classes decided to junk Marcos and go back to the old track of pseudo-democratic regimes.

The pseudo-democratic regimes, from that of Cory Aquino to her son Benigno III, have proven to be utterly servile to US imperialism, exploitative and oppressive, corrupt and brutal. They have imposed on the Filipino people the policies of neocolonialism and neoliberalism and have inflicted extremely terrible suffering on the people. A multiplicity of reactionary parties has not proven any better than the duopoly of the Nacionalista and Liberal parties or the one-party rule of Marcos. Bureaucratic capitalism has grown worse since the Marcos dictatorship. Thus, the Filipino people and their revolutionary forces have become ever more determined to overthrow the entire ruling system and consequently end US domination in order to fully realize national and social liberation.

IV. The Persistence of the Colonial Mentality

From the very start of its colonial rule in the Philippines, US imperialism was determined to dominate and control the Filipino people culturally aside from militarily, economically and politically. It sought to capture the hearts and minds of the people by misrepresenting itself as beneficent and altruistic and making the people forget about the extreme brutality of the US war of aggression through political propaganda and through the educational and cultural system. Thus, it dramatized the arrival of hundreds of American teachers on the ship *Thomas* and the conversion of some US troops to school teachers in pacified areas.

The US imperialists misrepresented themselves as far more gentle and kind than the Spanish colonialists whom they demonized. And yet they cleverly forged a compromise between their own cultural imperialism and the feudalism of the dominant Roman Catholic Church. The US controlled the expanding public school system and allowed the church and its religious orders to control in the main the private educational system. It propagated a conservative and pro-imperialist kind of liberalism, while the religio-sectarian schools continued religious instruction and accepted the new colonial dispensation. The US suppressed the expression of patriotism and anti-imperialism by political and mass leaders, by journalists, creative writers, artists and teachers.

A pro-US kind of colonial mentality supplanted the previous pro-Spanish version among those educated in the schools under the US colonial regime. The US colonial authorities established the pensionado system, providing scholarships to bright students for higher studies in various fields in the US. When the pensionados returned, they propagated their adulation of the US and were assured of promotions in the educational system, bureaucracy, business and professions. The supplanting of Spanish by English as the principal linguistic medium in the schools and in government guaranteed the predominance of a pro-US colonial mentality.

But such colonial mentality could never obliterate the patriotism and revolutionary aspirations of the Filipino people. In so many ways, the people demanded national independence and democracy and condemned the US colonial regime. Formations of the working people and the intelligentsia persevered in upholding and propagating patriotic and progressive ideas and sentiments. They were reinforced and revitalized by the establishment of the Communist Party of the Philippine Islands, which was avowedly guided by Marxism-Leninism and which demanded a national, scientific and mass culture.

The influences of the Great October Revolution and the revolutionary movements in China, Spain, Germany, US and elsewhere reached the Philippines, especially when the Great Depression worsened and fascist and anti-fascist movements arose in various parts of the world. The US colonial authorities tried to combine anti-communism with a colonial mentality to discourage the patriotic and progressive forces. But they failed because the economic and social crisis was worsening and the threat of fascism moved the people towards the struggle for national independence, democratic rights and social justice.

During their occupation of the Philippines from 1942 to 1945, the Japanese imperialists tried to ape the US imperialists by using the schools, mass media, puppet organizations such as the KALIBAPI, the Japanese language, and other cultural vehicles to impose on the people the most colonial aspect of their culture, including their fascist ideas and practices that carried markedly feudal vestiges—even their body language (e.g. deep bowing to show respect or submission). This aroused patriotic anger among the Filipino people. To keep them away from Japanese indoctrination, many Filipinos did not send their children to the Japanese-controlled public schools.

After their reconquest of the Philippines in 1946, the US imperialists misrepresented themselves as liberators of the Filipino people even as they were clearly reestablishing their military, economic, political and cultural dominance. They showed signs of wishing to postpone the granting of nominal independence, unless their unjust impositions were accepted. They were confronted by the old merger of the Communist and Socialist parties that had led the People's Army against Japan and by a broad Democratic Alliance of patriotic and progressive forces that demanded national independence and resisted the imperialist impositions.

Subsequent to the US granting of nominal independence in 1946, making the Philippine ruling system semi-colonial, the US tried to perpetuate a pro-US colonial mentality among the Filipinos and combine it with anti-communism. It used the dominant political parties, the schools, the mass media, the churches, the movies, pop music and stage entertainment to tout the US as the defender of democracy or distract the people from the cause of national and social liberation in the Philippines and from following the advancing forces of national liberation and socialism abroad.

The political ideas and sentiments generated by the duopoly of the Liberal and Nacionalista parties were pro-imperialist and reactionary. The higher political and educational authorities directed the school administrators and teachers to adopt the curricula and syllabi that they had approved. The US granted scholarships under the Fulbright and Smith-Mundt programs to maintain its influence in key universities and the entire educational system. It also used conferences, seminars and travel grants to promote pro-imperialist and anti-communist ideas and sentiments among academics, journalists, creative writers, artists, trade unionists and other people.

The Central Intelligence Agency became most notorious, through its front foundations (Asia Foundation, PEN and Congress for Cultural Freedom), in funding and manipulating cultural organizations and activities along the pro-imperialist and anti-communist line as a major part of the US-instigated Cold War. The reactionary authorities in state and religious schools were also notorious in trying to prevent the study of the works of the intellectual and political leaders of the old democratic revolution and to oppose the speeches and writings of contemporary anti-imperialists like Claro Mayo Recto.

When the mass organizations that espoused the new democratic revolution grew in strength in the 1960s and early 1970s, the US foreign aid and educational agencies and private US foundations like those of Ford and Rockefeller intensified their interference in the educational and cultural field in the Philippines. After declaring martial law in 1972, Marcos established draconian control over mass media and cultural channels, and deepened the propaganda of his fascist dictatorship through the educational system with its censored curricula and syllabi. The fascist regime and the US also started to use the World Bank to fund so-called reforms to align education to US policies.

The post-Marcos regimes have propagated anti-national and anti-democratic ideas and sentiments along the neocolonial and neoliberal line. US cultural imperialism has become even more pronounced. While one regime after another has increasingly channeled public funds to foreign debt servicing, bureaucratic corruption and military campaigns of suppression, all have reduced appropriations for state colleges and universities in order to press them to raise tuition fees and seek assistance from the private sector and US and foreign entities.

The US and other imperialist governmental agencies and private foundations fund and direct nongovernmental or so-called civil society organizations to subvert educational and cultural institutions and attack the cultural, educational and other works of the people's national democratic movement. US agencies like the US Agency for International Development (USAID), the National Endowment of Democracy (NED), the US Institute of Peace and the like are well known for funding groups engaged in subverting and attacking the endeavors and aspirations of the Filipino people for national and social liberation.

More than ever the Filipino people and their revolutionary forces demand and struggle for a national scientific and mass culture and education. The cadres and mass activists are propagating this patriotic and progressive type of culture and education and contributing creatively to its advance even in the schools and other cultural institutions of the ruling system. But certainly they are most effective in the mass movement, in the people's army and in the rural areas governed by the people's democratic government.

V. The National Liberation Struggle

The Filipino people and their revolutionary forces persevere in the struggle for national liberation and democracy under the leadership of the working class and its advanced detachment, the Communist Party of the Philippines. It is precisely through the revolutionary struggle that they build their strength to overthrow the ruling system and to establish a people's democratic state system. They are prepared to fight US imperialism as it escalates its military intervention and proceeds to a full scale war of aggression.

Both US imperialism and the ruling system of big compradors and landlords cannot persist forever in the Philippines. By their own unbridled greed and terrorism under the auspices of neocolonialism and neoliberalism, they increasingly expose their unjust character and bankruptcy and drive the people to intensify their struggle for national and social liberation. After winning the new democratic revolution, the Filipino people can proceed to the socialist stage of the Philippine revolution.

The betrayal of socialism by the modern revisionists since the late 1950s, culminating in their full restoration of capitalism in their respective countries from 1989 to 1991, led to the full sway of neocolonialism in the underdeveloped countries and neoliberalism in the entire world capitalist system. Since 2007-2008 when the US and other imperialist powers were hit hard by an economic and financial crisis comparable to that of the Great Depression, the conditions of exploitation and oppression have worsened as if without end, but have at the same time driven the broad masses of the people to wage resistance.

US imperialism has undermined its position as the sole superpower by becoming overdrawn to high tech military production and wars of aggression, by making China a major partner in neoliberal globalization, by relying on cheap Chinese labor to produce consumer goods, by undercutting manufacturing and employment in the US, by accelerating the financialization of the US economy and by becoming a debtor to China, Japan and a host of other countries. The full entry of China and Russia into the ranks of big capitalist powers has not strengthened the world capitalist system but has made it more cramped and more prone to the intensification of inter-imperialist contradictions.

Up to the first decade of the 21st century, China and Russia have been acquiescent to the US engaging in wars of aggression, as in Iraq and Afghanistan. But subsequently, they have become wary of US expansionism and have formed the Shanghai Cooperation Organization (SCO) to countervail the growing aggressiveness of the US and NATO. They have also promoted the BRICS as an economic bloc to serve as counterfoil to US arrogance in economic, trade and financial matters. The inter-imperialist contradictions are still apparently far from breaking out into direct or indirect war between any of the big capitalist powers, notwithstanding their involvement in civil strife, such as that in Syria and Ukraine.

In East Asia, China has moved from being the sponsor of the Chinese comprador big bourgeoisie collaborating with US and other multinational firms in sweatshop operations and private construction to being a rising industrial capitalist power, involving the nationalist collaboration of both state and private monopoly capitalism. But China is still avoiding being a full imperialist power that uses aggression to grab both economic and political territory. Even in UN peacekeeping missions, it prefers to contribute police advisors rather than military troops.

In maritime disputes over the South China Sea, China is conspicuously overreaching and potentially violent. But so far it has not engaged in any act of aggression for the purpose of subjugating any country. The submission by the Philippines of its maritime dispute with China to the International Tribunal on the Law of the Sea is a peaceful act and could be a peaceful way of resolving the said maritime dispute and similar disputes. A situation in which China can always insist on indisputable sovereignty over 90 per cent of the South China Sea is more fraught with violence.

The reactionary Aquino regime has boasted that the US will protect the Philippines from China and this is why it has allowed the US to have military bases, troops, facilities, war materiel (tanks, warships and attack planes) and even nuclear weapons on Philippine territory under the new Enhanced Defense Cooperation Agreement, in flagrant violation of the 1987 constitution. But in fact, the US has declared neutrality between the Philippines and China over their maritime dispute. It is deliberately maintaining a dual policy of cooperation and contention towards China. It is mindful that it has far more economic, trade, financial and security interests in China than in the Philippines. Even the Aquino ruling clique has lucrative relations with Chinese mining, construction, export-processing and marketing firms.

In the meantime, the long-running provocative thrust of neoconservative policy is to make the US dominant in the entire 21st century and use a broad spectrum approach to put down any imperialist rival. The more recent provocations resulting from the US pivot to Asia against China and the US-EU-NATO expansion into the Ukraine against Russia have pushed China and Russia to sign on May 21, 2014 a 30-year $400 billion natural gas agreement. This agreement solidifies the alliance of China and Russia against the hegemonic schemes of the US and is at the center of the most pertinent economic, financial and trade agreements and is concomitant to a greatly increased security alliance and cooperation between the two giant neighbors. The struggle for a redivision of the world among the great capitalist powers is steadily developing; it is only a matter of time before the huge earthquakes break out and serve as prelude to an unprecedented rise of anti-imperialist and socialist movements.

The Filipino people and the revolutionary forces have to grasp the complexity of the world capitalist system today and study how to make use of opportunities presented by inter-imperialist contradictions as did the Bolsheviks when there was no preceding socialist country to aid them. They must resolutely raise the level of their revolutionary consciousness and fighting capabilities. They must be determined to win the people's democratic revolution and proceed to the socialist revolution. They must be prepared to confront and counter the No. 1 imperialist enemy at every stage.

They can be confident that the turmoil of the world capitalist system, wracked by protracted, intensifying and widening crisis, marks the eve of renewed anti-imperialist and proletarian revolutions on a global scale. They must rely primarily on themselves in waging revolution as they have done successfully for so long, and intensify their efforts to win the solidarity and support of other peoples and revolutionary movements to take advantage of the worsening global crisis, inter-imperialist contradictions and the rise and spread of anti-imperialist and proletarian revolutions on a global scale.

VI. The Crimes of US Imperialism and its Puppets

US imperialism must be held accountable. When we speak of US imperialism, we refer to the US federal state and its various agencies, the corporations and banks which are impelled by monopoly capitalism to engage in aggression and plunder.

For the purpose of putting on trial US imperialism and its puppets, the people must be aware of the comprehensive range of crimes for which they are culpable:

1. The genocidal killing of 1.5 million Filipinos, amounting to 20 percent of the Philippine population of 7 million, is a horrendous crime. This was the brutal way by which US imperialism violated the national sovereignty of the Filipino and destroyed the Philippine republic.

2. The direct colonial occupation of the Philippines from 1902 to 1946, except for the interregnum of US occupation from 1942 to 1945, entailed the oppression and exploitation of the Filipino people. The people were taxed by the colonial state to pay for the costs of US aggression and colonial occupation.

3. The US monopoly capitalists extracted superprofits from the Philippine colony by plundering its natural resources, subjecting the workers to inhumanly low wages in public works and in US enterprises, promoting the unequal exchange of raw-material exports and manufactured imports and subjecting the country to debt peonage to US banks.

4. The US used the Philippines as a launching base for aggression against China and for getting a piece of the Chinese melon in the colonial game. This started the criminal use of US military bases in the Philippines for aggression against the neighboring countries of the Philippines, especially after World War II, against China, Korea, Vietnam, Laos, Cambodia and Indonesia.

5. The US engaged in cultural imperialism and perpetuated a colonial mentality. It imposed on the people not only the English language but also pro-imperialist ideas and values that obscured the blood debts of the US and misrepresented the exploitation of the people as beneficial. It bent the feudal and medieval belief system of the dominant Catholic church to serve the interests of US monopoly capitalism.

6. The US trained the bureaucrats, politicians and professionals to be servile to US imperialist power and to use the language of pro-imperialist liberal democracy to deceive the people. It was most responsible for promoting bureaucratic capitalism. It taught the children of the exploiting classes and the urban petty bourgeois to seek and hold power and mass private wealth through bureaucratic corruption.

7. The US has fostered the comprador big bourgeoisie as its principal trading and financial agents in the country. This class is responsible for ensuring raw material production for export and for importing foreign manufactures and distributing them in the country. The US has also retained the landlord class for the purpose of controlling food production and agricultural production for export.

8. When the US pretended to grant independence in the Philippines in 1946, it was sure of being able to rely on its puppets: the big compradors and landlords and bureaucrat capitalists. Since then it has retained control over the economy, the politics, the culture, security and diplomatic relations of the Philippines.

9. The US is culpable for the semi-colonial system of exploitation, underdevelopment and rampant poverty. The daily violence of exploitation has caused the untimely death of many more Filipinos than those 1.5 million killed from 1899 to 1913.

10. To this day, the US provides arms, indoctrination, training and strategic planning to the military and police forces of the reactionary state and is culpable for military campaigns of suppression and the gross and systematic human rights violations. It has forces of military intervention in the Philippines and uses these to dominate the Philippines and threaten neighboring countries under the US pretext of a permanent war on terrorism and the US strategic policy of pivot to East Asia.

US imperialism maintains hegemony over the Philippines because it is assisted by the big compradors, landlords and bureaucrat capitalists. These reactionary puppets are complicit with the US in grave crimes against the Filipino people and they take their own initiatives to oppress and exploit the people.

VIET NAM

ONE MAN'S ATONEMENT IN AN OCEAN OF GRIEF

Chuck Searcy

Decades after the fighting stopped, the war has not ended in Viet Nam. The struggle continues to rid the country of bombs and mines, and to overcome the legacy of Agent Orange.

More than four decades after the war in Viet Nam ended, unexploded ordnance remains a serious threat to communities throughout Viet Nam. Of the more than eight million tons of munitions used by the U.S during the war, an estimated 10 percent failed to detonate on impact. This means that thousands of unstable and dangerous munitions lie on the ground or inches under the soil. According to Viet Nam's Ministry of Labor, Invalids and Social Affairs, unexploded bombs (UXO) have been responsible for more than 100,000 injuries and deaths since 1975, with many of the survivors facing a lifetime of permanent disabilities. In Quang Tri Province, the former DMZ during wartime, about a third of the casualties have been children 16 years of age or younger.

Some 20 million gallons of Agent Orange were sprayed on jungle forests, crop lands, and rice fields in South Viet Nam (and Cambodia and Laos) from 1961 to 1971. The herbicide made by Monsanto, Dow Chemical, and other contractors contained the deadly chemical dioxin. It has caused major health problems, including cancers, birth defects, and severe psychological and neurological problems to American veterans and their children, and among a much larger population of Vietnamese families. Some of these families, comprising a population estimated by Vietnamese officials to total around three million victims, deal with the daily burden of two, three, in some cases even five, severely disabled children. These are children who may be unable to function in any normal way. Some are blind or deaf, some have cognitive limitations, they may be missing limbs or their arms and legs may be terribly misshapen, some must be watched constantly or restrained to prevent them from hurting themselves. These families are often among the poorest in Viet Nam, isolated from social services and medical care, dependent upon extended families and next-door neighbors for help.

My Return to Viet Nam

When I returned to Viet Nam in 1995 to work on a project sponsored by Vietnam Veterans of America Foundation (VVAF) with funding from USAID, I was unaware of the extent of the problem of war legacies here. Only as I became more engaged with the Vietnamese medical and rehabilitation professionals, providing orthopedic braces for children with polio, cerebral palsy, and other birth defects and illnesses, did I become aware from newspaper and TV reports that every week children, farmers, local villagers were being blown up by bombs and mines. The fact that countless families were struggling to care for severely disabled children, thought to be affected by Agent Orange, was a revelation for me.

I had been here as an Army enlisted man in 1967 and 1968 in a military intelligence unit in Saigon. I had seen the war, especially when the 1968 Tet Offensive changed history. But in the years after my return, though I was closely attuned to problems facing US veterans from Agent Orange, I was woefully uninformed about the extent of the damage still being done in Viet Nam today by Agent Orange and UXO, and the pain and sorrow that these consequences of war bring to Vietnamese families all over this country.

The war ended on April 30, 1975 for us Americans. We and the rest of the world witnessed televised images of the chaotic departure of the last US helicopter from CIA headquarters in Saigon (it was not the US Embassy, as is generally thought). The guns had fallen silent, after decades of war. America dropped a black curtain on Viet Nam, and we turned away.

The people of Viet Nam awakened on the morning of May 1, 1975, to the quietude of an exhausting and uncertain peace. The nation faced the grim challenge of cleaning up the damage and the devastation of the war, accounting for their nearly four million dead, caring for another four million wounded, and looking for 300,000 soldiers and civilians who were missing and unaccounted for.

Destruction Beyond Comprehension

The physical devastation was almost beyond comprehension at that time. Few images reached citizens of the US, so we were mostly unaware of the extent of the catastrophe, both damage to the physical infrastructure and the personal trauma Vietnamese had to face after years of warfare that divided families and loyalties.

Industry was virtually non-existent in both the north and south. The country's infrastructure, including critical agricultural production, had been badly damaged. In the South there were roughly 20,000 bomb craters. Among the 10 million refugees who swarmed into urban areas during and after the war were an estimated 250,000 drug addicts, 300,000 prostitutes, and three million unemployed—soon to be increased by the demobilization of half a million soldiers of the Army of the Republic of Viet Nam.

Relentless US bombing campaigns over nearly a decade took a terrible toll. Of 21,000 Vietnamese villages that existed before the war, 13,000 or 62 percent had been severely damaged or destroyed. Some 950 churches and pagodas were destroyed by bombing, along with 350 hospitals and 1,500 maternity wards, and nearly 3,000 high schools and universities. More than 15,000 bridges were destroyed while 26 million bomb craters were created, mostly by B-52s.

The people of Viet Nam woke up on May 1st to the arduous task of rebuilding their country, against overwhelming odds. Crops had to be planted in fields where the process might be a deadly one, due to landmines or cluster munitions or artillery rounds. Simple houses had to be constructed from the ground up, built on rubble from the war's destruction. Water systems and irrigation had to be restored. Roads had to be reopened. Schools had to be rebuilt or repaired, hospitals had to adjust from wartime emergencies to conventional civilian care, which would now include post-war medical consequences.

There may have been some hope among a few optimistic Vietnamese that the US would follow the enlightened approach of the Allies toward Germany and Japan after World War II, when the Marshall Plan was launched to help rebuild those countries after the destruction they had suffered in the war. That was a generous stroke of enlightened self-interest, intended to stabilize a troubled world, protect an uncertain peace, and provide a bulwark against Communism.

Some Vietnamese assumed that the US might be equally pragmatic and "generous" toward Viet Nam. They thought, at the very least, the US would stand by our pledge, documented in a letter from President Nixon to North Vietnam's leadership, to help rebuild the country from ruinous bomb damage.

Nixon promised to "contribute to postwar reconstruction in North Vietnam" in the amount of roughly $3.25 billion in aid over five years, to help rebuild Viet Nam. The funds were to become available once the Paris Peace Accord was signed which occurred on Jan. 27, 1973.

It Was Not to Be

Not only did the US renege on that promise officially, after Jimmy Carter became President, but the US had already imposed a crippling economic embargo against Viet Nam and persuaded other nations to follow. That meant that Viet Nam could not import or export goods and services as other nations did routinely, so the country's economic recovery was severely hampered. Viet Nam also became isolated politically, which was the goal of American officials.

It was not until February 1994 that President Bill Clinton lifted the US trade embargo against Vietnam. He tied the move to Viet Nam's unexpected cooperation in searching for the remains of missing American military personnel, most of whom had been shot down during bombing missions and whose remains had not been recovered.

Long after the embargo was lifted, a Vietnamese doctor complained to me about one of the injustices the embargo had caused. He noted that only in the year 2000 was Viet Nam able to eradicate polio, after the embargo was lifted and medical professionals could procure components needed for polio vaccine.

Normalization of Diplomatic Relations

Americans might be surprised that the US has driven hard bargains in our dealings with the Vietnamese, even after the political and military humiliation we suffered in "losing" the first war in our history (or maybe it's because of that historical indignity). Even in the early days of our engagement in Viet Nam, when the French were still ruling the country as colonial masters, the US provided some 80 percent of the funds and military equipment the French used in their desperate and losing battle against Ho Chi Minh's independence forces.

We never fully endorsed the Geneva Agreements, intended to bring peace to Viet Nam under Vietnamese rule for the first time in a thousand years. Instead, while espousing democratic traditions, President Eisenhower cancelled nationwide elections to choose a new government in 1956, because he knew that, in his words, Ho Chi Minh would have been elected with 80 percent of the vote. And that was unacceptable to the US. So much for democracy.

The bloody war years that followed were rife with examples of missed opportunities and misunderstandings that cost millions of lives and set the US on a path to perpetual war without congressional approval.

I remember how hopeful I was on April 30, 1975 when the war in Viet Nam was finally over. Though the experience for America had been a bitter one, at least we had learned a valuable lesson, I thought, and we Americans would never let something like this happen again.

How wrong I was! The wars continue, without congressional approval, in violation of the US Constitution, and usually with the full-throated endorsement of the mainstream media who seem no longer capable of asking probing and intelligent questions.

A Hard Bargain

In 1995, when the US and Viet Nam were very close to a comprehensive agreement to normalize diplomatic relations—something that both countries had sought to achieve—the US still stubbornly drove a hard bargain. Case in point: exchange of property and equipment belonging to the two sides during time of conflict. There were items such as the Vietnamese Embassy in Washington, DC which had been shuttered during the embargo, and now would be reopened as the Embassy of the Socialist Republic of Viet Nam. That was a no-brainer. And we got some property in Viet Nam that had belonged to us, including the former US Embassy site in Ho Chi Minh City which is today the US Consulate.

There were a few oddities. IBM Corporation was compensated for computers the company had left behind, in the final days before the end of the war in Saigon. A US government employee who had lived in a villa in the seaside town of Vung Tau was unable to take his ski boat and Evinrude motor with him in the final hours of April 30th. He was reimbursed several thousand dollars for the beach toys he had left behind.

Most significantly, the US insisted that Viet Nam must repay a debt incurred by the Saigon government, a government which no longer existed, of some $140 million USD in loans that had never been reimbursed. After protracted negotiations, the Vietnamese gave in, and made an initial down payment of $15 million. Luckily, sanity prevailed. When Sen. John McCain and then-Sen. John Kerry got wind of the deal, they intervened with special legislation that converted the debt to a scholarship fund enabling Vietnamese students to study in the US and American students to study in Viet Nam. That compromise softened some of the bitterness caused by our demand.

Remaining Legacies of the War

Now, after two decades of "normalized" relations between our two countries, the US is finally demonstrating unprecedented flexibility and sensibility, and earnestness, in dealing with the remaining legacies of the war—UXO and Agent Orange.

In Quang Tri Province, I have been associated with Project RENEW since the effort was launched in 2001 as an agreement between the provincial government and the Vietnam Veterans Memorial Fund (VVMF). When this agreement came to an end in 2011, the effort continued without interruption and now RENEW's main partner is Norwegian People's Aid (NPA), one of the leading humanitarian disarmament organizations in the world. Our mission is to make Quang Tri Province safe from unexploded ordnance such as mines, cluster bombs, grenades, and artillery rounds.

This is done through a survey methodology that consists of interviewing local people and comparing their knowledge on the ground with bombing maps provided by the U.S. Department of Defense. Demining teams then pinpoint the location of ordnance based on evidence, saving time and money. The ordnance is identified and safely detonated or removed to a demolition site.

In the past 10 years, RENEW and NPA teams have destroyed nearly 70,000 bombs. The number of accidents has gone down—from an average of around 70 a year going back to 1975 to one fatality in 2016. The year 2017 was the first year since 1975 without a single fatality in Quang Tri Province. (There were three minor injuries, not requiring hospitalization—luckily.)

Meanwhile, school children, farmers, local villagers are taught how to identify the ordnance they find, and how to report it immediately to one of the RENEW-NPA teams. The result has been an increasing number of reports, a growing number of UXO cleaned up, and a decreasing rate of accidents. Last year RENEW-NPA mobile teams received more than 1,000 call-ins, resulted in 4,175 bombs being destroyed.

RENEW also provides support including rehabilitation and prosthetic limbs and orthopedic braces to Vietnamese who have been disabled by bombs and mines. Some 1,800 amputees have received artificial limbs. There are still around 200 on the waiting list. RENEW also supports three blind workshops, providing incomes for UXO victims who lost their sight in bomb or mine accidents. They make brooms, toothpicks, incense sticks to sell and generate extra income for their families.

These projects have been supported by individual veterans and organizations such as Veterans For Peace (VFP), foundations and other institutions, and governments including Norway, Ireland, Japan, and Taiwan. From the first days of international cooperation in Viet Nam on the issue of unexploded ordnance, the US government—through association with NGOs—has been a willing supporter and donor, although modestly at the beginning. That has changed. Now the US government is by far the largest donor in the UXO cleanup effort, providing some $40 million in the past five years to RENEW and NPA, Mines Advisory Group (MAG), PeaceTrees, and Golden West Humanitarian Foundation (GWHF).

Agent Orange

The impact of Agent Orange lingers, and no one knows for how long into the future. The "herbicide" that the chemical companies concocted to strip the trees of leaves and to destroy food crops and other vegetation to expose the enemy was, we were assured, totally safe. No harm could come to human beings.

Now we know Agent Orange—specifically the dioxin by-product from its manufacture—is the most toxic substance known to man. It has caused terrible medical problems for thousands of American veterans and, according to the Vietnamese, an estimated three million Vietnamese. The U.S. Veterans Administration has budgeted more than $10 billion annually in medical benefits to American veterans affected by Agent Orange. No support, other than some funding for disability programs, has been directed to Vietnamese families suffering from Agent Orange.

However, after years of political posturing and public denials of any proven connection between Agent Orange /dioxin and problems believed to be associated with the chemical, the US government has moved in a more positive direction in recent years. Focusing first on the residual contamination that exists in Viet Nam, former US military bases where barrels of Agent Orange were stored, loaded onto airplanes, or otherwise handled (and often carelessly), the governments of both countries have agreed to cooperate in cleaning up the dioxin which has been found in the soil and water in the two largest and most immediate sites: the airport at Da Nang, and the former airbase at Bien Hoa. The Da Nang project has been completed, at a cost of $105 million, and the US has now committed to move next to the Bien Hoa airbase, which will certainly be even more expensive.

Meanwhile, in another important shift in direction, USAID is providing funds that can be channeled to efforts that will support families with members who suffer severe disabilities, presumed to be related to Agent Orange. That effort, hopefully, will bring additional balance to the picture and answer some of the critics who have accused the US of hypocrisy in recognizing medical problems among American veterans, but refusing to acknowledge that those same problems exist among the Vietnamese population.

Doing the Right Thing

Ironies abound as we look at woeful, sometimes overwhelming humanitarian needs that exist in places like Viet Nam, and among American veterans and their children, only because we are too eager to use the military as our first, and often our only, option. We act hastily, with inadequate information, without careful consideration of future consequences, and apparently with no concern for human, environmental, and financial costs. Then, when the enormity of the problems becomes apparent, and the bill comes due, we resort to denial, or outright lying to try to cover up the culpability—which usually should be spread widely.

There are times when the US does the right thing. It may be late, and that's unfortunate because much suffering has occurred because of such delays and indecision, or resistance among some in key positions of authority. We should get on with it. We still can introduce some sense of justice and fairness, some basic ethics, in our relations with Viet Nam. We can embrace, finally, the kind of old-fashioned morality that can make us a better people, and a better nation.

VIET NAM

LIFE AFTER AGENT ORANGE

Thomas Cox

The Interview took place in the town of Phong Nha, North Central Vietnam 145 kms north of the DMZ. It was mid December 2015 and I had been searching the past four months for an effective and reputable, Vietnamese, grassroots assistance program we could support financially once our OrangeAid Benefit Charity Concert for Agent Orange Victims series commenced. Tri, the video/IT wiz, and I were up until 3 am building websites. Come the morning the weather turned on us and he was a minute away from postponing our film shoot and heading back to Danang, from where he and his crew had traveled twelve hours from by bus, arriving late in the afternoon the day before. He came to film three possible concert site locations after I had gained support for the event from the Provincial People's Committee Vice Chairman, the same Authority that Hollywood had to court to be approved for filming scenes of the latest King Kong movie: Skull Island. Upon his arrival we were able to spend an hour over some BBQ goat and a few beers before hitting the computers hard that night. In that hour I had Hien from Hue, who worked at a tour outfit, come to meet Tri and bond a bit before our attempt to film locations the following day. As often the Vietnamese hit it off and our team was getting tight.

As the weather worsened I turned to Tri over the breakfast table and said, "Hey let's ask Hien if she can locate a village in the province that has a family that's been exposed to Agent Orange during the war." It was a long shot but we decided to give it a go. After all the concert could theoretically be at any one of a handful of terrific locations across the Vietnamese countryside.

The cause is about the four million plus victims that have all but been completely forgotten about. To Tri and Hien this was a seamless and natural change in direction.

Forty-five minutes after a phone call, Hien called back with an excited tone in her voice to say she's located a family right in Phong Nha and they agreed to an audio video interview, although being very reluctant to do it.

On our three motorbikes, driving through the increasing rain, we barked at each other how we would go about this "documentary" considering none of us had any first hand experience in this field.

Hien's English was perfect so we decided she would translate a series of questions that would come from me (while being reminded it was all my idea). I felt as nervous as Hien, and for that matter, Tri. They are both about thirty and have been working in tourism and marketing without any direct personal relation to the war—the illegal, immoral invasion waged on their previous generations. As many young Vietnamese, they try to look and move forward into the future.

Their ability to background the past atrocities committed on their people is dumbfounding.

Arriving in their rural commune just off the main road we came upon the family's house(shack).

I realized that I had seen the "boy" wondering the streets of Phong Nha over the past few weeks, the last living offspring of the parents that served their nation resupplying their army on the Ho Chi Minh Trail in Cambodia and Laos. The "boy" looked to be about twelve years old; he was twenty five.

His father and mother had lost three other children from the effects of their exposure to Agent Orange from the US planes above.

Here is a brief segment of the interview transcribed from the audio tape:

INTERVIEWER 1: Okay. Now what I want you to do is to ask them what happened to them, here? Where they were during the war? And why they were exposed to the airplane spraying Agent Orange? Anybody else in the family has the problem? Just a natural scenery and that they don't feel they are on 5TV. He'll fix it off. Everyone is happy, okay?

INTERVIEWER 2: Uhmm, this process, in general, is consequence of the war, isn't it?

FEMALE: Yes. I was voluntary youth.

MALE 1: She was voluntary youth and when she got back she was affected.

INTERVIEWER 2: Do you remember which year? When did you join the war?

FEMALE: From 1969 to 1971.

INTERVIEWER 2: Was Mr. or Mrs. affected?

MALE 1: Mrs. affected

FEMALE: No, Mr. affected, not me.

MALE 2: In Central Highland.

FEMALE: Yes, correct. It was in Central Highland. It was in Kon Tum that the chemical was sprayed where he got affected.

INTERVIEWER 2: Uhm, do you remember which year?

FEMALE: In 1969, he went to the battlefield and returned in 1971-72.

INTERVIEWER 2: In 1971-72 returned, right? In 1969 went to the battlefield, correct? Central Highland?

FEMALE: Southern Laos war. He was in Central Highland, yes.

INTERVIEWER 2: Did you both return at the same time?

FEMALE: No, he returned.... I returned first and he returned later.

INTERVIEWER 2: He returned later?

FEMALE: He returned in 1983.

INTERVIEWER 2: Went to the battlefield in 1969, returned 1972 and 1992 pregnant?

FEMALE: In 1992, I gave birth and got pregnant in 1991.

INTERVIEWER 2: In 1991, you got pregnant without knowing that you were affected with dioxin?

FEMALE: No, I didn't know.

INTERVIEWER 2: Only after your giving birth that you got to know?

FEMALE: Yes, that's correct. Four limbs of the infant showed.

MALE 2: After giving birth, the baby's limbs.

INTERVIEWER 2: Can you describe? What was the weight of the baby?

MALE 1: After being brought up for three years without observation of any growth.

INTERVIEWER 1: Can you tell me what the history was during the war and the development afterward in this condition?

INTERVIEWER 2: Can you tell about your participation in the war, your pregnancy and your giving birth to your child? You can speak in Vietnamese and I will interpret.

FEMALE: The history is that I was in the battlefield in 1969 and returned in 1972. In 1991, I got pregnant and gave birth in 1992. He was just a thing and very quiet. Only after three years that his eyes started blinking, lying down with little movement and never cried. As I gave birth to him so nurturing him is my responsibility. By then, a survey on poisonous/toxic chemical conducted by the Americans was carried out then my baby was sent to the hospital for examination to be concluded as affected by Agent Orange, therefore, he is entitled to the subsidies. He was growing up wandering around knowing nothing but obey what people telling him to sit or to eat. I and my husband both worked for the government before and are retired and entitled to subsidies, too, so just bringing him up without being able to do anything else in addition to us, sometime, having to look for him, terrified thinking he was missing through long night until two in the early morning before we returned to the house.

INTERVIEWER 2: She said she went to the south in 1969 and she came to the south of Laos in the same year without knowing their being exposed to dioxin until their return in 1971-1972, thought they were fine. In 1991, she got pregnant and gave birth in 1992. Until now he is almost 25 years old. And when he was first born, he was very small, only 1.7 kg with no eyes as you can see his face right now he looks like when he was young/little. Until he was three years old, his eyes opened a little bit, you know? And he has teeth but not so much like normal children. Since he was born until he was three years old, he could not active or move or something like that.

INTERVIEWER 1: Okay. Does he have any brothers or sisters in the same condition?

INTERVIEWER 2: Do you have any other offspring, his siblings, contaminated with the chemicals?

FEMALE: My last two children also. After gave birth to him and then the next two children also contaminated with the chemicals. They were teratogenic.

INTERVIEWER 2: This means three of your children?

FEMALE: Yes, three.

INTERVIEWER 2: Other children born earlier are not contaminated with the chemicals, aren't they?

FEMALE: Yes.

INTERVIEWER 2: How many children have you got?

FEMALE: Both before and after are nine.

INTERVIEWER 2: Your first six children are normal, aren't they? You lost two so how many do you have?

FEMALE: Seven. My last two were only sacs.

INTERVIEWER 2: Their first six children are ok as they were born before 1971, before their return in 1971-72 without knowing their bodies affected with dioxin, right? Yeah, and in 1992 when he was born, they didn't know he was affected with dioxin either. Only five year later, an American from Czech came in town conducting the examination and confirmed he is affected with dioxin. So by that time, they exactly know that he gets the dioxin. After him, she lost two more children because they were affected with dioxin and couldn't survive.

INTERVIEWER 1: We know, you and I both know, that there are certain aspects financially. How was the situation? How could they survive to take care of him? Well, I think it is more about the family. How do they manage to get by to nurture him?

INTERVIEWER 2: Can you tell what difficulties you faced during bringing him up?

FEMALE: My bringing him up was a challenge as I gave birth to him I should be responsible for bringing him up despite the fact that we were poor and to hide from people the fact that he was affected with the chemical. I deeply regretted at heart as I worked for the government and entitled to the subsidies. Tears flooded my eyes.

INTERVIEWER 2: So, she also gets the support from the government but then they take care of him until he's grown up, so it's so hard. It is really, really hard because he could not eat by himself. He could not learn. He could not hear anything and sometime they lost him until 2am as he was wandering around, left them no idea of where he was, but they think it is their responsibility therefore they must spend more time to take care of him. That's why both her and her husband couldn't do any other things like farming or anything else because they must spend more time to take care of him.

INTERVIEWER 1: There are 4.7 million people affected with Agent Orange because of the war. How many people have to take care of them? At least the father and mother of those families so may be ten million people beside the 4.7 million people affected. What's the alternative? What's the solution?

INTERVIEWER 2: The families' solution or the government's?

INTERVIEWER 1: The families of the 4.7 million people. They are innocent victims.

INTERVIEWER 2: (Whispering)

INTERVIEWER 1: What do you think, Tri? Are we ok?

TRI: Yup.

INTERVIEWER 1: He's very good.

TRI: He's playing with the animal.

INTERVIEWER 1: Okay. Get up. We have to do this seriously. He does it good. May be what you can do is speak to him a little bit. I am sorry I didn't get his name. What's his name?

INTERVIEWER 2: What's your name?

VICTIM: Hoa

INTERVIEWER 2: Okay, Hoa. Your full name?

FEMALE: Khai Van Hoa

INTERVIEWER 1: Maybe what you can do. Could you try to ask him a few questions? Now he is a little stressed.

INTERVIEWER: What's your name?

FEMALE: He doesn't know how to speak.

VICTIM: Hoa

INTERVIEWER 2: Oh, he can say it. Hoa.

FEMALE: (Giggling)

INTERVIEWER 2: Hoa, how old are you?

THE VICTIM: Twenty-six

INTERVIEWER 2: Twenty-five or twenty-six?

INTERVIEWER 2 + group: (Counting) One, two, three, four, five, six. (Giggling)

INTERVIEWER 2: Good job, right? Do you want to go to school?

THE VICTIM: Uh? Learning is better.

INTERVIEWER 2: He wants to come just for learning.

INTERVIEWER 1: When you have your place opened, maybe we can buy some...

INTERVIEWER 2: What do you like to eat?

THE VICTIM: Stew fish with pork.

INTERVIEWER 2: You like fish? Which fish?

THE VICTIM: Fish with pork.

INTERVIEWER 2: Fish with pork? (Giggling) Do you have girlfriend?

GROUP: (Giggling and laughing)

INTERVIEWER 2:
You are 26 already and you can get married. What do you like, Hoa?

THE VICTIM: Duck.

INTERVIEWER 2: Duck? (Giggling)

INTERVIEWER 1: Can you ask him what his dream is? What does he want the most?

INTERVIEWER 2: He said: "Duck".

INTERVIEWER 1: Duck? He wants the duck? Okay! Alright!

INTERVIEWER 2: What is your dream in the future, Hoa?

FEMALE: Dream? What is your dream?

VICTIM: Flying.

INTERVIEWER 2: Airplane or flying?

VICTIM: Flying.

INTERVIEWER 1: He wants to fly huh? He wants to fly an airplane huh? He's good boy huh? Okay.

INTERVIEWER 2: Helicopter.

INTERVIEWER 1: Helicopter.

INTERVIEWER 2: Flying an airplane, do you fly an airplane?

INTERVIEWER 1: Motorbike, airplane and then helicopter.

INTERVIEWER 2: Helicopter. He likes helicopter.

INTERVIEWER 1: How do you think, Tri? Do you want to continue or do you think it's enough?

Tri: Keep going.

INTERVIEWER 1: Okay. In the southern provinces during the war, what exact province is that?

INTERVIEWER 2: The province?

INTERVIEWER 1: Yeah, the province. In the south of Vietnam?

INTERVIEWER 2: Central Highland.

INTERVIEWER 1: Near Kon Tum or ...?

INTERVIEWER 2: Tay Nguyen.

INTERVIEWER 1: Tay Nguyen? Okay.

INTERVIEWER 2: He came to Tay Nguyen. I mean her husband and she was in the south of Laos.

INTERVIEWER 1: Okay. Would he be willing to talk with us a little bit about that period?

INTERVIEWER 2: Can you tell clearer about the war that you participated at the battlefield No. 95?

FEMALE: When I participated in Laos southern war, I carried goods for the soldiers through road No. 95 to Laos. The B52 were spraying toxic chemicals all over the road and into the village and calling for our youth volunteers' climbing up their ladder to their planes. Ignoring their calling, we moved under carrying foodstuffs such as: sugar, rice, salt, etc. gathered in a warehouse for the soldiers. We and voluntary youth from Thanh Hoa province were working diligently. For the affection, on our return, the B52 was spraying and we moved toward its direction and got affected. My limbs after being affected were paralyzed with staggering motion. After my return between 1972-1975/76, I was hospitalized for a long time. My assignment as a voluntary youth supplying foodstuffs and cartridge for the soldiers was tough with our daily physically carrying uninterruptedly in two years. Our little break was to rake the rice in the warehouse.

INTERVIEWER 2: So it was tough.

FEMALE: Yes, it was.

INTERVIEWER 2: So she was a volunteer working in the south of Laos at that time. She and many other volunteers from this area and in the north were carrying food, weapon, and everything from the north supplying to the south. The south was then showered with bombs. Speakers from B52 were calling for the voluntary youth and soldiers who were trained to shoot B52 down to join their team yet the volunteers keeps walking and carrying the goods under the green canopy of the jungle that hided them underneath. While B52, beside their dropping bombs, were also spraying Agent Orange that affected those who were under. I knew she and her team are among a lot of local female volunteers providing supports to the south of Vietnam.

TRI: Can you ask Hoa to look at the camera and smile so we can close the video?

INTERVIEWER 1: Can you ask him to look at Tri and say "Hello"?

INTERVIEWER 2: Will you look at the camera and smile for a nice picture?

TRI: Look at me/the camera.

INTERVIEW 2: Now let's look at the camera and smile.

INTERVIEWER 1: Thank you, Tri.

INTERVIEWER 2: Say thank you.

FEMALE: Say thank you. Thank you.

INTERVIEW 2: Look at the camera and smile for beauty.

GROUP: Smile.

TRI: It's okay. Nice job.

PALESTINE

HOW THE US PERPETUATES THE PALESTINIAN TRAGEDY

Sami Al-Arian

In his novel *1984* George Orwell introduced the lexicon of Big Brother's Doublespeak in which "War is peace, freedom is slavery, and ignorance is strength." In today's Western political circles and mainstream media coverage of the Israeli-Palestinian conflict, one may add a host of other phrases to this Orwellian Newspeak. Expressions that would fittingly describe this praxis might include "racism is democracy, resistance is terrorism, and occupation is bliss."[1]

If individuals were to rely solely on Western political leaders or media outlets as their source of information regarding the volatile situation in the occupied Palestinian territories, especially Jerusalem, they would not only be perplexed by the portrayals of victims and oppressors, but also confused about the history and nature of the conflict itself. For instance, one can hardly find mention of the words "Israeli occupation," or "illegal Israeli settlements" in official government statements or in most mainstream media outlets. Seldom if ever do they mention the fact that Jerusalem has been under illegal Israeli control for over 50 years, or that most confrontations in the holy city are provoked by Israeli attempts to change the status quo and impose its claim of jurisdiction on the Islamic and Christian holy sites within the walls of old Jerusalem.

Often Israel and its enablers in the political and media arenas try to obfuscate basic facts about the nature and history of the conflict.[2] Despite these attempts, however, the conflict is neither complicated nor has it existed for centuries. Dating from 1948, with the founding of the state of Israel, it is a century-old modern phenomenon that emerged as a direct result of political Zionism. This movement, founded by secular journalist Theodore Herzl in the late nineteenth century, has incessantly attempted to transform Judaism from one of the world's great religious traditions into an ethnic national colonialist movement with the aim of transferring Jews around the world to Palestine, while ethnically cleansing the indigenous Palestinian population from the land of their ancestors.[3] This is the essence of the conflict, and thus all of Israel's policies and actions can only be understood by acknowledging this fundamental reality.

It might be understandable, if detestable, for Israel and its Zionist defenders to circulate false characterizations of history and myths[4] to advance their political agenda. But it is incomprehensible, indeed reprehensible, for those who claim to advocate the rule of law, believe in the principle of self-determination, and call for freedom and justice to fall for this propaganda or to become its willing accomplices. In following much of American political leaders' rhetoric or media coverage of the conflict, one is struck by the lack of historical context, the deliberate disregard of empirical facts, and the contempt for established legal constructs and precedents. Here are the questions for which accurate answers seem so lacking:

- Are the Palestinian territories disputed or occupied?
- Do Palestinians have a legal right, embedded in international law, to resist their occupiers, including the use of armed struggle, or is every means of resistance considered terrorism?
- Does Israel have any right to old Jerusalem and its historical and religious environs as President Donald Trump recently declared?
- Is the protraction of the so-called "cycle of violence" really coming proportionally from both sides of the conflict?
- Is Israel a true democracy?
- Should political Zionism be treated as a legitimate national liberation movement (from whom?) while ignoring its overwhelmingly racist manifestations?

- Is Israel genuine about seeking a peaceful resolution to the conflict?
- Can the U.S. really be an honest broker between the two sides as it has persistently promoted itself in the region?

The factual answers to these questions would undoubtedly clear the fog and lead objective observers not only to a full understanding of the conflict, but also to a deep appreciation of the policies and actions needed to bring it to an end.

Covering for Israel's Crimes Politically and Diplomatically

In its pursuit of strategic objectives across the globe,[5] the United States has embarked on several policies and grand strategies, none of which explain the "special strategic partnership" it has established with the state of Israel. Mearsheimer and Walt[6] have comprehensively argued that Israel has become a domestic issue within American politics, where its outsized influence could not be understood if it were merely analyzed as a foreign policy issue subject to the classic national security interest theory for states or even empires. Since Israel's establishment, with few exceptions, its relationship with the U.S. has undergone several evolutions. The U.S. started as a political supporter of Israel, eventually becoming not only its chief financial benefactor and military supplier, but also its enabler, and ultimately becoming an accomplice and a full partner in its expansionist policies, aggressive activities, and criminal behavior.

In politics and diplomacy, the U.S. has been Israel's protector on the world stage to the consternation of most countries. After the passing of U.N. Resolution 3379 in 1975 that declared Zionism as a "form of racism and racial discrimination" because of its exclusivist ideology,[7] the U.S. worked relentlessly to repeal it. Indeed, it was revoked 16 years later under tremendous pressure from the U.S. in the aftermath of the first Gulf war in 1991. In subsequent years the U.S. has continuously shielded Israel from any action or meaningful criticism at the U.N. Human Rights Council and UNESCO, to the point of withholding its dues, or even withdrawing its membership from the latter because of the Palestinian Authority's symbolic admission into the U.N. cultural body.[8]

Furthermore, in contrast to the overwhelming majority of nations across the globe, the U.S. has doggedly defended Israel's destructive behavior, in many instances standing virtually alone in its stubborn support of the latter's fully documented illegal belligerent actions. Using its veto powers in the United Nations Security Council, the U.S. has cast, since 1973, forty-four vetoes[9] in order to shield Israel from any condemnation or enforcement of international law, or to hold it accountable for its aggressive posture dictated by international legal norms. Such blanket support has given the Zionist state a blank check to use its military power at will to occupy and seize land, declare war against its neighbors, commit atrocious human rights violations against civilians in Palestine, Lebanon, and other neighboring states, and to defy at will international law and scores of international treaties such as the Geneva conventions, which were designed to provide protection to people under military occupation. According to the former Israeli deputy national security adviser Charles Freilich, "Israel's relationship with the United States is a fundamental pillar of its national security. Militarily, diplomatically, and economically, American support has for decades been a vital strategic enabler (of Israel)."[10] But such support for Israel surpasses the enablement of any counter views via party politics in the U.S. Since 1973, every Republican and Democratic president has cast vetoes in the U.N. Security Council on behalf of Israel.[11].

The scope of crimes the U.S. has covered for Israel in these vetoes and the degree it was willing to protect it from accountability and compliance is mind boggling. Through its frequent use of vetoes, the U.S. has effectively emboldened the Zionist state to further disregard the will of the world. Because of the U.S. political shield, Israel was allowed to kill with impunity, commit assassinations, and murder civilians, including women and children. It has also been given a free pass in committing crimes against humanity, embarking on genocidal policies, and violations of countless U.N. resolutions and human rights conventions. All the vetoed resolutions would have easily passed and been enforceable had it not been for U.S. objections.

These vetoes included resolutions

- demanding that Israel apply the Fourth Geneva Conventions for people under occupation as well as comply with other human rights treaties [1976, 1984, 1985, 1989 (4)];
- demanding that Israel end its occupation and military rule or show support for the right of Palestinian self-determination [1973, 1976 (2), 1980, 1982, 2001, 2014];

- demanding the end of aggression or invasion against Gaza, the West Bank or Lebanon [1982 (3), 1985, 1986, 1988 (3), 2004];
- denouncing the killing of Palestinian civilians or U.N. workers [1987, 2002];
- denouncing the massacre of over two thousand Palestinians in Sabra and Shatila refugee camps, for which an Israeli commission had partially assigned the responsibility of the massacres to then Israeli Defense Minister Ariel Sharon [1983];
- denouncing the hijacking of a civilian airplane [1986];
- condemning the assassination or the protection against the assassination of Palestinian leaders [1982, 1988 (2), 2001, 2003, 2004];
- demanding the release of civilian prisoners or end of the siege against Gaza [2006];
- denouncing the construction of the illegal (as determined by the World Court) Separation Wall [2003];
- demanding the end of annexation of Palestinian and Arab lands and settlement activities [1982, 1995, 1997 (2)];
- demanding that Israel cease changing the character of Jerusalem or defying the implementation of U.N. resolutions on Jerusalem and the Aqsa Holy Shrine [1982, 1986, 2017].

The U.S. even opposed appointing a fact finding commission regarding harsh Israeli military policies during the first Palestinian intifada [1990] or assassinating defenseless and unarmed Palestinian protesters at the border with Gaza [2018].

Aiding and Abetting Israel's Colonialist Policies

But lending Israel its full political and diplomatic support for its aggressive behavior and brutal policies pales in comparison to the financial and military aid the Zionist state has been receiving from the U.S. For decades, Israel has by far been the recipient of the largest aid of any other country. According to the Congressional Research Office report,[12] the U.S. has provided Israel with more than $135 billion in direct aid since 1973, seventy percent of which was military. That figure does not even account for the tens of billions of dollars in loan guarantees and other special aid, as well as the permission to use advanced U.S military equipment stored in Israel by making them readily available during emergencies. In 2006, Mearsheimer and Walt estimated that aid to have been around $150 billion,[13] which would subsequently add up to almost $190 billion by 2018.

More than two decades ago, the U.S. set up a long-term program that guarantees military and economic aid to the Zionist state for ten years in advance, instead of being subject to the annual budgetary pressures. In 1997, President Bill Clinton signed a ten-year military and economic aid package to Israel exceeding $21 billion, while President George W. Bush subsequently signed another ten-year package in 2006 for $30 billion. Similarly, President Barak Obama signed, despite his public feud with Israeli Prime Minister Benjamin Netanyahu, another ten-year deal for $38 billion in 2016. In addition, Israel is the only country that receives all of its aid in cash at the beginning of the fiscal year in October in order to earn interest before it is even allocated, while the U.S. treasury pays billions in interest for the money it borrows in order to cover its budget deficit.

Moreover, the U.S. has been the main supplier of virtually all of Israel's military hardware including the most advanced state of the art technology and know-how, even when the closest U.S. NATO allies were denied access, such as the F35 fighter planes. All the sophisticated ammunitions, from the cluster and phosphorus bombs, to the tear gas and rubber bullets used against defenseless civilians, to the bulldozers and other heavy equipment destroying Palestinian homes, livelihood, and olive groves, are supplied for free by the U.S. In essence, the U.S has transformed itself in this conflict into a direct participant and an active Israeli partner in causing and perpetuating the pain and suffering of the Palestinians. Contrary to its claims, the U.S. has never been an honest broker searching for just peace in the Israeli-Arab conflict.[14]

Occupation, Self-Determination, and International Law

There should be no disputing that the territories seized by Israel in June 1967, including East Jerusalem, are occupied. Dozens of U.N. resolutions have passed since November 1967, including binding Security Council resolutions calling on Israel to withdraw from the occupied territories, which the Zionist State has stubbornly refused to comply with. In fact, if there were any "disputed" territories, they should be those Palestinian territories that Israel confiscated[15] in 1948, through a campaign of terror, massacres,[16] and military conquests,[17] which resulted in forcibly and illegally expelling over 800,000 Palestinians from their homes, villages, and towns, in order to make room for thousands of Jews coming from Europe and other parts of the world. Consequently, U.N. Resolution 194 mandated that these Palestinian "refugees wishing to return to their homes ... should be permitted to do so." This resolution has now remained unfulfilled for seven decades. There is also no dispute in international law that Israel has been a belligerent occupier[18] and as such, triggering the application of all the relevant Geneva Conventions, as the Palestinian people have been under occupation since their "territory is actually placed under the authority of the hostile army."[19]

Furthermore, the right to self-determination for the Palestinian people and their right to resist their occupiers by all means are well established in international law. In 1960, U.N. resolution 1514[20] adopted the "Declaration on the Granting of Independence to Colonial Countries and Peoples." It stated that, "All peoples have the right to self-determination", and that, "the subjection of peoples to alien subjugation, domination and exploitation constitutes a denial of fundamental human rights and is contrary to the Charter of the United Nations." Ten years later the U.N. adopted Resolution 2625[21] which called on its members to support colonized people or people under occupation against their colonizers and occupiers. In fact, U.N. Resolution 3246[22] reaffirmed in 1974 "the legitimacy of the peoples' struggle for liberation from colonial and foreign domination and alien subjugation by all available means, including armed struggle." Four years later U.N. Resolution 33/24[23] also strongly confirmed "the legitimacy of the struggle of peoples for independence, territorial integrity, national unity and liberation from colonial and foreign domination and foreign occupation by all available means, particularly armed struggle," and "strongly condemned all governments" that did not recognize "the right to self-determination to the Palestinian people."

As for occupied Jerusalem, the U.N. Security Council adopted in 1980 two binding resolutions (476[24] and 478[25]) by a vote of 14-0 (the U.S. abstained and did not veto either resolution). Both resolutions condemned Israel's attempt to change "the physical character, demographic composition, institutional structure, (and) the status of the Holy City of Jerusalem." It also reaffirmed "the overriding necessity to end the prolonged occupation of Arab territories occupied by Israel since 1967, including Jerusalem," and called out Israel as "the occupying power." It further considered any changes to the city of Jerusalem as "a violation of international law."

The Israeli Use of Violence, and the Palestinian Right of Resistance

Living under brutal occupation for over half a century without any prospect for its end, the Palestinian people, particularly in Jerusalem, have for years been protesting against Israeli incursions on their holy sites[26] and revolting against the ceaseless occupation. As a consequence, the Israeli army, aided by thousands of armed settlers[27] roaming the West Bank, have intensified their use of violence, which has resulted[28] in hundreds of deaths, thousands of injuries, and tens of thousands of arrests. The Israeli army and the settlements-based armed gangs, though forbidden under international law and the Geneva conventions, have regularly employed various violent means in order to force Palestinian exile or compel submission to the occupation. The Israeli harsh tactics have included:

- settler violence[29] and provocation[30] under full army protection,[31]
- targeting children,[32] including kidnapping,[33] killing,[34] as well as arresting children as young as five,[35]
- burning infants alive,[36]
- the constant use of collective punishment[37] and house demolitions,[38]
- the use of excessive prison sentences[39] for any act of defiance including throwing rocks,
- storming[40] revered religious sites,[41] and
- the deliberate targeting of journalists[42] who dare to challenge Israeli hegemony.

The Palestinian people, whether under occupation or under siege, in exile and blocked by Israel from returning to their homes, or denied their right to self-determination, have the legitimate right to resist the military occupation and its manifestations such as the denial of their freedom and human rights, the confiscation of their lands, or the building and expansion of Israeli colonies on their lands. Although most Palestinians opt for the use of nonviolent resistance as a prudent tactic against the brutality of the occupation, international law does not limit their resistance only to the use of peaceful means. In essence, *the right to legitimate armed resistance, subject to international humanitarian law, is enshrined in international law and cannot be denied to any people* including the Palestinians in their struggle to gain their freedom and exercise their right to self-determination. Furthermore, international law does not confer any right on the occupying power to use any force against their occupied subjects, in order to maintain and sustain their occupation, including in self-defense. In short, aggressors and land usurpers are by definition denied[43] the use of force to subjugate their victims. Consequently, as a matter of principle enshrined in international law and regardless of any political viability, strikes against military targets including soldiers, armed settlers, or other tools and institutions of the occupation are legitimate and sanctioned by international law, and thus any action against them, non-violent or otherwise, cannot be condemned or deemed terrorism.

Moreover, the moral argument regarding the validity of using armed struggle against oppression and denial of political rights by tyrannical and colonial regimes is well established. Patrick Henry rallied his countrymen in 1775 prior to the American Revolution in his famous call "give me liberty or give me death." Even civil rights and nonviolence icon Martin Luther King, Jr. rejected pacifism in the face of aggression. He only questioned the tactical utility of violence when he stated "I contended that the debate over the question of self-defense was unnecessary since few people suggested that Negroes should not defend themselves as individuals when attacked. The question was not whether one should use his gun when his home was attacked, but whether it was tactically wise to use a gun while participating in an organized demonstration." Mahatma Gandhi saw active resistance as more honorable than pacifism when he said "I would rather have India resort to arms in order to defend her honor than that she would, in a cowardly manner, become or remain a helpless witness to her own dishonor." Nelson Mandela reflected on this debate when he asserted that he resorted to armed struggle only when "all other forms of resistance were no longer open", and demanded that the Apartheid regime "guarantee free political activity" to blacks before he would call on his compatriots to suspend armed struggle. Accordingly, the debate over whether the use of armed resistance against Israeli occupation advances the cause of justice for Palestinians is not a question of legitimacy, but rather of sound political strategy in light of the skewed balance of military power and massive public support from peoples around the globe for their just struggle.

Yet, the reality of the conflict actually reveals that the Palestinian people have overwhelmingly been at the receiving end of the use of ruthless Israeli violence and aggression since 1948. With the exception of the 1973 war (initiated by Egypt and Syria to regain the lands they lost in the 1967 war) every Arab-Israeli war in the past seven decades ('48, '56, '67, '78, '82, '02, '06, etc.) was initiated by Israel and resulted in more uprooting and misery to the Palestinians.[44] Still, since 2008 Israel launched three brutal wars against Gaza[45] with devastating consequences.

- In the 2008/2009 war, Israel killed 1417 Palestinians and lost 13 people including 9 soldiers.
- In the 2012 war, Israel killed 167 Palestinians and lost 6 including 2 soldiers.
- And in the 2014 war, Israel killed 2104 Palestinians, including 539 children, with 475,000 people made homeless, 17,500 homes destroyed, while 244 schools and scores of hospitals and mosques were damaged. In that war Israel lost 72 including 66 soldiers.

In short, since late 2008 Israel killed 3688 Palestinians in its three declared wars and lost 91 including 77 soldiers. Shamefully the deliberate targeting of Palestinian children has been amply documented[46] as over two thousand[47] have been killed by Israel since 2000. This massive intentional use of violence by Israel against the Palestinians, especially in Gaza (which has been under a crippling siege for over a decade) was investigated, determined to constitute war crimes, and condemned by the U.N. in the Goldstone Report,[48] as well as by other human rights groups such as Amnesty International[49] and Human Rights Watch.[50]

The Deceptive Peace Process Brokered by the U.S.

The 1993 Oslo process gave rise to the promise of ending decades of Israeli occupation. But the process was rigged[51] from the start as many experts have since admitted.[52] It was an Israeli ploy to halt the first Palestinian uprising and give Israel the breathing room it needed to aggressively and permanently colonize[53] the West Bank, including East Jerusalem. It was an accord with a lopsided balance of power, between one side which held all the cards and gave no real concessions—aided and abetted by biased U.S. administrations masquerading as neutral mediators—and a much weaker side stripped of all its bargaining chips.[54] During this period the number of settlements in the West Bank more than doubled[55] and the number of settlers increased by more than sevenfold to over 700 thousand including in East Jerusalem.

The world has none other than Benjamin Netanyahu to acknowledge that Israel has no intention of withdrawing or ending its occupation. After serving his first term as a prime minister, Netanyahu was exposed in a leaked video[56] while visiting a settlement in 2001, where he admitted to his true intention of grabbing as much as 98 percent of Palestinian territories in the West Bank and halting the fraudulent Oslo process. Believing that the camera was off, he spoke candidly to a group of settlers about his strategic vision, plans, and tactics.

On his vision he assured them that, "The settlements are here. They are everywhere." He stated, "I halted the fulfillment of the Oslo agreements. It's better to give two percent than 100 percent. You gave two percent but you stopped the withdrawal." He later added, "I gave my own interpretation to the agreements in such a way that will allow me to stop the race back towards the 1967 borders." As for the tactics, Netanyahu freely confessed his strategy of causing so much pain to the Palestinians that they would submit to the occupation rather than resist. He said, "The main thing is to strike them not once but several times so painfully that the price they pay will be unbearable, causing them to fear that everything is about to collapse." When he was challenged that such a strategy might cause the world to consider Israel as the aggressor, he dismissively said, "They can say whatever they want." He also implied how he was not concerned about American pressure. To the contrary he asserted that he could easily manipulate Israel's main benefactor when he stated "America is something you can easily maneuver and move in the right direction. I wasn't afraid to confront Clinton. I wasn't afraid to go against the U.N." Even though world leaders consider Netanyahu a "liar" and they "can't stand him" as demonstrated in the exchange[57] between former French president Nicolas Sarkozy and former president Barak Obama, virtually no Western leader has ever stood up to Israel. This is also in spite of what a British parliamentarian stated, which is that 70 percent of Europeans consider Israel a "danger to world's peace."[58] However, the obstructionist posture and expansionist policies of Israeli leaders are not restricted to the Israeli right. Former Labor leader Ehud Barak was equally determined in 2000 at Camp David[59] not to withdraw from parts of the West Bank and Jerusalem, or dismantle the settlements.[60]

For decades, the world waited for Israel to decide its destiny by choosing two out of three defining elements: its Jewish national character, its claim to democracy, and its claim to the lands of so-called "greater Israel." If it chose to retain its Jewish majority and claim to be democratic, it would have had to withdraw from the lands it occupied in 1967 (two-state solution). If it insists on incorporating the lands and having a democracy, it would have to integrate its Arab populations while forsaking its Jewish exceptionalism in a secular state (one-state solution). Sadly but true to its Zionist nature, Israel has chosen to maintain its Jewish exclusiveness over all of historical Palestine, and to subjugate its Palestinian populations under a harsh military regime, and consequently structure itself as a manifestly Apartheid[61] state.

Political Zionism and the True Nature of the Israeli State

For over a century political Zionism has evoked intense passions and emotions on both sides of the Israeli-Palestinian conflict: from its ardent supporters as well as its critics and hapless victims. Zionists hail their enterprise as a national liberation movement for the Jewish people while its opponents condemn it as a racist ideology that practiced ethnic cleansing, instituted racial and religious discrimination, and committed war crimes to realize its goals. Often, the public is denied unfiltered information about the true nature of political Zionism and its declared state. And unfortunately the media conglomerates rarely cover that aspect of the conflict, which contributes to the public's confusion and exasperation.

Since its creation in 1948, Israel has passed laws and implemented policies that institutionalized discrimination against its Arab Palestinian minority. In the aftermath of its 1967 invasion, it instituted a military occupation regime that has denied basic human and civil rights to millions of Palestinians whose population now exceeds the number of Israeli Jews in the land within historical Palestine. In addition, in defiance of international law, Israel has obstinately refused to allow the descendants of the Palestinian people that it expelled in 1948 and 1967 to return to their homes, while granting millions of people of other nationalities the right to become citizens of the Israeli state upon arrival simply because they are Jewish. Meanwhile, millions of Palestinians who have been rotting in squalid refugee camps since 1948 are denied their right of return.

Zionist leaders from Ben-Gurion to Netanyahu have always claimed that Israel was a democracy similar to other Western liberal democracies. But perhaps the best way to examine this claim and illustrate the nature of the modern Zionist state is through a comparative analogy (a similar example could also be found in Israeli historian Shalom Sand's book[62]):

What if a Western country claiming to be a democracy, such as the U.S. or the U.K., were officially to change its constitution and system to become the state of the White Anglo-Saxon Protestants (WASPs)? Even though its African, Hispanic, Asian, Catholic, Jewish, and Muslim citizens as well as other minorities would still have the right to vote, hold political offices, and enjoy some civil and social rights, they would have to submit to the new nature and exclusive character of the WASP state. Moreover, with the exception of the WASP class of citizens, no other citizen would be allowed to buy or sell any land, and there would be permanent constitutional laws that would forbid any WASP from selling any property to any members of other ethnicities or religions in the country. Its Congress or parliament would pass laws that would also forbid any WASP from marrying outside his or her social class, and if any such "illegal" marriage were to take place, it would not be recognized by the state. As for immigration, only WASPs from around the world would be welcome. In fact, there would be no restrictions on their category as any WASP worldwide could claim immediate citizenship upon arrival in the country with full economic and social benefits granted by the state, while all other ethnicities are denied. Furthermore, most of the existing minorities in the country would be subjected to certain "security" policies in order to allow room for the WASPs coming from outside. So in many parts of the country, there would be settlements and colonies constructed only for the new WASP settlers and consequently some of the non-WASP populations would have to be restricted or relocated. In these new settlements the state would designate WASP-only roads, WASP-only schools, WASP-only health clinics, WASP-only shopping malls, WASP-only parks or swimming pools. There would also be a two-tier health care system, educational system, criminal justice system, and social welfare system. In this dual system for example, if a WASP assaults or kills a non-WASP he would receive a small fine or a light sentence that would not exceed few years, while if a non-WASP murders a WASP, even accidentally, he would receive a harsh or mandatory life sentence. In this system, where the police is exclusively staffed by WASPs, the Supreme Court would routinely sanction the use of torture against any non-WASP, subject to the judgment of the security officers. Such a system would clearly be so manifestly racist, patently criminal, and globally abhorred that no one would stand by it or defend it. But could such a regime even exist or be accepted in today's world? (I realize that some people may argue that many of these practices had actually occurred in the past against certain segments of the population in some Western societies. But no government today would dare to embrace this model or defend its policies.)

Yet, because of the Zionist nature of the Israeli state, this absurd example is actually a reality with varying degrees in the daily lives of the Palestinian people, whether they are nominal citizens of the state, live under occupation or under siege, or have been blocked for decades from returning back to their homes, towns, and villages. Such a system would not only be condemned but no decent human being or a country that respects the rule of law would even associate with it or tolerate it.

From its early days, prominent Jewish intellectuals have condemned the racist nature of the Zionist state.[63] Albert Einstein and Hannah Arendt wrote in 1948 condemning Zionist leaders of Israel who "openly preached the doctrine of the Fascist state."[64] Israeli scientist and thinker Israel Shahak considered Israel as "a racist state in the full meaning of this term, where the Palestinians are discriminated against, in the most permanent and legal way and in the most important areas of life, only because of their origin."[65] Renowned American intellectual Noam Chomsky considers Israel's actions in Palestine as even "much worse than Apartheid"[66] ever was in South Africa. Israeli historian Ilan Pappé argues that "The Zionist goal from the very beginning was to have as much of Palestine as possible with as few Palestinians in it as possible,"[67] while American historian Howard Zinn thought that "Zionism is a mistake."[68] American academic and author Norman Finkelstein has often spoken out against the racist nature of the Zionist state and condemned its manipulation of the Nazi Holocaust to justify its colonization of Palestine.[69] British historian Tony Judt described Israel as "an anachronism"[70] because of its exclusive nature in comparison to its "non-Jewish citizens." Former U.N. Special Rapporteur for Occupied Palestine Professor Richard Falk called Israeli policies in the Occupied Territories "a crime against humanity"[71] and compared Israel's treatment of the Palestinians to the Nazi treatment of the Jews and has said, "I think the Palestinians stand out as the most victimized people in the world." Recently, prominent American Jewish academics posed the question: "Can we continue to embrace a state that permanently denies basic rights to another people?"[72] Their answer was an emphatic call for a complete boycott against the Zionist state.

Furthermore, Israeli politicians and religious leaders regularly use racist rhetoric to appeal to their constituents and articulate their policies. In the last Israeli national elections in 2015, Prime Minister Netanyahu tweeted to the Israeli public, "The right-wing government is in danger. Arab voters are coming out in droves to the polls."[73] Defense minister Avigdor Lieberman advocated new ethnic cleansing through "the transfer" of Palestinian citizens from the state.[74] One prominent Rabbi considered "killing Palestinians a religious duty,"[75] while another declared that "It is not only desirable to do so, but it is a religious duty that you hold his head down to the ground and hit him until his last breath."[76] Former Sephardic Chief Rabbi Mordechai Eliyahu, one of the most senior religious leaders in Israel ruled that "there was absolutely no moral prohibition against the indiscriminate killing of civilians during a potential massive military offensive on Gaza."[77] Racism in Israel is so pervasive that a Jewish settler stabbed[78] another Jew, and another settler killed[79] a fellow Jewish settler not because the perpetrators were threatened, but because the victims looked Arab. Israeli racism is so widespread among its population that journalist Max Blumenthal, who investigated the Israeli society's attitudes towards the Palestinians,[80] was himself surprised about "the extent to which groups and figures, remarkably similar ideologically and psychologically to the radical right in the U.S. and to neo-fascist movements across Europe, controlled the heart of Israeli society and the Israeli government."[81]

In short, the ideology of political Zionism, as has amply been demonstrated within the state of Israel, with its exclusionary vision and persistent policies of occupying the land and subjugating its people, has proven without any doubt that it represents a relic of a bygone era that utterly lacks civilized behavior or claims to a democratic system. Therefore, any discussion, coverage, analysis, or debate of the Palestinian-Israeli conflict that sidesteps the nature and ideology of the Israeli state is not only disingenuous and lacks credibility, but also contributes to the deepening of the conflict, the continuous suffering of its victims, and the illusion of finding a potential just and peaceful outcome.

In the 1980s, the U.S. supported Apartheid South Africa and embarked on failed policies to rehabilitate the racist regime.[82] It was the last country to abandon the Apartheid government in Pretoria after a long global struggle that culminated in a powerful boycott campaign, including in the U.S., to irretrievably dismantle the immoral Apartheid system in 1994. Similarly, there is a growing world-wide movement to free the Palestinian people from the yoke of occupation, dispossession, and exile, called the Boycott, Divestment, and Sanctions or BDS movement.[83] But BDS supporters and campaigns need to expand and strengthen across the globe, particularly in the U.S. in order to pressure the power elite to abandon the critical U.S. support given to Israel, which has been sustaining a demonstrably racist regime for far too long. To dismantle the institutions of the Apartheid system[84] in Israel is for the American people to reclaim back their professed ideals of freedom, equality, democracy, dignity, and human rights. This is the true challenge.

In his farewell address in 1961, President Dwight Eisenhower warned the nation against the dangers of the military-industrial complex by calling for engaged and knowledgeable citizens to be involved. He noted that, "In the councils of government, we must guard against the acquisition of unwarranted influence, whether sought or unsought, by the military-industrial complex. The potential for the disastrous rise of misplaced power exists and will persist. We must never let the weight of this combination endanger our liberties or democratic processes. We should take nothing for granted. Only an alert and knowledgeable citizenry can compel the proper meshing of the huge industrial and military machinery of defense with our peaceful methods and goals."[85]

Likewise, George Washington pronounced in his own farewell address in 1796, a prophetic warning to the citizens of his young nation that appropriately describes the current state of affairs between the U.S. and Israel. President Washington said, "[A] passionate attachment of one nation for another produces a variety of evils. Sympathy for the favorite nation, facilitating the illusion of an imaginary common interest in cases where no real common interest exists, and infusing into one the enmities of the other, betrays the former into a participation in the quarrels and wars of the latter without adequate inducement or justification. It leads also to concessions to the favorite nation of privileges denied to others which is apt doubly to injure the nation making the concessions... And it gives to ambitious, corrupted, or deluded citizens (who devote themselves to the favorite nation), facility to betray or sacrifice the interests of their own country, without odium, sometimes even with popularity; gilding, with the appearances of a virtuous sense of obligation, a commendable deference for public opinion, or a laudable zeal for public good, the base or foolish compliances of ambition, corruption, or infatuation. As avenues to foreign influence in innumerable ways, such attachments are particularly alarming to the truly enlightened and independent patriot."[86]

If these words are taken to heart and acted upon, peace with justice could indeed be realized once again in the Holy Land.

ENDNOTES

1   Part of this essay appeared in CounterPunch on December 8, 2015 in an article by the author titled: "Back to Basics: Clearing the Fog of the Palestinian-Israeli Conflict." See: https://www.counterpunch.org/2015/12/08/back-to-basics-clearing-the-fog-of-the-palestinian-israeli-conflict/

2   See: Beit-Hallahmi, Benjamin, *Original Sins, Reflections on the History of Zionism and Israel*, Olive Branch Press, 1993.

3   See: Pappe, Ilan, *The Ethnic Cleansing of Palestine*, Oneworld Publications, 2006.

4   See: Pappe, Ilan, *Ten Myths about Israel*, Verso, 2017.

5   Friedman, George, *The Next 100 Years*, Anchor Books, 2010, pp. 40-46.

6   See: Mearsheimer, John J. and Stephen M. Walt, *The Israel Lobby and U.S. Foreign Policy*, Farrar, Straus, and Girdoux, 2007.

7   https://documents-dds-ny.un.org/doc/RESOLUTION/GEN/NR0/000/92/IMG/NR000092.pdf?OpenElement

8   https://www.washingtonpost.com/news/post-nation/wp/2017/10/12/u-s-withdraws-from-unesco-the-u-n-s-cultural-organization-citing-anti-israel-bias/?utm_term=.0d04a02e05ef

9   US Vetoes at UN Security Council: 1973 (1): 7/26; 1976 (3): 1/25, 3/25, 6/29; 1980 (1): 4/30; 1982 (7): 1/20, 2/25, 4/2, 4/20, 6/9, 6/25, 8/6; 1983 (1): 2/15; 1984 (1): 9/6; 1985 (2) : 3/12, 9/13; 1986 (3): 1/17, 1/30, 2/7; 1987 (1): 2/20; 1988 (5): 1/18, 2/1, 4/15, 5/10, 12/14; 1989 (4): 2/1, 2/18, 6/9, 11/7; 1990 (1): 6/1; 1995 (1): 3/17; 1997 (2): 3/14, 3/21; 2001 (2): 3/27, 12/14; 2002 (1): 12/20; 2003 (2): 7/14, 7/16; 2004 (2): 3/25, 10/5; 2006 (1): 7/13; 2014 (1): 12/31; 2017 (1): 12/18; 2018 (1): 6/1.

10 https://mosaicmagazine.com/essay/2018/02/has-israel-grown-too-dependent-on-the-united-states/

11 Republicans cast 39 vetoes, while Democrats cast 5, as follows: Nixon: 1, Ford: 3, Carter: 1, Reagan: 20, G.H.W. Bush: 5, Clinton: 3, G.W. Bush: 8, Obama: 1, Trump: 2.

12 https://fas.org/sgp/crs/mideast/RL33222.pdf

13 https://www.lrb.co.uk/v28/n06/john-mearsheimer/the-israel-lobby

14 See: Aruri, Naseer H., *Dishonest Broker: The U.S. Role in Israel and Palestine*, South End Press, 2003. See also: Khalidi, Rashid, *Brookers of Deceit, How the US Undermined Peace in the Middle East*, Beacon Press, 2013.

15 See: Flapan, Simha, *The Birth of Israel, Myths and Realities*, Pantheon, 1987.

16 https://occupiedpalestine.wordpress.com/2010/10/03/the-deathmasters-israeli-massacres-on-palestinians/. See also: https://occupiedpalestine.wordpress.com/2010/10/03/the-deathmasters-israeli-massacres-on-palestinians/; http://info.wafa.ps/atemplate.aspx?id=5037; http://ifamericaknew.org/stat/deaths.html

17 http://www.1948.org.uk/plan-dalet-and-the-nakba/

18 http://books.openedition.org/iheid/94?lang=en

19 https://ihl-databases.icrc.org/applic/ihl/ihl.nsf/ART/195-200052?OpenDocument

20   http://www.un.org/en/decolonization/declaration.shtml

21   http://www.un-documents.net/a25r2625.htm

22   https://unispal.un.org/DPA/DPR/unispal.nsf/0/C867EE1DB-F29A6E5852568C6006B2F0C

23   https://unispal.un.org/DPA/DPR/unispal.nsf/0/D7340F-04B82A2CB085256A9D006BA47A

24   https://unispal.un.org/DPA/DPR/unispal.nsf/b86613e7d92097880525672e007227a7/6de6da8a650b4c3b852560df00663826?OpenDocument

25   https://unispal.un.org/DPA/DPR/unispal.nsf/0DDE590C6FF232007852560DF0065FDDB

26   https://www.youtube.com/watch?v=HG2vZTcassE

27   https://www.youtube.com/watch?v=E0uLbeQlwjw

28   https://www.aljazeera.com/indepth/interactive/2015/10/mapping-dead-latest-israeli-palestinian-violence-151013142015577.html

29   https://www.btselem.org/topic/settler_violence

30   https://www.youtube.com/watch?v=T0kCX53YIcw

31   http://imemc.org/article/73371/

32   http://palestineun.org/1-may-2015-israeli-occupying-force-violations-against-palestinian-children/

33   https://www.youtube.com/watch?v=TWZy1eFT-Ow

34   https://www.youtube.com/watch?v=hOR0lXHKhBo

35   https://www.youtube.com/watch?v=Xs1fIjIKamo

36   http://www.dci-palestine.org/palestinian_toddler_burns_to_death_in_suspected_settler_arson_attack

37   https://www.i24news.tv/en/news/israel/diplomacy-defense/87868-151004-israel-police-restrict-access-to-jerusalem-s-old-city-amid-rise-in-violence

38   http://www.middleeasteye.net/news/israel-razes-west-bank-home-jailed-palestinian-arrest-hamas-leader-1302253076

39   https://sputniknews.com/middleeast/201507221024901235/

40   https://www.youtube.com/watch?v=-Lm4j0Do2hA

41   https://www.youtube.com/watch?v=HG2vZTcassE

42   http://imemc.org/article/israeli-soldiers-continue-to-target-journalists-60-violations-this-week/

43   http://www.jadaliyya.com/pages/index/8799/no-israel-does-not-have-the-right-to-self-defense-

44   https://www.ochaopt.org/sites/default/files/fragmented_lives_2016_english.pdf

45   http://www.bbc.com/news/world-middle-east-28439404

46   http://www.dci-palestine.org/child_fatalities_by_month

47   http://ifamericaknew.org/

48   http://www2.ohchr.org/english/bodies/hrcouncil/docs/12session/A-HRC-12-48.pdf

49   https://www.amnesty.org/en/countries/middle-east-and-north-africa/israel-and-occupied-palestinian-territories/report-israel-and-occupied-palestinian-territories/

50   https://www.hrw.org/news/2014/09/11/israel-depth-look-gaza-school-attacks

51   https://www.aljazeera.com/programmes/aljazeerawor
     ld/2013/09/2013910121456318891.html
52   http://www.ecfr.eu/publications/summary/rethinking_oslo_how_europe_can_
     promote_peace_in_israel_palestine_7219
53   https://www.btselem.org/topic/settlements
54   See: Said, Edward W., *Peace and Its Discontents*, Vintage, 1995; and *The End
     of the Peace Process, Oslo and After*, Vintage, 2001.
55   https://www.btselem.org/settlements/statistics
56   https://www.youtube.com/watch?v=3-5hUG6Os68
57   https://www.youtube.com/watch?v=JDJXWgVaFnk
58   http://theiranproject.com/blog/2015/09/04/israel-great-danger-to-world-peace-
     british-mp/
59   http://www.nybooks.com/articles/2001/08/09/camp-david-the-tragedy-of-er-
     rors/
60   See: Swisher, Clayton E., *The Truth About Camp David, The Untold Story
     about the Collapse of the Middle East Process*, Nation Books, 2004.
61   https://www.democracynow.org/2006/11/30/palestine_peace_not_apartheid_
     jimmy_carter
62   http://mondoweiss.net/2012/12/shlomo-sand-on-zionism-post-zionism-and-
     the-two-state-solution/
63   http://www.stopwar.org.uk/index.php/news-comment/1307-from-albert-ein-
     stein-to-noam-chomsky-famous-jews-who-have-opposed-israel
64   http://www.globalresearch.ca/albert-einsteins-letter-warning-of-zionist-fa-
     cism-in-israel/5438170
65   https://sites.google.com/site/jewsagainstracistzionism/shahak-israel-racist-na-
     ture-of-zionism-and-the-zionist-state-of-israel
66   https://www.democracynow.org/2014/8/8/noam_chomsky_what_israel_is_do-
     ing
67   https://palsolidarity.org/2013/07/interview-with-ilan-pappe-the-zionist-goal-
     from-the-very-beginning-was-to-have-as-much-as-palestine-as-possible-with-
     as-few-palestinians-in-it-as-possible/
68   http://jewishjournal.com/uncategorized/77435/
69   https://www.youtube.com/watch?v=5B7ijMjc2Js
70   http://www.nybooks.com/articles/2003/10/23/israel-the-alternative/
71   https://www.tni.org/es/node/9804
72   https://www.washingtonpost.com/opinions/a-zionist-case-for-boycotting-
     israel/2015/10/23/ac4dab80-735c-11e5-9cbb-790369643cf9_story.html?utm_
     term=.c1998af774d2&wpisrc=nl_wemost&wpmm=1
73   https://www.salon.com/2015/03/25/benjamin_netanyahus_racist_remarks_
     may_have_swung_israeli_election_pollster_suggests/
74   http://mondoweiss.net/2014/03/lieberman-transferring-palestinian/
75   https://www.middleeastmonitor.com/20151016-rabbis-killing-palestinian-re-
     sistance-fighters-a-religious-duty/
76   https://www.middleeastmonitor.com/20151015-620-palestinians-arrested-by-
     israel-in-just-2-weeks/
77   https://electronicintifada.net/content/top-israeli-rabbis-advocate-geno-
     cide/6974

78   https://www.independent.co.uk/news/world/middle-east/victim-describes-being-stabbed-by-fellow-israeli-jewish-man-shouting-you-deserve-it-arab-bs-a6693641.html

79   https://www.alternet.org/grayzone-project/israeli-stabbed-jew-anti-arab-violence

80   https://www.huffingtonpost.com/2014/07/10/max-blumenthal-israel-palestine_n_5574082.html

81   http://www.truth-out.org/news/item/19454-max-blumenthal-qa

82   https://www.salon.com/2011/02/05/ronald_reagan_apartheid_south_africa/

83   Barghouti, Omar, *BDS: Boycott, Divestment, and Sanctions, The Global Struggle for Palestinian Rights,* Haymarket Books, 2011.

84   Carter, Jimmy, *Peace Not Apartheid, Simon & Shuster, 2007.*

85   http://mcadams.posc.mu.edu/ike.htm

86   http://avalon.law.yale.edu/18th_century/washing.asp

AFRICA

AFRICA
AND WESTERN
MULTINATIONAL
CORPORATIONS

Baffour Ankomah

How Western Companies Rob Africa of its Natural Resources

It is now generally accepted that Africa is the richest continent in the world by natural resources but the poorest by bank balance. This "great conundrum" has been made possible by a skewed world economic and political order that ensures that African resources are exploited for a song by multinational companies, principally from the USA and Europe, who leave very little back in Africa for the development of the continent, so little that there is never enough to run the African economies without foreign aid, and without Africa begging for it.

How does it happen—that a rich man, super rich, in fact, in all the resources that create wealth, who is yet poor, living in abject poverty, who, without the grace of alms liberally begged from abroad, which are sometimes stingily given, cannot make ends meet?

One estimate, in fact, says the majority of all the world's natural resources are in Africa and yet most Africans are poor. And this is notwithstanding the fact that without these African resources, the world economy, including that of the Mighty USA, would suffer and would definitely not be what it is today. So why is Africa poor in the midst of these stupendous riches? That is the great conundrum of the modern era that Africans will have to collectively solve if there should be any hope for the continent and its future generations.

By dint of Africa's colonial and post-colonial history, and the refusal of the metropolitan powers, including the USA, to help the continent in a massive way to recover from the horrors of colonialism, as those powers have helped other countries since World War II, Africa does not have the requisite capital—human, financial, machinery, and knowhow—to exploit its own natural resources, and thus relies on multinational companies to extract those resources on its behalf—if it is on its behalf!

And this is where the problem lies. Because of Africa's lack of capital to exploit these resources, the multinational companies use the muscle of their capital to bamboozle individual African countries into granting them concessions that, in effect, give the companies a disproportionate, and some say unconscionable, share of the proceeds that accrue from the African resources.

The great sinners in this massive rip-off have been companies in the extractive sector. And they come from mostly Europe, the USA, Canada and Australia. They use their negotiating skills, honed over decades and centuries, and sometimes with the help of political and economic pressure by their home countries, to browbeat African governments into signing away mining concessions that ensure that Africans get very little for their God-given resources.

The Hows and Whys

Take the petroleum sector as an example. The average royalty that new African oil producers are given by foreign oil giants who come to exploit the petroleum resources of Africa is not more than 10% (sometimes as low as 5%). The rationale is that the oil giants need that much money (as much as 90% to 95% of the profits) over so many years, sometimes two or three decades, in order to recoup the initial financial investment they put into exploration, development and production. So though an African country may be seen to be producing oil, only a tiny fraction of the proceeds ever come to the country in the form of royalties and taxes.

This is the situation that so riled The Gambia's former president, Yahya Jammeh, that he ordered a representative of an American oil giant out of his country and threatened to arrest him if he ever set foot in the country again. As Jammeh explained to *New African* magazine:

> Some of the crimes I am supposed to have committed are to say we are not going to accept 5% from our petroleum resources, and the rest going to the foreign oil companies exploiting our resources.
>
> But they tell me that other African countries have accepted the 5%, and in fact no African country, except three, gets more than 3% from its minerals. So if other African countries have accepted that ridiculously low percentage, then you must be in the wrong not to accept the same ludicrous deal. To me, any talk about our countries taking a 3% or 5% royalty to exploit our resources is an insult.

The Gambia's President went on:

> So, they expect me to have diamonds in The Gambia and I go to my people and tell them, "Oh don't worry, we are getting only 5% of what God has given us, and a Western company is getting 95%." No, I can't say that. And so, this is the crime I am supposed to have committed. It's not only the minerals but also oil.
>
> But if you look at Dubai in 1990 and the Dubai of today, it's very different, and the change has come from their oil and gas resources. If you look at Qatar when I went there in 1996 and the Qatar of today, it is completely changed. But you look at some of the oil producing countries in Africa, I won't name them, it's a sad story. In fact the irony is that African countries are the richest in mineral resources, but our citizens are the poorest in the world. No, this state of affairs must change.

And what is his solution? Africa, according to Jammeh, should be tough in the pre-exploration negotiations and get what it rightly deserves, or the oil and other mineral resources should remain untapped in the ground and in the sea until such time that the foreign companies give Africa its due, or the continent develops its own capital, machinery and knowhow to exploit the resources for itself.

This quite revolutionary thought is worth considering and could even be what might bring sanity into the way the foreign companies treat Africa, a treatment that has so far bordered on a mixture of condescension and greed.

As Jammeh narrated to *New African*:

> Somebody told me: "Oh little Gambia, I will give you $400m a year, but that's too much for a small country". I said, "Are you going to give it to me for free". He said, "No, of course, the oil, your oil". I said, "You want to exploit our oil, and you tell me that giving us $400m a year is too much for The Gambia?"
>
> The surveys already carried out show that this country [The Gambia] has maybe 4 or 5 billion barrels of oil and they want to give us only $400m a year, by calculation of a 5% royalty, and even that they say is too much for The Gambia. So who is he to tell us that? The oil belongs to the Gambian people and then he tells me that he is going to give us just 5%. He thought he was doing me a favour, but I told him to go to hell. He didn't like it, but I told him that if he ever set his foot on Gambian soil again, he would regret it.

The man who was sent away from the sacred soil of The Gambia in that manner was an American oil executive!

But not many African leaders can say or do what Yahya Jammeh did when offered paltry percentages for their countries' resources. Yet when it comes to getting a better deal for natural resources, according to Jammeh, the solution lies in African leadership.

"There are some leaders who really fight for their people, and there are those who just say 'yes sir, yes sir' to foreign powers," Jammeh said. "These are the type of leaders we never hear being criticized by the Western media. These are their people!"

Jammeh continued: "Now it may not be physical colonization, but it may be in the exploitation of our mineral resources or whatever, and I find the deals they are offering us insulting. And if you stand up to them, they turn against you and call you a dictator. But it is better to fight for the rights of your people and be called a dictator than being a puppet they will discard when they don't have any need of you."

Recalcitrant Leaders?

Jammeh's story is not different from what Liberia's former president, Charles Taylor, experienced while negotiating for the production of Liberia's oil. Two years after coming into office in 1997, Taylor ordered a comprehensive aerial survey of Liberia's mineral resources. The results were quite promising, giving the government the advantage of knowing what minerals the country had, where exactly they were located, and in what quantities.

A few years later, an American oil giant with levers in the top echelons of George W. Bush's administration came by, wanting to exploit Liberia's oil, but offering the country 5 cents in every dollar from the proceeds of the oil resources. President Taylor refused to accept the deal but the company pushed and pushed until Taylor was indicted in 2004 to stand trial at the UN-backed Special Court for Sierra Leone for supporting rebels in Liberia's neighbouring country.

The American oil giant then offered a carrot to Taylor. "If you give us the rights to exploit Liberia's oil, we shall protect you from standing trial at the Special Court for Sierra Leone," they told him. It was a tempting deal. Taylor's trial was being pushed from behind the scenes by the USA and Britain to get him out of power. He knew it. But the oil deal, at 5 cents in every dollar, was a bad one for Liberia, so despite his personal liberty being at stake, Taylor still rejected the oil deal. "Then we can't help you, Mr President, we can't protect you," the American oil giant told Taylor.

The day Taylor narrated this story in court in The Hague (Netherlands) after the Special Court for Sierra Leone had moved its proceedings to the premises of the International Criminal Court, the place went deathly silent! The long and short of this story is that for rejecting the bad oil deal, Taylor could not be protected by the American oil giant, and today he sits in a British prison serving 50 years for what the court found to be "aiding and abetting" rebels in Sierra Leone.

In 1997, a not too dissimilar fate had befallen President Pascal Lissouba of Congo Brazzaville. When he came into office in 1992, having been democratically elected, he felt he had the mandate of the people of Congo Brazzaville to renegotiate the oil deal that Western oil giants had given the country under the previous government headed by a military leader.

The country was getting 15% from its oil resources. President Lissouba wanted this to be increased to 33%. All the oil companies were happy with the 33% deal except one French oil giant, which rushed to Paris and leaned on the government of President Jacques Chirac to force Lissouba to bend the knee.

In an interview in London in April 1998, President Lissouba told me that Jacques Chirac called him from Paris and ordered him to appoint the ex-military president as his vice president and head of the armed forces. This was, however, in contravention of the country's constitution, and also Lissouba deduced that Chirac wanted to use the ex-military president to checkmate him in the interest of the French oil company.

When Lissouba told Chirac that the constitution of Congo Brazzaville did not allow for what he was asking for, Lissouba said Chirac, now shrill on the phone, told him point-blank: "Chuck your bloody constitution in the dustbin!"

A few weeks later, Lissouba's government was no more, overthrown in a "mini civil war" in which rebel soldiers allied to the former military president who were supported by boats and other logistics provided by the French oil company, overthrew Lissouba's government. It came as no surprise that the rebels brought back the ex-military president to head the new government, which went on to reduce the 33% oil deal that Lissouba had pressed the multinational oil companies to pay, to 20%. Case closed!

In fact, 25 years before Lissouba's overthrow, a similar fate had befallen Niger's president, Hamani Diori, when his government was ousted in 1974 in comparable circumstances because Diori, a staunch pro-West leader, asked for a better deal for Niger's uranium ore resources, which were being mined by a French multinational company. Of course the official reason for the coup was corruption, allegedly perpetrated by President Diori, but if you believe that, you might also believe that pigs can fly!

Today, Niger is still producing uranium ore, which is still mined and purchased by the French, but the country has remained one of the poorest in Africa. A classic poverty-in-the-midst-of-plenty situation!

This is why President Yahya Jammeh had such a huge problem with the deals being given to Africa by the foreign oil giants. "Of course I do," he said. "I used to tell the Emir of Qatar that I was competing with him because our countries were both small, but I didn't know that they had such massive gas deposits which they are now exploiting, and using to improve their lives," Jammeh said.

> But we, African leaders, deprive our people of benefiting from their God-given resources because we accept ridiculous deals that prevent us from earning enough to improve the lives of our people. This is the problem. Because if they come and give us 5%, and tell us how much the president is going to get, we agree! But the oil resources do not belong to the president, [they] belong to the people of the Gambia. So I will not accept 5% or 10% on behalf of the Gambian people. If I do accept that ridiculous percentage, what am I going to tell my people? That we have 10% and they take 90%?

Jammeh then did the sums and showed how unfair the 5% deals were. "Today," he said, "in the case of oil, we know the cost per barrel is $100 [at the time of our interview]. So now if you tell me that there are, say, one billion barrels of oil in The Gambia, and you multiply one billion barrels by $100 per barrel, you have $100 billion. And what you used to drill your well and whatever, all the capital expenditure is less than $2 billion, so why do you expect me to accept 10% or 5% when it is $2 billion you need in maybe 5 or 6 years to recoup your capital expenditure. Why would they want me to accept 5% for 35 years, do you understand?"

The Other Africa

Unfortunately, not all African leaders have the same perspicacity as Jammeh. In fact sometimes African countries themselves, whether through sheer laziness, corruption, soft-headedness, or pure criminality, just hand over their natural resources to the foreign companies through bad national mining laws that should never be on any country's statute books.

An example of this was recently "discovered" in Ghana—of

all places! In September 2013, Ghana's Parliament suddenly woke up to the fact that the country's mining law in force since 2003 allows some foreign companies to retain virtually all their earnings in Ghana in offshore accounts.

This revelation stung Dr Tony Aidoo, the head of policy monitoring and evaluation in the President's Office, into saying that he would prefer Ghana's mining resources remained untapped in the ground, so that someday, local mining techniques, however primitive, could be developed to exploit them for the benefit of the nation, not foreign companies.

The Ghana case is so important to the discourse on how Africa can own its resources that it deserves to be retold here at some length. In fact, Dr Tony Aidoo was not the only one stung by the "discovery" of the rip-off. Mike Allen Hamah, Ghana's former minister for lands and natural resources, blamed the 2003 law, which was an amendment to the country's Mining and Minerals Law passed in 1986 by the military government headed by Flt-Lt Jerry Rawlings, for "the naked rape of Ghana's resources". The question then arose as to why Hamah did nothing about the 2003 law during his tenure as minister for lands and natural resources?

Ghana's extraordinary story goes back to 1986 when the then military government headed by Flt-Lt Jerry John Rawlings capitulated to pressure from the neoliberal Washington Consensus and enacted the first damaging mining law (damaging to Ghana) giving multinational mining companies what amounted to an official license to cheat the country of its natural resources.

Two pieces of bad legislation stand out in this drama. The first is the Minerals/Mining Law (PNDCL 153) which was passed in 1986 by the Rawlings' Provisional National Defence Council (PNDC) which ruled Ghana for 10 years, between 1982 and 1992.

The second is the Minerals and Mining Act (Act 703) which was passed in 2006 by President John Kufuor's New Patriotic Party (NPP) government in power from 2000 to 2008, a government which should have known better but didn't.

The first law (PNDCL 153) was passed as part of the IMF/World-Bank imposed Economic Recovery Programme (ERP) which was later converted into what became Africa's disastrous Structural Adjustment Programmes (SAPs). The second law (Act 703) was enacted by President Kufuor's government to deepen Ghana's neoliberal credentials. And all this was done supposedly to boost foreign investor confidence in the country, attract more foreign direct investment, and convince foreign investors of the safety of their investments in Ghana. In the process, Ghana gave away its resources for a song.

In fact, Act 703 literally gave international mining companies full freedom to market the gold they mined in Ghana without any Ghanaian institutional oversight. This meant the mining companies had total freedom to mine, process, package, ship and sell overseas all the gold they produced in Ghana without supervision or intervention by any Ghanaian authority—not the government itself or any of its relevant agencies.

"By so doing," says the Ghanaian academic Kwamina Panford, "the state of Ghana literally reneged on its duty to ensure proper accounting for the tonnage of gold produced and to ensure accurate assessment of taxes and other relevant fees owed the state."

Panford, an expert with intimate knowledge of Ghana's gold and oil industries, teaches at the Northeastern University in Boston, Massachusetts, USA. In his latest book, *Africa's Natural Resources and Underdevelopment: How Ghana's Petroleum Can Create Sustainable Economic Prosperity*, he shows how

> by 1994, Ghana had acquired a uniquely dubious distinction, by becoming the most economically liberalised country in the whole of Africa... But this created a paradox: while multinational companies' profits soared from 2003 to 2014, the proportion of state revenues shrunk substantially.
>
> Even worse, instead of setting the pace for an environmentally friendly and local community-centred agenda, Ghana, through the introduction of the post-1986 mining laws, policies and actual practices, embarked on what is known as the "race to the bottom, and set the bar so low that it was emulated by other African countries such as Sierra Leone which had a mining lease with a royalty of a miniscule 0.5% a year.

Panford reveals that "after other countries sought to catch up with Ghana's attempts to race to the bottom, it created a much lower standard to boost its competitiveness and to persuade Western donors that it was indeed their Sub-Saharan Africa's star pupil."

That notwithstanding, the gold companies still threatened Ghana that they would relocate to Tanzania if it did not offer even lower taxes and royalties.

This prompted President Kufuor's NPP government to enact Act 703 in 2006 that assured foreign investors of the safety of their capital by imposing a new ceiling of an absolute 10% on state ownership in foreign mining companies. That meant Ghana could not attain more than a 10% stake in any multinational mining company.

Act 703 also scrapped taxes on mining companies' extra profits, and introduced a new tax regime, ranging from 3% to 6%. However, in practice most companies paid the lower 3%. In subsequent changes to the law, and still under pressure from the mining industry, the government fixed a new royalty rate of 5%.

"As a result of global capitalist pressure," Panford reveals, "starting in 1986 with mining, especially gold and diamond, and since 2007 with oil, the Government of Ghana, acting on policy advice from the IMF and World Bank, seems to be forsaking Ghanaians."

In 2010, a new government headed by President John Atta Mills, in a bid to undo the harm done by Act 703, enacted the Minerals and Mining (Amendment) Act 794 after complaining publicly in its 2010 budget about the mining companies' bad dividend payments and excessive tax exemptions.

Three years later, (in September 2013), the Public Accounts Committee (PAC) of Ghana's Parliament expressed "shock" after "discovering" that mining agreements signed by various Ghanaian governments in the past and ratified by parliament itself were heavily tilted in favor of foreign mining companies. "As much as 100% of earnings from gold mined in Ghana by some foreign companies," the PAC discovered, "are lodged in offshore accounts. And all this is backed by Ghanaian law!" So, people asked, where was Parliament when all this was going on? Surprise, surprise, it is Parliament that ratifies the mining agreements before they become law!

The scandal forced the chief executive of Ghana's Minerals Commission, Ben Aryee, to explain that the situation had arisen because the country's 1986 Minerals and Mining Law made it possible for a "retention account agreement" to be signed by, and between, the Ministry of Finance and the Bank of Ghana on the one hand, and an applicant mining firm on the other hand.

Ten years after the 1986 law came into force, the "retention agreements" were found to be so distasteful that the "civilian" government of President Rawlings (he had now won democratic elections in 1992 as a retired soldier) was compelled to amend them in 1996 to force, in some cases, 20% of earnings of foreign mining companies to be kept in Ghana. Of all the retention agreements "discovered" in September 2013, one stood out like a sore thumb—and it was with a Canadian mining giant. The agreement allowed the company to keep abroad a full 100% of its earnings in Ghana!

As everybody expressed shock at this "naked rape of Ghana's resources", Ben Aryee, the CEO of the Minerals Commission, spoke for most Ghanaians when he said Parliament could not escape blame for the mess. It passed the 1996 retention agreement amendment, and also the 2003 law with its eyes wide open.

As one newly elected MP put it: "One of the 'discovered' retention agreements, signed on 17 December 2003, was ratified by Parliament on 23 December 2003—in a mere five days! This is curious, because under the parliamentary system, [the] ratification of laws should not happen in five days."

As a result there has been one glaring result: "Ghana has attracted substantial FDI, boosted gold and diamond output and exports, but with little or no job growth, technology transfer, improved quality of life, enhanced state revenues, or enhanced capacity to undertake more development," says Kwamina Panford who argues that "since 1986, Ghana's state of development and its mining conditions can be characterised as a classic case of growth without any positive transformation or shared prosperity. If there were indeed economic prosperity, it was not shared by Ghanaian workers and those living in mining communities."

Because of the near giveaway culture in the Ghanaian mining industry, there have been concrete examples of rising mining revenues and profits existing side by side with falling state incomes. Panford shows that "in 2013, for example, out of a total of $23 billion worth of gold produced, the state's revenue was $1.7 billion, or a paltry 7%. Newmont Gold [from Canada] made $931m in 2012, and $919m in 2011 in profits, plus another $2.5 billion. But in 3 years, it paid taxes of less than $500 million."

Panford quotes another report revealing that between 2005 and 2014, only 4 of 22 mining companies operating in Ghana did not evade paying dividends to the state. The other 18 paid zero dividends for the state's 10% carried interest. "This means the state got absolutely nothing for its 10% ownership of 18 separate gold mining companies all of which were raking in huge profits. The 4 companies that paid, contributed only GHc43.168m, approximately US$10m."

The same can be said of Ghana's nascent petroleum industry which came on stream in December 2010. According to Panford's investigations, state financial receipts since 15 December 2010 when commercial crude production started have not mirrored the earlier assumptions about plentiful revenues from corporate taxes. "Contrary to earlier projections of incomes ranging from $1bn to $1.4bn annually," Panford shows that,

> in the first 3 years of Jubilee Field production, Ghana has received less than half of the projected earnings while no corporate taxes were paid to Ghana in 2010, 2011 or 2012.
>
> While the multinational oil companies operating in Ghana, including American and British companies, have raked in billions and billions of dollars in the last 7 years, Ghana's earnings between 2011 and 2015 have been, as follows: 2011 - $470 million. 2012 - $541.623 million. 2013 - $846.767 million. And 2014 - $978.886 million.

If this could happen in Ghana, a country said to have grown firm democratic roots in the past 20 years, during which four governments have been changed peacefully in seven elections, imagine what goes on in the African countries that do not have Ghana's "democratic" credentials.

One of those countries is South Sudan. The multinational mining and oil companies use the same tactics all the time to control and loot African resources. And any time an African government tries to say no, the multinational companies run to their home governments for political and media support, and their home governments oblige them by bringing their immense political and economic power to bear on the African governments and break their will.

A classic example is the civil war that has torn South Sudan apart since 2013, which, according to the country's President, Salva Kiir Mayardit, is partly due to Washington wanting American oil companies to have a stake in South Sudan's oil industry. I interviewed President Kiir in June 2014 and October 2015, and on both occasions he told me in clear language that the USA was behind the civil war started by his former Vice President, Riek Machar Teny Dhurgon, because the USA wants Riek Machar to take over the country and hand over the exploitation of South Sudan's oil to American companies.

Washington has had an ambivalent relationship with South Sudan for quite some time. It started with Washington not liking the Sudan People's Liberation Movement/Army (SPLM/A) in the 1980s because America's geopolitical and strategic interests pushed it towards supporting a united Sudan, with capital in Khartoum, because of an alleged communist threat posed by neighboring Ethiopia under President Mengistu Haile Mariam.

"However, with the Cold War's conclusion and as [Khartoum] pushed Islamist extremism during the early and mid-1990s, American support for Khartoum quickly slackened," report Matthew LeRiche and Matthew Arnold in their 2012 book, *South Sudan: From Revolution to Independence*. South Sudan now became the new darling of the USA and the SPLM/A became a major beneficiary of Washington's political, economic and military largesse.

According to LeRiche and Arnold: "The best example of Washington's approach was the 2002 Sudan Peace Act [passed by the US Congress], which authorised $100 million a year from 2003 to 2005 for humanitarian relief in areas not controlled by Khartoum, and threatened economic pressure if [Khartoum] did not show itself as sincerely negotiating." In private, the elites of South Sudan talk about the huge war materiel, cash and political support that the USA and its many churches gave the SPLM/A during the war years, especially from the mid-1990s when Washington switched its support from North to South.

The story is told of how the American oil giant, Chevron, was the first multinational to prospect for oil in South Sudan where it discovered in the north of the country that fish actually die of old age in the Sudd region. The Sudd is a huge 35,000 sq km expanse of wetland in northern South Sudan where 30 or so rivers converge as they flow into the River Nile from the six neighboring countries bordering South Sudan. Because of the intensity of the waters that converge in the Sudd, it contains an overabundance of natural fresh-water fish, so many that the local people do not have the capacity to harvest them all. Therefore many of the fish grow and grow until they die of old age.

Today, however, there is no US oil company operating in South Sudan's oil industry. And Washington is not best pleased with the situation, especially after all the help the Americans gave South Sudan during the war with Khartoum. But, according to President Salva Kiir, this is not the mistake of Juba, it is the mistake of Washington.

Before 2005, as South Sudan battled to break away from the North, the USA had its own problems with the government in Khartoum, headed by President Omar al-Bashir, who became America's bête noire. Washington therefore pulled out its oil companies from United Sudan and imposed sanctions on President Bashir. It so happened that the largest chunk of United Sudan's oil resources were in South Sudan. Consequently, the American pull-out mostly affected South Sudan. Which explains why there is no US presence today in South Sudan's oil industry, an industry now dominated by America's new "economic enemy" from the East, China, and to a lesser extent by Malaysia via their oil giant Petronas.

You can imagine how this state of affairs rumbles stomachs and minds in Washington. Surely all the help extended to the SPLM/A by the USA during the war with Khartoum cannot be in vain. In January 2014, at the African Union (AU) Summit held in Addis Ababa, which was well attended by African presidents, several delegates talked about US collusion in South Sudan's civil war. Some delegates in fact accused the Americans of stoking the fires in South Sudan for their selfish ends, and further alleged that the Americans wanted to break the dominance of, if not completely dethrone, the Chinese from the oilfields of South Sudan. One delegate was actually bold enough to tell how Washington was behind the political conflict in South Sudan that broke out in the capital Juba on 15 December 2013 when troops loyal to President Kiir exchanged fire with Dr Riek Machar's followers.

The allegations at the AU Summit were being made a mere six weeks after the civil war broke out in Juba. Six months later, on 24 June 2014, President Kiir confirmed the allegations to me in an extensive interview held in his office in Juba. Kiir's take is that Riek Machar has assured the Americans that if they help him to become president, he would drive out the Chinese and the other Asian oil companies from South Sudan and hand everything over to American companies. "And they believe him," Kiir said, his words dripping with sarcasm.

In the interview, Salva Kiir clearly stated America's attempts to overthrow him: He told me:

There are many things that you can read into it. There are people who are looking for resources and they see South Sudan as a country full of resources, especially oil. With my government, they see that they cannot loot these resources. But if it is Riek Machar, they can play around with him and then take over. So it is the situation of Iraq that they want to happen here. These are strong nations, they can come in, throw away the elected government, and then install one of their stooges. That is the first thing.

The second is that those who talk about democracy are saying that the SPLM, as a party, is too strong to be challenged by any other political party. We have 19 political parties in this country, including the SPLM. So they say the other 18 political parties, even if they are combined, cannot challenge the SPLM. Therefore the SPLM has to be destroyed. It has to be divided. Their aim is to crush the SPLM into factions, to create so many factions.

When I asked President Kiir about forthcoming elections in South Sudan which were likely to be postponed to 2015 or 2016 because of the civil war, he responded:

When one examines the timeframe of when this war can be stopped and people can go back to the arrangements for the elections, it is clear that the elections cannot be held in 2015 but beyond that, yes; even in 2016. But the Troika—the Americans and the European Union— want the election to be pushed back three years. The reasons behind that are very clear. They think that in three years' time, they would be sufficiently prepared to have a candidate of their choice, and equip that candidate with whatever amounts of money he may need to win the election, so that they can have their man in Juba.

Kiir's answer intrigued me so I asked him why the Americans would do such a thing when they supported the SPLM/A during the war with Khartoum. "Why are they now turning their backs on you and undermining the very thing they fought for—an independent South Sudan," I asked Kiir. His answer was straight forward. "They say the government in Juba has ignored them, it has turned its back on them."

"Is it in connection with China's role in South Sudan's oil industry?" I asked the President. He answered:

Yes. They [the Americans] say that their companies are not allowed to invest in the oil industry here. But it is not our mistake. When we signed the Comprehensive Peace Agreement with Khartoum in 2005, we wanted to review the oil agreements that had been signed by Khartoum and China. The Americans refused. They said "No, don't touch the already signed agreements, we [the Americans] will be given access to the files later so that we will know what has been done. But we have nothing to say on it just now. If there are new contracts to be awarded, yes we will sit down and sort them out, but not the existing agreements."

So we left the existing agreements alone. And the Americans went on to impose sanctions on President Bashir and pulled out their companies from South Sudan. I appealed to them to bring back their companies when I became the First Vice President of Sudan. I said to them: "Those companies that were operating in the oil fields in South Sudan, let them come back." They said: "No, if this is done Bashir will benefit from this money. So we are not coming back". They wanted Bashir to fall. But Bashir cannot fall because he is with his people.

Now when South Sudan became independent in 2011, I called the Americans again. "Let your companies come back, so that if there are oil blocks that have not been awarded to any companies, I will give them to you—including Block 5B which was originally awarded to an American company that later pulled out. Up to now that block is still not awarded to anybody". So I called them but they said no. Riek Machar had told them that, "if you help me to become president, I will chase away the Chinese and the other Asian oil companies in South Sudan, and I will give everything to you". And they believe him. So this is my crime. I haven't offered them what Riek has offered.

"Is that why they want you out of power?" I asked President Kiir. He answered in the affirmative. "Yes, out of power." "So are you saying all the talk about a transitional government is just a smokescreen?" I asked him again. He replied: "It's just how to get me out of power. It's a smokescreen."

That was in June 2014. In October 2015, I went back to Juba to interview President Kiir again, and America's dirty hands behind the country's civil war came up yet again in our discussions. This time my wife, Elizabeth, was with me at the interview as the official photographer. While I asked the questions, she took the photos of President Kiir. It was a powerful husband-and-wife team, which Kiir liked. And this time he was blunter than when I first interviewed him in June 2014. It was no holds barred.

"I said to you last year," he told us, "that the Americans were here, and are still here, with what they call regime change. Their ambassador who was here before the Riek Machar coup of 15 December 2013 was actually working with Machar on the coup. He was the one who actually helped Machar, facilitating everything. I know them all—those foreign diplomats who were involved with Machar. I don't think [the Americans] have changed their mind. This is why they want to impose UN Security Council sanctions on us, because they think that the African Union is not bold enough to push us out."

President Kiir again took us through the story of the American absence in South Sudan's oil industry. "You remember I told you last year that in 2005 when we were negotiating with Khartoum," he said, "we had wanted all the oil agreements and contracts that had been signed by Khartoum to be revisited. It was America that refused to let us do it ... Today, it is the same America that has accepted Riek Machar, a rebel, because he has promised to kick out the Chinese and the other countries that have oil contracts in South Sudan and give them to the Americans if they help him to power. So it is the Americans who are actually encouraging Riek Machar to do what he is doing." Kiir brought a light moment to the grave matter of the American involvement in the conflict when he said: "I think they love Riek Machar." I laughed and asked him: "Just for the sake of it?" He replied: "Yes, but what can I say. Both Riek and I have black faces but they love his black face, not mine."

This "love affair" is what has sustained South Sudan's crisis, and until America is made to understand how harmful that love affair is to the general good of South Sudan, not much can be achieved by way of a lasting peace. I reported this to the world in *New African* in December 2015.

On the second visit to Juba, I picked up more background information that I had not known on my first visit. From the outside, the conflict in South Sudan appeared very stereotypical: two powerful African men (in this case President Salva Kiir and his former deputy Riek Machar) and their followers were fighting and killing themselves and destroying the country in the process. But from inside the country, the picture was totally different. Interference by outsiders, particularly the dirty tricks by the USA, was stoking the fires and ensuring that a peaceful and quick solution was difficult to find. Therefore, for the conflict to end any time soon, the USA would have to remove itself from the scene or be brought to attention.

I knew then that the window-dressing in the shape of enforced peace agreements, transitional governments, threats of UN sanctions, and biased mediation by the member-countries of the Inter-Governmental Authority on Development (IGAD) would not bring a lasting peace if the crux of the matter—the behind-the-scenes meddling by the USA—was not stopped. The American connection was poisoning the atmosphere for all concerned as it was putting pressure on even neighboring countries such as Ethiopia and Kenya to take biased positions unhelpful to the pursuit of peace in South Sudan.

Therefore, if real peace was to be reached, America had to be told to pack up its ill-intentions and ship out. But who was to tell the elephant to behave properly at the common drinking pool? Yet anything short of that was tantamount to playing a cruel joke on South Sudan, a nation that had, save for the 11 years between 1972-1983, been at war since 1955 (first with the British and Egyptian colonial overlords, and later with Khartoum, and now with itself). I learned on my second visit to Juba that there were even more to the American connection than President Kiir had cared to tell me on my first visit. I learned that despite the massive military and diplomatic assistance that the Americans had given the SPLM/A during the war with Khartoum, things began to go awry when Kiir's government refused to allow the USA to set up a military base in South Sudan at a time when African continental opinion was, and is still, stridently against such American bases on African soil. As if that was not enough, there was another bone of contention. South Sudan has huge deposits of uranium which are yet to be mined. And the Americans wanted to mine and control it. Kiir's government said no. And it was one "no" too much for Washington's liking. So Kiir had to be replaced. And the Americans chose his deputy, Riek Machar. So war broke out on 15 December 2013. That is the real genesis of South Sudan's post-independence civil war, but don't expect to find it in any of the newspapers and 24-hour TV news channels near you. Because of the lack of truthful reporting, South Sudan's conflict has been painted as a power struggle between Kiir and Machar. But it goes beyond them. It is an American regime change agenda gone bad and mad. But no one wants to say that publicly.. But I did. I came back from my second trip to Juba and reported these matters in a big special report in the December 2015 issue of the London-based *New African* magazine, of which I was editor at the time, under the banner headline: "South Sudan: American Connection is Making Peace Difficult to Achieve." But the world read my article and chose to ignore one of the main reasons why the 2013 civil war in Africa's youngest country kept going.

South Sudan became independent on 9 July 2011 and its post-independence experience makes it imperative that Africa, as a collective, must find an alternative way to control its natural resources. So far no better "alternative" has surpassed what Zimbabwe tried to do with its indigenization program, which was aimed at giving the people of Zimbabwe control over their God-given natural resources. Reduced to its lowest denominator, Zimbabwe's indigenization law wanted the country to retain 51% of all foreign companies exploiting Zimbabwe's natural resources while the foreign companies keep 49% of the equity.

Indigenization and the Power of the Zimbabwe Example

There is no doubt that if Zimbabwe had succeeded in pushing indigenization to its logical conclusion, it would have had a huge impact on how Africa in general did business with its natural resources in the future. Africa could have even rewritten the principles of a world economy that had grown fat on cheap resources from Africa. But alas Zimbabwe failed!

This made the former South African president Thabo Mbeki's admonition to Africa in 2013 not to let Zimbabwe fail in the implementation of its indigenization program all the more important.

He said: "I think we should ask ourselves the question: Why is Zimbabwe such a major issue for some people? Zimbabwe is a small country by any standard; there is no particular reason why Zimbabwe should be a matter to which *The New York Times*, the London *Guardian* and whoever else ... why are they paying so much attention to Zimbabwe?"

Mbeki answered the question himself by telling a story:

Towards the end of last year [2012], they asked me to speak at a conference on Zimbabwe diamonds. So I went, and what surprised me about the conference held at Victoria Falls [Zimbabwe] was that everybody and anybody who has anything to do with diamonds in the world was there. From America, from Israel, from India, from Brussels, everybody! [The conference] was not about diamonds in the world, it was about Zimbabwe diamonds! So I was puzzled, saying, but why have they all come?

Maybe two hours before we left the conference to come back, we sat in a session which was addressed by one of the Indian diamond people. In the course of his presentation, he explained why. He gave an answer to this query in my head. He said in a few years' time, Zimbabwe would account for 25 per cent of world production of diamonds. So I said, "I now understand. I understand why everybody is here."

Mbeki also understands well the resistance from the metropolitan powers when a country like Zimbabwe tries other ways to own its resources. According to him, "powerful players" say openly that the Zimbabweans "have set a bad example [with land reform] which we don't want anybody else in Africa and the rest of the world to follow. So they must pay a price for setting a bad example."

But bad example for whom? Mbeki responded:

Bad in the instance of the interests of these other people; not bad in terms of the interests of the people of Zimbabwe! So I think this is part of the reason that there is so much attention, globally, on a country in a continent which is actually in itself—never mind the diamonds—not particularly important, but it is important because it is setting in the minds of some a bad example which must be defeated.

Mbeki then came to the crux of the matter: "I am using all of this talk about Zimbabwe," he said, "as an example about our continent because [with] all of these things I am saying relating to Zimbabwe, you can find the same [or] similar examples on the continent, but we are not challenging it as intellectuals. We are not challenging a narrative, a perspective about our continent which is wrong and self-serving in terms of the interests of our people.

The Zimbabweans are now talking about indigenization and I can see that there is a big storm brewing about indigenization. But what is wrong about indigenization? What is wrong with saying: "Here we are, as Africans, with all our resources, sure we are ready and very willing to interact with the rest of the world about the exploitation of all these resources, but what is the indigenous benefit from the exploitation of this, and even the control?"

You have seen examples of this, all of us have, when Chinese companies, in terms of all this theory about free markets, have sought to acquire US firms [and] they got prohibited. No, [it is] indigenization of US intellectual property! We can't allow it to be owned by the Chinese, so no!

So when the Africans say "indigenization," why is this a strange notion? And yet when we talk about solutions to Africa's development, one of the issues that we have to address is exactly this indigenization. How are we utilising our resources to impact positively on African development? I am saying this because I can see that there is a cloud that is building up somewhere on the horizon when Zimbabweans say "indigenization." But we have to, as intellectuals and thought leaders, address that and say: "Yes, indeed as Africans we are concerned

about our own renaissance, our own development, and
we must as indigenous people make sure that we have
control of our development, our future, and that includes
our resources. And therefore indigenization is correct."
We must demonstrate it even intellectually, which I am
quite sure we can.

If only Africa could have 100 people with the clarity of Mbeki.

The Challenges

All said and done, Africa must not expect anything to be easy
on the "alternative" course. There is bound to be resistance and spoiling
tactics by the metropolitan powers and their multinational companies,
which have grown used to getting African resources on the cheap. They
will do everything in and outside the law to prevent Africa from freeing
itself from the shackles of the current world economic order.

Which should inspire the Africans to question the motivation of
these powers in helping countries such as Germany, Japan, South Korea,
Taiwan, Singapore, Malaysia and the others to rise from the ashes of the
Second World War and the Cold War, while at the same time frustrating
African attempts to be a Japan, a South Korea, a Germany, a Taiwan
or even miniature versions of them. Why do they resist or kill African
attempts to be like these countries?

This is exactly what the Henry Kissinger-inspired American
national security memorandum, NSSM 200, of 1974, recommended.

That document, whose aim was to control a so-called
uncontrollable growth of the world population from 4 billion to 13
billion by 2000, clearly states that as the West lives off the resources
of Africa and other developing countries, a large population in Africa
would lead to the Africans controlling their natural resources, and this
would have implications for American national interest in the form of the
Africans asking for better terms of trade for their resources or using them
for themselves. And this had to be fought by the Americans!

Thus, if Africa should embark on an "alternative" way, it should
not be surprised to find multinational companies refusing to invest or
threatening to pull out of Africa, a horror that orthodox economists and
other like-minded Africans will recommend that Africa should avoid,
especially in this day and age where capital has many places to fly to.

But if Africa collectively stands its ground and acts in the manner suggested by President Jammeh and Dr Tony Aidoo of Ghana— namely, letting the resources remain in the ground—the multinational companies will come willy-nilly, if indeed the majority of the world's natural resources are in Africa.

Besides, the current generation of Africans will have to learn to sacrifice for the economic emancipation of the continent and its teeming generations yet unborn. After all, if the resources are exploited today at a 3% royalty, we get basically nothing and remain poor; and if the resources remain in the ground, we get nothing, but at least we will know that there is some capital in the ground to be inherited by our sons and daughters who will someday be able to exploit them.

This is why Africa will have to listen to ex-President Mbeki about the metropolitan resistance to African progress. He said on 23 August 2013: "As you can see, I get very, very agitated about Zimbabwe, because it's very, very clear that the offensive against Zimbabwe is an offensive against the rest of the continent...

> That offensive is not in the first instance about Zimbabwe, it's about the future of our continent. So the Zimbabweans have been in the frontline in terms of defending our right as Africans to determine our future, and they are paying a price for that. I think it is our responsibility as African intellectuals to join them, the Zimbabweans, to say "No"! We have a common responsibility as Africans to determine our destiny and are quite ready to stand up against anybody else who thinks [otherwise]. We stand up as Africans to say [there must be] an end, and really an end, to [the] contempt for African thought! We have to. If we don't, Africa will never be able to own its own resources.

SOMALIA

IS SOMALIA THE US TEMPLATE FOR ALL OF AFRICA?

Cynthia McKinney

Introduction

Currently, I am teaching at a US-accredited university in Asia. About 50 students from Somalia[1] and Somaliland attend the school and every one of them is working to complete their studies and return to Africa to make their country better. They are graduate level students seeking their Masters Degrees in Environmental Science, Law, and Development Studies. And every time I see them, my heart cries because I know what the United States is currently doing in their country to destroy it. And if that isn't enough, I know that the US has been working to destroy Somalia for a very long time.

Moreover, in 2011 while visiting Libya, I had a meeting with around 20 Somali students who were in Libya attending university. I asked them how they were treated during their studies in Libya and they were grateful to the Libyan Jamahiriya because all of their needs were taken care of: they had access to all of the resources of the university and the country, including free health care and free university tuition. And in 2011, while meeting with these Somali students, I felt guilty because I knew that the US had done everything in its immense power to prevent self-determination of the Somali people. Of course, that's true of the entire African Continent, but Somalia has been a country of particular interest to the US since the Cold War where every country on the world's "chessboard" had something of value—if only its geo-strategic location—to be owned and controlled by the US or one of its proxy states, the former colonial powers of Western Europe.

While I was in the Congress, I was very active on African issues—much to the chagrin of the US Deep State, at that time embodied in the public personages of Madeleine Albright, Susan Rice; Condoleezza Rice, Colin Powell, and others. I decried the US provision of weapons to Ethiopia in its border war with Somalia. I accused the Clinton Administration of having an even more anti-Africa African foreign policy than that of even President George Herbert Walker Bush. Bill Clinton readily admitted that it was the Black vote that awarded him the US Presidency, but his admission did little to transform US foreign policy into the anti-imperial, pro-justice values that the Civil Rights Movement gifted to the US as a whole. Instead, the lessons learned from the Civil Rights Movement were chucked into the dustbin of forgotten history. Little did I realize at that time that US policy would get even worse for Africa in the future!

I was able to secure funding for the Somali community so that they could start a community center and begin to resolve the many issues they faced as emigrants now expected to automatically just blend into a strange, new US culture. Shockingly, the money, $250,000, and the center, soon came under Zionist Jewish control and the Zionist Jews of DeKalb County, Georgia served as the front line for Zionist Jews throughout the State of Georgia and in the entire US who opposed my tenure in Congress and my reelection to it. They orchestrated the political theater of having dark-skinned Somali faces hold campaign signs for my Zionist Jewish opponent! I know the purpose of the deception was to trick the voting public into thinking that the Black voter support for my opponent was higher than it actually was. When I spoke to the Somali sign holders about their signs, they couldn't even read them and didn't even know the candidate whose signs they were holding. They didn't even know that *I*—standing in front of them in flesh and blood—was the other candidate in the race! They had merely been told to stand in front of the rapid transit station and hold the signs and so, they did it. I knew they had been tricked, but sadly, there was little I could do about it at the time. Despite the deliberate confusion, I went on to win my reelection effort to the Congress in that year.

However, before I even entered the Congress, I had read John Stockwell's transformational book, *In Search of Enemies*.[2] This book made me so aware of the pernicious and punitive policies of the US against the so-called "Third World" in general and Africa, in particular. It was the reading of that book (along with my extensive training in International Relations) that compelled me to ask for the House International Relations Committee when I began my service in the US Congress. I detail my experiences in the Congress on that Committee, along with the resistance I encountered from the Zionist, pro-Israel Lobby extensively in my 2013 book, *Aint' Nothing Like Freedom*.[3]

Oh, if I had just been like all of the other Members of Congress and asked for a "money committee" which would have ensured lots of campaign cash every election—provided, of course, that I voted the right way. Sigh . . .

Thus, writing this Chapter is my way of officially apologizing to all of those Somali students who have crossed my path in Africa and in Asia—and even in my own Congressional District—that I wasn't able to save you from a fate predetermined for you by Washington, D.C. This Chapter is my way of saying "I'm sorry." I'm sorry for my past failures and I'm sorry that even today, in 2018, the United States military still has Somalia in an illegal chokehold and is squeezing so tight that Somalia, and quite frankly, all of Africa can't breathe. The US to Africa is just like that New York cop who put Eric Garner in a chokehold and choked the life him while he was saying over and over again, "I can't breathe, I can't breathe." It is US policy to not allow Africa to breathe and Somalia is an illustrative case in point.

Somalia's Colonial Past

The United States wasn't the first country to victimize the Somali people, although it might be the last, if we—the pro-peace forces around the world—are successful. Before the US landed troops in Somalia, its people were victimized in the infamous 1899 "Scramble for Africa" by Europeans seeking to regulate their own intra-continental competitions. These Europeans decided to carve up the Continent of Africa among themselves so as to staunch any in-fighting that would erupt over colonies. Therefore, Somalia was colonized by the European colonial powers of the day—Britain and France—and Italy, an upstart country trying to flex its muscles in the colonial game being played at that time.[4] Interestingly, the Somali people share the same identity, language, and religion. They view themselves as a nation whose history goes back thousands of years: *the Somali nation*. They lived together in the past as one and would like to do so again. This didn't matter to the Europeans. So, when the British suggested that Italian Somaliland and British Somaliland join and become one independent state, that is exactly what happened in 1960 when the independent state of the Republic of Somalia was born—without, however, a portion of the Somali nation that was located in Ethiopia. Moreover, the French did everything to obstruct the reunification of the Somali people and return them at least in form if not in function to their existence as they were before the European colonial intrusions.

The French territory was known as Affars and Issas. After voting for independence in 1967, the former French Somaliland became the independent state of Djibouti. But, before the 1967 referendum, French Somalia had a chance to reunite with its British and Italian parts. That vote, however was marred with rigging and election fraud, even including a sizable number of Europeans living there on the voter rolls. French Somaliland was thus prevented from joining in the reunited Somalia, despite a majority of Somalis voting in that election choosing reunification over continued domination by France.

Unfortunately for the freedom fighters who struggled to decolonize their countries, support from the US was rarely to be had. I remember reading that Ho Chi Minh started imploring the US for help in liberating Vietnam from French colonialism in 1919 in Versailles. The US rebuffed his entreaties until the very end, with Ho having to militarily defeat France in 1954 at Dien Bien Phu. Ho died a decade and a half later in 1969. Even then, the US could not accept the freedom of peoples it deemed inferior: after the 1963 murder of US President John Kennedy, the US entered the war against the Vietnamese people, only to suffer ignominious defeat a decade later.

US treatment of other peoples wanting to enjoy freedom has always been along the lines of US treatment of its own imported African colony and consistent with the treatment by Europeans of their own colonial subjects. Today, the US military still acts as a guarantor of sorts to maintain the global apartheid order that keeps the US Deep State and Western Europeans at the top of the international power game and in full control of the geopolitical chess board. Even in its relations with former European colonies, the US is satisfied to serve as the ultimate enforcer while allowing the European former colonial masters to lead US policy. CENTCOM and AFRICOM, whose jurisdictions fall in Eurasia and Africa, are headquartered respectively in the USA and Germany.

And so it has been ever since with others struggling to throw off the yoke of Western European colonialism, neocolonialism, and neoliberalism: while mouthing freedom, democracy, and liberty, the United States has denied these very aspirations to others, especially when it inconvenienced the US or its allies. In Mozambique and Angola, the US stood with Portugal until it was the Portuguese people, themselves, who threw off their government and voted in a socialist government that vowed to free Portugal of its colonies.

The United States is hardly an honest supporter of truth, justice, peace, or freedom—at least not when it comes to Western Europe's former colonial subjects. When they want freedom, they are forced to pay a very high price, indeed. So it was with Haiti ever since it defeated Napoleon's Army in 1803, and so we shall see again in the case of Somalia.

And Somalia Has Oil!

Of course, the British, French, and Italians weren't in Somalia because they love the Somali people! The colonizers were in Somalia to get rich—the Africans be damned! (Especially since slavery was outlawed, not even African bodies were valuable to the Western European colonizers any more.) Today, there's a showdown going on in Africa between the major contenders in a unipolar world (the US and its allies who are also former colonizers), and their counterparts trying to make global politics more multi-polar (that would be Russia, China, Iran, and Brazil before the coup against the Workers Party). It is no secret that Africa is bestowed with riches in abundance; and that includes Somalia: Somalia not only has a strategic location on the Indian Ocean, the Gulf of Aden, and the Red Sea; Somalia has oil.

It has long been believed that Somalia shares oil reserves along with its neighbors which, interestingly given events there, also include

Yemen. "The Buzz" began in earnest in 2015, when *The National Interest*[5] headlined, "Somalia: The Next Oil Superpower?" in its "The Buzz" section. In 2016, *The Danish Institute for International Studies*[6] focused one of its Working Papers on Somalia's oil, its contested boundaries with Ethiopia and Kenya, and its offshore prospects. Its research focused on the "resource curse" outcomes of increased violence, corruption, and diversion of funds that accompany oil exploration and extraction in low- and middle-income countries. Later in 2016, in December, *Offshore* magazine called Somalia "East Africa's Oil Province" and wrote "this is the part of East Africa where hydrocarbon wealth will not just be defined by the development of long-term gas projects, but from the discovery of earth's richest natural resource prize—oil."[7]

"One of six US conditions for recognizing the Federal Government of Somalia (FGS) in 2012 implied a demand for the FGS to recognise and honour the *force majeure* concession rights of the US oil majors." This is how the Danish Working Paper begins. And throughout it is a reading of a delicious fictional plot that pits family against family, city against city, state against state, region against region, and all of them against the federal government. Except, it's not fiction in Somalia, it's real. As an example, the Danes write:

> Letters from 2013 Khaatumo State president and the chairman of Khaatumo Forum for Peace, Unity and Development, both addressed to the oil company DNO, illustrate the widespread disputes permeating the area. DNO is harshly criticised for making an agreement with '(...) the renegade one-clan secessionist enclave calling themselves "Somaliland,"' concerning SL18, which is "rightfully" owned by Khaatumo State, and DNO is thus urged to immediately withdraw from the void agreement as tensions and conflict in the area might otherwise intensify.[8]

And exactly as predicted by the Danish Working Paper, Kenya and Somalia are at odds with each other with oil contracts bringing the dispute to a boil. OilPrice.com headlined, "Tensions Spike As Kenya And Somalia Battle For Oil Rich Offshore Blocks."[9] Thankfully, they took the matter to the International Court of Justice[10] and not to their militaries.

Somalia's Tough Neighborhood

Compounding Somalia's "resource curse" as discussed in the Danish Working Paper, is Somalia's extremely important location. Its location becomes even more important once one realizes that all of the oil traffic from the Gulf States that is headed for Europe or the US comes into proximity to Somalia's territorial waters.

In addition to that, China's New Silk Road, One Belt One Road Maritime route incorporates Africa into the ambitious global trading, communication scheme. President Obama's "Pivot to Asia" guaranteed that one part of US policy would be the containment of Chinese influence in Asia; President Donald Trump has built on that containment policy by expanding the US military presence in Africa. After all, Africa has "belonged" to Europe and the US since the days of Western European colonialism. China helped many countries in their liberation struggles, but was never really a competitor on the African Continent. The Maritime Belt of the New Silk Road dramatically changes that. Africa is an integral part of China's global New Silk Road plan. China has even done something it has never done before—established a base outside of the country—and that base is in Djibouti, the former French Somaliland.

Yemen

Geo-strategically speaking, Somalia is in a very tough neighborhood. First of all, Somalia commands the littoral along one side of the Gulf of Aden (Yemen), also known as the Gulf of Berbera (Somalia). Just across the Gulf is Yemen which until recently, was artificially divided, like the Koreas and the Vietnams, purely on political, colonial, and ideological grounds. This positioning makes Somalia and Yemen both extremely important for commerce going along the Red Sea route through the Suez Canal and on to Europe or the Americas. Persian Gulf oil makes its way to its destination by way of this very route. In fact, approximately 4 million barrels of oil per day pass this way, headed on to Europe and the US Before the Suez Canal, remember, it was Cape Town and the Cape of Good Hope that was so important for global shipping. Today, it is the Suez Canal; tomorrow it will be China's New Silk Road, which is an overland and maritime project. And of course, the US wants to stop it at all costs.

Unacceptable turmoil in this area could cost millions to the companies in the shipping business. I say, "unacceptable," because US ally Saudi Arabia's fight to subdue Yemen is "acceptable" conflict—as long as the shipping lanes remain free for navigation. So, when Yemen's Houthi faction, supported by Iran, threatened to block this vital shipping lane, retribution was swift and decisive by the U.K. and Saudi Arabia. Today, the U.K. and Saudi Arabia closely monitor the shipping traffic in the area. In 2017, Trump ramped up US bombings in Yemen from 34 to 120, according to *Middle East Eye*.[11] Those whose business depends on access to the Red Sea commercial shipping lanes continue to keep an eye on the situation in this tough neighborhood.[12] As Saudi actions against Yemen dovetail nicely with US/Israel plans for containment of Iran, I'm certain that Saudi Arabia will be allowed to continue prosecuting its war against Yemen (and Iran) as long as these vital sea lanes are not threatened.

Ethiopia

Once-proud, never-colonized, but once-occupied Ethiopia, became a rendition and torture destination in the US Global War On Terror. That meant that Ethiopia was also a recipient of US weapons; Ethiopia used those weapons to fight its neighbors and in some cases, its own citizens. In fact, Ethiopia and Somalia have had several border skirmishes and outright wars! In 1964, and again in 1977, 1998, and in 2006—mostly arising from the Somali desire to be reunited in one true nation-state, as they were before the intrusion of the Europeans. In 2011 and 2012, the US-backed government of Somalia joined forces with Ethiopia and Kenya to fight Al Shabab, Somalia's branch of US-created and funded Al Qaeda. Add to this Ethiopia's internal changes that bode well for the largest ethnicity in the country, and that involve a huge identity changes as well for the state. In seeming recognition of the demographic political facts in the country, the ruling party just nominated an Oromo Muslim as its leader, meaning that the country is beginning to acknowledge its Muslim community as a part of the Ethiopian identity.[13]

Enter the Somali "Pirates" and Al Shabab

Now, one might wonder, why would the US create an Al Qaeda branch in Somalia? In just a few short paragraphs, we shall see . . .

So, you've got important sea lanes, geo-strategic importance, border issues, oil, and interest from both China and the US What a combustible mix! You just know there are going to be some problems. And, they surfaced around the "pirate" issue and the Somali version of the US-created and financed geo-strategic tool[14]—the Al Qaeda/ISIS phenomenon.

Around the year 2000 the world became aware of "Somali Pirates." The "pirates" were trying to prevent western dumping of toxic chemicals that interfered with fish catches in Somalia's waterways. Since Somalia didn't have a government, the "pirates" were the Somalis who responded to this direct threat to their lives and livelihood. In fact, according to at least one local non-governmental organization, Common Community Care, Somali fishermen were dying due to health conditions in the waters after a 2004 tsunami washed up containers of toxic waste, including radioactive material, washed ashore. Before that, after the collapse of the Barre government in the early 1990s, it was reported that European mafia-related companies were dumping toxic waste off the Somali coast. The *Environmental Justice Atlas* lists the conflict as one of waste management involving nuclear waste, uncontrolled dump sites, uranium, chemical products, lead, and industrial waste. Human health effects include birth defects and cancerous growths. The *Environmental Justice Atlas* writes:

> An Italian government investigation in the 1990s found that 35 million tonnes of waste had been exported to Somalia for $6.6 billion, but this figure would not include other countries whose waste ended up being illegally dumped in Somali waters. What is clear is that the cost of exporting waste is a far cheaper option for developed countries: a UNEP report states that it costs $2.50 per ton to dump toxic waste in Africa compared to $250 per ton to dump waste in Europe.[15]

Of course, the US responded vociferously and belligerently with the military and stepped up patrols to curb "Somali Pirates" infringing on the right of navigation on the high seas. The Western media, complicit in the deception, rarely informed its public the real reasons that the phenomenon of "Somali Pirates" existed.

Adding insult to injury, the US, led by Ethiopia, invaded Somalia in 2006. The Ethiopians didn't leave until 2009 and the US military is still in Somalia. As one of my interviewees so aptly put it: "Each locality has its own ingredients to apply to the same paradigm: Al Shabab is the Somali version of Al Qaeda and what is happening in

Somalia is the same thing that happened in Libya, Yemen. The formula is the same everywhere." Thus, Al Shabab is the Somali Al Qaeda/ISIS version created in the "terrorism laboratory" of the US and its allies. Interestingly, the US has tied Yemen insurgencies to Somalia—justifying its bombings of each.[16] We can rest assured of one thing: whatever the US says it is doing in Somalia and why is a lie.

And Back to Black Hawk Down

Somalia first came into the consciousness of the US public when two US Black Hawk helicopters were shot down by Somalis who then paraded one US soldier's white-skinned body throughout the streets of Mogadishu. That was in 1993. It was just a few years earlier that the outgoing US President, George Herbert Walker Bush, had traveled to Somalia to proclaim the New World Order in Africa.[17] What could possibly have caused such interest in Somalia from the US, and what did George Herbert Walker Bush mean by his remark?

In 1969 Siad Barre, a military man, seized power in Somalia in a bloodless coup. Barre declared Somalia to be a socialist state aligned with the Soviet Union. But, in 1974, a communist government in Ethiopia came to power. At first, the Soviets wanted to broker a peace between its two allies. But, the Somalis had the dream of unification with the British-ceded Somali land called the Ogaden that was now a part of Ethiopia. Thus, the Soviet Union abandoned Somalia and supported Ethiopia, which forced Barre to switch sides and invite the US military to back Somalia. The US came and never left. According to Mahdi Nazemroaya, "In the end Mogadishu would lose the war, but its new Cold War alliance with Washington would prove to be much more fatal, with a direct bearing on the future breakdown of the African country."[18] Just how devastating this realignment was is further highlighted by Nazemroaya: "Mogadishu opened its doors to the IMF and World Bank which would impose a neoliberal structural adjustment program on the country. These put an end to important public services and government investment in the public sector and in effect destroyed the foundations of Somalia's economic structure."[19] Adding fuel to the fire that was destroying Somalia's economy was the US designation of *hawala* (a money transfer system) as terrorist finance, thus eliminating an important Somali internal and international economic institution. Thus, the people began to tire of Siad Barre after having been in office for almost 30 years.

What was unknown at that time, however, is that foreign oil companies were also tired of the nationalism of Siad Barre, who refused to renew the oil contracts on their terms. This was exactly the scenario that later led to Libya's dissolution as a state in 2011. Thus, the people's unrest with Siad Barre was aided and abetted by the oil multinationals. It turns out that, according to my interviewees, the unrest was orchestrated, although the participants thought it was real (like the so-called "Arab Spring"). The oil contracts were due to expire in 1982—just when the International Monetary Fund (IMF) and World Bank arrived in town to demand even more austerity from the government. This, combined with the drought and the wars against Ethiopia, drained the coffers of the government and tried the patience of the people. And the more the IMF demanded of the government, the more the people demanded that the Barre government go! In 1981, the IMF demanded that the Somali government devalue its currency. IMF policy, combined with the food aid from the West, sent Somalia in to an economic tailspin. Somalia's agricultural sector was annihilated as a result of the double-barreled policies from the government, the IMF, and international donors—coordinated by the US Somalia's debt to those same Western countries had to be serviced and thus Somalia was caught in a vise with little way to escape. It had to borrow money from the West in order to pay the debt that it recognized that it owed to the West. It was around this time that Fidel Castro began to utter the unthinkable: the debt is a trap—walk away from it.

Food security in Somalia took a turn for the worse when food "aid" became a weapon that totally destroyed Somalia's agriculture sector. IMF-forced austerity combined with the effects of the Ogaden War with Ethiopia, which Somalia lost, and a natural drought all converged to create a crisis in Somalia's agriculture sector. According to Michel Chossudovsky[20] as quoted in Nazemroaya:

> The devaluation of the Somali shilling imposed by the IMF in June 1981, was followed by periodic devaluations, leading to hikes in the prices of fuel, fertilizer and farm inputs. The impact on agricultural producers was immediate particularly in rain-fed agriculture, as well as areas of irrigated farming. Urban purchasing power declined dramatically, government extension programs were curtailed, infrastructure collapsed, the deregulation of the grain market and

the influx of "food aid" led to the impoverishment of farming communities.[21]

The government went along with the austerity program and reluctantly signed the oil contract renewals. They would next come up for renewal in 2002.

It wouldn't take long before the government agreed to the IMF "structural adjustment" program that the Barre government would fall. And, of course, Barre was expendable after he had signed the oil contracts. In 1991, the Barre government fell and in December 1992, George Herbert Walker Bush ordered 28,000 US troops into Somalia—ostensibly to protect the Somalis from starving to death in the ongoing famine. But delivering food was not the only purpose US troops served: the US wanted to determine who the Barre successor would be—and the Somali contending factions would have none of that. The result is the spectacle that we all remember so vividly and the resulting humiliation that the US military will never be able to live down. The Somalis shot down two US helicopters, killing 18 personnel, with one of the corpses being dragged through the Mogadishu streets. The US "recovered" by shutting down the Somali *hawala*. The US shut down the Somalia Internet Company. The US intervention morphed into a military mission to ensure denial of victory to one of the contending factions in Somalia vying to succeed Barre. As I have found in previous research, then the United Nations peacekeeping force arrives. I call it *Pax Americana*-keeping.[22] Belgian and Canadian troops committed torture and war crimes against the Somali people as well as the contending factions. United Nations Pax Americana-keepers shot at civilians using United Nations helicopters.[23]

It was around this time that a little-known provision in the contracts was discovered that stated that the contracts would automatically renew should there be no government in Somalia to sign them. And of course, in 2002, there was no government in Somalia and so the oil contracts automatically renewed—again.

And there hasn't been much of a government in Somalia since—until the US-approved one that is seated now. Let's see if they dare to demand more for the Somali people as Somalia tries to sort out its myriad problems. And, of course, if there's no government in 2022 . . .

As he was wrapping up his tenure as President of the United States, Barack Obama dropped more than 26,000 bombs on Afghanistan, Pakistan, Libya, Yemen, and Somalia, and engaged in a covert drone war killing twice the number of civilians previously announced.[24] Somalis that I interviewed overwhelmingly believe that the real objective of the US military is to deny China access to Africa.

Enter China's New Silk Road

The Chinese are making huge investments in Africa: in Djibouti, a military installation; in Kenya, a rail line; in Tanzania, a new port; and industrial zones in Egypt along the Suez Canal. Currently, the Chinese are reportedly trying to decide if they will extend their overland corridors in Africa into Central Africa. The US, of course, is not taking these developments lightly. After all, Africa has been the private preserve of Western Europe and the US from the human trafficking during the Trans Atlantic Slave Trade to the neocolonial relations with state and non-state actors, including illegal relations resulting in the pillage of Africa's resources. The US warns the Africans that China is trying to "colonize" them!

China has lifted more people out of dire poverty than any other country in the world. The figure hovers around 300 million, according to Hong Kong government statistics.[25] In March 2018, the World Bank announced that extreme poverty in China will fall below 1% for the first time![26] In 2015, China declared that it had nearly wiped out urban poverty.[27] Meanwhile, poverty in neoliberal Hong Kong is growing in the opposite direction with 20% of its residents experiencing poverty and inequality being among the highest in the world.[28]

On March 22, 2018, President Trump declared a trade war on China accusing China of "harming" US "intellectual property right, innovation, or technology."[29] China responded by rejecting Trump's accusations, stating that if such a trade war were to ensue, "China would fight to the end to defend its own legitimate interests with all necessary measures."[30] China placed new levies on 128 products including pork and aluminum.

Unfortunately for Somalia, according to Evgeny Satanovsky, founder of the Middle East Institute, outside contention will only get worse in Somalia before the situation sees any improvement.[31] In fact, the region has received so much attention from China that the US Congress—the House Intelligence Committee—has decided to investigate China's military "footprint" on the African Continent.

Enter, Oil Contracts 2.0: Somalia's Predicament With Its Ports

The United States *Voice of America* Radio Station describes

Somalia as "a society deeply divided along clan and family lines, with no allegiance to a central authority."[32] And under the watchful eye of the United Nations, an organization which reflects the power configuration of today, with five states having the power to veto the desired policies of two hundred states, ensures that the rich and powerful countries and their smaller allies will maintain hegemony (or lawlessness) over smaller, victim states. Thus, the Constitution of Somalia was drafted in such a way as to exacerbate, rather than ameliorate, the tendencies described by the *Voice of America*. While the *Voice of America* broadcast focused on religion, (of course, since virtually all Somalis are Muslims), the Somalis focused on the heavy-handedness of the so-called International Community (meaning the rich and powerful countries) instead of building a consensus for the new Constitution by including the Somali people in the process of Constitution writing. The reasoning by April Powell-Willingham, head of the Joint Constitution Unit at the United Nations Political Office for Somalia (UNPOS) and United Nations Development Program (UNDP) for Somalia at the time went as follows: "The fact is that in a deeply globalized world, it is often true that Constitution making and democratization is no longer solely a national exercise. There are multiple local, national, regional and international influences at play at any given time."[33] And thus, the people of Somalia would be saddled with a Constitution that many characterized as did one Somali quoted by *Voice of America*: "It is not our constitution and it's never going to be." The International Policy Digest does not mince words describing the Constitutional process, using characterizations like "all-but Somali led," "corrupt," and concludes that the entire Constitutional process, as run by the United Nations:

> instigate[d] all sorts of negative social, political, security and legal drawbacks such as social fragmentation and conflicts, secession or separation, foreign claims over Somali territory, primacy of international laws over Somalia laws, long term foreign military occupation, installation of bogus Federal Government (FG), protracted stalemate over the formation of Federal Member States (FMSs), corruption, terrorism and radicalism. Some of the factors that give rise to those negative developments are the imposition of federalism, creation of bogus FG and FMSs.[34]

Thus, Somalia had imposed on it a system of governance not desired by the majority of its people and that bestows foreign policy making power on individual states created in the Constitution. This is the situation that gave rise to what I'll call the Oil Contracts 2.0: the predicament with Somalia's ports. The Constitution gives the individual states the power to negotiate with external interests for the extraction or use of Somali resources in contradiction to any desires of the central Federal Government. Thus, this imposed system of governance pits state versus state and states versus Federal Government in the matters of resource extraction (like oil leases) and operation of the ports (port licenses). Ahali and Ackah conclude that this set of circumstances sets Somalia up for interminable turmoil. They write: "This puts Somalia's stability at high risk as she does not have a nationwide framework that will enable her [to] oversee and equitably distribute rents accumulated from her natural resources."[35]

With this as a backdrop, the predicament with Somalia's ports is proving as devastating as is the situation with its oil leases, leaving foreigners completely in charge. I will use the example of the port of Berbera, the ancient port of Somalia, as an example. Lying within the Somaliland FMS and serving as its commercial capital, the political leaders of Somaliland negotiated an arrangement with DP World of Dubai to upgrade the major class port there. DP World then announced that the state of Ethiopia was also a part of the deal. On March 2, 2018, *Asharq Al-Awsat* reported, in a misleading headline, that the Ethiopian Foreign Minister announced, "after a year of serious negotiations, Ethiopia has concluded an agreement with the Somaliland Ports Authority and DP World that will give the Government of Ethiopia [a] 19 percent stake in the joint venture developing the Port of Berbera."[36] The FG of Somalia was nowhere in the picture and a foreign country had purchased its way into Somalia's port operation! The Somali government has objected and the disputed lease has predictably pitted the FG against the Somaliland FMS. The controversial lease is for 30 years; and if the same or similar provisions as the oil contracts are in this and other port contracts, Somalis may not ever again have 100% control over their own ports!

Somalia has been effectively Balkanized by the US and the former colonizers under the guise of Constitutionalism and democracy. Interestingly, the "solutions" for Somalia that they imposed are the exact same solutions rejected by the United States as it debated its own Constitution two hundred years ago.

Somalia-ization Is US Policy

It seems that many controversial recent events in which the United States played a negative part were tested first in Somalia. Arab Spring—check. Refusal to negotiate oil deals with patriotic leaders who want better terms for the resources of their people like Libya. Check.[37] Sociocide—Elimination of all functioning institutions of society—like, Iraq. Check. Using a tragedy to move in the military, like Haiti. Check. It's not the Libyanization of other countries, but in fact, even Libya was Somalia-ized!

The US is still bombing Somalia; the US prevented the Somalis from having a government, for generations. The US still seeks to control the Somali state in order to steal Somalia's resources. The US and its allies have robbed and pillaged Somalia blind. The prediction made by one of my Somali interviewees is that the 20-year oil contract comes up for renewal in 2022 and the election has been scheduled for 2021.

With all of the built-in traps that have been set for Somali politicians having to deal with the clan issue, the federal government versus state issue, the Somaliland issue, and the Ogaden issue, and more—not to mention Al Shabab and foreign troops on its soil—it will be hard for Somalia to emerge as anything other than its designation by President Donald Trump. That is the condition that serves the interests of the US Deep State very well. They get resources and they don't even have to pay for them. Think about that when you're admiring US and Western European wealth.

In fact, since the Berlin Conference of the late 1800s, every interference in Somalia by Western Europeans and the US has been one with negative outcomes for the Somali people. Somalia is a very profitable "shithole" for those who created it. The endless intrusion of colonizers, neocolonizers, globalizers, neoliberals, and occupiers has only worsened Somalia's affairs. The only way the outlook can change is for the people of the US to call off their dogs of war, domination, greed, and occupation and allow the Somali people to breathe again. In the meantime, I must acknowledge the sheer tenacity and resilience of the Somali people who still stand as a proud Somali nation despite all of these facts. Or do they? One of my interviewees from Somaliland expressed sadly that Somalia's treatment at the hands of the successive waves of colonialism, neocolonialism, globalization, neoliberalism, and now a Constitution and Federal Government that don't represent them, have all combined to effectively kill the idea of the Somali nation. In his words, "It is dead." I hope that is not irreversibly the case. Ironically, while today struggling to preserve their own identities, the Europeans and the US have had no problem killing those of others.

Somalia's recent history is a sad one of outside interference—yet hope in the future—that Donald Trump probably never cared to know as he made his derogatory remarks about such an ancient, 4,000 year old civilization.

ENDNOTES

1   Map of Somalia is from the *CIA World Facebook*, Central Intelligence Agency located at https://www.cia.gov/library/publications/the-world-factbook/geos/so.html accessed on March 23, 2018.

2   John Stockwell, *In Search of Enemies*, (Toronto: George J. McCloud, Limited, 1978). The book can be found online at https://www.scribd.com/document/243591231/In-Search-of-Enemies-A-CIA-Story-John-Stockwell accessed on March 22, 2018.

3   Cynthia McKinney, *Ain't Nothing Like Freedom*, (Atlanta: Clarity Press, 2013).

4   Italy was only united as a country in 1861, less than 40 years before the infamous Berlin Conference and its ensuing "Scramble for Africa" where Europe's planned to devour Africa and carve it up into pieces to be consumed like the Thanksgiving Turkey is in the U.S.

5   Alex Dick-Gregory, "Somalia: The Next Oil Superpower?" *The National Interest*, January 15, 2015 located at http://nationalinterest.org/blog/the-buzz/somalia-the-next-oil-superpower-12041 accessed April 3, 2018.

6   Jakob Grandjean Bamberger and Kristian Skovsted, "Concessions and Conflicts: Mapping Oil Exploration in Somalia and Ethiopia," *Danish Institute for International Studies* located at http://pure.diis.dk/ws/files/576720/DIIS_WP_2016_2.pdf accessed on April 3, 2018.

7   Neil Hodgson, "Somalia awakens as East Africa's oil province," *Offshore* located at https://www.offshore-mag.com/articles/print/volume-76/issue-12/geology-geophysics/somalia-awakens-as-east-africa-s-oil-province.html accessed April 3, 2018.

8   Banberger and Skovsted, op. cit., 15.

9   Zainab Calcuttawala, "Tensions Spike As Kenya And Somalia Battle For Oil Rich Offshore Blocks," *OilPrice.com,*September 21, 2016 located at https://oilprice.com/Energy/Energy-General/Tensions-Spike-As-Kenya-And-Somalia-Battle-For-Oil-Rich-Offshore-Blocks.html accessed April 3, 2018.

10   To see video of the ICJ ruling in Round One of the Kenya–Somalia border

dispute please visit https://www.youtube.com/watch?v=O82c7ielqiM accessed April 3, 2018. Video of the entire proceedings can be seen located at https://www.youtube.com/watch?v=TE9KDnULWyE accessed April 3, 2018.

11   *Middle East Eye*, December 20, 2017 located at http://www.middleeasteye.net/news/us-tripled-number-air-strikes-yemen-2017-809615374 accessed March 24, 2018.

12   "Red Sea commercial shipping in danger of becoming 'collateral damage' in Yemen conflict," *Seatrade Maritime News*, October 11, 2016, located at http://www.seatrade-maritime.com/news/middle-east-africa/red-sea-commercial-shipping-in-danger-of-becoming-collateral-damage-in-yemen-conflict.html accessed on March 24, 2018.

13   For more analysis of this development, please see Andrew Korybko, "Ethiopia: 'Deceptive Facelift' Or 'Full-Blown Change?'" *Oriental Review*, March 29, 2018 located at https://orientalreview.org/2018/03/29/ethiopia-deceptive-face-lift-or-full-blown-change/ accessed on April 3, 2018.

14   Remember, General Wesley Clark had told FOX News audiences that ISIS was used by the U.S. as a "geo-strategic tool."

15   "Somalia toxic waste dumping," *Environmental Justice Atlas* located at https://ejatlas.org/conflict/somalia-toxic-waste-dumping-somalia accessed April 3, 2018.

16   Mark Mazzetti, Jeffrey Gettleman, Eric Schmitt, "In Somalia, US Escalates a Shadow War," *New York Times*, October 16, 2016 located at https://www.nytimes.com/2016/10/16/world/africa/obama-somalia-secret-war.html accessed on April 3, 2018.

17   According to a March 23, 2018 interview conducted by the author with a Somali national.

18   Mahdi Darius Nazemroaya, *The Globalization of NATO*, (Atlanta, Clarity Press, 2012) 224.

19   *Ibid.*, 224.

20   Michel Chossudovsky *The Globalization of Poverty and the New World Order, 2nd edition* (Pincourt, QC: Global Research Publishers, 2003), p.95.

21   Nazemroaya, *op. cit.*, 226–227.

22   Cynthia McKinney, "A Deeper Look At Peacekeeping Operations: Peacekeeping or Pax Americana-Keeping?" *Dialogue of Civilizations Research Institute*, June 29, 2016 located at https://doc-research.org/en/a-deeper-look-at-un-peacekeeping-operations-peacekeeping-or-pax-americana-keeping/ accessed on April 3, 2018.

23   Alex de Waal, "US War Crimes In Somalia," *Social Science Research Council*, February 28, 2007 located at http://hornofafrica.ssrc.org/de_Waal3/printable.html accessed on April 3, 2018.

24   As an example of the reportage, see Jessica Purkiss and Jack Serle, "Obama's Covert Drone War In Numbers: Ten Times More Strikes Than Bush," *The Bureau of Investigative Journalism*, January 17, 2017 located at https://www.thebureauinvestigates.com/stories/2017-01-17/obamas-covert-drone-war-in-numbers-ten-times-more-strikes-than-bush accessed April 3, 2018.

25   "Analysis of poverty situation in Hong Kong in 2016 announced" Hong Kong

Government, November 17, 2017 located at http://www.info.gov.hk/gia/general/201711/17/P2017111700634.htm accessed March23 2018.

26 *People's Daily Online*, March 5, 2018 located at http://en.people.cn/n3/2018/0305/c90000-9433193.html accessed March 23, 2018.

27 *The Guardian, International Edition*, August 19, 2015 located at https://www.theguardian.com/business/economics-blog/2015/aug/19/china-poverty-inequality-development-goals accessed on March 23, 2018.

28 *The Guardian, International Edition*, November 20, 2017 located at https://www.theguardian.com/world/2017/nov/20/hong-kong-20-of-residents-live-in-poverty accessed on March 23, 2018.

29 "Presidential Memorandum on the Actions by the United States Related to the Section 301 Investigation," located at https://www.whitehouse.gov/presidential-actions/presidential-memorandum-actions-united-states-related-section-301-investigation/ accessed March 23, 2018.

30 *South China Morning Post International Edition*, March 23, 2018 located at http://www.scmp.com/news/china/article/2138521/read-chinas-furious-response-donald-trumps-us60b-tariffs-full accessed March 23, 2018.

31 Evgeny Satanovsky, "AFRICA SHOWDOWN: Major Players Involved, Including Russia," *South Front*, March 26, 2018 located at https://southfront.org/africa-showdown-major-players-involved-including-russia/ accessed on April 3, 2018.

32 "Drafting Somalia's Constitution Opens Debate on Religion, Law," *Voice of America*, March 28, 2012 located at https://www.voanews.com/a/drafting-somalias-constitution-opens-debate-on-religion-law-144862645/180622.html accessed on April 18, 2018.

33 Ibid.

34 Mohamud Uluso, "Provisional Constitution Heightens Tensions in Somalia," *International Policy Digest* August 8, 2012 located at https://intpolicydigest.org/2012/08/08/provisional-constitution-heightens-tensions-in-somalia/ accessed April 18, 2018.

35 Aaron Yao Efui Ahali and Ishamel Ackah, "Oil Resource Governance in Somalia: Are they Susceptible to the Resource Curse?" *Munich Personal ReEc Archive* December 20, 2014 located at https://mpra.ub.uni-muenchen.de/61211/2/MPRA_paper_61211.pdf accessed April 18, 2018.

36 "DP World Signs Agreement with Ethiopia, Somalia to Develop Port of Berbera," *Asharq Al-Awsat*, March 2, 2018 located at https://aawsat.com/english/home/article/1191896/dp-world-signs-agreement-ethiopia-somalia-develop-port-berbera accessed April 18, 2018.

37 For the entire story of how the U.S. and its allies took Libya from the wealthiest African country with zero homelessness, etc. to the utter state of lawlessness that it is now, please see Cynthia McKinney's *Illegal War on Libya* (Atlanta: Clarity Press, 2011).

DEMOCRATIC REPUBLIC OF CONGO

DISASTER CAPITALISM'S GREATEST CARNAGE OF THEM ALL

Keith Harmon Snow

"It was madness, it was brutal, but it was the Congo,
and it should not have surprised anyone."
Major (then) Thomas P. Odom
Dragon Operations in Congo,
1964-1965

"Africa is beset with many dormant, inactive conflicts.
Like sleeping volcanoes, they wait patiently
for their day of reckoning."[1]
William G. Thom
Chief, Defense Intelligence Agency
1987-2002

"NO CONFLICT since the 1940s has been bloodier, yet few have been more completely ignored."[2] So begins the standard mainstream media piece about Africa manufactured by *The Economist*. This one is about the Congo. It appeared 15 February 2018, a month after the supreme leader of the United States uttered his scatological remarks demeaning Haiti and certain unnamed countries in Africa.

The cataclysm in Africa's great lakes countries of Burundi, Congo, Rwanda and Uganda—and *ditto* Sudan—amounts to the greatest destruction of human lives in all recorded history. No matter what argument you might try to make to the contrary, overall this is *genocide* against African people of diverse ethnicities, and it is genocide perpetrated by white power interests.[3]

The dystopian dispatches in western magazines or newspapers imply that it is hopeless to try to figure out the root causes of the conflicts and ongoing violence in central Africa, but these mostly fictitious accounts are examples of fake news billed as principled journalistic reportage.

The Economist and other assorted western media brands— *Bloomberg, New York Times, Atlantic Monthly,* Reuters, CNN, *The Guardian, Der Spiegel,* VICE, *New Yorker, Nation, Business Insider, Democracy Now*—all serve some kind of interests or other, whether it be the interests of Wall Street executives or Downing Street diplomats, liberals or conservatives, and most of them serve the interests of assorted inter-linked multinational multi-passport white-collar arms dealers, minerals cartels, plantation slaveholders, timber barons, war criminals, *genocidaires,* a multitude of other unscrupulous diamond-studded profiteers and, of course, toilet paper manufacturers.

There is nothing unique about such reportage: it is packed with *boilerplate* warlike racial terminology, tropes, stereotypes, distortions, unstated insinuations, intentional omissions and outright lies. The Congo is nothing like you might think, should you consume the propaganda as you are expected to, and there's no knowing Congo, even for those of us who have spent a long time there.

Perception Management

The titling of *The Economist's* [15 February 2018] Congo fiction is disingenuous at best. The language of both the title and contents is based on a long lexicology of deeply racist symbols, writings and meanings that have appropriately been described as "warlike racial operations".[4]

Africa's broken heart
Congo is sliding back to bloodshed
How to stop a catastrophe

Rather than demonstrate humanitarian concern, *The Economist's* subtitle "How to Stop A Catastrophe" rather reflects a directive based on the modern day political doctrine of humanitarian intervention, relabeled Responsibility to Protect, or R2P. This doctrine is the contemporary cornerstone of the old tried and true imperialist narrative that "We can save these people from themselves"—the equivalent of a rapist insisting that he is the one who must protect his victims. At the hands of these very imperialists, posing as ethical humanitarians and righteous saviors, the R2P doctrine is used to project imperial power and disguise the deployment of imperial storm troopers all over the world. That is the real purpose of this article by *The Economist*—to manipulate public opinion in support of further western interventions in central Africa and everywhere.

The black and white photograph that attends *The Economist's* fictitious story about Congo supports a deeply entrenched narrative about child soldiering in Africa that serves the white power military-industrial complex and our Western interventionist narratives.[5] It depicts a black African guerrilla in the photo wearing rather new fatigues and a beret and he is looking back at the camera-cum-reader menacingly. There's a giant gun slung over the young man's shoulder dangling a string of bullets into an aluminum can. The soldier might be 16.

The image projects the imminent menace of the coming anarchy, of barbarism and savagery overflowing their confines, similar to how widely disseminated propaganda/reports about disease in Africa play on the western psyche's fear of pathogens and bodily fluids.[6] It seeks to disorient and disconnect the reader from any and all awareness not only of conditions where the man is struggling to survive, circumvent and prevail, but also from the West's benefit in and responsibility for creating and sustaining these very conditions.

This photo was taken somewhere in eastern Congo. It might be of a Rwandan soldier in a Congolese uniform or it might be a Congolese soldier. The spectator-consumer-viewer learns nothing from the photo even while they assume an (erroneous) understanding. The editors don't tell us anything further about the photo's source. Even if they did, most readers would not understand what they have been told, or why the exact identification of the nationality of the combatant(s) is crucial. Rather they would think that they have learned something useful or truthful about what is really going on. On the other hand, the uncaptioned photo is also clearly branded: *Polaris/Eyevine* to insure private property rights.

The branding of the photo speaks to the western production of imagery about Africa and African people being an industry in and of itself.[7]

To the white and even to the African-American mind, this uncaptioned iconic photograph misrepresenting another people is the epitome of what such viewers, with their falsified African consciousness, perceive Africa to be, and its subhead offers a clear implication: "We can save them." That is part of the interventionist message, reminiscent of the deft UK Orientalist distorted portrayals of the Islamic world. More precisely it implies: "We can save those (read: other and dark-skinned) people *from themselves.*"

The great white hope, the bloody heart, the broken heart, the heart of darkness, apocalypse now, the coming anarchy—all these epithets add up to a very long and simple though equally sophisticated history of managing the perceptions of the Western commodities consumer about our destructive relations with such places as Congo or Papua New Guinea or Haiti.

The Economist begins its tale by explaining how the war has gone on for some years, that no one has any idea how many people have died or what the fighting is about or who was killing whom. Anarchy, get it? But nothing could be further from the truth.

The "Congo Wars" did not begin in 1998: they began in 1996, when the U.S. proxy armies of Uganda and Rwanda openly invaded the Congo, with complete U.S. military involvement. The planning preceded the September '96 invasions by at least two years: the September '96 date is only valid if we exclude the certain presence of U.S. Special Operations Forces operating on the ground before then. The crucial period 1996-1998 is specifically and intentionally excluded to protect and exonerate the United States, Israel and the United Kingdom for their involvement in the war crimes, crimes against humanity and genocide that occurred in Central Africa during this period. The story of war and plunder in Congo has been censored, manipulated, and covered up even while it is ostensibly being told, and this by both right-wing and left-wing, conservative or liberal, even so-called progressive media. For the Congolese people, it is one long contiguous war that began in 1996 and continues—with some 120-armed groups and multinational corporations getting away with murder in eastern Congo as this book goes to press.

In *Business Insider* in December 2015, reporter Armin Rosen revealed a map produced by an organization introduced to readers as the Congo Research Group.[8] This is a western intelligence organization masquerading as an independent non-profit non-governmental organization that was born back in the 2000's era as the western defense and intelligence establishment grappled with the changing realities on the ground in Central Africa. Rosen falsely claimed that it is hopeless to try to understand the complexity of "the conflict" calling it senseless violence concerning only small time Congolese (artisanal) miners (who pillage the Congo's minerals) and the government which cannot enforce the law. These are some of the main themes of the propaganda system as regards Central Africa. One would be hard pressed to perceive the *business* angle of this *Business Insider* article.

In another article Rosen purports to explain "the origins of war in the DRC"—this from a man who spent one week in Congo. Mr. Rosen focused the reader's attention on what he called "small unregulated mines" but he said nothing about the big transnational corporations and how they are exporting riches while importing and manufacturing violence, mayhem and suffering.[9]

Rosen uses the modern ploy of hiding the root causes of resource plunder, obscuring the funding and aiding of forces to attack their neighbors and manufacture chaos. While Rosen cites Congolese voices stating (correctly) that Rwanda and Uganda are destabilizing and occupying DRC, he then cites Congolese voices supplemented by his own dismissing such ideas as conspiracy theories. Rosen's selected sources are in actuality blaming the victims.[10]

Splashed over the pages of the world's premier financial magazines and pumped into global consciousness by some of the world's foremost liars, such propaganda is the vanguard for the empire and it's campaigns to scrub clean the image of people like Donald Trump and Hillary Clinton and so many other men and women whose names we never hear, who initiate and implement the West's ongoing plunder of Africa.

Many of these agents of repression, almost never mentioned, are profoundly dirty and deeply culpable in organized crime. But if and when they are seen in the public eye they are characterized as playboys, humanitarians, politicians, philanthropists, compassionate capitalists, or "leaders" of high moral and ethical repute. There is a hierarchy of exploitation (and exploiters), just as there is a hierarchy of suffering.

Public relations firms like Young & Rubicam, Hill & Knowlton Strategies, Ogilvy PR, Goodworks International, Cohen and Woods International, Burson-Marstellar and Bell Pottinger have all conspired in influence-peddling, corporate whitewashing and the prettying up of blood-spattered regimes both in and out of Africa. These firms protect the interests of the most powerful.

If there were any justification for the *shithole* label to be applied to Africa it would go beyond these giant PR firms to the direct but often media-invisible involvement of politician statesmen (e.g. Hillary Clinton, Donald Trump, Madeleine Albright, William Cohen, Samantha Power, Johanna König, Karl Heinz Albers, Tony Blair, Avigdor Liberman), celebrity actorvists (e.g. Ben Affleck, Bono, George Clooney, Mia Farrow), business tycoons (e.g. Maurice Tempelsman, Philippe De Moerloose[11], Louis Michel, Walter Kansteiner, John Bredencamp, Arnold Kondrat, Marc Rich), military and/or intelligence operatives (Larry Devlin, William Thom, Richard Orth, Thomas Odom, John Prendergast, Jason Stearns, Daphne Park[12], David Kimche[13]) and so-called humanitarians and philanthropists (e.g. Henry Gates, Eve Ensler, Paula Green, Warren Buffet), and many more.

As a lay reader, you probably don't know who any of these people are, or you might know some of them, but you likely have no idea why we are pointing the finger at them. That is precisely the point. We can name names. In most cases we know who done it, when they done it, and how they done it. Naming names, corporations or individuals does not make one a conspiracy theorist, it makes one a conspiracy researcher and muckraker of the most honorable kind.[14]

The invisibility of white agents of violence (and their comprador black allies) to media like *The Economist* and *The New York Times* in turn renders them invisible to most African-Americans and even Africans. The Western public is kept unaware and confused about what is happening on the ground while white power agents and their embraceable African-American and African agent-functionaries commandeer resources, re-enslave black labor, and either foster or permit massive depopulations on a scale threatening to match or exceed the European slave trade.

The western academic establishment plays a pivotal role in maintaining this structural violence and permanent exploitation. The dictates and prerogatives of academia lead to pressures placed on academics to conform to the general silence, misrepresent or hide the violence, and whitewash the oppressors, the systems of oppression and the institutions that enable them to proliferate. Academics seldom link the realities of the exploitation with the (obvious) presence of the exploiters, and they often skirt around the truth to protect their interests:

their prestigious careers, academic appointments, research grants, and peer-reviewed publications.[15]

One academic after another—all these huge and skinny volumes on Central Africa—has whitewashed reality to serve and advance the imperial agenda. The most notable culprits include such prominent names as Samuel Totten, Gerard Prunier, Gerald Kaplan, Adam Jones, Phil Clark, Eric Reeves—academics that unabashedly present themselves as the arbiters of truth, meanwhile shielding the interests of the most powerful and reaping the rewards of empire. Most all of these offer limited if any discussion about any and all involvement of either the U.S. military or U.S. mercenaries or their intelligence and defense allies in the central African conflicts and they universally exclude all but the most specious references to the powerful transnational corporations that are there on the ground in plain sight.

Guerillas in the Mist

Underpinning the white man's arsenal of superficial Hollywood films like *Black Panther* and *Hotel Rwanda* is an unacknowledged racialized identity of whiteness which penetrates, controls and exploits Africa—regardless of its geographical location—by posturing itself as politically neutral and allocating unto itself the implementation of an arsenal of non-negotiable rights that in actuality extend dominion over Africa through a multitude of political, economic, military, ideological and cultural means. In lay terms, there are a lot of white people (and colored allies) making a lot of money off the massive death and destruction of African people all over the continent and at this very moment.

On one hand the white-owned corporate power structure demands guaranteed access to populations that can be induced—and this generally involves coercion given the horrible working conditions—to provide cheap and easily replenished labor. On the other hand there is the need for "willing" populations to be used, for example, for "consensual" testing of pharmaceutical products. While corporations seek to maximize sales of certain globalized commodities (e.g. Coca Cola) through market expansion in Africa, we are also seeing the massive depopulation of vast territories, whether for multinational mining, agribusiness or so-called environmental conservation, i.e. the gazetting and "protecting" of national parks and reserves. The current state-sponsored repression, dislocation and retaliation against the indigenous Maasai but backed by elite conservation interests from Boston (USA) is a perfect example.[16]

Coca Cola is available almost everywhere in Africa, in the most rural places, even while medicines are often unavailable in the same locations. This illustrates the nature of structural violence. Similarly, foreign owned western mining companies like Banro Gold Corporation operate clean shiny new mining facilities in areas of eastern Congo and the gold (and we don't know what other minerals) is shipped out by helicopter and then transported through Rwanda while blood is practically dripping off the grass and skeletons are barely submerged beneath the surface of the land. Banro Gold could not achieve such plunder without the overt and covert support of the terrorist military regime in neighboring Rwanda, one of the U.S., Canada and Israel's mainstays of military power on the continent.

It is interesting to examine how these parallel economies are portrayed. On the one hand the media imply an economy predicated on supposed black African savagery where people are portrayed as hopeless, lazy, diseased, ignorant, sexually licentious, culturally backward and other things; on the other they celebrate a parallel economy of shiny clean white expatriates predicated on the gracious and caring provision of jobs, medicine and schools to the needy people.

What are the relationships between Coca Cola or Banro Gold directors and black African functionaries? Well, in short it is a master-slave relationship. It could also be portrayed as white-collar war criminals and their black African fall guys.[17] How, as instances, does Coca Cola achieve market saturation or Banro Gold maximize bullion exports in the midst of calamities, droughts, famines, and so-called civil-wars in rural Africa? Where and how does the Pentagon, *inter alia*, come in (and go out)? This is the system that exists today all over the world, and it is a system of managed inequality, with prodigious suffering, despair and death. What follows are a few examples in limited detail.

The Horror, the Horror

Reality does not matter. Instead, we have blockbuster box-office hits like *Avatar, Black Panther, King Kong* and *Tarzan*, reproduced in a more technologically sophisticated Special F/X version every decade or so, repeated in sequel and prequel, *ad nauseam*.

The stereotypes, themes and mythologies invented in the minds of white invaders and supplanted in the minds of arm-chair travelers and theater spectators both proscribe and inform a contemporary mass media culture that deploys shape-shifting versions of the original civilizing discourses used by the early missionaries, conquerors and settlers. Contemporary discourses are repackaged and reconstituted using the evolving syntax and lexicon of modernity and globalization that today are formulated in white elite terms. The Western discourses of development, conservation, human rights and humanitarianism all deploy elaborate rhetorical arguments about the importance of indigenous autonomy, national sovereignty, human rights and cultural heritage. But the rhetoric and propaganda do not hold water so the Western media cloaks the realities on the ground in Africa—which in actuality facilitate a cyclical, self-reinforcing structure of power, exploitation and profit.

Beyond the word "Africa" and all that it conjures up in the minds of outsiders we have numerous subconscious and now programmed or conditioned associations with words that demean and subordinate the *othered* peoples, cultures and places of Africa. These associations universally revolve around stereotypes, essentialized constructs and other fictional or imagined re-presentations that likely emanate from identity-based fears concerned with a loss of power, even as the power relations are enhanced in the process. The lexicon of *Dark Continentalism* deployed in and by white public space is rich with labels like savage, Hutu or Tutsi, dictator, Janjaweed, Mai Mai, Mau Mau, ebola, anarchy, zombie, Ju-Ju, Killmonger, voodoo, *genocidaire*, tribal chief and *Interahamwe*.[18]

Louis Leakey, his wife Mary, and their son Richard "made the key discoveries that have shaped our understanding of the first men." Leakey's actions and interests facilitated the production of a huge body of knowledge—an industry—whose locus of power resides in white Western institutions whose importance cannot be overstated. These include such notable entities as the National Geographic Society, the Dian Fossey Gorilla Fund International, the Smithsonian Institute, the International Gorilla Conservation Program, and the multitudinous academic, corporate and non-governmental organizations (NGOs) that today constitute a billions-of-dollars economy in conservation and captive-breeding interests. Zoos, tourism, taxonomy, GIS and remote sensing are but a few of the peripheral interests involved, and each is an industry in its own right. For most conservation programs the gorillas or elephants or rhinos are merely the brand adopted by corporate entities: if any of these species went extinct the corporate entity (e.g. Jane Goodall Institute) would merely adopt a new brand (e.g. species) and reinvent itself. It has very little to do with saving wildlife or habitat, and—no matter what they say—it is never about helping *the people* that inhabit these landscapes.

Louis Leakey served as a British spy in colonial Kenya and his son has in the past headed a white paramilitary organization that deployed armed forces for conservation projects and "primatology" research in numerous African countries. Richard Leakey's Wildlife Direct[19] is incorporated and funded out of Washington, DC, and its affiliated sponsors and board members at one time included, for example, Walter Kansteiner III, formerly on staff at the White House who was also a director of Moto Gold,[20] a mining company that was in control of vast tracts of blood drenched eastern Congo[21]—a country invaded by the United States military (1996-1997) and its African allies (esp. Rwanda, Uganda) during Kansteiner's White House tenure.[22]

Walter Kansteiner III is one of the shadiest architects of Congo's troubles. The son of a coltan trader in Chicago, Kansteiner was Assistant Secretary of State for Africa under G.W. Bush and former National Security insider and member of the Department of Defense Task Force on Strategic Minerals under Bill Clinton. Kansteiner's speech at The Forum for International Policy in October of 1996 advocated partitioning the Congo (Zaire) into smaller states based on ethnic lineage; the Pentagon was at that precise time backing an insurgency to overthrow the long time dictator Colonel Joseph Mobutu.[23]

Kansteiner is a former director of the precious metal firm Titanium Resources Group, a company deeply tied to Sierra Rutile Limited, a firm pivotal to the bloodshed in Sierra Leone. Sierra Rutile Ltd. director Sir Sam Jonah reportedly helped finance Rwandan (Congolese Rally for Democracy) rebel groups in DRC while he was a CEO of Ashanti Goldfields; Jonah was also a director for Moto Gold. Sierra Rutile is owned by Max and Jean-Raymond Boulle and Robert Friedland, "Friends of Bill" Clinton who were linked to clandestine networks of offshore holdings and front companies involved in weapons trafficking, money laundering and human rights atrocities from Burma to the Congos to Indonesia to Mongolia.[24]

In Central Africa the average life span for men and women hovers around 42 years of age (2007). Treatable diseases are in "beyond epidemic" proportions, including malaria (for which a vaccine was developed only for the U.S. military and its selected partners[25]), river blindness, tuberculosis, yellow fever, tetanus and typhoid. Weapons and landmines produced in white privileged economies proliferate, and the corporations hired, for example, to de-mine landscapes and deactivate unexploded ordinance come from the same white economies that produce them. Hundreds of millions of dollars of mineral exports occur monthly, scores of billions of dollars annually, yet the scale of poverty, devastation and war is unprecedented with upwards of 7 million dead between 1996 and 2007.[26] After 2007 some 1000 people continued to die monthly in eastern Congo, and the war is ongoing in 2018. This is a region long coveted by westerners for its gorilla forests and since the very beginning of colonialism for its minerals. Famine, malnutrition, parasites and diarrhea are widespread, while even the most basic staple food sources become increasingly compromised or unavailable due to land grabs (mining, petroleum, plantations) by Western-owned-and-run multinational corporations routinely empowered by intelligence operatives and private military companies from outside Africa.

Meanwhile, elites operate through non-governmental organizations (NGOs) aligned with animal rights, wildlife conservation, environmental protection and humanitarian charities to consistently produce, re-inscribe and further entrench white cultural practices and institutions self-defined as "neutral," "apolitical" and "progressive" that nonetheless target and punish resident populations in central Africa for pursuing their day-to-day struggle to survive. The white agents of conservation, development, human rights and "humanitarian" relief flock here and there (not only in Africa) with little oversight or accountability, and they deploy an arsenal of non-negotiable rights and privileges to further their agenda, including lucrative research projects, funding instruments, "expeditions" in the "uncharted" "wilderness" or "jungle", and policies that universally discriminate against local populations, people with little agency, with whom often they have never communicated.

Countless examples of this can be found in the exclusive field programs of the Jane Goodall Institute, the Dian Fossey Gorilla Fund International or Wildlife Conservation Society in Central Africa.[27] These entities emerge from an increasingly privatized white public space to penetrate black Africa where they then peddle programs of birth control in the target (subaltern) populations. Uneducated, illiterate Congolese women who nonetheless speak three or four of some 400 native languages are informed without discussion or concern for their needs that they must reduce the size of their families. After a cursory "education" program by some local health agent empowered with a small stipend that temporarily offers a meal and blanket and a means of day-to-day survival, the target women are offered "choices"—backed by some economic or material reward—which include three or four contraceptive devices, permanent sterilization and Norplant.

Another example: armed with huge budgets, equipment and research regimens, the agents of these white institutions descend on rural forest areas and implement long-term research projects to collect data on intestinal parasites in non-human primate populations. In the end the researchers generate huge scientific reports peer reviewed in white scientific space, while the people in the forest continue to die of starvation, intestinal parasites, diarrhea, and the side effects of the implanted contraceptive devices that the poor, black women cannot remove from their arms, or have removed, because there are no trained medical personnel.

While arguing that the locals are uneducated, the white enterprise never questions why that might be, but rather merely proclaims the need for education, as if savagery and isolation are to blame for its absence, with no duty owed by the agents of modern technology and scientific endeavor, who have no problems at all arriving, taking what they want, and leaving. The white man's "middle of nowhere" is the black tribal's middle of somewhere—their homeland, a familiar place that can't be understood by the invading hordes of western researchers layering it with their own psycho-spiritual projections and justifications that amount to nothing less than their acquiescence to, if not participation in, genocide.

Beyond this the white unseeing "I" of everyone from the individual to the institution remains studiously blind and stubbornly resistant to anything that might challenge their *I*-nterests, their mobility or their status, and it would never cross their mind that they might be complicit in genocide, except in those multitudinous cases where the invader-conquerors hear (but ignore) a little voice in their head that says *this is wrong*. The white skin serves as a badge and a shield, which, like the uniform of any "good-intentioned" law enforcement agent, deflects interrogation, and is hostile to any suggestion that something, anything, might warrant any questioning at all.

Plantation Slavery

A major theme advanced to inform and shape recent white power discourses on "third world" labor, "development" and the proliferation of the *maquiladora* or multinational sweat-shop enterprise can be summed up with the statement attributed to British Economist Joan Robinson that "under capitalism, the only thing worse than being exploited is not being exploited at all." *New York Times* columnist and Pulitzer Prize recipient Nicholas D. Kristof cashed in on this in a column titled "Two Cheers for Sweatshops" where he pressed the idea that "the only thing worse than exploitation is no exploitation."[28]

Kristof pressed this original theme in column after column and in speaking engagements, and the exploitation theme proliferated in the U.S. media as an argument for multinational corporations to set up business in Africa (which they had already done). Kristof actually advised G-8 leaders to "start an international campaign to promote imports from sweatshops, perhaps with bold labels depicting an unrecognizable flag and the words 'Proudly Made in a Third World Sweatshop.'" More recently, presumably after a visit to Africa, Kristof shifted his argument to buttress international capital's claims about the need to manufacture (process, refine) in other places without the intractable problems of Africa. Kristof pointed to the "headaches" across much of the continent including "red tape, corruption, political instability, unreliable electricity and ports, and an inexperienced labor force that leads to low productivity and quality." Kristof then went on to promote the deeply protectionist and destructive *African Growth and Opportunity Act*, passed by the Clinton Administration.

An example: The Busira Lomami plantation is 100 miles down the Congo River from the city of Kisangani—the very heart of the *heart of darkness*—the colonial outpost that served as a center for blood rubber collection overseen by Henry Morton Stanley. Busira Lomami was incorporated in Isangi in 1889, and in the beginning it produced rubber for the Royal House of Belgium. Today it produces some coffee and cocoa beans (chocolate), but primarily produces palm nuts (palm oil and palm paste).

Busira Lomami is one of at least six plantations (rubber, palm oil, coffee, cocoa) transitioned from Belgian colonial and postcolonial ownership to the Belgo-American Blattner family. James Blattner built a business empire in Congo, which was then Zaire, under the client state and CIA-supported dictator Colonel Joseph Mobutu, and the empire expanded greatly during the latter decades of Mobutu's reign.

The plantation land was acquired from Congolese chiefs by bribery, coercion, trickery and outright theft. Always being promised schools, health care, employment and roads, plantation communities benefited somewhat under Belgian colonial rule but today have nothing after more than 100 years of exploitation. Meanwhile the company continues to usurp community lands. Minimal taxes are paid to the DRC "government," corrupt practices abound, and regular payments are sent direct from Blattner headquarters in Kinshasa to insure that plantation interests are protected by the Governor, the Chief of the Territory, and other black officials whose participation is guaranteed by corruption. Any chief or high official who complains will be replaced, driven out of the territory or country, or killed.

At the height of the war in Congo, from 1998-2004, the Blattners worked with both "rebel" and "government" forces to secure plantations and capital equipment, and to insure that shipments of products to international markets would continue. There was a working relationship with top military officials and allegations that commodities were shipped out on planes that returned with weapons. The Blattners spent huge sums of money to support their candidates of choice in the 2006 elections. State-of-the-art Robo-Cop equipment purchased with international elections funds was transferred to paramilitary forces now operating in plantation areas, and the World Bank supported Blattner plantation and logging projects in Congo.

The Western mass media and international human rights organizations have never reported on plantation conditions anywhere in Congo in the past three decades (at least). In sharp contradistinction to the idea of the media "reporting" or "exposing" the conditions on these plantations we find that Monique Stauder, the fiancé of Jean-Claude Troupin,[29] a European overseer of plantations, is a Swiss-American woman whose photographs—romanticized portraits of plantation workers—are sold for $600 apiece internationally; this photographer has freelanced with *National Geographic*, *Time*, *GEO* and *The New York Times*. The photographer and the Belgian overseer of plantations regularly fly in and out of Congo for international travel, conferences, photography exhibitions and vacations. In her on-line biography the photographer bills herself as a person concerned about "humanizing political science," formerly dedicated to investigative reporting on behalf (or with) international humanitarian NGOs.[30]

The Blattner plantations employ between 18,000 and 25,000 Congolese workers under the most severe and exploitative conditions. However, plantation operations affect far more people due to the radiation of power to families and communities both within and beyond the physical borders of the plantation. The actual numbers of people impacted by exploitative plantation relations might well be an order of magnitude larger.[31]

Health conditions include epidemics of tuberculosis, malaria, river blindness, intestinal diseases, diarrhea and other maladies. Famine and malnutrition are systemic. Palm nuts (oil) provide a staple source of vitamin A—nutritionally essential for children under five years old—but plantation security tightly controls palm products (even raiding houses at times) and people in possession of palm nuts are accused of theft. International humanitarian NGOs (World Health Organization, UNICEF, CARE, Medicins San Frontières) have supported Vitamin A vaccination campaigns, benefiting multinational pharmaceutical corporations, but coverage has been inadequate and irregular, though the concomitant public relations campaigns (posters) advertising the international NGO brand names have proliferated.

Housing conditions vary from crumbling dirt-floor exoskeletons of cement shacks constructed during colonial years, to mud-and-stick shacks. Those who occupy plantation housing are taxed. Women and children are turned out of plantation housing if the male workers die. Mosquito nets are universally absent.

Wages are heavily taxed (for services not provided), and routinely unpaid on trumped up disciplinary grounds. Thousands of non-contract "daily" workers "earn" between three and fifteen dollars a month and though they are "daily" workers they are subject at times to gross injustices and are not paid for months at a time. The system uses structures of power to exploit workers in every which way, always to the advantage of the company, while offering numerous instances to workers of how it is going out of its way to help and support them.

The private Blattner enterprises are backed by state security services, including police and national army, and the plantations employ a private security force, an "industrial guard", whose payment in part comes from predation against the plantation communities. In fact, the industrial guard is rewarded with what amount to "bounties" for every person arrested, no matter the veracity of the charges against the victims. Blattner and his chief of plantations utilize black paramilitary forces that are themselves members of a traumatized, desperate labor pool seeking to maximize opportunity for personal and familial survival. These empowered (clothed, armed) black agents of white power are used to suppress all forms of social or labor protest and to instill fear in the labor pool. Arrests, extortion and thefts by security forces are routine and both arbitrary and systematic. The industrial guard, police and soldiers routinely prey on women and girls (and sometimes boys). During periods of extreme conflict women and girls were abducted from plantation villages for forced marriages and prolonged sexual slavery. Rapes and survival sex are common, and perpetrators include plantation management. There are numerous concomitant practices that increase vulnerability and destitution amongst females, including pregnancies, disease and social ostracism.

Without doubt, the white capitalist has an active interest in reducing the feasible set of choices available to the worker, or in other words, an active interest in reducing their real freedom. Exploitation here means that one group of people (white, privileged, affluent, mobile, multi-national) has a positive interest in doing harm to others. Exploiters—plantation owners and overseers—not only have a material interest in protecting their own property from redistribution; they have a positive material interest in preventing the exploited from gaining resources which would make them less dependent upon the exploiter. The combined economic, social, labor, health and security climate foster a state of terror and absolute slavery for Congolese men, women and children.

Enter the Misery Industry

A case examination of specific operations of one international NGO in one location offers insights into the problematic of international AID and charity as arbiters of white public space that proliferate and advance white power interests through their assumption and assertion of non-negotiable discourses, rights and activities.

The international humanitarian NGO *Medicins Sans Frontieres* (*MSF*) and their American branch Doctors Without Borders (*DWB*), are widely and unquestionably perceived to be a "neutral" and "apolitical" non-governmental organization serving a humanitarian agenda which is premised in selfless, compassionate, dedication to the prevention and alleviation of human suffering. Public perceptions about *MSF/DWB* both within and outside the international NGO "community" or enterprise, generally credit *MSF/DWB* with the highest moral standards, and the suggestion that *MSF/DWB* might be at all compromised generally invokes immediate hostility and dismissals. The following case study is based on visits to an *MSF* operation in rural Congo, reports generated by *MSF/DWB*, communications with former *MSF* staff from the project, and numerous communications with *MSF* officials after the visits there.

The Belgium offices of *MSF* supported a public hospital in Basankusu, an area in rural western Congo that abuts the Blattner's Commercial Plantations Company (Compagnie Commerciale des Plantations)(CCP) concessions. *MSF* operated in Basankusu from circa 1987 to 2006, but *MSF* never raised an alarm about plantation conditions. Commodities from the CCP plantation are exported to Belgium through international transport; cocoa beans are turned into luxury Belgian chocolate under the brand names Callebaut and Cote d'Or.

In 2005 *MSF* published a research report declaring a "complex emergency" in the Basankusu region, but their research was intentionally de-linked from the issues of health-related conditions (labor conditions, income security, protection against violence, infringements of human rights) associated with the CCP plantation, even though a large percentage of CCP workers were forced to make the difficult trek to the *MSF*-supported hospital for medical care, and even though health conditions in plantation areas were worse than non-plantation areas studied.[32] When Basankusu hospital workers went on strike to protest the huge disparity in salaries and other perks between white ex-patriot doctors/nurses and Congolese doctors/nurses (who were well trained, expected and required to work harder and longer hours) *MSF* pulled out of the area. After some 15 years of operations backed by massive external funding the conditions at the public hospital had deteriorated; one (white) Belgian *MSF* doctor resigned in protest of the structural violence inherent in *MSF* policies and operations.

MSF pulled out of Basankusu on the grounds that *MSF* has supported the zone since 1987, other actors were ready to get involved, and *MSF*—being a medical emergency humanitarian organization—was providing little added value—no matter that their own report had identified Basankusu as undergoing a complex medical emergency. Professional Congolese doctors who are producing reports about these and other catastrophes do so under inhuman working conditions, with the most meager resources, and their resultant reports are generally ignored.

Attempts to clarify the *MSF* programs in, or reasons for withdrawal from, Basankusu were met with a combination of bureaucratic stalling, public relations, obtuse responses, and institutional denial. *MSF*

Belgium was asked why they pulled out of Basankusu after their own report exposed a complex and catastrophic emergency. Attempts were made to explore the *MSF* rationale and decision-making process that led to the skewed research study that did not account for the impact of plantation operations on the health conditions in and around plantations, or the increased patient caseload at the *MSF*-supported hospital. At the root of the obstructionism by *MSF* officials are certain assumptions of their non-negotiable rights and privileges that are not open to question by "unauthorized" or "unsanctioned" external agents (like this journalist). White public space positions international NGOs in frameworks where accountability and transparency are wholly absent and the cycle of closure is perpetuated by a Western corporate media that, under most circumstances, neither investigates nor challenges the "humanitarian" enterprise. Hundreds if not thousands of Western NGOs like *MSF* are freely afforded access to resources and, therefore, generation of profits, in Africa, under structural terms that amount to nothing more than managed inequality and the perpetuation of structural violence. *MSF* represents the *crème* of the ethical NGO crop—the No. 1 humanitarian brand—and it offers a very conservative example, but in the end serves as a rather mild testament to the scale and nature of the problem.

NGOs have been charged with—and some are directly involved in—arming combatants, trafficking in children, prostitution and survival sex scandals, and more general racketeering and money-laundering that all exist and occur behind the façade of international charity.[33] There is also the unaccountable adoptions industry—more trafficking in children by the white power system, tearing apart African families.[34]

The processes of development serve the task of assimilation well. Assimilation has been defined as "making the different similar; smothering cultural or linguistic traditions; forbidding all traditions and loyalties except those meant to encourage conformity and the new and all-embracing order; promoting and enforcing one, and only one, measure of conformity."[35] Anyone who documents or reports on the actual, verifiable realities of the white power enterprise in/with/over Africa is ostracized from white public space and relegated to the unemployable, limbo, or criminalized status reserved for unembraceable blacks. They will be banned for life from elite western colleges or universities.[36] Or, equally common, they will be cast as conspiracy theorists.[37]

According to a regional World Health Organization doctor who was interviewed while working there, conditions on plantations and for plantation communities are significantly worse than conditions for people in areas where plantations are not operating. It is notable that this doctor is a Congolese doctor, and I suggest that the very attachment of the label "Congolese" in this writing increases the bias against this doctor and, in the minds of most affluent white listeners/readers, invalidates his research and his authority as a medical professional, provoking the suggestion of inadequacy, inexperience, lack of education and other negative stereotypes, and that this invalidation and denial is further projected onto the messenger (the author). It does not matter that the doctor works for the World Health Organization when there exists predetermined—prejudged—binary markers of superiority and inferiority premised on the deeply entrenched and inculcated racial aggression pervasive in the white public space and its adamant racialized assumptions of dominance.

The Coming Anarchy

In September 1996, the armies of Rwanda and Uganda, with lesser numbers of troops from Eritrea, Ethiopia and South Sudan, invaded Zaire from Rwanda and Uganda. The invasion forces were armed, trained, funded, and supplied by the United States, Canada, Britain and Israel. The Pentagon's primary military agents overseeing the invasion included covert low intensity warfare operatives Roger Winter,[38] Major (then) Rick Orth,[39] Lt. Col. Thomas P. Odom,[40] and William G. Thom.[41] USAID administrator J. Brian Atwood was also involved at some level.[42]

Reporting on Central Africa at the time of the U.S.-sponsored invasion of Zaire was British journalist Michela Wrong, "a correspondent who witnessed firsthand Mobutu's last days, traces the rise and fall of the idealistic young journalist who became the stereotype of an African despot."[43] Ms. Wrong worked in Africa for six years reporting for Reuters, the BBC and *Financial Times*. Ms. Wrong's book *In the Footsteps of Mr. Kurtz* was published in 2001 and it covers the fall of the long time U.S. puppet Colonel Joseph Mobutu.[44]

Michela Wrong's text must have made some of the prime agents of the neocolonial enterprise uncomfortable. While offering nuggets of previously tabooed truth that help us better understand at least some of these agents and their actions, Michela Wrong also mistakenly repeats the establishment narrative that inverts the truth about victims and killers in Rwanda and Congo/Zaire. That said, Ms. Wrong's text nonetheless offers a unique starting point to explore and unpack the hidden realities of the Mobutu era and the transition period of 1996-1997, and it provides (both accidentally and on purpose) some insights into the white-on-black structural dynamics at play.

Michela Wrong briefly delves into the Central Intelligence Agency operations in Congo and she mentions (which is more than some authors have done) its most notorious agent Lawrence Devlin, the CIA's Chief of Station in Congo-Zaire in the 1960s. Ms. Wrong weaves Larry Devlin in and out of her story. Indeed, it would be political and career suicide to explore such topics in any depth: no journalist would be allowed to maintain favorable relations with the bastions of foreign corporate capital and its media vanguard (e.g. *Financial Times*, BBC or Reuters) if they unearthed any real skeletons and all foreign journalists (on the *career path*) know that.

There are few books that explore or expose the CIA's fomenting or perpetrating its signature 'dirty tricks' in Zaire (1960-1997) or Congo (1997-2018), and very few hard accounts of how the United States and its partners have deployed absolute terrorism inside and outside the country's borders during the removal (and murder) of the country's first leader, Patrice Lumumba, during the CIA's stage-managed installation of Colonel Joseph Mobutu, and during the decades of Mobutu's reign. Of course, the CIA's operations have to some great extent been approved or supported by Britain's SIS (MI-6), Belgium's Veiligheid van de Staat (VSSE), the French Direction générale de la sécurité extérieure (DGSE) and the Israeli Mossad.[45]

Rwanda's Tutsi president, Paul Kagame, and Uganda's Hima president, Yoweri Museveni and their crime syndicates are at the root of all of Central Africa's problems. These are the black African dictators that serve the prerogatives of western imperial plunder and depopulation and the white beneficiaries of same. *The New Yorker* and CNN consistently manufactured the pro-Rwandan (Rwandan Patriotic Front/Army or RPF/A) propaganda, reported by Christiane Amanpour and Philip Gourevitch—one of the most notorious agents of disinformation on 'genocide in Rwanda.' Amanpour is married to James Rubin, president Bill Clinton's former Assistant Secretary of State and Madeleine Albright's right-hand man, and who was later an economic adviser to president Barack Obama. Gourevitch produced the celebrated establishment chronicle, *We Wish To Inform You That Tomorrow We Will Be Killed With Our Families*, and he remained a close friend of Paul Kagame. He was also a conduit for U.S. State Department disinformation passed by James Rubin, who was also Chief Spokesman for the Clinton State Department (1997-2000). Rubin's sister, Elizabeth Rubin, was dating Gourevitch. *The New Yorker* and Gourevitch also played a stellar role in covering up the crimes of the Rwanda Patriotic Front and Uganda People's Defense Forces in the Congo/Zaire.[46]

From the very beginning, Israeli-trained shock troops became Mobutu's bodyguards, and Israeli military intelligence advisors trained Mobutu's shock troops, both the elite Division Speciale Presidentielle (DSP), and the dreaded Service d'Action et de Renseignement Militaires (SARM), created in 1985. Mobutu received paratrooper training in Israel in 1963, and he prevailed and persisted in power under the guidance of Mossad advisers (notwithstanding the brief public severance of relations with Israel in 1973).[47] As the American Jewish Committee noted: after 1980 "Mossad agents, military emissaries, and a small group of private businessmen… replaced diplomats as Israel's main interlocutors with African leaders and political (mainly opposition) groups."[48]

Israel's involvement on the continent was extensive: Israel was virtually built on the blood diamonds stolen from Africa.[49] One of the Mossad agents involved in secretly courting African dictators was David Kimche, Israel's version of Mr. Africa[50], who was also the former director-general of the Israeli Foreign Ministry.[51] During the RPA/F invasions, he was the Israeli counterpart to U.S. covert operative Roger Winter (whose cover was the seemingly benign U.S. Committee for Refugees): while details are few and far between, it seems certain that both were directly involved in supporting the terrorism committed by the Rwandan Patriotic Army as it marched from Uganda into Rwanda and Congo-Zaire.[52]

The policies and actions of the International Monetary Fund and the World Bank were and are devastating to Congo-Zaire. The United Nations deployments in Congo, past and present, represent foreign military occupations on Congolese soil. The mercenary "Dragon Operations" and "Hostage Rescues" of the United Nations Peacekeeping (*sic*) forces in Congo of the 1960s were further examples of how the newly independent Congo-Zaire was crippled by foreign interests and shackled like the thousands of slaves that were shipped out of the Kingdom of the Kongo during the first relations with Europeans.

What we don't know enough about, either past or present, are the secret defense and intelligence operations conducted by the CIA, the Pentagon and their allies, and by private military companies and their mercenaries, all having tight ties to the power establishment.

Larry Devlin, Zaire's notorious CIA Chief of Station, began his tour of duty in Zaire as an attaché and political affairs officer on 10 July 1960 and by November 1960 he was Chief of Station. In September 1975 Devlin testified under the pseudonym Victor Hedgeman to the Senate Select Committee on Intelligence (the Church Committee) on the CIA's massive Congo operations, the true extent of which remain shrouded in secrecy and classified documents.

In the 1970s the CIA (alone) counted up to 109 clandestine CIA operatives working through the Kinshasa station.[53] During the first years of so-called "independence", the time of the assassination of Patrice Lumumba, another one of the top CIA assets in Congo—working directly under Larry Devlin—was Frank Carlucci, the second secretary of the U.S. Embassy in Congo from 1960 to 1962, a man whose career has taken him to the apex of international subterfuge and foreign interventions (read: U.S.-brokered terrorism).[54] These two agents of "The Company" [CIA] worked closely with U.S. Ambassador Clare Timberlake. Devlin and Carlucci were the two primary U.S. CIA operatives most directly involved in the assassination of Patrice Lumumba.[55,56] These two CIA assets in Congo must have also worked under the direct supervision of Montgomery "Monty" Rogers, Chief of the CIA Clandestine Service's Africa Division, a man whose public persona is even more completely hidden than Maurice Tempelsman's. Devlin was no casual bystander to covert operations nor a disinterested confidant who knew little of consequence—as all these spooks try to make us believe—about the assassinations of Lumumba and others. Having decided it was impossible to poison Lumumba with the lethal toxins that the CIA dispatched to him for that purpose, Larry Devlin, for example, cabled CIA headquarters (circa September 1960) requesting a "High Power Foreign Made Rifle With Telescopic Scope And Silencer" be sent to him via the diplomatic bag from the U.S.[57]

Indeed, it's becoming well known that the CIA "has acted as a secret mafia engaged in assassinations, levying war in other countries, and organizing mercenary forces in order to overthrow lawfully established governments and to destabilize societies, governments, and organizations that did not meet with its *approval*."[58]

In 1967 Larry Devlin left Congo for Laos, "where he was to win the Distinguished Intelligence medal he wore with quiet pride for a particularly risky battlefield operation."[59] Devlin's rotation to the CIA operation in tiny land-locked Laos in 1967 occurred at the time when Indochina was deep in the throes of America's criminal war, and Laos in particular was under the most horrible and devastating aerial bombardment—the likes of which no country had ever seen, not even Korea. The U.S. and allied bombing of both was unprecedented; turning productive agricultural land and ancient cultural architectures and innocent people into scorched earth and skeletons.[60] The legacy of the Laotian people's suffering, dismemberment and death due to unexploded ordinance lives on to this day.

"Not only does the 2.1 million tons of bombs dropped on Laos from 1965 to 1973 rank among the largest air wars of the twentieth century, exceeded only by the 2.7 million tons dropped on Cambodia," wrote then journalist Alfred W. McCoy, in the foreword to the heartbreaking testimonies of Lao survivors amassed in *Voices From the Plain of Jars*, "but it also was a precursor for the ways wars would be fought in the twenty-first century and beyond."[61]

And then there was Phoenix. Laos was one of the main Indochina staging operations for the clandestine U.S. military-intelligence 'counterinsurgency' black program named 'Phoenix', and the CIA ran Phoenix with Federal Bureau of Investigation (FBI) and Michigan State University support throughout the 1960s and into the 1970s.[62]

The term "counterinsurgency" is highly problematic: Phoenix was a pacification program, with all the gory aspects of tortures and assassinations and massacres that pacification programs (run by white people from Europe and North America) have perpetrated against their targets. As CIA Chief of Station in Laos in 1967, Lawrence Devlin was immediately plunged into the high-level day-to-day decision-making that determined the horrible fate of scores of thousands of innocent people.

> There's no dispute that the CIA has used assassination as a weapon lower down the political and social pecking order... Phoenix was aimed at 'neutralizing' [Viet Cong] political leaders and organizers in rural South Vietnam. In congressional testimony [CIA director William] Colby boasted that 20,587 NLF activists had been killed between 1967 and 1971 alone. The South Vietnamese published a much higher estimate, declaring that nearly 41,000 had been killed...[63]

Those killed outright in Phoenix operations may have been more fortunate than the 29,000 suspected NLF members arrested and interrogated with techniques that were horrible even by the standards of Pol Pot and Mobutu. In 1972 a parade of witnesses before Congress testified about the techniques of the Phoenix interrogators: how they interviewed suspects and then pushed them out of planes, how they cut off fingers, ears and testicles, how they used electro-shock, shoved wooden dowels into the brains of some prisoners, and rammed electric probes into the rectums of others.[64]

In Vietnam, the CIA built an archipelago of secret torture centers to process the hundreds of thousands of suspects that were kidnapped by its mercenary army of "counter-terrorists". All around the world, CIA officers and their military sidekicks teach modern torture techniques and design the torture centers concealed within the National Security Establishment's network of military posts. Along with the CIA's stations, those posts are the secret government's infrastructure for Full Spectrum Dominance.[65]

Lawrence Devlin was not so clean as his autobiography might lead us to believe. Zaire in the 1960s and 1970s, even the 1980s, may seem like the distant past. But people like Devlin have been replaced and the terrorism against the Congolese lives on. What about Maurice Tempelsman, the diamond and cobalt kingpin who was always so close to Colonel Joseph Mobutu and Lawrence Devlin, and who hired Devlin to run the diamond cartel after Laos? Any and all discussion of Maurice (and Leon) Tempelsman is studiously omitted from Larry Devlin's dishonest autobiography, but Michela Wrong properly situates Maurice Tempelsman as "the secretive diamond dealer."[66,67]

It is impossible to overstate the absolutely devastating impact that Maurice Tempelsman has had on Africa.[68] When William Jefferson Clinton conducted his victory tour of Africa circa 1998 his close friend Maurice Tempelsman was part of the president's entourage.[69] Like the CIA's many other "assets" in the Congo-Zaire, Tempelsman and Devlin maintained the cobalt connection. Far more important than diamonds, cobalt is an essential element for super alloys used in nuclear reactors, nuclear weapons, submarines, tanks, spacecraft, industrial blast furnaces, oil rigs, UAVs, UUVs, jet turbines, satellites, and many other technologies deemed essential to and for the military industrial complex. Even today, any journal or magazine that mentions cobalt relegates this precious metal purely to cell phone and computer applications, thus ever underplaying the strategic importance of this mineral.[70]

Perhaps even more substantial was Maurice Tempelsman's role as uranium broker to the U.S. government: recall that the raw material for the atomic bombs dropped on Hiroshima and Nagasaki came from the Congolese mine at Shinkolobwe.[71]

Everything that can be said about Maurice Tempelsman's shady roles in Africa can be said, even if differently, about Belgian business tycoon Philippe de Moerloose, British tycoon John Bredencamp, Israeli tycoon Dan Gertler, and so many more.

Like Dan Gertler and Beny Steinmetz, two similar untouchables, Maurice Tempelsman's interests in Central Africa are advanced in part through the support of the Committee of the Jewish Community of Kinshasa—*le Comité de la Communauté Israélite*—that is tightly coordinated with the power structure in New York, Brussels, London, Tel Aviv and Kinshasa to exert influence and assure control of Israeli-Belgian-Anglo-American interests over the geopolitical arena.[72]

The white power forces involved in Congo today have a pedigree of exploitation in many cases, with some new players, so that many of the same people, institutions and corporations, or their contemporary compatriots, companies and subsidiaries, can be identified and their activities documented.

The way to judge the veracity and integrity of any text on Central Africa is to open to the Index and look for certain key terms, names, locations, programs, or corporations. French academic Gerard Prunier, for example, goes out of his way to discredit and demean any writer, academic or journalist that discusses the Rwandan and Ugandan militaries as proxy forces for the United States. It is clear that the U.S. was deeply involved, and when the Rwandan Patriotic Front invaded Zaire in 1996, they marched across the country with both overt and covert Pentagon support and were "reinforced by a contingent of U.S. mercenaries."[73]

Let's look briefly into the role of William G. Thom, the Mr. Africa of the Defense Intelligence Agency (DIA), whose entire professional life was spent with DIA as an Africa specialist. (The DIA is far more significant than the CIA, for anyone who does not know of the DIA's role in the intelligence and warfare complex.) "During his long career, he [Thom] maintained a front row seat regarding sensitive information on African countries and, as he became more senior, he affected decision-making and policy implementation on key Africa issues and events."[74] Thom's connections went way beyond the DIA to the principals of the super-secretive high-level mercenary firms Executive Outcomes and Military Professional Resources Inc., and some of the people known to be involved in organizations that were considered nothing more than deaths squads.[75]

"During the latter half of 1996 and early 1997," wrote Wayne Madsen in *Genocide and Covert Operations in Africa, 1993-1999*, "U.S. military, mercenary and intelligence operatives continued to provide the Tutsi rebels in Zaire with advice." Madsen then spelled out their deeper involvement, including the presence of a parallel U.S. embassy being run by the DIA (read: Thom & Orth) in eastern Zaire.[76] The "Tutsi rebels in Zaire" were the Rwandan Patriotic Army forces led by Paul Kagame and James Kabarebe, who were committing massive war crimes, crimes against humanity and genocide under the watchful all-knowing eyes of the western intelligence apparatus and its satellite surveillance networks.[77]

One of dictator Mobutu Sese Seko's right-hand men was Albert-Henri Buisine, a French mercenary-pirate who worked on the *Kamanyola*, the luxury yacht floating on the Congo River where Mobutu arrived by helicopter to receive foreign backers and "VIP" cronies. While Mobutu frequently visited the White House, Brussels, Paris, Tokyo, Geneva, London—and sometimes Tel Aviv—he regularly received his cronies and patrons on his yacht in Zaire.[78]

Protected by Albert-Henri Buisine and Israeli mercenary Meir Meyouhas—and a slew of crack black intelligence operatives—Mobutu received his guests. Hundreds of high profile people came and went from Zaire over the years. These included Secretary of State Henry Kissinger; Vice-President George H.W. Bush; Ambassadors Andrew Young and Jean Kirkpatrick; and of course the many CIA mercenaries like Larry Devlin and Frank Carlucci. Diamond tycoon Maurice Tempelsman dined often with Mobutu on the *Kamanyola*, sometimes with his lover, Jacqueline Kennedy Onassis, often with his Zaire-based diamond agents like Jerry Funk or James Barnes, and with De Beers agents like Nicky Oppenheimer or Nick Davenport.[79] Of course, Mobutu's personal physician for many years was Dr. William T. Close, the father of Hollywood actress Glenn Close, and one of Mobutu's closest confidantes.[80]

The Tempelsman and De Beers empires exist today in Congo in their modern forms, and many of the same agents of the Mobutu period are connected to policies or actions that perpetuate suffering and violence all over Africa today. It is important to note, also, that the Tempelsman blood minerals machine has heavily subsidized the campaigns of the Democrats, including recent manifestations, Barack Obama and Hillary Clinton. In the final counting, Bill and Hillary Clinton did more damage to Africa than Barack Obama or Donald Trump (but there is still time).

On May 11 and 12, 1990, Mobutu's shock troops—including the Israeli-trained DSP, the SARM and National Gendarmerie—attacked the campus at the University of Lumumbashi, and they killed hundreds of students, at least, while countless more were tortured and brutalized. The U.S. Central Intelligence Agency station in Lumumbashi supported the atrocities and cover-up. It may sound like a long time ago, but these agents of repression are still around and their impact is still being felt.

What was Albert-Henri Buisine's role in protecting the Mobutu dictatorship and perpetuating such atrocities and what happened to Mobutu's old mercenary bodyguard? Well, Mobutu's French mercenary bodyguard Albert-Henri Buisine surfaced in October 2007, in a *Harper's* magazine article by Bryan Mealer, a journalist who formerly freelanced with the *Associated Press* and *The Independent* (London). Buisine is no longer a private military agent serving the terror apparatus of a Cold War dictator: he is the loquacious captain of a barge pressing 2600 tons of cargo up the Congo River (for his private shipping company and substantial personal profit). One hundred years after Joseph Conrad's *Heart of Darkness* we still have a white American *AP* journalist retelling the (racist) tale of his *unfathomable* voyage up the Congo.

And there's the nostalgic Captain, a reluctant French mercenary-terrorist-turned-pilot-profiteer, who for 16 years, against his will, Mealer tells us, served Mobutu reluctantly. "He was chained to Mobutu's shadow at all times, even living four straight years aboard the lavish presidential yacht, the *Kamanyola*, as it drifted aimlessly down the Congo River."

Drifted aimlessly? Chained to Mobutu's shadow? This is fiction. There are deep cultural stereotypes and subliminal fault lines at work here that have been inculcated through decades of propaganda about Congo/Zaire. There is nothing but dross in Mealer's account, no mention of the brutalities suffered by Congolese people, the strike-breaking and student massacres, or the rented crowds chanting "Mobutu! Mobutu!" and the empty slogans of Mobutu's *Movement Populaire de la Revolution* party. There is no mention of the hated Special Presidential Division terror apparatus, the illegal arrests and detention without trial, the tortures at underground dungeons like the "OAU-2" or the underground "corridor of death" or Camp Tshiatshi in Kinshasa. It is all rendered nostalgic, and the plunderers of the past are painted as unwitting victims who missed their lot in life. The story casts the standard dispersions of pathos on the white exploiters, and this works to displace the attention from their past and often current criminality.

"Buisine now led the simple life of a river rat," Mealer tells us, "making his run six or seven times a year," pointing out "whirlpools roiling in the deep spots, crocodiles camouflaged in the mud, or, along a wooded island, a tree whose leaves cured hemorrhoids."[81]

The *Harper's* production mirrored the obliviousness of white men in Congo and the even greater obliviousness of white editors to the brutal truth of the Congolese history as suffered by its people. These and other propaganda themes proliferate to this day and they serve the falsification of African consciousness (so aptly described by Dr. Amos Wilson).[82]

The New Old Peacemakers

Beyond the involvement of private military companies (e.g. Sandline International, Branch Energy, Executive Outcomes, Erinys, etc.) and western military agents documented by this and other journalists, imperialism's genocidal onslaught in Africa includes the most seemingly benign agents of change. Consider the progressive sounding Karuna Center for Peacebuilding, a U.S.-based NGO that projects its work as politically neutral. According to their own public relations:

> [W]e bridge divides to build sustainable peace…Civil wars, political instability, and environmental challenges are an increasing threat to human security across the globe. Our multi-dimensional approach to peacebuilding builds the social resilience that is required to adapt to 21st century challenges.[83]

The Karuna Center for Peacebuilding sits at the center of a network of white power imperial forces that serve as the vanguard for interventionist pro-war and intelligence interests, assimilation programs and military operations. Karuna everywhere peddles the U.S. establishment's false narrative about genocide in Rwanda and Sudan.[84] The fact that Karuna is deeply involved with the Kagame dictatorship and is also operating in eastern Congo says it all: only those interests that gain the direct protection or indirect approval of Kigali and Kampala and their western and Israeli backers are able to operate successfully in the eastern Congo.

Karuna's partners, affiliates and colleagues include some of the leading intelligence agents involved in central Africa, Sudan, or elsewhere. One of Karuna's partners is the ENOUGH organization, the U.S. intelligence front group pretending to be concerned about violence around the world but instead serving very subversive imperial interests, including the R2P project, and the entire false and inverted global politics of genocide.[85] Counted on the board of directors of ENOUGH is Colonel Rick Orth, one of the architects of the U.S. invasion of Congo-Zaire.[86]

Many of Karuna's partners and affiliates are deeply tied to the softer arms of the Pentagon, institutions such as the National Democratic Institute (NDI), USAID, National Republican Institute (NRI), National Endowment for Democracy (NED), and the equally deceptive U.S. Institute for Peace.[87] Karuna is also close with the International Peace and Security Institute, an organization with dubious agents of imperialism sitting on its boards (e.g. David Crane, Gareth Evans, John Prendergast, Chester Crocker).[88] Again, if you have not heard of these people it is because your sources of "news" are not news sources at all.

Most of Karuna's partners, employees and advocates are involved in the intelligence sector, with the U.S. State Department, or with some other highly compromised politico-military-intelligence interest. These links can be easily discovered and documented. Amongst the most obvious conflicts of interest—for an organization that claims to be involved in peacemaking—Karuna's partner AECOM is a Private Military Corporation whose contract base includes U.S. Army, U.S. Air Force, NASA, FEMA, USAID, World Bank, Department of Homeland Security and SPAWAR.[89] With an $899 million contract with the Pentagon's Cyber Command, AECOM is quite literally at the heart of the beast of western terrorism and permanent warfare.

Karuna works with AECOM in Cote d'Ivoire, Senegal and other

places. In Afghanistan, Karuna is "building peace" in partnership with the Washington D.C.-based Initiative for Public Security. Coincidentally, AECOM provides combat support for the U.S. Army and Coalition forces in Afghanistan.[90]

The Initiative for Public Security is an intelligence front group whose partners include all the complicit think tanks, foundations, councils and PACs, including the Council on Foreign relations, National Democratic Institute, the Center for a New American Security, and others, and these are staffed, directed or advised by military and intelligence and political people of dubious repute.[91]

Like most of those people and organizations and interests that feed from the trough, the Karuna Center for Peacebuilding will not challenge its ideological peers, the U.S. government, the Pentagon, the C.I.A., or the black power interests installed as dictatorships or in key gatekeeper positions that it relies upon and partners with. Instead, Karuna applauds the terrorist regimes of Paul Kagame, Yoweri Museveni, and Congolese president Hippolyte Kanambe (alias Joseph Kabila)[92] just as they applaud their western benefactors and pat themselves on the back for orchestrating peace and security.

Karuna epitomizes the white power interests that situate themselves as neutral, always operating from the epistemologies of ignorance, arrogance and innocence, always claiming the moral high ground, always presenting their white selves as innocent, while projecting their moral superiority, but in reality perpetuating violence, often at the deepest levels, because they are actually in the business of war.[93]

Similarly, over the past decade, a slew of glossy reports have been produced out of eastern Congo purporting to identify the perpetrators and victims of war. These reports universally whitewash the western corporations, such as Banro Gold or Loncor or Moto Gold, and they blame the victims—usually nationalist Congolese militias such as the Mai Mai—for taking up arms in defense of themselves, their families and their lands. Many of these reports are funded by western interests—e.g. USAID, ENOUGH, Humanity United, Open Square, or one or another of the diverse tentacles of the Open Society Institute— masquerading as peace and justice truth-tellers, and the reports are collaborative efforts that serve select, powerful interests.[94]

Are there covert U.S. Special Operations Forces and CIA operatives all over Central Africa today? Of course there are. US Special OPs are routinely sighted near the airport in Goma, North Kivu.[95]

Reports from Goma on 14 March 2018 placed U.S. troops just over the border in Gisenyi, Rwanda, with another group based out of Mubambiro, some 10 kilometers from Goma town, in North Kivu. These forces are not building schools, or coddling babies. AFRICOM now has major bases in Uganda, Rwanda and South Sudan, and SOCOM operatives are routinely deployed from these.[96]

The violence in the eastern Congo today—snatch and grab kidnappings, targeted killings, massacres, political assassinations, tortures and mutilations, and disappearing all over the Kivus, Orientale and Maniema Provinces—shows similarities to the clandestine Phoenix program. The difference might be that the terror in eastern Congo is orchestrated by Rwanda and Uganda, the Pentagon's surrogate or client or proxy warriors involved in Congo, rather than by the Pentagon or CIA directly.

This brings us back, full circle, to the nasty propaganda that is peddled by all those media venues allowed to participate in the spectrum of debate, from the *New York Times* to *Democracy Now*, and to the many insights into the petulant and juvenile mind of Donald Trump. When *The Economist* said: "Yet scarcely any outsider has a clue what the fighting was about or who was killing whom," they couldn't be telling a bigger lie. We know who is fighting whom and we know what the fighting is all about. The Congolese people know what it is about. The Rwandans, the Ugandans, the Burundians, the people of Africa and Afghanistan and Haiti and Papua New Guinea[97] know what it is all about and who is responsible.

It is not a question of "was": none of this is passé. The militarization in eastern Congo is about conquest and assimilation, and this is genocide. The killing in eastern Congo has become a way of life. "We have learned to adapt to it," one Congolese survivor, working on human rights issues, told me.

The regimes of Rwanda and Uganda are responsible for crimes and atrocities beyond description or quantification. The United States and its allies back these regimes. Western corporations operate with the sanction or in direct partnership with these client regimes and/or with the organized criminal syndicate in power in Kinshasa. President Hippolyte Kanambe—alias Joseph Kabila—and his compatriots in Kigali (Kagame/Kabarebe *et al*) and Kampala (Museveni, Kazini *et al*)—has arguably caused more death and destruction than Mobutu could ever have dreamed of. Mobutu promised the worst—"*Apres moi, le deluge*"—and the United States and its partners in crime made sure the promise came true.[98] This is the shit show that the United States has created in Central Africa, and the Trump administration is completely engaged in the terrorism and war crimes and genocide that continue to occur.

The indigenous Congolese militias operating in Congo arise out of the imperatives of survival and because of the humiliation and atrocities committed against them again and again and again. Confronted with the onslaught of imperialism, destruction of homes, villages and communities, widespread massive depopulation, and the occupation and plunder of the land—insult upon insult, loss upon loss—the Congolese people are fighting for their lives, their loves, their children and their families, everything that has ever meant anything to them, and the survival of their traditions, cultures and people.

There is an African proverb that says: "Until the story of the hunt is told by the Lion, the tale of the hunt will always glorify the hunter.[99] Until the Africans tell the history of Africa, the stories of greatness, humanity and courage will always glorify the imperialists.

What should the people of Congo do? Well, read Franz Fanon, *concerning violence,*[100] and consider every white and non-white foreigner in Central Africa as the enemy.

ENDNOTES

1   William G. Thom, *African Wars: A defense Intelligence Perspective,* University of Calgary Press, 2010: p. 179.

2   Unsigned, "Congo is Sliding Back to Bloodshed," *The Economist,* 15 February 2018: https://www.economist.com/news/leaders/21737027-how-stop-catastrophe-congo-sliding-back-bloodshed.

3   Not the genocide you have probably read about, the hysterical mass media accounts of, for example, the Janjaweed in Darfur, Sudan; or Joseph Kony and the Lord's Resistance Army in Uganda; or the Forces for the Democratic Liberation of Rwanda (FDLR) in Congo; or the Devil who came on Horseback, and all that *shite.* There is a very clear political economy of genocide and human rights at work.

4   Helan Page, "'Black Male' Imagery and Media Containment of African American Men," *American Anthropologist,* Vol. 99, No. 1: pp. 99-111.

5   See, e.g.: Kasper Hoffmann, "The Ethics of Child-Soldiering in the Congo," *Young Nordic Journal of Youth Research,* 18:3, 2010: 339-358; and David M.

Rosen, "Child Soldiers, International Humanitarian Law, and the Globalization of Childhood," *American Anthropologist,* Vol. 109, Issue 2, 2007: p: 299.

6   The 1994 *Atlantic Monthly* feature story titled "The Coming Anarchy" was a major splash: President Bill Clinton reportedly recommended the article to White House staff. Robert D. Caplan, "The Coming Anarchy: How scarcity, crime, overpopulation, tribalism, and disease are rapidly destroying the social fabric of our planet," *Atlantic Monthly,* February 1994.

7   For an excellent deconstruction of the western-based image industry and how it operates, see the documentary film Enjoy Poverty by Dutch filmmaker Renzo Martens.

8   Armin Rosen, "A rare map of the most complex conflict on Earth," Business Insider, 14 December 2015: http://www.businessinsider.com/map-congo-conflict-2015-12 (accessed 12/14/2015).

9   Armin Rosin, "The Origins of War in the DRC," *Atlantic Monthly,* 26 June 2013: http://www.theatlantic.com/international/archive/2013/06/the-origins-of-war-in-the-drc/277131/ (accessed 10/15/2015).

10   Ibid.

11   https://philippedemoerloose.com/?lang=en

12   Daphne Park was the British MI-6 intelligence agent and counterpart to CIA agent Lawrence Devlin. See, e.g.: Susan Williams, Spies in the Congo: America's Atomic Mission in World War II, *PublicAffairs,* 2016: 259-260.

13   See, e.g.: David Kimche, "Lessons From Rwanda, the 'Israel of Africa," *Jerusalem Post,* 9 August 2007: http://www.jpost.com/Opinion/Op-Ed-Contributors/Lessons-from-Rwanda-the-Israel-of-Africa; and (unsigned), "David Kimche: Spymaster who established Mossad as a Force in International Espionage," *The Independent,* 28 April 2010: https://www.independent.co.uk/news/obituaries/david-kimche-spymaster-who-established-mossad-as-a-force-in-international-espionage-1957199.html.

14   See, e.g.: Nancy Rose Hunt, "An Acoustic Register: Rape and Repetition in Congo", ed. Anne Laura Stoler, *Imperial Debris: On Ruins and Ruination,* Duke University Press, 2013. In writing about rape in the Congo in a very circuitous, unemotional and indirect way, Nancy Rose Hunt cited my work for its exceptionalism in naming names, thus allowing her to reference my concepts and the poignancy of my reportage in her own work, but to protect her career and academic peer-review status, she subsequently denigrates my work in the footnotes by describing me as a conspiracy theorist.

15   A perfect example is the academic 'genocide' scholar Samuel Totten, whose latest publications' ·projections of his insecurity serve the prerogatives of power and propaganda.

16   See: Mittal & Fraser, *Losing the Serengeti: The Maasai Land that was to Run Forever,* The Oakland Institute, 2018: https://www.oaklandinstitute.org/sites/oaklandinstitute.org/files/losing-the-serengeti.pdf.

17   See, e.g.: Keith Harmon Snow, "Merchants of Death: Exposing Corporate Financed Holocaust in Africa," Global Research, 5 December 2008: https://www.globalresearch.ca/merchants-of-death-exposing-corporate-financed-holocaust-in-africa/11311.

18   The concept of white public space was formulated by Dr. Helan Page in the following works: 2000: "No Black Public Sphere in White Public Space",, *Transforming Anthropology*. 8(1&2): 111-128; 1994: "White Public Space and the Construction of White Privilege in U.S. Health Care: Fresh Concepts and a New Model of Analysis", *Medical Anthropology Quarterly*. 8(1):109-116. Co-Authored with Brooke Thomas; 2015: "The Gender, Race, and Class Barriers Enclosing Yoga as White Public Space", *Yoga and the Body: An Intersectional Analysis of Contemporary Body Politics, Mindfulness, and Embodied Social Change*. Rowman & Littlefield: Lanham, Maryland. Deemed "excellent" by the editors and under review by the publisher. Melanie Klein, Beth Berila and Chelsea Jackson, eds., pp. 1-33. The term *Dark Continentalism* was coined by Keith Harmon Snow in his paper presented at the American Anthropology Association annual symposium in 2008 and titled *Towards an Anthropology of White Man in Africa: A Call to Explore the Militarized White Project of "Dark Continentalism"*.

19   Wildlife Direct funders and/or partners in 2018 include U.S. Department of the Interior, U.S. Embassy, USAID, UNDP, and others: https://wildlifedirect.org/#.

20   Moto Gold was acquired by Randgold Resources in 2009.

21   The Moto Gold Project was located in the Kilo Moto goldfields in the north east of the DRC, some 150 kilometers west of the Ugandan border town of Arua.

22   Ibid.

23   "Genocide and Covert Operations In Africa, 1993-1999," United States One Hundred Seventh Congress, Subcommittee on International Operations and Human Rights, First Session, 17 May 2001.

24   Wayne Madsen, *Genocide and Covert Operations In Africa, 1993-1999*, Mellen Books, 1999.

25   Teneza-Mora et al, "A malaria vaccine for travelers and military personnel: Requirements and top candidates," *VACCINE*, Vol. 33, Issue 52, 22 December 2015: https://www.ncbi.nlm.nih.gov/pubmed/26458800 .

26   See: Keith Harmon Snow, "The War that did not make the Headlines: Over Five Million Dead in Congo?" Global Research, https://www.globalresearch.ca/the-war-that-did-not-make-the-headlines-over-five-million-dead-in-congo/7957

27   See the numerous publications on these organizations by Keith Harmon Snow.

28   Nicholas Kristof and Sheryl Wudunn, "Two Cheers for Sweatshops," *New York Times*, 24 September 2000; and Nicholas Kristoff, "In Defense of 12-Hour Days," *New York Times*, 31 May 2007.

29   See: Jean-Claude Troupin, Lynx Connections: http://www.lynxconnections.com/jean-claude-troupin-cv.

30   Monique Stauder: http://www.moniquestauder.com/main.php.

31   The full scope of plantations and plantation concessions in DRC far exceeds the concessions held by the Blattner family alone, including such big name long-tern exploiters as George Forrest Groupe. See: "DRC: Belgian mining giant lied over bulldozing homes," Amnesty International, 24 November 2014: https://www.amnesty.org/en/latest/news/2014/11/drc-belgian-mining-giant-lied-over-bulldozing-homes/ .

32   Access to healthcare, mortality and violence in Democratic Republic of the Con-

go: Results of five epidemiological surveys: Kilwa, Inongo, Basankusu, Lubutu, Bunkeya, March to May 2005, *Medicins Sans Frontieres*, October 2005.

33   Ibid.

34   Jennifer Fierburg and Keith Harmon Snow, "Christian Saviors and the Adoptions Industry in Congo: Exploiting Africa's Most Precious Resource: Children," Conscious Being Alliance, 26 June 2013: http://www.consciousbeingalliance.com/2013/06/christian-saviors-the-adoptions-industry-in-congo.

35   Zygmunt Bauman, *Postmodernity and Its Discontents*, Polity Press.

36   E.g. Keith Harmon Snow was banned for life from Smith College, Mt. Holyoke College, and Hampshire College (the latter two of which he had not visited for years) based on a mild challenge to Eric Reeves, the Smith College English professor who has been situated by the media and academia as the world's foremost expert on genocide in Sudan, but who has inverted the realities of victim and perpetrator to serve the U.S., NATO, Israeli warfare agenda.

37   See, e.g.: Nancy Rose Hunt, "An Acoustic Register: Rape and Repetition in Congo", ed. Anne Laura Stoler, *Imperial Debris: On Ruins and Ruination*, Duke University Press, 2013.

38   See: Keith Harmon Snow, "Special Report: Exposing U.S. Agents of Low-Intensity Warfare in Africa: The 'Policy Wonks' Behind Covert Warfare and Humanitarian Fascism," Conscious Being Alliance, 13 August 2012.

39   Ibid.

40   See, e.g.: Thomas P. Odom, "Guerrillas From the Mist: A Defense Attaché Watches the Rwandan Patriotic Front Transform from Insurgent to Counter Insurgent," *Small Wars Journal*, Vol. 5, July 2006; and Thomas P. Odom, *Journey Into Darkness: Genocide in Rwanda*, Texas A&M University, 2005.

41   Ibid.

42   Ibid.

43   Michela Wrong, *In The Footsteps of Mr. Kurtz*, Harper-Collins, 2000: book jacket blurb.

44   Ibid.

45   On Israeli support for Mobutu, see, e.g.,: Israel and Africa: Assessing the Past, Envisioning the Future, The Africa Institute of the American Jewish Committee, May 2006; see also: Wayne Madsen, *Genocide and Covert Operations In Africa, 1993-1999*, Mellen Books, 1999.

46   See: Robin Philpot, "An Open Letter to the New Yorker's Philip Gourevitch on the Congo," Counterpunch, 6 June 2003: https://www.counterpunch.org/2003/06/06/an-open-letter-to-the-new-yorker-s-philip-gourevitch-on-the-congo/.

47   Madeleine Kalb, *The Congo Cables*, Macmillan, 1982: p. 381.

48   Israel and Africa: Assessing the Past, Envisioning the Future, The Africa Institute of the American Jewish Committee, May 2006.

49   See, e.g.: Keith Harmon Snow, "Gertler's Bling Bang Torah Gang: Israel and the Ongoing Holocaust in Congo," Dissident Voice, 9 February 2008.

50   The term "Mr. Africa" was originally applied to Jacques Foccart (31 August 1913 – 19 March 1997), the nationalist French spymaster who masterminded coup d'etats, assassinations and other covert operations—serving Francophone

interests—in Africa. The British version of 'Mr. Africa' was Roland (Tiny) Rowland (November 27, 1917 – July 25, 1998) of Lonrho Corporation. Maurice Tempelsman is (arguably) the U.S. version.

51   Benjamin Beit-Hallahmi, *The Israeli Connection: Who Israel Arms and Why,*, Pantheon, 1987: p. 73.

52   See: Keith Harmon Snow, "Special Report: Exposing U.S. Agents of Low-Intensity Warfare in Africa: The 'Policy Wonks' Behind Covert Warfare and Humanitarian Fascism," Conscious Being Alliance, 13 August 2012.

53   Ellen Ray *et al*, Eds, *Dirty Work II: The CIA in Africa*, C. I. Publications, pp. 350, 512.

54   See: Tim Shorrock, "Company Man," *The Nation*, 25 March 2002 Issue: https://www.thenation.com/article/company-man/.

55   Ibid.

56   See: Lucy Komisar, "Carlucci Can't Hide His Role in Lumumba," *Pacific News Service*, 14 February 2002: http://www.constantinereport.com/frank-carlucci-and-the-murder-of-patrice-lumumba/.

57   Janine Roberts, *Glitter & Greed: The Secret World of the Diamond Cartel*, Disinformation Press, 2003, p. 178, and fn 26 and fn 22 citation of "Alleged Assassination Plots Involving Foreign Leaders", Senate Intelligence Committee Report, p. 32.

58   Ellen Ray *et al*, Eds, *Dirty Work II: The CIA in Africa*, C. I. Publications, p. xvi.

59   Ibid.

60   See, e.g.: Keith Harmon Snow, "Democracy and Dictatorship in Korea: The Korea Problem: This is What Democracy Looks Like," Conscious Being Alliance, 28 March 2017, http://www.consciousbeingalliance.com/2017/03/democracy-dictatorship-in-korea/.

61   Foreword by Alfred W. McCoy in Fred Branfman, Ed., *Voices from the Plain of Jars: Life Under an Air War*, University of Wisconsin Press, 1972.

62   Douglas Valentine, *The Phoenix Program*, William Morrow & Co./An Author's Guild Backinprint, 1990/2000: p. 32.

63   Jeffrey St. Clair and Alexander Cockburn, "Meet the CIA: Guns, Drugs and Money," Counterpunch, 26 January 2018.

64   Ibid.

65   Douglas Valentine, *The CIA As Organized Crime*, Clarity Press Inc., 2017: p. 146.

66   Larry Devlin, Chief of Station, Congo: *Fighting the Cold War in a Hot Zone*, PublicAffairs, 2007.

67   Ibid.

68   Ibid.

69   Ibid.

70   Todd C. Frankel, "THE COBALT PIPELINE: Tracing the path from deadly hand-dug mines in Congo to consumers' phones and laptops," *Washington Post*, 30 September 2016: https://www.washingtonpost.com/graphics/business/batteries/congo-cobalt-mining-for-lithium-ion-battery/.

71   See, e.g.: Susan Williams, *Spies in the Congo: America's Atomic Mission in World War II*, PublicAffairs, 2016.

72   Ibid.

73   See, e.g.: Tom Cooper, *Great Lakes Holocaust: The First Congo War, 1996-1997, Africa @ War*, Vol. 13, Helion & Company, 2013: p. 49

74   Foreword by William T. Stoakley, in: William G. Thom, *African Wars: A defense Intelligence Perspective*, University of Calgary Press, 2010: p. xiii.

75   Ibid.

76   Ibid.

77   See, e.g.: DEMOCRATIC REPUBLIC OF THE CONGO, 1993–2003: Report of the Mapping Exercise documenting the most serious violations of human rights and international humanitarian law committed within the territory of the Democratic Republic of the Congo between March 1993 and June 2003, UNHCR, August 2010; Reuters, "Congo Killing Seen Persisting," *Los Angeles Times*, 11 June 1997: http://articles.latimes.com/1997-06-11/news/mn-2324_1_congo-killing-kabila; and Keith Harmon Snow, "Pentagon Produces Satellite Photos of 1994 Rwanda Genocide," Conscious Being Alliance, 9 April 2012: http://www.consciousbeingalliance.com/2012/04/pentagon-reveals-satelitte-photos-of-1994-rwanda-genocide.

78   On Mobutu in Tel Aviv see, e.g.: "Mobutu and Israel," *Journal of Palestine Studies*, Vol. 15, No. 1, Autumn 1985: pp. 171-175.

79   See: Jerry Funk, *Life is an Excellent Adventure: An Irreverent Personal Odyssey*, Trafford, 2003.

80   See, e.g.: Curtis Abraham, "How Glenn Close's Father Became Mobutu's Personal Doctor," *New African Magazine*, 10 January 2012: http://newafricanmagazine.com/how-the-father-of-glenn-close-became-mobutus-personal-doctor/; and Larry Devlin, Chief of Station, *Congo: Fighting the Cold War in a Hot Zone*, PublicAffairs, 2007: 105.

81   Bryan Mealer, "The River Is A Road: Searching for Peace in Congo," *Harper's*, October 2007.

82   See: Dr. Amos Wilson, *The Falsification of African Consciousness: Eurocentric History, Psychiatry, and the Politics of White Supremacy*, African World Infosystems, 1 July 1993.

83   The Karuna Center For Peacebuilding, website accessed 28 March 2018: http://www.karunacenter.org/.

84   See, e.g., Keith Harmon Snow, "White Slaughter in Black Africa: Genocide and Denialism," Conscious Being Alliance, 11 May 2013: http://www.consciousbeingalliance.com/2013/05/white-slaughter-in-black-africa-the-politics-of-genocide-denialism.

85   See: Keith Harmon Snow, "Special Report: Exposing U.S. Agents of Low-Intensity Warfare in Africa: The 'Policy Wonks' Behind Covert Warfare and Humanitarian Fascism," Conscious Being Alliance, 13 August 2012.

86   See Rick Orth's LinkedIn profile: https://www.linkedin.com/in/rick-orth-6354b04/; also: The Enough Project press release: Lexi Briton, The Enough Project Announces the Launch of its Non-Resident Senior Fellows Program, 29 March 2013: https://enoughproject.org/blog/enough-project-announces-launch-its-non-resident-senior-fellows-program.

87   On the roles such institutions play in statecraft and foreign covert and overt interventions, see, e.g., Joan Roelofs, *Foundations and Public Policy: The Mask*

of Pluralism, SUNY Press, 2003.

88   International Peace & Security Institute, web site accessed 28 March 2018, http://ipsinstitute.org/about-us/.

89   See, e.g., AECOM, GWAC/IDIQ Contracts Center of Excellence, https://om.govwin.com/aecom/contract/index accessed 28 March 2018.

90   AECOM: Maintenance and Operational Support Contract – Afghanistan, AECOM web site accessed 28 March 2018: https://www.aecom.com/projects/maintenance-operational-support-contract-afghanistan/.

91   See, e.g., the directors of the Center for a New American Society, https://www.cnas.org/people?group=board-of-directors.

92   See: Dr. Yaa-Lengi M. Ngemi, "Joseph Kabila," Identity Thief, Impostor, and Rwandan Trojan Horse in Congo, Yaa-Lengi M. Ngemi, 2017.

93   See: Shannon Sullivan and Nancy Tuana, *Race and Epistemologies of Ignorance*, State University of New York Press, 2007.

94   For a single example, see: Jason Stearns and anonymous, *Mai Mai Yakutumba: Resistance and Racketeering in Fizi, South Kivu*, The Rift Valley Institute, London and Nairobi, 2013.

95   Private communication to the author, March 2018.

96   The AFRICOM base that was established in the late 2000 era near the airport in Kisangani, DRC, has been relocated; AFRICOM troops were redeployed to Ango in northern Congo but as of April 2018 their exact location is unknown.

97   See: The Neglected Genocide: Human Rights Abuses Against Papuans in the Central Highlands, 1977-1978, Asian Human Rights Commission 2013.

98   See the 26 minute video by Keith Harmon Snow and Ada Shaw, *"Le Deluge,"* Conscious Being Alliance, December 2012: http://www.consciousbeingalliance.com/2012/12/le-deluge-the-deluge.

99   African proverb.

100   Frantz Fanon, *The Wretched of the Earth*, Présence Africaine, 1963.

RWANDA

THE UNITED STATES AND THE RWANDA GENOCIDE

Charles Onana

For more than twenty years, researchers, journalists, and several human rights organizations have repeated the misperception that the conflict that was occurring in 1994 in Rwanda was a "genocide inflicted on the Tutsi by the Hutu." This view of the events is that of a number of Hollywood films opposing good guys against bad, but it has little to do with the actual situation.

What in fact transpired is a good deal less simple, and some of us are disturbed by what the British researcher Barry Colins calls the "dominant narrative". What has been accepted as the official story is today considered to be cast in bronze and over with. It is imposed on the world in dogmatic, authoritarian terms, and is not to be questioned. Nobody demands that the archives be opened, and new firsthand accounts, even when discussed or written by reliable witnesses, are dismissed as ancient, irrelevant history, and ignored.

The architects of those official views, and their gurus and militants, are not subject to debate, questioning, or contradiction, especially when attention is focused on certain errors that call the dominant narrative into question. Defenders of the Official History of the conflict in Rwanda reiterate their conviction that the subject is covered and done with, and will not consider any crack in its armor.

It would seem however, that History is rarely that clear cut, and can be considered solid only when the sources are. Any position of personal interest must be compared with other positions if we are to avoid twisting of meanings, even outright falsification and dissimulation. The official history of the tragedy in Rwanda over the past twenty years is touted as a 'scientific reference,' but it is based on unverifiable figures, dubious declarations, and improbable opinions, and above all, emotion. Deeply felt, unquestioning emotion. Its claim to be scientific has little to do with any scientific method of investigation and verification, and stands in great need of rectification. It is the purpose of this report to provide that.

When the murderous civil war reached a peak in 1994, the UN peacekeeping forces were already present in Rwanda, authorized by Resolution 872 of October 5, 1993, which created UNAMIR, the United Nations Assistance Mission for Rwanda.[1]

But the extent of the massacres, and especially the failure of a cease-fire between the Hutu government troops and the rebel Tutsis' RPF (Rwandan Patriotic Front), led UN Secretary General Boutros Boutros-Ghali to ask for urgent reinforcements. The French daily *Le Monde* announced on May 2, 1994:

> In a letter to the Security Council during the night of Friday April 29th and Saturday April 30th, Mr. Boutros-Ghali informed the Council that over the previous three weeks more than two hundred thousand people had been massacred in Rwanda. He requested emergency measures to put an end to the killing. Mr. Boutros-Ghali's message was greeted with a deafening silence. Only one diplomat on the Security Council admitted "Events in Rwanda are clearly abominable...."

Mr. Boutros-Ghali decided to draw the attention of the international community to its responsibilities, but the discussions remained purely academic; no country felt ready to send thousands of soldiers into Rwanda.

In fact, as the French daily *Libération* reported in its publication of the same date, "in spite of the ongoing killing and fighting, the Security Council rejected the request of Boutros-Ghali that reinforcements be sent in."

It went on to say:

> Saturday, after nine hours of negotiations, the ambassadors of the Member Nations settled for condemning the massacres, but did not go so far as to send troops into the country to reinforce the UN peacekeepers. They did, however, express their intention to "urgently" consider Boutros-Ghali's request, and asked him to keep them informed, in collaboration with the OAU [Organization for African Unity] of developments that might be considered to help reestablish order in Rwanda and insure the security of displaced persons. While it's surprising that the UN Security Council refused to increase the peacekeeping forces to a level that might have been sufficient to control the armed encounters and massacres among the Rwandese populations, it's even more surprising that the Tutsi rebels, who had initiated the complaint against the genocide they were suffering, opposed the reinforcement of the UNAMIR.
>
> In their declaration of April 30, 1994 under the title of "Statement by the political bureau of the Rwandan Patriotic Front on the proposed deployment of a UN intervention force in Rwanda", which can be obtained from the Archives of the US State Department, they say "In view of the foregoing the Rwandese Patriotic Front calls upon the UN Security Council not to authorize the deployment of the proposed force, as UN intervention at this stage can no longer serve any useful purpose as far as stopping the massacres is concerned."

Had it been the Hutu who had long been committing a planned genocide against the Tutsis, as the Official Version of events would have us believe, would it not be elementary logic that at least the Tutsi rebels, if not the United States, Great Britain and the whole of the international community would unite to urge the UN to intervene and put a stop to it?

Unfortunately that's not what happened in the Security Council. What we saw was a clear violation of the fundamental principle of the Council to "maintain international peace and security." And why, one might ask? At the time, there were those who wondered, considering how these UN forces were equipped and what they were expected to do, whether occupation was a good way of solving problems. Still, since the peacekeeping forces were already there, should they not have been supported?

The French communist daily *L'Humanité*, after having obtained statements from RPF leaders, explained in its May 2, 1994 issue that "its representative in New York, Claude Dusaidi, had refused the offer of support 'on the grounds that Mr. Boutros-Ghali should have recommended the emergency intervention he had requested two weeks ago,' adding that 'such an intervention at this point in time would be catastrophic.'" This would suggest, wouldn't it, that the RPF rebels were then in a position to end the civil war, the massacres, and the genocide, themselves? Yet *l'Humanité* never mentioned that the Tutsi rebels had suggested such a solution. It did note that "the RPF condemns all those who maintain relationships with this 'group of murderers,'[2] and is particularly virulent against the French government, [which had received a delegation of] 'these criminals at the highest level, thereby supporting their policy of extermination and inhuman actions.'" Via reports from Secretary General Boutros Boutros-Ghali, and other sources, the UN Security Council had been regularly alerted to the seriousness of the situation; yet it never did take effective measures to end the conflict. There is yet to be an investigation of the hesitations and blocking that might objectively explain the absence of any clear response to the pleas for adequate troop reinforcement to the horrifically suffering country, and very few researchers have taken the time to look into this fundamental question concerning the handling of the emergency.

One who did was Michael Barnett of George Washington University, in June 1994,[3] after the partial declassification of the UN archives concerning Rwanda, deploring the casual attitude of the Security Council in the face of what amounted to genocide. Professor Peter Erlinder, Defense Lawyer of the ICTR (United Nations International Criminal Tribunal for Rwanda), also collected documents supporting criticism of the Security Council and the Clinton administration.[4]

Some researchers were content to wonder whether or not the civil war had been avoidable, and did not go so far as to lay blame on the international community. And others diluted responsibility of the administrative powers by scattering it throughout what appeared to be the general apathy of the world.

The report of an independent inquiry into the action of the UN in Rwanda, the Carlson Commission, also avoided passing judgement on this delicate controversy, but it did admit that the international community "did not prevent the genocide, nor did it stop the killing once the genocide had begun."[5]

These ways of going about the reporting did little to clarify the situation. One might even say they simply dodged the assigning of political and criminal responsibility to those whose mandate it was to intervene and assist a population in grave danger, which was visibly the case in Rwanda in 1994. A close examination of facts might well have made it possible to end the genocide, and in particular, the civil war. But the declassification of US government documents reveals a clear intention on the part of the United States to avoid UN intervention.

The US Ambassador to the UN, Madame Madeleine Albright, had said, at the time when the UN Secretary General was pressing the Security Council to take measures to end the armed struggle and the massacres, that "a skeletal staff that might be able to facilitate a cease-fire and any future political negotiations" should be left in Rwanda.[6] The British supported the US position, even though that position had drawn the ire of the non-aligned and several other African countries.

While the American press was saying virtually nothing about the indecisive role that Washington was playing in the plight of Rwanda, or the possibly shared villainy of the RPF, it was verbose in its accusations of French intervention and the atrocities committed by the Hutus. Only very recently, that is, twenty years later, has an article by Helen C. Epstein appeared in *The Guardian*, under the title "America's secret role in the Rwandan genocide," suggesting the implication of the United States in the civil war.

"During this period," Epstein states, "officials at the US embassy in Kampala knew that weapons were crossing the border, and the CIA knew that the rebels' growing military strength was escalating ethnic tensions within Rwanda to such a degree that hundreds of thousands of Rwandans might die in widespread ethnic violence. Washington not only ignored Uganda's assistance to the Rwandan rebels, it ramped up military and development aid to Museveni, and then hailed him as a peacemaker once the genocide was underway."

Mrs. Epstein goes on to say, "In Washington a few days later, Museveni told the State Department's Africa chief, Herman Cohen, that he would court martial the Rwandan deserters if they attempted to cross back into Uganda. But a few days after that, he quietly asked France and Belgium not to assist the Rwandan government in repelling the invasion. Cohen writes that he now believes that Museveni must have been feigning shock, when he knew what was going on all along."

> When Museveni returned to Uganda, Robert Gribbin, then deputy chief of mission at the US embassy in Kampala, had some "stiff talking points" for him. "Stop the invasion at once," the American said, "and make sure no support flows to the RPF from Uganda."
>
> Museveni had already issued a statement promising to seal all Uganda–Rwanda border crossings, provide no assistance to the RPF, and arrest any rebels who tried to return to Uganda. But he proceeded to do none of those things and the Americans appear to have made no objection.
>
> When the RPF launched its invasion, Kagame, then a senior officer in both the Ugandan army and the RPF, was in Kansas at the United States Army Command and General Staff College at Fort Leavenworth, studying field tactics and psyops, propaganda techniques to win hearts and minds. But after four RPF commanders were killed—I know of three—Gisa, Chris and Dr. Pete, he told his American instructors that he was dropping out to join the Rwandan invasion. The Americans apparently supported this decision, and Kagame flew into Entebbe airport, traveled to the Rwandan border by road, and crossed over to take command of the rebels.

Cohen's censorship—and no doubt a good deal of self-censorship—in the American media seems to have been accepted unquestioningly by public opinion.

As Mrs.Epstein further observed,

> At least one American was concerned about this. The US ambassador to Rwanda, Robert Flaten, saw with his own eyes that the RPF invasion had caused terror in Rwanda. After the invasion,

hundreds of thousands of mostly Hutu villagers fled RPF-held areas, saying they had seen abductions and killings. Flaten urged the George H.W. Bush administration to impose sanctions on Uganda, as it had on Iraq after the Kuwait invasion earlier that year. But unlike Saddam Hussein, who was routed from Kuwait, Museveni received only Gribbin's "stiff questions" about the RPF's invasion of Rwanda. "In short," Gribbin writes, "we said that the cat was out of the bag, and neither the United States nor Uganda was going to rebag it."

"Sanctioning Museveni might have harmed US interests in Uganda," he explains. "We sought a stable nation after years of violence and uncertainty. We encouraged nascent democratic initiatives. We supported a full range of economic reforms."[7]

Another taboo in the Rwandan war that would have serious repercussions throughout the Central African region,[8] concerned the immense flight of civilian populations both inside the country and toward neighboring countries, particularly the Congo (ex-Zaire).

The reasons for these mass flights of populations have never been seriously investigated by researchers, journalists, or human rights organizations, except by the Belgian researcher De Schrijver Dirk,[9] who analyzed the conditions of civil war that necessitated them. What is needed now is a study of the objectives and motivations of the instigators of the Civil War, and the consequences that persist long after the interest of the International Community has faded.

The fact that the massive exodus of the Rwandan Hutu population, harassed by the RPF, fled to the Congo (Zaire), is confirmed in the report of the CIA on August 13, 1994.[10] If it had been a Hutu government that persecuted the Tutsi population, why would 85% of the refugees who fled to the Congo have been Hutu, as many press reports claimed? There were those in the press, notably the French, who tried to inform the world more accurately and dispassionately. For example, Libération, on May 2, 1994, asserted that "this exodus is proof of the pressure of the RPF, which, above and beyond its insurrection in the northern part of the country, has conquered several localities in the eastern part, notably the province of Kibungo. In Kigali, where there were exchanges of artillery fire over the past weekend, thousands of people were 'displaced' without leaving the capital."

Le Monde, in its May 5 issue, noted that "the rebels of the Rwandan Patriotic Front (RPF) declared, on Tuesday May 3, that no cease-fire is possible in Rwanda as long as the shelling of the capital, Kigali, by the government forces continues. Jacques Bihozagara, RPF head of international affairs, in a press conference in Brussels, doubted that a cease-fire could stop it." He declined to comment on the UN Secretary General's request for peacekeeping forces. "The international community cannot put an end to the massacres. Only the Rwandans can do that," he declared.

Yet it is well known that the civil war and the massacres continued until the RPF's conquest of the country was complete, a month and a half later. It is just as clear that they continued on both sides. The hesitation of the Security Council at the time when it was asked for help, enabled the RPF to achieve an unconditional military victory over the Hutus, and it was never obliged to share power with them, as provided for in the peace accords in Arusha in 1993.

These accords, signed by the RPF and the Hutu government and witnessed by the United States, France, Great Britain and Belgium, were intended to settle once and for all the political transition of the country and the sharing of authority between the Hutus and the Tutsis in Rwanda. But power sharing was never on the RPF's agenda, nor was it apparently on that of the United States. Ambassador Albright made eloquent statements and sent diplomatic cables that explain clearly the US's position re-enforcing the status quo. For example: " Two of the alternatives proposed by the UNSYG are clearly unacceptable to the US, ie.... alternative 1: 'immediate and massive reinforcement of UNAMIR' to enforce a ceasefire with its possible conversion to a chapter VII operation; or... alternative 3 : 'immediate and complete withdrawal of UNAMIR with the corollary risk of killings of persons currently under UN protection...'"[11]

Another example is Rwanda's talking point "Given the chaotic conditions in Rwanda, it is impossible for UNAMIR to fulfill its mandate. It is our view, therefore, that the force should withdraw from the country now..."[12] The non-intervention of the UN is also interesting in that it forces us to question the real intentions of the two permanent member nations of the Security Council—the United States and Great Britain, and those of the RPF representatives, at the time when the UN Secretary General himself asked for help. By insisting on the responsibility of the Hutus and covering up the power grab and crimes of the RPF and Tutsi rebels, and those of the indigenous Twa, who are never mentioned in the Official History of the conflict, the international instruments for world peace failed to call the attention of the world to the actual state of affairs. By holding the Hutu exclusively responsible, they in effect saw to it that the other ethnic groups got away with their crimes.

One must ask why civil war should break out in this small region. Who started it and in whose interest were the murders committed? Observations of preparations for armed insurrection, the delivery of arms to the belligerents, and the actual carrying out of military operations on the ground, which had begun in 1990, flagrantly demonstrate the error of the narrow and emotional information that has emanated from this suffering country over more than twenty years.

As early as April 29, 1994, even before achieving its total military victory over the Hutus, the RPF was urgently demanding that the Security Council summon its Hutu adversaries before the international court, and pointing out the individual Hutus they wanted to be accused. The United States supported these demands without reservation. American leaders refused to meet with any of the Hutu leaders (Jerome Bicamumpaka), although the Rwandan had been a member of the Security Council since 1994.[13] The Hutu troops in the Rwandan government's forces were ill prepared for armed struggle, and unceasingly called for an end to the massacres and assistance from the Security Council to get them under control. Correspondence beginning April 12th from the Hutu leaders to the Security Council and the American Department of State called repeatedly for assistance in enforcing a cease-fire. Strange to imagine a government intent on genocide asking the UN for help to prevent or to stop it.

There are those who claim that the Hutu had help from France in committing genocide of the Tutsi, but there is not a single page of proof or documentation of this claim. Among them, Human Rights Watch, who issued the first scoop to this effect, cannot produce the slightest verification, nor can any of the other sources repeating the claim over twenty years. And it must be recalled here that France's Prime Minister at the time, Edouard Balladur, didn't like to confront the United States directly. France's foreign policy did not include back-chatting Washington, and no one was risking opposing both the US and the RPF. France even voted resolutions that were a far cry from its normal socio-political stances to avoid conflict with the US.

When this claim first saw the light of day in April-May 1994, the American leaders immediately asked all their intelligence services to look into it. George Moose admits in a memorandum that the services had found no proof of France's having helped the Hutu to wipe out the Tutsi population, and the Hutu had not yet lost power in 1994.

The attitudes of the two main parties is obvious. The RPF wanted to overthrow the Hutu regime, and it did. The Hutu majority wanted to stay in power but it accepted power sharing with the Tutsi and signed the Arusha accords. The massacres took on the proportions of a genocide because the Tutsi rebels refused power sharing and preferred a battle to the death.

The error of the presses and human rights organizations was in accepting the genocide as a motivation, whereas, as the documents confirm, it was rather a consequence than a cause. A better examination of the hundreds of ill-informed articles and films about the tragedy of Rwanda would suggest they be round-filed, since they have done nothing more constructive than reinforce the official story. As things now stand, many students of Europe, the US, and Africa have been fed a clearly one-sided history of the two decades, with the result of installing the RPF solidly in charge in Rwanda with the support of the United States and some other actors in the international community.

If any doubt remains, we suggest looking into the autobiographies of Bill Clinton, Boutros Boutros-Ghali, and Carla del Ponte, the Chief Prosecutor of the ICTR. And along with these, of particular pertinence are the works of Jacques Roger Booh Booh, Special Representative of the Secretary General of the UN in Rwanda;[14] General Dallaire, Commandant of the peacekeeping forces in Rwanda; and Colonel Luc Marchal, Commandant of the Belgian forces in Rwanda;[15] Amadou Deme, Information Officer of UNAMIR; the presidential archives of the French Republic; and those declassified by the United States government and the ICTR (International Criminal Tribunal for Rwanda). Other reliable sources, much less energetically searched out by the English-speaking media, include Barrie Collins, Allan Stam, Christian Davenport, and the recently deceased Edward Herman. And there are many others.

It's no easy task reading all these people, but it's a small price to pay for a fair-minded, clear look at the civil war in Rwanda, which was fought in the media as well as on East African soil. And among the most important trophies of regime change in Rwanda, the riches of the Congo area far outranked the hearts and minds of the Rwandan people. When the Tutsi rebels exiled in Uganda crossed the border and attacked

Rwanda in 1990, and occupied the northern provinces of the country through the three years between 1991 and 1993, their objective was the fall of the Habyarimana government. On April 6, 1994, the Rwandan President was assassinated, triggering the surge that would put them in power over the whole country. There was no question of a cease-fire or negotiations with the Interim Government between April and July 1994. The takeover and subjection of the Hutu was complete by July 17, 1994, and the United States immediately recognized the new Tutsi regime.

Jacques-Roger Booh Booh, then special representative of the UN Secretary General, said of the Tutsi rebels' strategy in a diplomatic cable dated April 18, 1994 to Kofi Annan, UN Chief of Operations for Maintaining Peace at the time:

> In my opinion, the government forces have clearly demonstrated their intention to impose a cease-fire.... the RPF remains uncompromising...... They have given us orally their non-negotiable conditions, and they do not include a cease-fire at this time. This would appear to indicate their intention to attain military objectives they had heretofore not expressed, and I drew their attention to the seriousness of the humanitarian situation, which can be corrected only by the immediate imposition of a cease-fire.

According to documents in the United States archives, the American officials also asked the rebels to cease and desist immediately. The Military Attaché at the US Embassy to Rwanda and Burundi, Kevin Aiston Deskoff, had informed Charles Murigande, the representative of the Tutsi rebels in Washington, that the continuation of the conflict was unacceptable, and the government of the United States was calling for an immediate cease-fire. Also noted were the contradictions in the RPF rebels' position. A ceasefire, in his view, was the only way to ease the suffering of the populations and finally put an end to the disaster. All of these sources strongly indicate that the United States was aware of the atrocities committed by the RPF, and of its large share of responsibility for failing to end them.

A declassified secret document from the Assistant Secretary of

State in charge of information and research, Toby Trister Gati, addressed to Secretary of State for African Affairs, George Moose, states:

> There is substantial circumstantial evidence implicating senior Rwandan government and military officials in the widespread, systematic killing of ethnic Tutsis, and to a lesser extent, ethnic Hutus who supported power-sharing between the two groups. The Rwandan Patriotic Front (RPF) has also killed Hutus in the battle and has admitted targeting massacres of Tutsis. Unlike government forces, the RPF does not appear to have commited Geneva Convention defined genocidal atrocities.[16]

This document from Toby Trister Gati is interesting in that it recognizes unhesitatingly that the massacre of Tutsis is a violation of the Geneva Conventions, but while the execution of "Hutu extremists" was just as premeditated, it is not so considered. As they themselves admitted, the Tutsi rebels targeted and massacred Hutus, but at this stage, were not judged guilty of violation of the Convention by the American authorities or courts.

Already in April 1994, we see that killings, both premeditated and unpremeditated, were committed by both sides. But according to which researcher, journalist, or humanitarian organization you consulted, you could get a very different view of the events.

This approach, besides the fact that it is unscientific, appears to be mainly concerned with maintaining an artificial, even authoritarian disqualification of researchers who have done a serious job of researching, examining, and assessing the relevance of the official version. The positions it defends are deemed "negativist," or "revisionist," and in lieu of serious argument, documents, and scientific analyses, brushes off any new information with the sort of vocabulary we recognize as typical at the end of the Second World War. That other war, not subject to doubt or question from outside, when applied to the war in Rwanda, led the late professor Edward Herman, in his work with the journalist David Peterson, to declare that "it is extraordinary to see to what degree the principal sectors of the western establishment have been able to fall into line behind propaganda that paints the aggressors as victims and the victims as aggressors." Their work, "Rwanda and the Democratic Republic of Congo in the Propaganda System," is included in this present anthology.

At this writing, more than twenty-three years after the events, thanks to testimonies of officials and firsthand observers such as Boutros Boutros-Ghali, that have only now been made available, we have a more balanced view of the tragedy of civil war and internecine murder that tore the society of Rwanda to shreds. It is to be hoped that this better understanding of that tragedy will lead to an improvement in the current and future deliberations and actions of the international community.

ENDNOTES

1 Security Council, S/RES/872 (1993), 5 October 1993

2 The formulation "group of murderers" is used by the Tutsi rebels and the RPF leaders when referring to the representatives of the essentially Hutu government that lost power on July 17, 1994, three months after the assassination of President Juvenal Habyarimana. The RPF used the same expression when speaking of the Hutu militias, commanders, and in a general way the soldiers of the Rwandan Armed Forces.

3 "The United Nations Security Council and Rwanda, International Decision-making in the Age of Genocide."

4 http://www.rwandadocumentsproject.net/gsdl/cgi-bin/library

5 S/1999/ 1257, Report of the Independent Inquiry into the Actions of the United Nations during the 1994 Genocide in Rwanda, 15 December, 1999, p. 3

6 USUN N 01503 121743Z, from US Mission, subject: Future UNAMIR and French Roles in Rwanda, April, 1994, p.2.

7 Ibid.

8 "A million war refugees had just crowded into the slums on the hills around Kigali. The coalition government had vigorously defended the claim that the RPF's only purpose was to recover the social and political rights of the Tutsis exiled in Uganda, and that its good faith could be counted on in negotiations; but these claims were considered naive and ignored. The position of the Habyarimana regime and its hardline fringes was that the RPF was a gang of bloodthirsty feudal warlords, and it suddenly appeared to be plausible and rational to a number of people. Fear of an RPF conqueror—who was known to have unhesitatingly sought revenge by executing not only criminals like the mayor of Kinigi, Thaddée Gasana, in Ruhengeri, but their wives and children—bolstered the position of the opposition and the President of France, and weakened that of those in favor of a negotiated settlement."
This quotation is drawn from a Report of the French National General Assembly on Military Operations undertaken by France and other Member Nations of the UN in Rwanda between 1990 and 1994, Paris, 1998, Volume 1, page 114.

9 Les réfugiés rwandais dans la région des Grands Lacs en 1996 in l'Afrique des

Grands lacs, annuaire 1996-(dir. Reyntjens, F. Marysse, S.), Paris, l'Harmattan, 1997, pp. 221-224.

10   National Intelligence Daily, 13 August 1994.

11   United States Department of State, Confidential Memorandum from Arlen Render to Prudence Bushnell, April 21, 1994.

12   United States Department of State, Confidential Briefing Memorandum, from Douglas J. Bennet to The Secretary, April 13, 1994.

13   Jerome Bicamumpaka was Foreign Minister for the Interim Government from April to July 1994. Since January of that year Rwanda has been seated on the UN Security Council and represented there by its FM.

14   Booh Booh, Jacques-Roger, Le patron de Dallaire parle, Paris, Editions Duboiris, 2005, 208p.

15   Marchal, Luc, Rwanda : La descente aux enfers, Brussels, Labor, 2001, 334p

16   United States Department of State, Geneva Convention violations, secret document, from Mr. Toby Gati to Mr. Moose.

EL SALVADOR

WHAT GOES AROUND, COMES AROUND

S. Brian Willson

Historical Roots of Conflict

When the Spanish conquistadors conquered Latin American lands almost 500 years ago, they forcefully introduced a new concept—ownership of property (the fiction of "title"). Land with access to water is the most sacred and indispensable resource enabling sustainable human culture. The historic Indigenous occupants of the land lived and farmed communally. Thus, the idea of protected (with military dictatorships and oligarchic-created Constitutions) private, versus communal land was one introduced from outside—a foreign, alienating value. The consequent tensions have been played out ever since: private profit/individualism versus public/social/community; planter (oligarch) versus peasant/ Indigenous (serf); competition/greed versus cooperation/sharing. If this structural "sin" of private versus social good is not addressed, the modern version being state-protected "capitalism," nothing of substance will really change.

Learning Directly from the Salvadoran Guerrillas in the 1980s War Zones

In November 1988, I traveled with four other US military veterans to investigate the deadly civil war in El Salvador funded largely by the US government. One of our early meetings was with members of the Central Front of the FMLN guerrillas (Farabundo Marti National Liberation Front) in the "conflict zone" mountains of northern Chalatenango Department.

This meeting required an arduous journey that began with hiring a trusted driver with a van to take the five of us to Chalatenango. To increase chances of successfully passing through numerous military checkpoints, we traveled in the middle of the night, often with lights out. If stopped by soldiers, we would say we were traveling to San Pedro Sula, Honduras, 220 miles further north.

There were 12 army checkpoints on the route and we creeped with lights out over *each* of the checkpoint's speed bumps. Always, the soldiers were asleep on their ponchos next to the road. Phew! Three hours later, we arrived about 6:30 am in the small city of Chalatenango (15,000), only 50 miles from the capital, San Salvador. Quickly, we observed a US-supplied Huey helicopter gunship strafing a cluster of houses in the distance, reminding me of my wartime experience in Viet Nam. We hailed a reluctant taxi driver to take us to the small city of Guarjila, a few miles east. He said the trip was dangerous due to the active presence of guerrillas. He asked if we were part of the US advisory group at the military headquarters in Chalatenango. We told him the truth, that we were US military veterans examining the use of a large amount of US military aid. He agreed to drop us off in Guarjila.

From there we walked vigilantly toward the nearby small municipality of beautiful San Jose Las Flores. We spotted an army patrol on the next hill, and several Huey helicopters circling around. We became invisible behind vegetation until it seemed all clear. Because this walk was over rugged terrain, there was a pre-arrangement that local campesinos were to provide me with a mule, since my two artificial legs only function on relatively level ground. Continuing to be vigilant to avoid army patrols or helicopters, we soon were met by a young man and older woman on the trail with a mule. The others walked as I rode the mule until we saw a person on a distant bluff waving an identifiable FMLN flag. We were now in a safe part (at least for the moment) of guerrilla territory. We had walked less than 4 miles, within sight of proximal Honduran territory.

Thus began a crash course in the history of the war. Our first teachers being FMLN fighters, both men and women, mostly young, some in olive green uniforms, others in civilian clothes, all armed. We learned of daily indiscriminate bombings from US-provided A-37 jet fighter bombers, AC-47 gunships, O-2 Spotter planes, and Huey gunship helicopters, all aircraft like those the US had used in Viet Nam, but now piloted by Salvadorans. They were dropping white phosphorous that burns hotter than napalm at 3,000 degrees, 500 pound bombs, and rockets, while firing thousands of rounds of machine gun fire. Doctors had reported treating wounds that resemble those caused by phosphorous and napalm.[1] US advisers had been spotted carrying M-16s next to 105 mm artillery. Many civilians were being murdered every day by Salvadoran army units and patrols, as well as by the air war-in addition to widespread death squad murders.

These guerrillas, accompanied by three leaders of the Joint Command for the Central Front, took a night off. They organized a party for us that lasted all afternoon and night, with music on a borrowed sound system, dancing, and testimonies at a microphone. It was an incredible visceral as well as intellectual experience, equaling or surpassing many of my formal years of education.

I asked one teenage soldier missing part of an arm, an M-16 strapped to his shoulder, what keeps him going? His response: *"If you struggle for justice, you may die, but with dignity ("dignidad"). If you don't struggle, you die of slow starvation. We have no alternative."*

As we learned more of the 20th century history of El Salvador, the young soldier's response summarized the plight of the country's majority peasants.

Meeting with US and Salvadoran Military Personnel/ Human Rights Director

Two days later we returned by foot and mule to Chalatenango city. Casually dressed, we walked to the heavily fortified Salvadoran/ US military headquarters in the center of the city. Because we walked with an air of confidence, with one of our members being Mexican American, and another fluent in Spanish, the Salvadoran guards waved us through without hesitation. "At ease" we said, as he saluted us.

Perhaps he assumed we were CIA or other friendly civilian operatives assigned to consult with the US advisers whose office was at the rear of the building. Strangers don't just wander into military headquarters in "conflict zones".

We opened a rear unlocked door and surprised two US uniformed military advisers standing in front of large wall maps decorated with color-coded pins identifying specific locations of FMLN units and their recent attacks, and Salvadoran military units and their supportive US field advisers. We immediately introduced ourselves as US war veterans assessing the cost-effectiveness of the one million dollars a day of US military aid going to El Salvador. Like the Salvadoran guard outside, the advisors were not used to gringos walking through to their unlocked room inside a supposedly secure building. At first, they welcomed us and willingly discussed the latest intelligence reports, and details of the latest FMLN attacks, in which they said the "communist guerrillas" dragged their fallen comrades with them like the "dirty VC" had done in Viet Nam to conceal accurate casualty figures. A visible pallet of USAID bags of rice was being used, they said, to reward communities which professed allegiance to the government. Finally, after 30 minutes, one of the advisers called his boss in San Salvador, US Military Attaché Colonel Wayne Wheeler, who then ordered us by phone to immediately return to see him at the US Embassy.

Before departing Chalatenango, however, we visited the gravesites of Maryknoll Sisters Ida Ford and Maura Clark, two of the four US missionaries who had been raped and murdered on December 2, 1980, by Salvadoran National Guardsmen who, later we learned, were directed by an officer trained at the US Army School of the Americas (SOA), Fort Benning, Georgia. The church workers had been invited by Archbishop Romero to assist thousands of displaced children due to war and death squad activity, before he himself was murdered by an assassin on March 24 earlier the same year.

We subsequently learned that Roberto D'Aubuisson, graduate of the SOA, had planned and ordered Romero's assassination, which was carried out with complicity of other SOA graduates. The 1993 United Nations Truth Commission report after the war concluded that D'Aubuisson was the primary death squad organizer from 1978-1992. He was a friend of the oligarchy and the United States, always welcome at the US Embassy. US Senator Jesse Helms (R–NC) proclaimed: "All I know is that D'Aubuisson is a free enterprise man and deeply religious."[2]

In San Salvador, we indeed visited US Military Attaché Colonel Wayne Wheeler at the US Embassy on his second tour in El Salvador. Shocked that we had traveled to the dangerous war zones without a permit, we explained that as unarmed gringos we were not perceived as any threat. He was equally appalled that we had met with members of the FMLN. "How did you do it?" he asked. A Viet Nam veteran like three of our five-member delegation, he began to warm up to us. He was frank as he admitted the war was extremely frustrating, that the US–funded Salvadoran security forces were involved in too many massacres. He confessed that there were in fact 125 US advisers in country, despite a Congressionally-imposed limit of 55, made possible by manipulating titles and using "temporary duty" as a cover for long term assignments.

In 1981, President Reagan had limited the number of Green Beret trainers in El Salvador to 55. They were forbidden from carrying M-16s or being in combat. Nonetheless, we know that 21 US US soldiers died in combat in El Salvador during the 1980s, and some carried M-16s.[3]

Our meeting concluded when one of our members, 73-year old WWII veteran and ex-CIA man Phil Roettinger, involved in the 1954 coup ousting Guatemalan democratically-elected President Arbenz, admonished Wheeler: "You are confusing communism with people's need for land reform. One day you will live with what I do every day— that I participated in a grand lie leading to murder of 200,000 innocent people! You are on the wrong side." Wheeler was stunned.

Incidentally, one year after our interview with Wheeler, he and his family were barricaded inside their home in November 1989 as guerrillas and government forces fought each other near Escalon Circle in the wealthy San Salvador area of Avenida Escalon. One of the three leaders of the Joint Command, Dimas Rodriguez, with whom we had just met, was killed in the offensive.

We visited the recent September 21, 1988 massacre site at remote San Francisco, San Vicente Department, 25 miles east of San Salvador, where ten unarmed peasants had been murdered. The army denied guilt, attributing it to guerrillas. We subsequently learned the massacre was directed by a unit commanded by General Adolfo O. Blandon, another graduate of the SOA.

We then arranged a visit with Colonel Rene Emilio Ponce, chief of staff of the Salvadoran Armed Forces, and General Juan Rafael Bustillo, commander of the Salvadoran Air Force. We asked if the military had been involved in the San Vicente massacre. Of course, they denied responsibility, blaming the guerrillas. Ponce stressed that "it was imperative that El Salvador not go the way of neighboring revolutionary Nicaragua."

Our meeting with Ponce occurred one year before *he* orchestrated the massacre reported around the world on November 16, 1989 of six Jesuit priests, their housekeeper, and her teenage daughter, at the Central American University (UCA). They attempted to blame the FMLN for the murders. This assassination occurred five days after the FMLN began their offensive that had sent fear throughout the Salvadoran and US governments. Ponce, Bustillo, and a majority of officers involved in the massacre, were graduates of the SOA, and members of the US–trained Atlacatl Battalion.

The FMLN offensive had a powerful psychological impact, similar to that of the 1968 TET offensive in Viet Nam. It convinced the right-wing ARENA government, one that had dominated the political scene in El Salvador during the 1980s, to go to the peace table.

The gruesome murder of the Jesuits provoked Viet Nam veteran and Maryknoll priest Roy Bourgeois to begin a campaign to close the US Army's School of the Americas (SOA) at Fort Benning, Georgia, a campaign that continues to this day.

To learn more of the human rights violations, we arranged a visit with Reynaldo Blanco, president of the *non*-governmental Human Rights Commission (CDH) in El Salvador. His predecessor, Herbert Anaya, had been murdered nearly a year earlier, the second CDH president to be murdered in four years. Both he and Anaya had been captured and tortured in 1986, spending nine months in prison.

We were instructed to take detours to ensure we were not followed to Blanco's office. His office had recorded, in 1988 alone, over 1,800 violent political deaths (average 5 per day), over 1,000 assassinations, nearly 1,000 civilians captured, and nearly 275 disappeared. He showed us gruesome photographs of torture and murder victims, and current lists of over 400 torture victims by name and date of capture. Prisoners in the draconian La Esperanza (called "Mariona") prison in San Salvador had smuggled out hand drawings of the forty torture techniques being inflicted. *The New York Times* reported Green Berets overseeing tortures in El Salvador.[4]

Before leaving Blanco's office we asked him how and why he chose to take on such dangerous work. He calmly smiled, saying "This is my work for the people. Whatever happens, happens. I try to be careful and plan carefully how and when to travel while moving my office and sleeping quarters from place to place. I try to have others around me. The work is very dignified."

Farabundo Marti's 1932 Uprising

The name FMLN itself is a constant reminder of this tortured history. Farabundo Marti (1893-1932) was a Salvadoran peasant born in a poor farming community in southwest El Salvador. In his twenties he had developed a deep understanding of how the political-economic power of a small oligarchy had profited by maintaining a system which enforced impoverishment for the majority. His political activities led to his deportation several times. During his exile, he had met with Augusto Cesar Sandino, leader of the peasant rebellion in neighboring Nicaragua.

After a military coup in 1931, a new dictator, Maximiliano Hernandez Martinez, emerged. Marti returned to El Salvador and helped organize a revolt of peasant farmers and trade unionists. In January 1932 in western El Salvador, as many as 40,000 rebellious peasants, many Indigenous, armed only with machetes, were massacred ("La Mantanza") by General Martinez' well-armed forces and hacienda police using machine guns, cavalry and artillery. Hernandez Martinez, a vegetarian, called the peasants "bolsheviks" and thought "killing an ant was a greater crime than killing a man."[5] Fear of communists and Indians were used to justify brutal repression. Peasant leaders, including Marti, were immediately shot or lynched. Martinez became a hero of the feudal-like oligarchy. A lengthy period of fierce repression targeted those found with a machete or those with Indigenous facial features or who wore native dress, or spoke native tongues. Thousands were shot and buried in mass graves they were forced to dig themselves. This nearly exterminated the Nahua-Pipil Indigenous. Their collective memory was lost for four decades.[6]

In the early 20th Century, expansion of coffee, sugar and cotton plantations by a few large landowners had virtually eliminated Indigenous use of their productive lands which had provided the food supply for their oligarchic overlords. Staple foods like maize, beans, and fruit grew scarce. A nation that had imported less food than most of its Latin American neighbors, now depended on its neighbors and the US for food. Investors in the US took advantage of this new "opportunity" and became substantial controllers of Salvadoran markets. They provided millions of dollars in loans, assumed control of the Salvadoran railroad as collateral, and appointed a US fiscal agent to oversee collection of export and import duties from which the loans would be repaid.[7]

Meanwhile, the "forty Salvadoran families" continued their profitable plantations, protected by military dictatorships. Their serfs were fed two tortillas and two spoonfuls of beans twice a day.[8] "Success" depended on US food imports and quiet workers. Nothing else would enable profits. In 1931, a US Embassy officer observed that on streets in San Salvador "there appears nothing between these high priced cars and the oxcart and its barefoot attendant...Thirty or forty families own nearly everything...The rest of the population has practically nothing."[9] In 1932, a US spokesman observed that farm animals possessed more commercial value than the workers.[10]

In 1934 US President Franklin Roosevelt recognized dictator Maximiliano Hernandez Martinez as the duly selected President of El Salvador. This despite a 1923 treaty that prohibited recognition of governments formed from coups ("golpes"), which the Martinez government had achieved in late 1931. This is not surprising given an understanding that the US government violated every treaty made with original Indigenous Americans since the late 1700s.

**President Kennedy's Alliance For Progress:
Economic Development With a Catch**

El Salvador, a country the size of the state of Massachusetts, had a population of 2.8 million in 1961 when the ten-year, US$100 billion Alliance For Progress was launched by President Kennedy. Twenty years later in 1980 when the civil war started, the population was 4.6 million, but the basic socio-economic conditions remained virtually the same. (Today's population is nearly 6.5 million). Large landowners controlled the government. Two percent of the people owned 58 percent of the productive land. Average monthly income of peasant families was 12 dollars; half of them were illiterate. Nearly half the people were unemployed/underemployed. The controlling families lived in opulence with servants, protected by phony elections and an oligarchic-created Constitution. A priest proclaimed that the people "live like serfs in Europe four hundred years ago."[11]

Ostensibly to correct this injustice, President Kennedy

announced in 1961 the Alliance For Progress, intended "to complete the revolution of the Americas,"[12] fostering material progress and dignity for all Hemispheric citizens.

El Salvador was considered the pride of the Alliance. The CIA identified the country as "one of the Hemisphere's most stable, progressive republics."[13] This conclusion had been bolstered by a young officer's coup in 1961 that overthrew a "reformist" government considered "dangerously" influenced by Communism and on the other hand, Castro's recent revolution in Cuba. President Kennedy approved a civil-military type government in El Salvador as being the most effective at restraining communist advances, allowing the "success" of the Alliance. In 1965, President Johnson announced El Salvador was "a model for other Alliance countries."[14]

During a March 1963 meeting of the six Central American presidents in Costa Rica, Kennedy declared that "Communism is the chief obstacle to economic development in the Central American region."[15] The Presidents agreed to restrict movement of their citizens to and from Cuba, and to terminate trade with it. Rabid fear of the bogeyman communism was still driving policy.

The US had already been training Salvadoran soldiers since the late 1940s. Thousands of military personnel from Latin America, including El Salvador, had been trained at the US Army's School of the Americas (SOA) established in 1946 at Fort Sherman, Panama. Its goal was to teach "anti-communist counterinsurgency training."[16]

In 1984, the SOA moved to Fort Benning, Georgia. Since many of its graduates over the years were proven participants in numerous massacres, its critics were calling it the School of Assassins (SOA), demanding the school be closed. In 2000, its name was changed to the Western Hemisphere Institute for Security and Cooperation (WHINSEC) in an (unsuccessful) PR attempt to dilute its critics. It is still referred to as the SOA, and over 60 Salvadoran military graduates have been identified as participants in horrible human rights violations.[17]

National Security State

So, ironically, as the decade of the Alliance For Progress was intended to develop material progress and promote dignity for all Hemispheric citizens, it did nothing more than entrench the class status of societies, while exposing the majority of people to more severe threats to their safety and dignity. Creation of the National Security State (NSS) became the primary policy.

In El Salvador, the CIA's model as a "stable, progressive republic," the aggrieved population experienced control from an incredible network, much of it coordinated by the CIA itself. The CIA, US Embassy, Green Berets and other military advisers, Defense Intelligence Agency (DIA), and the US State Department through their "humanitarian" Agency for International Development (USAID), coordinated intimately with a beefed up Salvadoran army, Treasury Police, National Police, and two newly created Salvador national security agencies—ORDEN and ANSESAL. AID's Development Office of Public Safety conducted much of the security training, including "interrogation," as it had done in Viet Nam.[18]

ORDEN (National Democratic Organization) was created in 1961, coinciding with creation of the Alliance. It served as a rural intelligence network, keeping a finger on the pulse of peasant restiveness in every local village. Guided by the CIA, it became a paramilitary unit and death squad, commanded by Colonel Jose Alberto Medrano, a CIA payrollee, assisted by the Green Berets.[19] It used terror against anyone deemed an opponent of the government, i.e., those who mentioned poverty, "insulted" authority, discussed "imperialism" or problems with the "oligarchy," or organizers of peasants such as students or priests or nuns. Suspect lists were created, many listees were threatened, often kidnapped, tortured and murdered. The assassins became known as the "Mano Blanco" (White Hand) death squads,[20] an offshoot of the White Warriors Union (see below).

ANSESAL (National Agency of Salvadoran Security) was formed in the early 1960s as an elite intelligence unit with assistance from the CIA, coordinating directly with the Salvadoran President's office. It collected information from local ORDEN detachments, regularly sharing information with US officials. Elaborate personal histories were kept on leaders throughout the country such as student organizers, church leaders, teachers, professors, journalists, human rights workers, union leaders, and peasant leaders. Information included videotapes and photos of "suspects", daily whereabouts of "troublemakers", including students in other countries.[21]

The US agencies, including Embassy officials, were involved in training Salvadoran security leaders in personal surveillance techniques (often of people later murdered by death squads), use of combat weapons, explosives, sabotage methods, ambush strategies, physical and psychological torture. They provided technical and intelligence advisers who worked directly with ANSESAL in the Salvadoran President's office. Intelligence was gathered from the air as well as on the ground. Some key operatives, in addition to Medrano, were on the CIA payroll.[22]

By 1969, as repression increased, 300,000 Salvadorans (1 in 8) had fled this "model" Alliance nation seeking safety in neighboring Honduras.[23] The "revolutionary" Alliance model was starving the poor. In 1970, the first peasant-based armed resistance efforts sent fear through the Salvadoran oligarchy. Hacienda owners relied evermore on a number of the 3,500 Salvadoran military officers, virtually all trained by the US, who were profiting as their personal armed protectors. Many would later be implicated in atrocities.[24]

The 1980 Trauma, and the Revolutionary Civil War, 1979-1992

The purpose of the 1980s war was, in effect, to determine whether a few Salvadorans could continue to dominate and impoverish the many. The US predictably chose to support the few against the many, under the guise of stopping communism. President Reagan aimed to prevent at all costs creation of a "Soviet beachhead" in Central America.[25]

An officer's reformist coup in October 1979 overthrew the repressive Salvadoran government of General Carlos Humberto Romero, almost three months after the fall of US-supported dictator Somoza in Nicaragua. Unstable conditions under dictator Romero were threatening the existence of the oligarchy itself, thus convincing President Carter to support the coup. Ironically, this support marked the beginning of an escalated the US commitment to fund an extremely violent counter-revolution. A five-member junta formed, promising to control the worst of the behaviors of ORDEN, and to institute modest land reform. But internal divisions led to collapse of the junta in 1980, leading Carter to re-establish closer ties with Salvadoran military leaders, assigning three dozen advisers to assure a "clean counterinsurgency."[26] Moderate Christian Democrat Jose Napoleon Duarte returned from exile in Venezuela to become Salvador's new president, hoping to be elected in 1982 and bring peace to the country. Such was not to be the case.

March 24, 1980: Beloved Archbishop Oscar Arnulfo Romero was assassinated by a lone gunman as he finished a sermon mourning the murders of parishioners. Despite death threats, Romero was becoming bolder. In a Sunday sermon the previous day, he had appealed to Salvadoran soldiers—"No one has to fulfill an immoral law...I beg you, I ask you, I order you in the name of God—Stop the repression!" In February, in a letter to President Carter, he pleaded for cessation of military aid because "it is being used to repress my people."[27] It was ignored, and aid increased. Romero's funeral was attended by 250,000, one of the largest demonstrations in El Salvador history. Terrified government security forces fired into the crowd, killing over 40, while injuring 200.[28] During 1980, 10,000 Salvadorans were murdered, as Carter faced a contradiction: reform without revolution meant alienating the wealthy elite needed to carry out reforms.[29]

Many investigations of Romero's assassination, one of the most notorious murders of the 20th Century, revealed the likely killers and mastermind, but nobody has been prosecuted. A cabal of wealthy business owners, many living in Miami who fled the war, politicians, and death squad commanders who felt threatened by the Archbishop and other critics, bankrolled death squad activity, including Romero's assassination. Roberto D'Aubuission, the believed mastermind, was a graduate of the SOA, of the International Police Academy in Washington, DC, and had founded ARENA (Nationalist Republican Alliance) Party shortly after Romero's assassination.[30]

He was also noted as founder of the White Warriors Union in late 1970, specializing in murdering priests.[31] The Union published widely distributed leaflets, and wrote graffiti, "Be a patriot, kill a priest." After each priest on his list was assassinated, D'Aubuisson declared, "Once the dog is dead, we won't have to worry about rabies."[32] Scholars in the US National Security Archive have discovered a declassified document of a conversation in which Roberto D'Aubuisson bragged about planning the murder of Archbishop Romero, mentioning a lottery between members of his death squads, with the "winners" chosen to assassinate Romero.[33]

May 14-15, 1980: The Salvadoran army in coordination with ORDEN death squads, and cooperating Honduran military, massacred some 600 villagers at Las Arados in Chalatenango on the Sumpul River.[34] The River, separating Salvador from Honduras, ran with blood for days.

It was one of the first of *at least* 27 major massacres,[35] many committed by the Atlacatl Battalion, including El Mozote Massacre, 1981 (800-1,200 murdered), Lake Suchitlan, 1983 (117);[36] Los Llanitos, 1984 (68, most under 14 years of age);[37] and Chalatenango Guerrilla

Field Hospital in Los Encuentros, 1989 (10 medical staff and guerrilla patients).[38] Attacking the hospital violated the Geneva Conventions and Salvadoran law. The latter massacre occurred only days after US Vice-President Dan Quayle visited El Salvador, warning the army that continued aid depended on their respect for human rights.[39]

In October 1980, the FMLN formed as an umbrella organization from five different armed guerrilla groups to combat the hegemony of army, security forces, death squads and the US.

November 27, 1980: Six leaders of the Revolutionary Democratic Front (FDR) were meeting in a strategy session at a Jesuit high school not far from the US Embassy in San Salvador when they were seized by security forces, then murdered. President Duarte acknowledged the military was responsible, but the army was out of his control. The FDR had recently formed as the political, unarmed, component of the revolution, joining the armed FMLN in a united effort.[40]

December 2, 1980: A month after the election of Ronald Reagan, three US nuns and a Catholic lay worker were found in a shallow grave near the international airport; each had been raped and desecrated. Subsequent investigations revealed the murders were planned by Major Lizandro Zepeda Velasco, a graduate of the SOA, and carried out by National Guardsmen under command of another SOA graduate, General Edgardo Casanova. The latter went on to become Minister of Defense in the "reformist" government of José Napoleón Duarte. Tragically, President Carter again chose to increase military aid. President Reagan's future Secretary of State, General Alexander Haig, suggested the women were killed in an "exchange of gunfire" as they tried to "run a road block."[41] His future Ambassador to the United Nations, Jean Kirkpatrick, condemned the women as not just nuns, but "political activists."[42]

December 10-13, 1981: One of the worst single-event massacres in Latin American history occurred in the small community of El Mozote, and several small neighboring villages, in the mountains of northeastern Salvador. Soldiers of the army's US-trained Atlacatl Battalion participated in a scorched earth slaughter of anywhere from 800 to 1200 unarmed men, women, the elderly, and at least 145 children. Women and young girls were raped before being murdered. The murders occurred through mass shootings, hangings, grenades, slit throats and decapitations. It was code-named "Operación Rescate"/Operation Rescue, despite there being no combatants in the area. The Operation was ordered by Lieutenant Colonel Domingo Monterrosa Barrios, an SOA graduate, commander of the Atlacatl Battalion.[43]

As I studied the gruesome accounts of the massacre, I was reminded of the US army massacre at My Lai on March 16, 1968 by units of the US Army's "Americal" 23rd Infantry Division, murdering in cold blood 504 unarmed civilians, of whom 182 were women (17 pregnant), 173 children (56 under one year of age), and 60 old men. Twenty of the women had been raped. Not one bullet was fired at the US soldiers, but the killing was relentless nonetheless.

The US military had trained the murderers at My Lai, just as it had trained the murderers at El Mozote. The Atlacatl Battalion, comprised of 1,100 men wearing red berets, had been trained as an elite rapid-response counter-insurgency unit by US trainers from the School of Americas (SOA), Fort Benning, Georgia, and specialists in anti-communist counter-insurgency from the Special Warfare Center, Fort Bragg, North Carolina. Designed to be engaged in mass murder, it was described as "particularly ferocious."[44] Many SOA graduates were in its command structure.

President Reagan belittled the reports as "gross exaggerations."[45] He continued certifying to Congress that El Salvador "was making progress on its human rights record" as a required condition for seeking more aid.[46] He ignored the US Embassy's knowledge of death lists prepared by the Salvadoran high command identifying hundreds of targeted "subversive" peasants in the El Mozote region.[47] During Reagan's first year in office, 13,000 Salvadorans were murdered, an average of 35 every day.

The End of the War—Finally

The war witnessed violence breeding more violence in a vicious spiral, a conscious policy of elite oligarchs, military, death squads, and the US. By 1987, the US-funded Salvadoran army numbered 55,000, with nearly 25,000 additional paramilitary.[48] Finally a cease-fire was brokered in 1992 by the United Nations. Over 80,000 Salvadorans lay dead, 8,000 missing, countless maimed, and over 1,000,000 displaced in a country of 5 million people. The US had facilitated it *all* with 6 billion dollars,[49] spending an average of US$41.7 million each month, and $1.4 million every day for 12 years, to instill fear, murder, maim, torture and destroy the social fabric.

The Alliance For Progress, launched in 1961 "to complete the revolution of the Americas" by fostering material progress and dignity for people, instead created a regional terror machine. The years 1979-1991 were the most violent and bloodiest period of Central America's post-1820 history. Minimum estimates of total killed and "disappeared" are 200,000, likely more. El Salvador alone witnessed at least 80,000 of those murders, with millions more displaced or becoming refugees, with well over 500,000 fleeing to the United States.[50]

As long as the fanatical obsession with private ownership and profits, versus social re-construction, remains paramount to US foreign policy, imperialism and the repression necessary to enforce it, will be central to the continuation of the United States political economy (in essence, capitalism). And fear is the greatest weapon to coerce obedience to indignity.

The surprise November 11, 1989 offensive of 2,000 to 3,000 FMLN guerrillas, shocking both the Salvadoran and US governments, forced the policy to outgun the guerrillas to be reconsidered. The offensive lasted into early December and for the first time in the war, San Salvador city center itself was penetrated by guerrillas, as they stormed the Sheraton Hotel, holding more than 100 people hostage, including several Green Berets in the city for training missions. But the offensive also attacked military facilities in other major departments. It was during this offensive that a unit of the Atlacatl Battalion entered the Central American University (UCA) in the middle of the night on November 16, 1989, executing six Jesuit liberation theology priests, their housekeeper, and her teenage daughter. The priests, strong advocates of Liberation Theology, were considered by the Salvadoran right as motivators for the guerrillas. As mentioned above, Colonel Rene Ponce, chief of the Salvadoran armed forces, with whom our veteran's delegation had met exactly one year prior, planned the attack. But twenty-six Salvadoran officers altogether were involved, nineteen of whom were SOA graduates.[51]

By April 1990, representatives from the government agreed to meet with the FMLN in Geneva under auspices of the UN Secretary-General. An opening agreement was reached in July 1990, a cease-fire declared in September 1991, and preliminary peace agreement signed on December 31. A comprehensive settlement was signed on January 16, 1992, at Chapultepec Castle in Mexico City, thus called the Chapultepec Accords. The agreement included substantial reduction in Salvadoran armed forces, and complete dissolution of the rapid deployment forces, including the US-trained elite Atlacatl Battalion, the National Guard, the

National Police, and the Treasury Police, as well as all armed FMLN units.

A Truth Commission for El Salvador, July 1992-March 1993, issued its report, "From Madness to Hope: The 12-Year War in El Salvador: Report of the Commission on the Truth for El Salvador." It received 22,000 formal complaints: 60 percent involved extrajudicial killings, 25 percent involved disappearances, and 20 percent, torture. Collected testimony revealed 95 percent of the acts of violence were committed by state agents; only 5 percent of acts of violence were attributed to the FMLN. A number of actors were identified, including 69 key military officers and noncommissioned officers, including 49 of whom were graduates of the SOA.[52]

The Salvadoran government and its armed forces unsurprisingly rejected the report and no follow-up mechanism was established. Five days after the report was released, the legislature passed a general amnesty law covering all crimes related to the war. In 1999, the Inter-American Commission ruled that the amnesty law violated international law.

The largest criticism of the report is that it failed to identify the United States as the chief funder and trainer for the state agents. Knowingly instilling fear to compel obedience to repressive policies is a terrible thing, even diabolical. Thousands of Salvadoran families had been divided, disappeared, murdered, and tortured. Fear and silence ruled the country as the social fabric and bonds of society were destroyed, while the basic historical political-economic system remained.

Nonetheless, the US remains fanatically committed to private enterprise, no matter the cost to social fabric or human rights. US Assistant Secretary of State for Inter-American Affairs under Reagan, Elliott Abrams, 1985-1989, who was convicted of withholding information from Congress about the Iran-Contra affair, and is currently senior fellow for Middle Eastern Studies at the Council on Foreign Relations (CFR), proudly declared "the administration's record in El Salvador is one of fabulous achievement."[53] There you have it.

Long Term Effect: Violence Born in the USA[54]

El Salvador is now considered the murder capital of the world. In 2015, there were 6,556 murders, or an average of 547/month/18/day, rivaling the death rates of the 12-year civil war, 556/month/18.5/day.

Most of these killings are attributed to gang violence. But many of these gangs were born in the Pico neighborhood in Los Angeles in the 1990s. Why were they there?

During the war, at least 500,000 Salvadorans fled the incredible violence beginning in the late 1980s, seeking safety in the United States. With the broken social fabric those numbers escalated further after the war. Many lived in neighborhoods of central Los Angeles. The entire experience was disorienting and anxiety producing for the families. Presumably, most suffered from Post Traumatic Stress Disorder (PTSD) as the medical community recorded extraordinary rates of hypertension, diabetes, insomnia, stomach disorders, and inability to focus.

Additionally, many were greeted with hostility by existing local residents. The young family members felt lost and created a new secure "family"—the MS-13 street gang, rivaling an older 18th Street gang (Barrio 18) comprised of other alienated Central American youth. As the gang violence in Los Angeles escalated, the Los Angeles police worked closely with US authorities to begin mass exportations to El Salvador in the late 1990s. But now there are MS-13 gang members active in 44 US states. Of course those exported brought their gang patterns back with them to their home country of El Salvador that had no history of street gangs. The culture of gang violence became a way of life in Salvador as well.

The right-wing ARENA government resorted to military-style methods in attempts to (unsuccessfully) control the violence. ARENA remained in power until 2009, when it was replaced by an FMLN presidency. A truce among the gangs with support of the new FMLN government in 2012, cut homicides in half. But after eighteen months of controversy over the government's role, the government with 22,000 well-armed police officers, 14,000 soldiers, and special forces rapid response teams similar to those used by the repressive ARENA government of the 1980s, switched in 2014 to a renewed military-style crackdown. Violence continues unabated. Even US troops are now visible on "training exercises."

There are 70,000 gang members in the country representing an impoverished social base of 500,000 (1 of 8) Salvadorans. Over 15,000 gang members are in prison, and the country's homicide rates continue to lead the world. Salvadorans therefore continue to flee the violence, including gang members, fleeing for their lives toward the US. People are trapped in traumas upon traumas provoked by the 1980s US-financed war and death squads. Without an economic and political system committed to assuring a relatively class-free social fabric, supported by substantial reparations, there seems no end to this cycle of violence. Fear and Impunity have set in motion a deadly combination, as no real security and justice can prevail.

El Salvador is a case study of the three classical steps in the spiral of violence:

(1) Preservation of a repressive oligarchy dependent upon forceful impoverishment of a "serf" class—the ultimate structural violence;

(2) The aggrieved people organize for relief, sometimes using violence as a last resort, are identified as criminal subversives threatening stability of the "state" and its accessories; and

(3) The oligarchic political-economic structure violently repress the expressions of the aggrieved peasants, including murdering them, using fear to enforce obedience to the horrible system from which they originally sought relief.

Is another armed revolution in the making? In shithole El Salvador, or shithole USA?

ENDNOTES

1   Wayne Biddle, "Salvador Officer Said to have Told of Napalm Use," *New York Times*, October 9, 1984, http://www.nytimes.com/1984/10/09/world/salvador-officer-said-to-have-told-of-napalm-use.html, accessed, February 20, 2017; Sandra C. Smith—Nonini, *Healing the Body Politic of Salvador's Popular Struggle for Health Rights – From Civil War to Neoliberal Peace* (New Brunswick, NJ: Rutgers University Press, 2010), 107.

2   Patrick Martin, "Jesse Helms to retire from US Senate: a career based on racism, bigotry and contempt for democratic rights," https://www.wsws.org/en/articles/2001/08/helm-a31.html, August 31, 2001, accessed February 1, 2018.

3   Robert Parry, *Lost History* (Arlington, VA: The Media Consortium, 1999), 268.

4   Raymond Bonner, "US Advisers Saw 'Torture Class', Salvadoran Says," *New York Times*, January 11, 1982; The Department of Defense also issued torture manuals used in teaching Latin American military personnel at the SOA, SEE Greg Grandin, *Empire's Workshop: Latin America, The United States, and the Rise of the New Imperialism* (New York: Henry Holt and Co., 2006), 265, n50-56].

5   Eduardo Galeano, *Open Veins of Latin America: Five Centuries of the Pillage of a Continent* (New York: Monthly Review Press, 1973), 126.

6   Theodore Macdonald, "El Salvador's Indians", *Cultural Survival*, March 1982, https://www.culturalsurvival.org/publications/cultural-survival-quarterly/el-salvadors-indians, accessed February 10, 2017; Walter LaFeber, *Inevitable Revolutions, The United States in Central America*, 2nd ed (New York: W.W. Norton & Co., 1993), 75.

7   LaFeber, 73.

8   *Wikipedia*, 1932 Salvadoran Peasant Massacre.

9   LaFeber, 73.

10   *Wikipedia*, 1932 Salvadoran Peasant Massacre.

11   Penny Lernoux, *Cry Of The People: The Struggle For Human Rights In Latin America - The Catholic Church In Conflict With U. S. Policy* (London: Penguin Books, 1980), 62-3.

12   *Wikipedia*, Alliance For Progress,

13   LaFeber, 173-4.

14   LaFeber, 175.

15   Allan Nairn, "Behind the Death Squads: An Exclusive Report on the US Role in El Salvador's Official Terror," *The Progressive*, May 1984, http://www.historyisaweapon.com/defcon1/nairnelsalvadorbtds.html, accessed February 10, 2018.

16   *Wikipedia*, Western Hemisphere Institute for Security Cooperation.

17   "Notorious Salvadoran School of the Americas Graduates," http://www.derechos.org/soa/elsal-not.html, accessed February 1, 2018.

18   Alfred McCoy, *A Question of Torture: CIA Interrogations, From the Cold War to the War on Terror* (New York: Henry Holt and Company, 2006), 10-11, 61; Michael McClintock, *Instruments of Statecraft: US Guerrilla Warfare, Counter-Insurgency, Counter-Terrorism 1940-1990* (New York; Pantheon Books, 1992), 181, 188-190.

19   David Kirsch, "Death Squads in El Salvador: A Pattern of U.S. Complicity," *Covert Action Quarterly*, Summer 1990, reprinted in Third World Traveler, http://www.thirdworldtraveler.com/US_ThirdWorld/deathsquads_ElSal.html, accessed, February 10, 2018.

20   Nairn.

21   Nairn.

22   Nairn.

23   LaFeber, 177.

24   Victor Vaughn, "Cold War Killer: the Death Squads of El Salvador – Part 1", *The Red Phoenix*, August 12, 2012, https://theredphoenixapl.org/2012/08/12/cold-war-killer-file-the-death-squads-of-el-salvador-part-1/, accessed February 10, 2018.

25   President Ronald Reagan Address Before a Joint Session of Congress on the State of the Union, January 27, 1987, *The American Presidency Project*, http://www.presidency.ucsb.edu/ws/?pid=34430, accessed, February 10, 2018

26   LaFeber, 249.

27   "Oscar Romero Remembered on Centenary of His Birth," *Telesur*, August 15, 2017, https://www.telesurtv.net/english/news/Oscar-Romero-Remembered-on-Centenary-of-his-Birth-20170812-0015.html, accessed February 1, 2018.

28   John Dear, "Romero's Resurrection," *National Catholic Reporter*, March 16, 2010, https://www.ncronline.org/blogs/road-peace/romeros-resurrection, accessed February 9, 2018; The Center For Justice and Accountability "El Salvador: 12 Years of Civil War." *The Center For Justice and Accountability*, http://cja.org/where-we-work/el-salvador/, accessed February 10, 2018.

29   Raymond Bonner, "Bringing El Salvador Nun Killers to Justice," *Daily Beast*, November 9 2014, https://www.thedailybeast.com/bringing-el-salvador-nun-killers-to-justice, accessed, February 1, 2018.

30   Nina Lakhani, "Details of Plot to Murder Archbishop Oscar Romero Revealed in New Book," *The Guardian*, January 19, 2017, https://www.theguardian.com/world/2017/jan/19/archbishop-oscar-romero-murder-el-salvador-book, accessed February 8, 2018.

31   LaFeber, 250.

32   Linda Cooper and James Hodge, "Assassination Case Reopened in El Salvador," *National Catholic Reporter*, June 1, 2017.

33   Transcript: "School of the Americas: School of Assassins," Maryknoll World Productions (1995: 13 minutes), http://www.informationclearinghouse.info/article13436.htm, accessed February 10, 2018.

34   Warren Hoge, "Slaughter in Salvador: 200 Lost in Border Massacre," *New York Times*, June 8, 1981, http://www.nytimes.com/1981/06/08/world/slaughter-in-salvador-200-lost-in-border-massacre.html?pagewanted=all, accessed, January 29, 2018.

35   *Wikipedia*, List of Massacres in El Salvador, https://en.wikipedia.org/wiki/List_of_massacres_in_El_Salvador, accessed February 6, 2018.

36   Associated Press, "Salvadoran Troops Reported to Kill 100 Rebel Supporters," *New York Times*, November 18, 1983.

37   SOA Watch, "Notorious Graduates From El Salvador," http://www.soaw.org/about-the-soawhinsec/soawhinsec-grads/notorious-grads/238-notorious-graduates-from-el-salvador, accessed February 10, 2018.

38   SOA Watch.

39   Robert Pear, "Quayle Pressed Salvador for Inquiry on Massacre," *New York Times*, February 15, 1989, cited in William Blum, *Killing Hope: U.S. Military and CIA Interventions since WWII* (Monroe, Maine: Common Courage Press, 1995).

40   John Lamperti, "Enrique Alvarez: Presente!", *Truthout*, November 26, 2010, http://truth-out.org/archive/component/k2/item/93030:enrique-alvarez-presente, accessed February 20, 2018.

41   Bob Ford's Letter to the Editor, "Film Preserves Haig's Words on Murders," *New York Times*, April 12, 1993, http://www.nytimes.com/1993/04/12/opinion/l-film-preserves-haig-s-words-on-murders-563593.html, accessed February 10, 2018.

42   LaFeber, 277.

43   Mark Danner, "The Truth of El Mozote," *The New Yorker*, December 6, 1993, https://www.newyorker.com/magazine/1993/12/06/the-truth-of-el-mozote, accessed February 10, 2018.

44   James Goldston, *A Year of Reckonings: A Decade After the Assassination of*

Archbishop Romero (New York: Human Rights Watch, 1990), 225; Victor Vaughn, "Cold War Killer File: The Death Squads of El Salvador – Part 1", August 12, 2012, https://theredphoenixapl.org/2012/08/12/cold-war-killer-file-the-death-squads-of-el-salvador-part-1/, accessed February 20, 2018.

45 "Remembrance of a Massacre — El Mozote," Photographs by Susan Meiselas/ Magnum Photos Introduction by Raymond Bonner, *RetroReport.org*, https:// www.retroreport.org/multi-media/remembrance-of-a-massacre-el-mozote/, accessed February 1, 2018.

46 Bernard Weinraub, "Reagan Certifies Salvador For Aid," *New York Times*, July 28, 1982.

47 Richard Kreitner, "December 11, 1981: The Salvadoran Army Murders More Than 800 Civilians in El Mozote," *The Nation*, December 15, 2015.

48 CRS Report For Congress, "Central America: Major Trends in U.S. Foreign Assistance Fiscal 1978 to Fiscal 1990," (June 19, 1989), CRS-8.

49 Rand Institute Report, "American Counterinsurgency Doctrine and El Salvador," 1991, accessed January 28, 2018.

50 LaFeber, 316; *El Salvador - Overview of the history of international migration in El Salvador,* http://www.migracionoea.org/index.php/en/sicremi-en/282-el-salvador-1-si-ntesis-histo-rica-de-las-migracio-n-internacional-en-el-salvador-2.html, accessed February 14, 2018.

51 The Center For Justice and Accountability, citing "Statement of Representative Joe Moakley Chairman of the Speaker's Task Force on El Salvador", November 18, 1991, accessed February 10, 2018, see n22 above.

52 JP Sottile, "School of the Americas Morphs Into US Training Industrial Complex," *Truthout,* November 21, 2014.

53 Guy Gugliotta and Duglas Farah, "12 Years of Tortured Truth on El Salvador," *The Washington Post*, March 21, 1993, accessed February 5, 2018.

54 All information herein from: Robero Lovato, "El Salvador's Gang Violence: The Continuation of Civil War by Other Means, Poverty, the Politics of Impunity and the Long History of US-funded Oppression Are Creating a New Wave of Refugees," *The Nation*, June 8, 2015; Cora Currier and Natalie Keyssar, "El Salvador's Youth Trapped Between Gang Violence and Police Abuse," *The Intercept*, January 12, 2018; Hector Silva Avalos, "El Salvador Violence Rising Despite 'Extraordinary' Anti-Gang Measures," *Insight Crime*, October 3, 2017; Lisa Haugard, "El Salvador: Gang Violence and Growing Abuses by State Security Forces," *Latin American Working Group*, November 13, 2017; Dan Harris, Adam Degiderio, Jenna Millman, and Laura Effron, "In El Salvador, Gang Violence Becomes a Way of Life," *ABC News*, May 17, 2016; Robert Muggam, "It's Official: El Salvador is the Murder Capital of the World," *Los Angeles Times*, March 2, 2016. All sources accessed January 25–February 10, 2018.

VENEZUELA

FROM RELIABLE US OIL SUPPLIER TO EXTRAORDINARY THREAT

Alba Carioso

Geography, history and oil mark the relations between the United States and Venezuela. These three factors enable the "Americanization" of Venezuelan society and its structures, and enable a greater degree of cultural and economic connection than in any other Latin American nation.

Transformation of Venezuela into a reliable supplier

Although since 1878 Venezuela's oil was commercially exploited by the Venezuelan Petrolia del Táchira Company, that company's activities and markets had little influence on the subsequent development of the industry. At the end of the 19th century, Venezuela remained a mainly agricultural country, with coffee as the main export product.

Overwhelmed by the war and the decline in the price of coffee, the government of Cipriano Castro sought help from bankers, who denied it and were prosecuted. The ensuing conflict (1901-1903) aimed at the overthrow the government was headed by the banker Manuel Antonio Matos, supported by the transnational companies New York & Bermudez Company, asphalt dealership of Sucre and Orinoco Steamship Company, a concessionaire of maritime transport, which were facing Venezuelan government licensing and new taxes. These events forced the Castro government to suspend payments to the foreign debt. In December of 1902, the navies of Great Britain, Italy and Germany blocked Venezuelan shores, demanding the immediate payment of the debts, and attacking the coast, leading to numerous casualties.

With no fleet of his own, President Castro responded with a resounding proclamation: "The insolent plant of the Foreigner has profaned the sacred soil of the motherland!" With this call, a national popular self-defense movement was born, which faced the blockade of all the ports.

Across Latin America, news of the aggression resounded and the blockade was repudiated, while the United States disregarded its own Monroe Doctrine, arguing that its prohibitions would only apply to attacks by European powers interested in recovering American territories and colonizing them, but not in debt-related attacks. Argentina, on the other hand, issued a declaration signed by its Minister of Foreign Affairs, Luis María Drago, arguing the illegality of the violent collection of debts by the most important powers of the earth to the detriment of the sovereignty, stability and dignity of weak States. Later it would be known as Drago Doctrine.

The press and the liberal sectors of the US also condemned the aggression against Venezuela. The US proposed itself as mediator, Castro appointed Ambassador Bowen as representative to the invaders; the blockade was lifted at the signing of the Washington Protocol on February 13, 1903. As a consequence, North American influence in Latin America increased, clearly expressed in the Roosevelt Corollary of 1904, a substantial "amendment" to the Monroe Doctrine.

Theodore Roosevelt announced the Corollary on December 6, 1904, which decreed:

> All that this country desires is to see the neighboring countries stable, orderly, and prosperous. Any country whose people conduct them well can count upon our hearty friendship. If a nation shows that it knows how to act with reasonable efficiency and decency

in social and political matters, if it keeps order and pays its obligations, it need fear no interference from the United States. Chronic wrongdoing, or an impotence which results in a general loosening of the ties of civilized society, may in America, as elsewhere, ultimately require intervention by some civilized nation, and in the Western Hemisphere the adherence of the United States to the Monroe Doctrine may force the United States, however reluctantly, in flagrant cases of such wrongdoing or impotence, to the exercise of an international police power.

Latin America thus became a territory protected by the US and a favorable space for its commercial interests, in addition to the original purpose, to keep European hegemony from expanding into the hemisphere. Theodore Roosevelt enunciated the Politics of the Big Stick, and used to say: "I have always liked the proverb of West Africa: 'Speak softly and carry a big stick, and you will go far'." This policy was based on the so-called US Gunboat Diplomacy, due to the custom of sending a warship to the coasts of the countries that the US wanted to intimidate. At the beginning of the twentieth century, the US already thought that it could legitimately attack where and when the interests of its companies were threatened.

After the rise of Juan Vicente Gómez in 1908, Venezuela's international relations quickly improved, especially with the United States, which sent to the Venezuelan coasts, at the request of Gomez himself, the battleships *Maine*, *Des Moines*, *North Carolina* and *Dolphin*, to support his government—a virtual occupation of the country, during which the government desisted from three claims against US companies, and compensated them.

In 1914 a large amount of oil was discovered in Maracaibo Lake during the Gomez presidency, and Venezuela's external debt diminished promptly, by granting concessions to foreign oil companies. To obtain new income through taxes and mining fees, Gomez officially invited foreign investors to exploit Venezuelan resources (Edwin Lieuwen, 2016). This growth of the oil industry led to the strengthening of economic ties between the US and Venezuela.

On July 31, 1914, the commercial exploitation of oil began in Venezuela with the blowout of the Zumaque I well (technically known as Mene Grande 1, MG-1). From that moment, Venezuela would be a focus of interest for oil companies. During the Gómez period a good number of concessions were granted to Venezuelan businessmen, who soon sold them to foreign companies. The first positions were held starting in 1912 by Royal Dutch Shell. Standard Oil (the parent company of Creole Petroleum and today ExxonMobil) arrived in 1919, and Gulf Oil Corporation (Mene Grande Oil) entered in 1923. The three of them controlled 99% of the oil production in Venezuela.

During the First World War, oil became a vital strategic material, and the struggle between the oil companies became a struggle between countries. In Venezuela, the commercial war between England and the US for Venezuelan oil took place, and that competition was not always clean. In 1912, President William Howard Taft and his Secretary of State, Philander C. Knox, established Dollar Diplomacy based on the axiomatic principle that the United States government should extend all appropriate support abroad to every legitimate and beneficial American enterprise. The US exercised in Venezuela, through its minister Preston McGoodwin, strong pressure on the government to eliminate British concessions and secure their own. On April 25, 1927, President John Calvin Coolidge reiterated the US position that "... there is a distinct and binding obligation on the part of self-respecting governments to afford protection to the persons and property of their citizens, wherever they may be."

On June 30, 1920, the Venezuelan Congress approved the first Petroleum Law. Article 3 provided that the concession did not grant any property, but only a temporary right of exploitation (Edwin Lieuwen, 2016), taxes were increased, the concessions for exploration and exploitation were separated, and companies were held responsible for health of their workers. The US redoubled its pressure, and in 1922 an amendment was approved that included all its demands, affording greater privileges of concession and exploitation: low fees and leases, no drilling rules or expropriation rights, broad exemptions from customs duties and no cumbersome additional tax. There was no provision on refining and production of derivatives. The concessions continued to be given to Venezuelans close to the government who immediately transferred them to foreign companies. In 1920, 175 concessions were delivered and sold to US companies.

By 1928, Venezuela was the second largest oil producer and a world leader in its export, after the US. It also became the main supplier of the United States. Production doubled every year from 1922 to 1928; the companies increased production in fields that were easy to extract, and without any supervision from the Venezuelan State. Rómulo Betancourt (1956/2007) states in his book, *Venezuela, Política y Petróleo*:

> The millions applied by the companies to bribe venal officials and to increase the private money of Gomez came, by far, from the mouths of the wells. The returns on their investments were typical of a colonial country. The statement of the Minister of Development Gumersindo Torres—"Venezuela's oil laws are the best in the world for companies"— was absolutely true. The long terms of validity of the contracts, some of which reached half a century, the very low royalties, the absence of any state surveillance in the production processes and the defenselessness in which the Venezuelan worker was prevented from organizing and without labor laws that protected them, these were the many characteristics of the legal regime under which the exploitation of the Venezuelan subsoil was carried out.

As a byproduct of the extractive boom, the oil fields were surrounded by poverty belts. Food prices increased, crops declined, and as the industry developed, Venezuela imported more and more food. The relationship of the oil companies with the country was totally colonial; it was about extracting the wealth as quickly as possible. The names of two US magnates are indissolubly linked to this story: John D. Rockefeller of Standard Oil and Andrew Mellon, principal shareholder of the Gulf Oil Company, and then Treasurer of the US Government, under the administrations of Harding, Coolidge and Hoover.

Upon the death of Gómez, one of his generals, Eleazar López Contreras, assumed power. In December 1936, the first and longest oil strike broke out in which more than 10,000 workers participated for 47 days. It ended with López Contreras decree ordering the resumption of work, due to pressures from foreign companies on his government, which then adopted harsh measures against the agitators. This is how the ground was prepared for more friendly relations. "During the night of March 13, the oil executives met at the home of Alejandro Pietri, the Venezuelan lawyer for Standard Oil of New Jersey, to celebrate the exile of the 47 'radicals and communists' and the end of political freedom In Venezuela". The conquests of the strike were reduced to the increase of a daily bolívar (Venezuela's currency) in the wages of the workers and the commitment to place cold water with ice in the work centers. The insecure working conditions in the oil fields were maintained, and caused the fire at the lake community of Lagunillas on November 13, 1939, in which between 50 and 800 people died (according to differing figures from the companies and the press), in addition to two thousand injured. (Roberto López Sánchez, 2016)

In May of 1941, General Isaías Medina Angarita assumed the presidency. On December 7, 1941, the United States entered the Second World War, and the need to secure sources of oil for the allied cause became evident. The Venezuelan government's oil policy focused on obtaining benefits for the country; tariffs, taxes and production quotas were established, as well as extraction and refining obligations. In 1943, a new Petroleum Law was approved, which constituted a reform and increased the oil revenues of the Venezuelan State. However, the law did not establish improvements in the relations between companies and workers. By 1945 Standard Oil produced more oil than all the other companies combined. US entrepreneurs acquired growing control over trade in Venezuela, and not just over oil. Their companies provided more than half of Venezuelan imports, which quadrupled after the war.

On October 18, 1945, a civic-military coup d'état took place that evicted Isaías Medina Angarita from power, and established a Government Board composed of military and civilians. The US recognized the new government. In 1947, a document prepared by Mr. Pigott, an official of the Petroleum Division of the State Department, recommended special treatment for Venezuela because of its strategic oil importance. The document expressed concerns about activities of the Embassy of the USSR in Caracas and recommended improving relations between companies and the country, cooperating and giving better educational health support to their workers, so as to increase the link of the US's conservative unions with the Venezuelan trade unions, to ward off the phantom of communism. In this same report, Pigott warned:

> Unless the US reserves increase significantly in the
> near future, an unlikely possibility, any emergency

will find us short of two million barrels per day, with only Venezuela as a nearby alternative source with production of sufficient magnitude to fill the deficit. Hence, the importance of its industry and the tranquility of it is obvious. (cited by Margarita López Maya, 1996)

Venezuela drafted a new constitution, and the great writer, Rómulo Gallegos, was the first president elected by universal vote. Having been elected in 1947 for a period of five years, he governed for eight months, but was overthrown in November 1948. In his "Manifesto to the Nation," written by Gallegos himself before leaving the country, he said that the blow that deposed him *"smells like oil."* A few days before the so-called "fifty-fifty" had been approved, through which the benefits derived from the sale of oil would go from the 43/57 distribution in favor of the companies to a peer deal with the Nation. The overthrow opened the door to a period of military government, covering a decade, until 1958.

Venezuela was entering a process of progressive "Americanization" and its government's relations with the United States became more complex. A growing number of actors came between them: the oil companies and their workers (increasingly organized), political parties, chambers of commerce, entrepreneurs, adventurers, universities, intellectuals, social organizations. In 1968, Rodolfo Quintero defined the "culture of oil" as a culture of conquest that establishes standards and creates a new philosophy of life to adapt a society to the need to maintain it as a source of raw materials. That culture implied regarding all that was imposed by the oil companies as progress, maintaining the segregation of foreign workers and Venezuelans, and of industrial workers from the rest of the Venezuelan population.

Inferiority and incapacity of the natives were consolidated by segregration, driven discreetly by the creole elites. Foreigners received their salaries in dollars, lived in better houses and did not share their clubs and cinemas with Venezuelans. The vice president of Gulf, William T. Wallace, confirmed the meaning of segregation: "It is impossible to expect the native mind to adapt, after centuries of dirty and unhealthy life, to the accepted way of life in more developed countries" (quoted by Judith Ewell, 1996: 140). The American way of life was becoming more and more admired and emulated by many Venezuelans, especially in its consumerist aspects. The country became one of the most lucrative markets for American businessmen, while large masses remained in a state of poverty. The production of coffee and cocoa continued its downward trend, and the oil industry employed only 3% of the labor force.

A crucial event for business between both countries was the creation of the Venezuelan-American Chamber of Commerce (Venamcham) in 1950, by subsidiaries of US companies and some Venezuelan companies that depended on trade with the United States. In 1945, the *Caracas Journal*, later renamed *Daily Journal*, was founded by prominent members of the American business community in Venezuela to promote values and the culture of business. This medium afforded an intervention in public policy. For example, in 1955 it advised the Labor Minister to reject a proposal to cut the five-day work week, as it would raise the companies' costs and the Venezuelans "were not prepared for such comfort."

The Venezuelan government took pains to pave the way for the companies, while the American government spared no recognition and praise. In an international scenario dominated by the struggle of the United States against communism, the Venezuelan elite responded favorably and US officials highlighted Venezuela as an example for the region, for its political stability and economic growth.

The members of the Venezuelan elite participated with the Americans in clubs, neighborhood associations, Venamcham, the Venezuelan American Center, baseball teams, the YMCA, the Boy and Girl Scouts, charities and binational schools. The wealthy families began sending their children to study in the US. People like the Bottoms and the Coles, along with the Dale Carnegie courses, shaped the values and preferences of the executives and elites of Caracas. (Judith Ewell, 1996: 189). The oil multinationals were the most important companies in Venezuela; their influence was decisive both in the period of military government headed by Marcos Pérez Jiménez, and during the post-overthrow democracy after 1958. Some historians say that the US allowed the fall of Pérez Jiménez, because it was sure that the parties that would integrate the new government were similar.

The new president, Rómulo Betancourt (1959-1964), had a foreign policy based on the promotion of a hemispheric anti-dictatorship alliance, the defense of Venezuelan oil and the insistence on seeking multilateral solutions to regional problems through the mechanisms of the OAS (Organización de los Estados Americanos). On the other hand, Venezuela supported the program of the Alliance for Progress and the policy of confrontation towards Cuba, although it did not agree with a military invasion of the island. The Venezuelan conduct towards the United States in those years focused on obtaining the support of Washington for its internal affairs and was successful in this. There was American indifference to the successive wave of military coups in the region and despite the promulgation of the so-called Betancourt Doctrine, Venezuela was not threatened by a change of attitude towards Caracas by the White House. OPEC officially emerged on September 14, 1960, driven by downward price pressure, which was then felt in an inclement way.

The Venezuelan oil industry was nationalized on January 1, 1976, during the first presidency of Carlos Andrés Pérez. The state-owned company, Petróleos de Venezuela (PDVSA), was founded, which from then on reserved the rights of exploration and exploitation of deposits in the country. Between 1974 and 1976, tax revenues from oil revenues tripled, but at the same time external indebtedness increased due to the solvency guaranteed by the resources. Venezuela's share of oil income from exports between 1958 and 1985 was on average 93%. (Héctor Malavé Mata, 1987)

After the nationalization of the oil industry in 1976, PDVSA became something like a state within the state. Its Venezuelan executives, who had worked for years for international oil companies, shared their views, and maintained the same business ideology and the same links with their old headquarters (Carlos Mendoza Potellá, 2016). The multinationals were awarded millions in compensation for the 8 remaining years of operations, as well as contracts in marketing and technology that, except for details, assured the hitherto concessionaires control over the nascent national industry, and failed to create a new and efficient fiscal and regulatory regime, implementing instead disastrous development policies, characterized by poor planning and waste. This finally led, after 1989, to the Oil Opening Policy (or simply 'Opening'). Privatization was promoted at a forced pace, through internationalization, association agreements, strategic partnerships, outsourcing and the fortunately frustrated proposal to sell part of PDVSA's share capital. All this led Venezuela's oil policy towards re-privatization of the industry, and at the same time, towards the minimization of oil tax revenues.

From 1958 to 1999, Venezuela and the United States established relations which considered the Venezuelan case different from the rest of the Latin American countries, given the economic weight of oil and the stability of the political system. The friendly relations of the political and business elite with the US, and their cultural and economic dependence, the government's docility to the Washington lines, accompanied by an advantageous geographical proximity, kept Venezuela as a safe and strategic supplier in oil matters.

The local economic elite oriented its business towards the United States: the world trade of Venezuela was carried out 50% with the northern country, the imports that come from it revolve around 45%, the state oil company PDVSA invests in the USA and it establishes strategic alliances with American companies and a strong placement of private Venezuelan money in the banking of that country. Similarly, the Venezuelan military sector was trained and had an institutional culture with much influence from Washington, and the political sector maintained good relations with the American political elite. During this period, Venezuela was an exclusive democracy, with the agreed-upon conciliation of the elites of two parties. The Social Democratic Action (AD) and the social Christian COPEI (Committee of Independent Electoral Political Organization) shared power, alternating in the exercise of the government, and excluding the left parties. The oil rent was used to please the upper classes and create a clientelist model, which activated a mass consensus through a populist development model built on oil rent. The Punto Fijo Pact (1958) represented the agreement of the upper political crust that made possible the appropriation of the oil rent by the elites.

Breaking the illusion of stability

At the beginning of the 1980s, a strong economic crisis began. After many years of stability, in 1983 there was a great devaluation of the currency. The percentage of the poor population increased from 26% in 1975 to 66% in 1995. (Matías Riutort and María Orlando, 2001)

By 1988, the situation for the poor was dramatic, inflation was around 100%, there was a shortage and speculation with food, and the sector of the population with scarce resources did not even have enough to eat. When President Carlos Andrés Pérez in 1989 implemented a program of austerity and structural readjustment following IMF guidelines followed by an increase in transport prices, the accumulated discontent was transformed on February 27 into a popular rebellion, known as "El Caracazo," which is seen by a large part of the Venezuelan population and by many authors as a breaking point in the history of Venezuela. The unstoppable decline of the "puntofijista" system began.

In February and November of 1992 there were two civil-military rebellions, received with great sympathy by social movements and the impoverished population, without further explanations. The bipartisan political system was totally discredited in the eyes of the majority of the Venezuelan population. The rebellion led by Hugo Chávez on February 4, 1992 gained immediate affection and identification with its leaders, young officers who led the uprising. His speech did not speak of order, but of freedom, justice and the fight against marginalization.

At that time Ambassador Michael Skol warned that "any extra-constitutional action in Venezuela would be unacceptable to the United States." The pressure groups, the academic sector and the business sector insisted that for the United States it was preferable to "negotiate with a democratic government and not with a de facto government". In 1993, Caracas was visited by Undersecretary of State for Inter-American Affairs, Alexander Watson, who at a conference in Venancham said: "Maintaining Venezuela's brilliant democratic tradition is an indispensable prerequisite for normal relations between the United States and Venezuela". In 1996, President Clinton reiterated that ... "Venezuela is a bulwark of Latin American democracy. It is also our main supplier of oil and one of our main economic partners in the Hemisphere." In 1997, Venezuela became the foremost oil supplier of the United States.

Since the beginning of the '90s, PDVSA had been developing a process called Petroleum Opening, which involved association with international companies to develop several areas of the industry. PDVSA planned to increase production from 3.3 million barrels per day to 6 million for the year 2005 with the help of US companies, in the framework of operational contracts for the reactivation of marginal fields, and to do this in association with private companies to exploit deposits in the Orinoco Belt, under the scheme of shared profits, and the opening of the domestic market for fuels and other petroleum products. Thus, the strategic value of Venezuela for the United States was made greater.

But the need for redemption and social justice, strongly felt by the excluded majorities, which by the end of the 20th century represented more than two thirds of the Venezuelan population, was the magma in which the Bolivarian ideological process generated a movement and political action strongly against the dominant political class at the time. From that impetus, and with the appearance of Hugo Chávez, the people emerged as a political actor, as a subject that recognized itself. The key element has been the recognition of a popular "us" and a privileged or élite "them". It is assumed that there is a conflict between the powerful and weak, and the latter can then meet and recognize each other.

Luis Bonilla-Molina and Hayman El Troudi (2004) call the forces from which the process of the Bolivarian revolution is nourished as a historical current for change, an amplitude of political, social, cultural and even religious influences that nourish Bolivarianism. Chávez assumed not so much the role of giving a political line, but rather that of opening a political framework. New political subjects emerged: generated from the broad swath of the oppressed. The extraordinary revolutionary potential of Chavism derives from this multiplicity of subjects, which implies the multiplication of the battlegrounds of struggle, the diversity of strategies put in place to fight for the radical democratization of Venezuelan society, and the Bolivarian ability to mobilize to defend the revolutionary process.

1998, the first year of Chávez's term, was used to elaborate a new Constitution, which at the end of 1999 was accepted in a popular referendum with 72% of the votes. Starting in 2000, the Government began implementing social measures and restructuring the state oil company, PDVSA, to gain control of the most important source of financing, which was in fact acting as a transnational company, avoiding the delivery of resources to the State.

According to the Constitution of the Bolivarian Republic of Venezuela (1999), PDVSA cannot be privatized even partially. In addition, in 2001 the Organic Law on Hydrocarbons was approved, which allowed the increase of royalties or taxes to be paid to the State for the extraction of crude oil and, most importantly, fixed the mandatory participation of PDVSA in any operation with a minimum of 51%. All this was accompanied by a return to the active role of Venezuela in OPEC and through it in the oil market, restricting its flow and achieving a rise in prices. In this way, if "in 1998 the price of the barrel was at 11.2 dollars, in 1999 it increased to 14.3 dollars and in 2001 it reached 23.3 dollars. In the course of 6 years the price of a barrel of oil exceeded $100". (José Honorio Martínez, 2011)

Until then, relations between the US and Venezuela had not suffered apparent wear and tear. Beyond that the political projects of both countries seemed to go by different routes. Some of the foreign companies did not accept the increase of royalties and the majority participation of the State, although the new Constitution and Law of Hydrocarbons granted legal security and business possibilities. During its first years, the Chávez government assumed nationalist and independent positions, although in some cases it expressed its willingness to adapt to the interests of the United States. After the devastating floods of December 1999 on the Venezuelan coast, Chávez rejected the US offer to send engineers from the Navy Corps and bulldozers to repair the affected areas, and at the same time removed Defense Minister Raúl Salazar, who had accepted the proposal. (Steve Ellner, 2009)

Conversion of Venezuela into an Unusual and Extraordinary Threat

Almost from the beginning, the Bush administration hardened the United States' position toward the Chávez government by consistently criticizing its policies and positions, accusing it of destabilizing the region and increasing links to the drug trade. But it is in 2001 that the first public controversy arose with the then newly elected US President George W. Bush (from the Texas oil lobby).

After the attacks of September 11, 2001, Chavez's actions clashed with the "with us or against us" position assumed by Bush in his speech of September 20, 2001 on the fight against terrorism. The State Department characterized the televised appearance of Chávez, in which he showed photographs of the victims of the US bombing in Afghanistan, which he described as "a massacre of innocents" as completely inappropriate. In response to the incident, Washington temporarily withdrew its ambassador, Donna Hrinak. Subsequently, Secretary of State Colin Powell expressed doubts about Chavez's understanding of what a democratic system is. (Steve Ellner, 2009)

The United States began to give material support to the opposition. Between 2000 and 2001, Venezuela rose from tenth place to first among the largest recipients of NED funds in the region. The National Endowment for Democracy (NED) had been created in 1983, with a neoconservative agenda that prioritized the global struggle against communism over the democratic concepts of sovereignty and self-determination. The bitter opposition began to grow aggressively. The International Republican Institute (IRI), considered the international arm of the Republican Party of the United States, and one of the four "key groups" of the National Endowment for Democracy, had—as was recognized by its President George Folsom—intervened in the short-lived coup of 2002. In a press release celebrating the coup, he stated that: "The Institute has served as a bridge between the nation's political parties and all civil society groups to help Venezuelans build a new democratic future..." (Eva Golinger, 2005)

The United States gave its recognition to the government of Pedro Carmona Estanga, who briefly overthrew Chávez. After returning to power, Chávez claimed that a US plane, whose American registration numbers he had, had flown over and been in Venezuela at the air base on the island of La Orchila, where he had been held captive. He claimed there was evidence of US military involvement, with radar images indicating the presence of warships and aircraft in the territorial waters and airspace of Venezuela. US Senator Christopher Dodd called for an investigation in Congress, showing his concern over the presumption that Washington seemed to tolerate the removal of Mr. Chávez, but later concluded that "US officials have acted properly and have done nothing to encourage the coup of April against the president of Venezuela."

After the coup in 2002, the Venezuelan opposition continued to receive US support. By the end of 2002, the oil sabotage began, which consisted of a strike or paralysis of labor and of economic activities of a general and indefinite nature against the government of Venezuela of Hugo Chávez, promoted mainly by the Fedecámaras big bosses and seconded by the board of directors and high level workers of the largest payroll of the company, Petróleos de Venezuela (PDVSA). The strike was called on December 2, 2002 and lasted until the end of February 2003. In mid-2002, a group of active and retired military officers involved in the April coup spoke out openly against the government in Plaza Altamira, in the wealthy neighborhood east of Caracas; and for several months every day, for 24 hours, this square was the center of concentration of those who protested against the Chávez government. The paralysis climaxed on December 5, 2002 when practically all the list of executives and administrators left their work. Multiple acts of sabotage were carried out, such as stopping the refineries completely, anchoring an oil tanker in the navigation channel in Lake Maracaibo, destruction of equipment, but above all, sabotage of the electronic brain of PDVSA, managed by the company INTESA, constituted 60% by SAIC (Science Applications International Corporation), and 40% by PDVSA. SAIC counted among its directors former US military intelligence. Through INTESA, national storage, transportation and fuel distribution systems were paralyzed. Finally, relying on oil workers who did not join the strike, the government of President Chávez managed to regain control of PDVSA.

The harsh attacks by the Chávez government against the Bush administration began in 2003, as a reaction to Washington's interference during the previous two years, which broke with Clinton's more tolerant line. In 2003, Chávez began to use the term "imperialism" to describe the position of the United States. Chávez pointed to Washington as his main enemy, which eclipsed his internal adversaries and contrasted with the good relations of Venezuela with almost all the other governments of the world. The NED and its purported promotion of democracy served as a tool to infiltrate civil society. (Steve Ellner, 2009). In 2002, the Office of Initiatives for Transition (OTI), part of USAID, was created in the US Embassy. It worked there until 2011, when it moved to Miami; it is estimated that the OTI assigned five times more money to Venezuelan opposition organizations than the NED.

In 2004, the Recall Referendum took place, and President Chávez was victorious. That same year the Bolivarian Alternative for the Americas (ALBA) was created, which amplified the international influence of the Bolivarian Revolution. Then, the pressure of the US against the Venezuelan government become stronger. The researcher Edgardo Lander affirmed in 2004:

> In addition to the repeated "warnings" and denun-
> ciations made by the most representative officials
> of that government and support for the coup of
> 2002, the political and financial support to virtu-
> ally all the parties and social organizations that are
> part of the opposition has been systematic, and in-
> creased significantly after the defeat of the coup.
> In March 2004, General James T. Hill, Chief of
> the Southern Command of the United States, char-
> acterized the government of Venezuela as part of
> a "radical populism" that represents *a growing
> threat to the interests of the United States.*"

It was in 2003 that the Albert Einstein Institute, founded by Gene Sharp, touched ground in Venezuela for the first time. A trip made by Colonel Robert Helvey and another institute official, Chris Miller, took place in April 2003 for nine days in Venezuela.

The purpose of their consultations was to provide members of the Venezuelan opposition with the ability to develop a strategy based on soft-stroke techniques to "restore democracy" in Venezuela. According to the annual report of the Albert Einstein Institute, participants in the workshop included members of political parties and unions, NGO leaders and other activists and was sponsored by the Citizen Offensive organization. This workshop led to continuous contact with Venezuelans and new requests for consultations. Let us emphasize that AEI qualified President Chávez as authoritarian (The Albert Einstein Institute, Report on activities, 2000-2004). The nonviolent action, which applies against dictatorial governments, is described by Gene Sharp himself as a method of struggle that can be used for good actions and also for bad actions. It can produce powerful coercive effects and can force opponents to give up or destroy their power. The method describes nonviolent actions that must be carried out in stages that delegitimize and undermine the base of support of the governments, until finally they end up falling; these methods are qualified as "soft power". See also Galina Sapozhnikova (2018) about Sharp's methods.

In 2006, the student movement inspired and trained in the strategies of Gene Sharp, by Colonel Helvey and the young experts of OTPOR (Serbia), began to act openly, united by the symbolism of painting their hands white. Since 2005, it has been working within the universities with an agreement between USAID and the "Educando País" Foundation, whose objective was "the formation of student and youth leaders". From then on there would be a line of work from the US with the student movement "Manos Blancas"; according to the 2009 annual report on USAID activities in Venezuela, 32% of its multimillion-dollar funds were invested in student groups and youth linked with the opposition. "We have white hands and we are raising them towards peace," Freddy Guevara, one of the leaders of the movement, who ten years later, in 2017, would be the leader in driving violent actions, told BBC Mundo in 2007.

A fundamental milestone in relations between the US and Latin America was the IV Summit of the Americas in 2005 in Argentina. The clear intention of the bloc headed by the United States was to set concrete deadlines for the Free Trade Area of the Americas (FTAA) negotiations. Concretely and even only symbolicly, the reinstatement of this agreement would have meant a triumph for the objectives of the United States. The MERCOSUR countries, led by Venezuela, blocked the US initiative.

George Bush left Argentina empty-handed, while a massive People's Summit was taking place at the same time. In his speech, Chávez would reaffirm his commitment to the cause of the sovereignty of peoples against the empire. (Héctor de la Cueva, 2006)

In 2004, at the 3rd South American Summit of Presidents, the South American Community of Nations was created, which later became the Union of South American Nations: UNASUR, to form strategic plans of regional scope.

The enmity between Venezuela and the United States was shown in all its tension at the 2006 General Assembly of the United Nations in New York, a scenario in which Chávez expressed himself in these terms:

> .. the greatest threat that looms over our planet: the hegemonic pretension of the North American Imperialism puts at risk the very survival of the human species. ... This table where I must speak still smells like sulfur! Yesterday, ladies and gentlemen, from this rostrum, the President of the United States, whom I call "El Diablo", came here, speaking as the owner of the world. ... Wherever he looks he sees extremists. ... The imperialists see extremists everywhere. No, it is not that we are extremists, what is happening is that the world is awakening and we, the peoples, are rising up everywhere. (Chávez, Speech September 20, 2006 in UN Assembly).

In addition, he proposed the restructuring of the United Nations, the relocation of its headquarters to a southern country, and denounced US support for the 2002 coup and continued destabilization. These words catapulted him as an anti-imperialist spokesperson worldwide, earning him a greater ovation than Ernesto Guevara received for his speech in 1964.

Focused on the effort to promote a multipolar world, President Hugo Chávez developed a cooperative framework with Russia. Venezuela underlined the coinciding visions regarding the need to build a multipolar world, the reform of the UN and its Security Council, as well as fair trade, the creation of a new financial architecture and other issues, such as the fight against terrorism and drug trafficking, among others. The vision of common interests between Russia and Venezuela in the field of the use of energy resources and the stability of the oil market strengthened. In 2004, President Chávez signed the Energy Cooperation Agreement with Russia. The collaboration between the Russian oil company Gazprom and Venezuela has been ongoing since 2005. That year, the Russian gas consortium and state oil company Petróleos de Venezuela signed a memorandum of understanding for the exploration and exploitation of crude oil. Rosneft Oil Company has interests in five joint ventures with Petróleos de Venezuela, S.A. (PDVSA): PetroMonagas (40%), Petrovictoria (40%), Boquerón (26.67%); Petromiranda (32%) and Petroperijá (40%).

Russia and Venezuela signed their first technical-military cooperation agreement in May 2001, in Moscow, during one of the trips of President Hugo Chávez. The first contracts for the acquisition of Russian arms were made at the end of 2004. Since then, equipment for the Bolivarian Armed Forces has arrived in Venezuela, such as Kalashnikov machine guns, helicopters, Sukhoi fighters, anti-aircraft defense system units, and others. In 2006, the United States completed the ban on the sale and transfer of US military technology and weapons to Venezuela and most of the countries of the companies involved adhered to the US embargo. Given this circumstance, Chávez strengthened Venezuela's military ties with its new strategic allies: Russia, China, Belarus and Iran. In 2008, joint maneuvers between Russia and Venezuela took place. (Rocío San Miguel, 2016).

Relations between China and Venezuela have experienced a broad and rapid development in recent years, both economically and politically. The cooperation between China and Venezuela was developed as a plural collaboration, with energy as an axis, and extended to infrastructure, high technology, agriculture and other sectors, within the framework of intergovernmental cooperation, financed by banks or Chinese oil companies in the form of credit or investment. In 2000, the Economic and Technical Cooperation Agreement was signed. China granted large loans for the construction of infrastructure. The increased relationship with China caused great concern in Washington. Caracas supported the Chinese intention of creating an international currency that would put an end to the hegemony of the dollar, calling for the urgency of making changes in the prevailing financial system to make it more fair and inclusive.

China has become the second largest buyer of Venezuelan oil in the world. The Bolivarian Revolution has applied an oil policy model that seeks the international defense of oil prices, the strengthening of OPEC, new cooperation schemes with strategic allies and the diversification of markets with a vision towards the Asian market, specifically China and India. Between 2000 and 2016, there was a progressive decrease in the export of oil to the US (from 1 million 457 thousand barrels per day, to 796 thousand) and an increase in exports to China (from 5 thousand barrels per day in 2001, to 496 thousand). (Aymara Gerdel, 2018). In 2007, the China-Venezuela Joint Financing Fund was created for the development of large projects. In 2016, Venezuela was already China's foremost oil supplier, providing 5% of what China consumes.

In 2008, Venezuela expelled the US Ambassador, in solidarity with Bolivia, which had denounced Washington's interference in its internal affairs. In 2010, the Venezuelan Foreign Ministry withdrew the acceptance of Larry Palmer as ambassador and described as "unacceptable" his views on the internal affairs of the country. This happened after Palmer sent a message to the US Congress in which he said that the morale of the Venezuelan military was low and that it was necessary to investigate the presence of guerrillas from the Revolutionary Armed Forces of Colombia (FARC). Reciprocally, the US withdrew the visa of Venezuela's ambassador, Bernardo Álvarez. Since then, ambassadors have not been reappointed; instead in 2017 a Business Manager was appointed.

On March 5, 2013, President Hugo Chávez died after a two-year battle against cancer. A significant portion of the leadership and people are convinced that it was a murder, although confirming evidence has not been acquired. President Obama, in his note of condolence, pointed out that a new stage is opening for Venezuela, and called for a constructive relationship between the two countries. However, several congressmen expressed their relief at the death of the commander, wished the alliance of anti-US leftist leaders in South America was weakened, and expressed their hope that this would afford a democratic opportunity for Venezuela. On April 14, 2013, Venezuelans indeed exercised that democratic opportunity, electing Nicolás Maduro as President, and assuring Bolivarian continuity in power.

In January 2014, the Venezuelan opposition began a period of violent demonstrations to force the resignation of President Maduro, using a strategy called "La Salida." Streets were blocked, attacks were carried out on government offices and properties, on political parties, against the Subway, etc. The bulk of the protesters were young, mobilized by the above-mentioned student movement "Manos Blancas". In addition to the breakdown of peace and daily life, the 2014 protests left 43 dead and more than 800 injured. Opposition leader Leopoldo López was accused of public instigation of violent acts, and imprisoned.

On March 9, 2015, President Obama issued an Executive Order, which declared Venezuela an "unusual and extraordinary threat" to national security and US foreign policy, and imposed sanctions on seven officials. This document is a directive to "sanction" any citizen, including the President of the Bolivarian Republic, and the institutions of the Bolivarian Government and the State, according to the criteria of the US Treasury Secretary, in consultation with the Secretary of the Treasury. The sanctions process is effectively a sentence without a trial, because penalties can be applied by these two high officials, without their targets having any right to defense.

In 2017, the opposition began another series of violent protests, which lasted for more than two months, with a death toll of 142, and a significant number of injuries and destruction of state property and infrastructure. These actions come to an end when President Maduro called for a National Constituent Assembly, for which elections were held in July 2017. Then director of the CIA, Mike Pompeo, declared that he was working in coordination with the governments of Mexico and Colombia for a regime change in Venezuela. For his part, Rex Tillerson said: "We want it to be a peaceful change, which is always better than the alternative, a violent change."

While the hostile statements by Congress people and other US officials against Venezuela continue, the accusations of drug trafficking and pressure through the OAS followed the path opened by the executive order of Obama. President Donald Trump renewed it in 2017 and began further sanctions against officials and the financial transactions of the Venezuelan government, under which new debts with a maturity of more than 90 days from PDVSA are forbidden, and the assets of a significant number of Venezuelan officials are frozen, including those of President Maduro, the Minister of Defense, and the President of the Supreme Court of Justice, among others.

For the US, Venezuela has become one of the favorite enemies of the moment, viewed as a bad influence on other Latin American countries, challenging the hegemony of the US in Latin America and the Caribbean, and an inconvenient spearhead of Russia and China in the region.

And this is how a country in the Americas goes from being "a model of stability and democracy," to "an extraordinary threat to national security and foreign policy" of the United States.

Bibliographic references

Allard, Jean-Guy y Golinger, Eva. (2009) USAID, NED CIA LA AGRESIÓN PERMANENTE. Caracas: MINCI

Azzellini, Dario (2007) La Revolución Bolivariana: "o inventamos o erramos". Claves para leer el proceso de transformación social venezolano. In: Revista Herramienta N° 36, Octubre de 2007. Available in http://www.herramienta.com.ar/ Accessed: 27/3/2018.

Betancourt, Rómulo (2007) Venezuela, política y petróleo. 6 ed. Caracas: Academy of Political and Social Sciences and Andrés Bello Catholic University.

Bonilla-Molina, Luis/El Troudi, Haiman (2004): Historia de la Revolución Bolivariana. Caracas: MINCI

Chávez, Hugo (2006) Address to the General Assembly of the United Nations. New York, September 20th 2006. Available in http://www.panorama.com.ve/hugochavez/Discursos-memorables-Aqui-huele-a-azufre--20150720-0083.htm. Accessed: 3/4/2018

De la Cueva, Héctor (2006) Mar del Plata: El ALCA no pasó. Una victoria de la Cumbre de los Pueblos. En OSAL, Observatorio Social de América Latina (año VI no. 18 sep-dic 2005) Buenos Aires: CLACSO. Available in biblioteca.clacso.edu.ar/gsdl/collect/clacso/index/assoc/D3850.dir/7delaCueva.pdf. Accessed: 3/4/2018

Ellner, Steve. (2009) La política exterior del Gobierno de Chávez: La retórica chavista y los asuntos sustanciales. Venezuelan Journal of Economics and Social Sciences, Caracas, v. 15, n. 1, p. 115-132, April 2009 .

Ewell, Judith (1998) Venezuela y los Estados Unidos: desde el hemisferio de Monroe al imperio de petróleo. Caracas: Andrés Bello Catholic University.

Gerdel, Aymara (2018) Venezuela: ¿Alianza o Amenaza? Galicia: Observatory of Chinese policy.

Golinger, Eva (2005) El código Chávez Descifrando la intervención de Estados Unidos en Venezuela. Caracas: Monte Avila Editores.

Lander, Edgardo (2004) Venezuela: proceso de cambio, referéndum revocatorio y amenazas internacionales. En OSAL Nª 13. Buenos Aires: CLACSO.

Lieuwen, Edwin (2016) Petróleo en Venezuela, una historia. Caracas: Editorial El perro y la rana.

López Maya, Margarita (1996) EE.UU. en Venezuela, 1945-1948: revelaciones de los archivos estadounidenses. Caracas: UCV-CDCH

López Sánchez, Roberto; Paredes Valecillos, Lorelli y Moreno, Kerli (2016) La Industria Petrolera en Venezuela: Relaciones de Trabajo y Conciencia de Clase (1914-2015) En Revista Cuadernos Latinoamericanos, Vol. 28, N° 50, de la Universidad del Zulia. Centro Experimental de Estudios Latinoamericanos, CEELA. Julio-Diciembre/2016. Maracaibo (Venezuela). http://www.produccioncientifica.luz.edu.ve/index.php/cuadernos/article/view/22224

Malavé Mata, Héctor (1987) Los extravíos del poder. Caracas: Universidad Central de Venezuela.

Malavé, José (2009) Una ilusión de modernidad. Los negocios de Estados Unidos en Venezuela durante la primera mitad del siglo veinte. Caracas: Institute of Advanced Management Studies (IAMS).

Martínez, José Honorio (2011) La política petrolera del gobierno Chávez o la redefinición del estado ante la globalización neoliberal. En Historia Actual On Line, Núm. 24 (Invierno, 2011), 7-15. México: UNAM.

Mendoza Potellá, Carlos (2016) Vigencia del nacionalismo petrolero. Dos ensayos. Caracas: Fundación Editorial El perro y la rana.

Quintero, Rodolfo (1968) La cultura del petróleo. Ensayo sobre estilos de vida de grupos sociales de Venezuela. Caracas: Fundación Editorial El perro y la rana, 2018 (digital).

Riutort, Matías y Orlando, María B. (2001) Las cifras de pobreza en Venezuela. IIES. UCAB. Caracas.

Roosevelt, Theodoro. El corolario Roosevelt a la Doctrina Monroe, 6 de diciembre de 1904. En Rodríguez, M. (2002). Memorias de América Latina. Venezuela: Humanities and Education Editorial Fund.

San Miguel, Rocío (2016) Acuerdos de cooperación militar 2005-2016. Caracas: Asociación Civil Control Ciudadano para la Seguridad, la Defensa y la Fuerza Armada Nacional. Available in: controlciudadano.org Accessed: 3/4/2018.

Sapozhnikova, Galina (2018) The Lithuanian Conspiracy and the Soviet Collapse: Investigation into a Political Demolition. Available at http://www.claritypress.com/Sapozhnikova.html.

The Albert Einstein Institution, Report on activities, 2000-2004. Available at https://www.aeinstein.org/wp-content/uploads/2014/04/2000-04rpt.pdf. Accessed: 2/4/2018.

Vázquez Puente, Unai (2013) Las relaciones entre Estados Unidos y la República Bolivariana de Venezuela: de la dependencia mutua a la emancipación. En Trabajos y Ensayos Nª 17, Julio de 2013. Departamento de Derecho Internacional Público. Universidad del País Vasco.

PUERTO RICO

"SH*THOLING" A US COLONY BEFORE AND AFTER HURRICANE MARIA

Maribel Aponte-García

Introduction

Last year, when hurricanes hit the Greater and Lesser Antilles, as well as Mexico and the state of Florida, unsustainable capitalism and climate change exacerbated poverty and redefined inequalities (those with or without water, gas generators, adequate housing); interrupted the supply chains of basic foods and petroleum products on which the logistics of distribution depend; destroyed the productive multi-sectorial ecosystem around tourism and fishing; razed new vulnerable social sectors; and unleashed waves of climate change and environmental refugees. The disaster also reordered the priorities of daily life and heightened community resilience and solidarity.[1]

This time the atmospheric phenomena of Irma and Maria impacted several Antilles that share a particularity, being colonies or overseas territories of diverse empires: Puerto Rico and the Virgin Islands (St. Thomas, St. John and St. Croix) of the USA; Saint Martin of

Holland and France. Independent islands such as Antigua and Barbuda, Dominica and Cuba were also affected.[2]

Puerto Rico, the smallest of the Greater Antilles located in the Caribbean Sea, has been a US colony since 1898. But it is neither the only nor the last colony, since in the Caribbean there are about twenty colonies. However, it is an exception worldwide because it is the only colony with a population of around 8 million US citizens, of which more than half reside in the US. Also, because in 2016 it became the first-ever bankruptcy case of a U.S. territory (through a 2016 law that created a process akin to Chapter 9 municipal bankruptcy of the US), as will be explained below.

Hurricane Maria hit Puerto Rico on September 20, 2017 as a category 4 phenomenon (with some areas hit with category 5 winds). The communications system, which had been privatized, and the electric service system completely collapsed, leaving the private sector paralyzed and the government unable to coordinate the logistics of water, food, and petroleum products distribution. When the port of Jacksonville in Florida wasn't able to operate after Irma, it became clear that the dependence on imports threatened the supply chains of these products in PR. A rapid transition to solar energy and food sovereignty cannot be postponed.[3]

Waves of climate change and environmental refugees impacted both the independent countries and the colonies. The island of Barbuda was left uninhabited after the population residing there had to move to Antigua. Similarly, thousands of Puerto Ricans have migrated to the US, most noticeably elderly people who need health care in the post-hurricane situation and people who have been left homeless or without work due to the impact on the economic system but who have relatives in the USA. In the case of San Martin and the Virgin Islands, Puerto Ricans (after Irma's scourge and before Maria's) navigated in small boats to rescue people in neighboring islands and the PR government temporarily relocated refugees to San Juan.[4]

In the colonies, the disaster generated outcries for help from the metropolitan government and the solidarity of the diaspora as a solution to the crisis. The crisis showed that the government of PR did not have a plan to deal with these disasters and the lack of it culminated in a cry of *Gringo, Come Home!* But when the US government took over the distribution and logistics operations, it led to a new process of pseudo-militarization. The help that Cuba and Venezuela honorably offered was rejected by the US government.[5]

The colonial government placed the axis of reconstruction in federal aid and in new loans, despite the situation of colonial bankruptcy that PR faces with a present debt of US $72 billion.[6] This must be understood within the historical and political context of Puerto Rico's shattering in 2016 by bankruptcy and its consequences. In the aftermath of Maria, the political economy of how matters were run in PR was dramatically signaling that the Island was not a priority for the US.

That came as a crude reality to many on the Island. A brief note is in order to enable an understanding of why the crisis and Maria are restructuring the political economy of Puerto Rico.

Until 1948, Puerto Rico was run by a governor designated and imposed by the US. The Puerto Rican flag was prohibited under the Gag Law (*Ley de la Mordaza*) in the 1950's, and displaying the Puerto Rican flag or campaigning for independence was made illegal. Through the years, opposition leaders were assassinated (Pedro Albizu Campos, Filiberto Ojeda) or incarcerated (Óscar López Rivera, Rafael Cancel Miranda and Lolita Lebrón, among others). People were politically persecuted (*the carpeteo*) and even massacred at political events, such as the Ponce Massacre (1937); ambushed and killed as in Cerro Maravilla (1978); and killed by Navy bombs as in Vieques (1999). Recent legislation (against constitutional rights) threatens to criminalize public protests again.

During the 1950s and until the seventies, the pro-colonial Popular Democratic Party (PPD) dominated the political scene. In 1952, the *Estado Libre Asociado* was created as a Commonwealth. This turned out to be a misnomer because it made the island neither a sovereign state (*Estado*), nor a free (*Libre*) or freely associated (*Asociado*) nation. But for many party followers, this imagery remained dominant until the 2016 Sánchez Judicial decision of the Supreme Court of the United States held that PR did not constitute a "sovereign" state (for double jeopardy purposes).[7] This case highlighted what some politicians had never explicitly acknowledged: that Puerto Rico was in actuality a colony of the US.

During the seventies, the newly founded (1967) pro-statehood New Progressive Party (PNP) claimed political space and both parties have since taken turns at governing the Island, i.e. managing the colony. Independence parties were strong in the fifties with the Nationalist Party and the Independence Party gaining strength for several decades. At present, neither independence parties have significant power or following, especially the Nationalist Party, which has only a few members still active. The Independence Party has not been able to make its membership grow significantly but still participates in elections. Independence groups also include non-electoral organizations, such as *Movimiento Independentista Nacional Hostosiano, and Movimiento Unión Soberanista,* among others.

This creates a situation that permeates almost every aspect of life in Puerto Rico. As the two "dominant" political parties often switch power every four-year election cycle, people seek political favors in order to secure economic positions and gain advantages depending on who is in power. Thus, everything becomes politicized. Examples of this are government offices where directors are frequently designated based not on merit but on political connections. The public university is also affected by this because every four years the administration might change if these two political parties switch turns at power. This generates a spiraling process of people stepping up and down that lasts usually 1-2 years and disrupts many aspects of academic life.

What Hurricane Maria made evident is who really holds power in the colony. To some of us this has always been evident, but it hasn't been for politicians and people in general who belonged to the two dominant political parties. It has also made many people realize that only by cultivating sustainable sovereignty in food, energy and finance and strengthening international and Caribbean solidarity will we find the resilience that this age of climate change forces us to undertake.[8]

The Collapse of the Development Model[9]

Until the 1990s, four important traits distinguished Puerto Rico (PR) as a United States colony in the Caribbean and Latin American region: 1) duty-free trade with the US; 2) subjugation to the imposition of the Jones Act requiring transport of maritime trade only on US- flagged vessels, known as the Cabotage Laws; 3) US federal tax incentives (Section 936 of the Internal Revenue Code) that until 2006 allowed U.S. corporations to repatriate profits without paying taxes in the US; and 4) an education system with tertiary education rates and public universities' rankings among the highest in the region.[10]

This landscape changed dramatically after 2000, as the US extended PR's preferred terms of trade to other Latin American and Caribbean countries, leaving PR without its prioritized status. Open regionalist schemes based on the attraction of foreign investment, capital flight, production for export and low wage employment, mirrored PR's model and characterized US policies in the region during the 1990s neoliberalism. Among the problem areas of this model are: capital flight, negative trade balances, migration, debt, food insecurity and problematic issues around employment, poverty and unequal income distribution.[11]

Regional alternative schemes, identified as new strategic regionalism or post-hegemonic regionalism, grew significantly in the post-2000 period. The new regionalism included the Bolivarian Alliance-Treaty of the Peoples, the Union of South American Nations (UNASUR), the Community of Latin American and Caribbean States (CELAC) and a series of sectorial/industrial agreements such as Petrocaribe, the energy integration agreement promoted by Venezuela where 18 Caribbean members participated (but not Puerto Rico). These alternative schemes marked a departure from U.S.-controlled agreements but only sovereign countries were able to join. These alternative schemes promoted food, energy and financial sovereignty from US multinational corporations.[12]

This left colonial Puerto Rico in a complex situation. Puerto Rico neither adapted to the changing scenario of open regionalism nor integrated into alternative schemes, and still worst, it remained attached to its existing economic development model. As other countries gained what had distinguished PR earlier on—duty free trade with the US—the island lost an important competitive advantage while continuing to be constrained by the Jones Act and the Cabotage Laws. The Jones Act prohibits direct or indirect transportation of cargo between a foreign port, and points in the United States which are subject to coastwise laws, in vessels that are not: (1) built in the United States (2) documented under the laws of the United States, and (3) owned by citizens of the United States (Santos, 1997: 5). These laws impose cumbersome costs on Puerto Rico that affect its competitive position and increase prices for goods. The elimination or moratorium of the Cabotage Laws has been proposed as an alternative many times since it would encourage local businesses to internationalize and export their products by lowering marketing and transportation costs.[13]

Congress repealed Section 936 of the Internal Revenue Code in 1996 and ordered a ten-year phase-out period. This phase-out generated a contraction of Puerto Rico's economy after 2006, as many MNCs divested, increasing unemployment and migration (with over 300,000 persons migrating to the U.S. after 2009, even before Hurricane Maria hit).[14]

Tertiary education remained important but wasn't heralded as the new focus of a development strategy. The University of Puerto Rico, the island's top university system comprised of eleven campuses, should play a pivotal role in generating alternative development models because this is the only positive characteristic still distinguishing the Island in the region. According to Scimago's Institutions Ranking for 2016, the UPR is the only Puerto Rican institution that achieved a top 13th rank in Latin America and 503th internationally, among 5,147 institutions.[15]

While advocating the abandonment of the "development mandate" in the WTO, President Donald Trump is inclined towards protectionism and bilateral negotiations under the motto of "Make America Great Again". The protectionist stance favors renegotiation and conversion of regional to bilateral agreements. This is clearly manifested in the renegotiation of the North American Free Trade Agreement (NAFTA), a regional agreement among the United States, Mexico and Canada, implemented in 1994. The following issues stand out in the renegotiation: greater access to markets for agriculture; greater investments and intellectual property objectives; and increases in the local content of certain products.[16] Once NAFTA is renegotiated, it is expected that the Free Trade Agreement of Central America-Dominican Republic (CAFTA-DR) will enter the Trump administration window. Among the possible areas of renegotiation are those of e-commerce and intellectual property rights, areas that are discussed in the rounds of the WTO.[17]

In Puerto Rico, some pro-statehood politicians thought that these moves could be beneficial because they considered that the Island was part of "Trump's America". But not even the American colonies are saved from the Trumpian attack of "Make America Great Again". Recently, the US government approved tax reform that includes an excise tax on goods produced by the offshore subsidiaries of US companies. The repercussion of this measure would encourage the relocation to the US of some companies established on the Island, generating greater disinvestment and unemployment in Puerto Rico. Although diverse stakeholders lobbied in Washington so that exclusions for Puerto Rico be introduced, their plight was not taken into consideration.

Vulture Funds in a Colonial Context[18]

Puerto Rico shares many problems with the countries of the region. Among these are the vulture funds; the uncertain outlook under Donald Trump's presidency; and the attack on social spending, particularly education, as we consider next.

The Island is burdened with a debt of 72 billion US dollars. This debt is called public debt and not sovereign debt due to the colonial condition of Puerto Rico. The traditional bipartisan leadership—one favoring a colonial stance and the other pro-statehood—that has administered the colony for decades, both indebted the country while they had access to capital markets. The socioeconomic model was exhausted, recession worsened, and the financial options of Puerto Rico were disappearing. The government could no longer resort to debt issuance because the classification of its financial instruments was degraded (almost to junk category) in the capital markets.

Then the country found itself at a crossroads never experienced before. As a colony, it could not access loans from international financial institutions such as the International Monetary Fund or the New Financial Architecture structure built by New Regionalism. But neither could it declare bankruptcy because as a colony, the United States denied the government of the Island that alternative. The decision of the First Circuit Court of Appeals in Boston on *Puerto Rico v. Franklin California Tax-Free Trust* of July 6, 2015, held that under Chapter 9 of the Federal Bankruptcy Law, Puerto Rico cannot declare bankruptcy because it is not a state.

Of the total debt of 72 billion, it is estimated that at least half can be claimed to be unconstitutional and/or illegal for three possible reasons. The Constitution of Puerto Rico:

1) prohibits the government from borrowing to cover budget deficits, and it is estimated that up to $30 billion may fall into this category;

2) states that the debt service cannot exceed 15% of the central government's average domestic revenue (though for the two fiscal years preceding the debt issued[19] this limit has been exceeded); and

3) establishes that Puerto Rico can not issue any debt for more than 30 years, when in practice this has been done by refinancing debt.

Months before Donald Trump was elected president, in June 2016, the US Congress enacted the Puerto Rico Oversight, Management, and Economic Stability Act (PROMESA, PL 1140187), a US federal law that established a process to restructure the public debt of the Island's government and a federal fiscal control board to "oversee" the country until its "fiscal crisis stabilizes," (read: until the vulture funds manage to collect their debt). PROMESA and the Fiscal Oversight Board highlight the collapse of the colonial development model. The members of the Board were appointed by Barack Obama and their power is above that of the legislature and the governor of Puerto Rico.

The Fiscal Control Board has asked the PR government for a balanced budget for 2019 and the restoration of access to capital markets. The colonial structural adjustment focused on five main areas:

1) improvements in revenues;
2) efficiency and government downsizing;
3) reduced spending on health care;
4) drastic cuts to higher education; and
5) pension reform.

The government must achieve savings of one billion dollars in health, and a reduction of $300 million in the public university's budget, among others. Ricardo Rosselló, newly elected governor in November 2016 who favors annexionism (statehood), was required to present a fiscal plan by March 31, 2017 in accordance with these requirements.

In his first weeks as governor, Rosselló established several neoliberal measures that sought to guarantee debt payment to vulture funds at the expense of social spending and workers. Among these, the following stand out: a labor reform that reduces the benefits and rights of workers; changes to the Criminal Code that penalize social protest; and an attack against education, requiring the public university to cut its budget by more than $300 million—despite the fact that the government then owed the public university more than $400 million dollars and that the institution had already significantly cut its spending in recent years.

Although it attacks workers and education, the government does not question the unconstitutionality of the debt or fight its default. In 2015, a Commission for the Comprehensive Audit of Public Credit was created (Law 97). Rosselló, son of one of the governors who increased the debt in the past, dismissed members of the Commission and aims to eliminate the budget allocated to it, a clear effort to derail the process of citizen auditing to clear the way for payment to the vulture funds. Vulture funds do not favor the audit of the debt because they might then risk not collecting their money. In reaction, a petition was created that gathered more than 100,000 signatures of citizens demanding both auditing the debt and reinstating Commission members.

What has Donald Trump said about the situation confronting

Puerto Rico? During the election campaign, he said that Puerto Rico had to solve its financial problem and define its political status. Afterwards, reminding the island of its debt to Wall Street during his visit to Puerto Rico on October 3, after Hurricane Maria, he said "I hate to tell you, Puerto Rico, but you have thrown our budget a little out of control, because we have spent a lot of money in Puerto Rico and that's fine, we have saved many lives".

Still, the pro-statehood party in power bets on statehood as a way out of the crisis. But it is almost unimaginable that a bankrupt colony would be annexed to the US empire. Instead, we face, as a colony in bankruptcy, a program of structural adjustment dictated by a colonial junta.

On May 5, 2017, Judge Laura Taylor Swain was appointed to preside over the bankruptcy of Puerto Rico. *USA Today* reported, "She will have significant sway over the first-ever bankruptcy of a U.S. territory, which was made possible through a 2016 law that created a legal process akin to Chapter 9 municipal bankruptcy."[20] Judge Swain has already ruled on some important matters. Among these: the dismissal of a case filed by a bond insurer, that "threw cold water on bondholders' hopes of boosting their claims by challenging the island's fiscal plan;"[21] and denying a grant to the Puerto Rico Electric Power Authority (PREPA) of a $1 billion loan, but later approving a $300 million loan petition. Taylor Swain added that the commonwealth should not have a significant priority as it concerns payment of other creditors. Loan terms should not preclude bondholders or the court from participating.[22]

Judge Swain's decision on PREPA is particularly important at present. Five months after Hurricane Maria, the government claims that 85% of customers have their electric service restored, but these numbers are shaky and unreliable. PREPA has been plagued by inefficiencies, scandals, and is practically bankrupt. The government has announced its privatization. Furthermore, on March 5, 2018, the government, in a clear abuse of power, has even "threatened" to impose a tax on citizens if we opt for solar power. It seems that as PREPA loses its customers to migration and solar energy, the government can only think of imposing more taxes on an already burdened and impoverished population.

Since its formation in the 1940s, the Fluvial Sources Authority (the former name of PREPA) was a vital corporation for the industrial and social development of Puerto Rico. At present, PREPA faces a process of restructuring its debt (to respond to a classification by the credit fund according to Moody's Investors Service, reflecting the possibility that PREPA cannot fulfill its payments or carry out its plan to convert its "generating" plants to natural gas. In addition to the financial crisis it faces, PREPA is in breach of the provisions of Law 83 of 2010, which requires that 12 percent of the energy used in the country be renewable by 2015.

PREPA is bankrupt. Some mayors of the 78 municipalities have established local town Recovery Authorities and recruited retired certified electricians, some of whom once worked with PREPA. As months go by, the mayors have been moved to demand answers, but the channels of authority are disrupted and nobody seems to know what's happening or who's in charge. Even the rapper-philanthropist Akon tried to help Puerto Rico but the US Government stopped him from restoring power on the Island after he presented a plan to restore electricity in under 30 days. When his proposal was rejected, Akon stated: "It's politics, propaganda, and special interests." "They didn't care about the people. If that was the case, they would've allowed us to go in and just provide the solution. But, I think it was bigger than 'numbers' at that point."[23]

The Whitefish-Cobra scandal plunged Puerto Rico government's credibility further. In the aftermath of Hurricane Maria, instead of activating state and local protocols to manage the electrical system's collapse, and "entering into the mutual-aid agreements usually favored by utility companies, which allow them to contract with other utility companies in other states for rebuilding services,"[24] the government issued expensive contracts to two US companies –Whitefish Energy and Cobra Acquisitions. "On October 2, PREPA granted Whitefish Energy, a small power company based in Whitefish, Montana, a $300 million contract to rebuild Puerto Rico's power lines. That contract, which is now the subject of multiple federal inquiries, has only opened the door to broader scrutiny of PREPA, including a contract with another entity, Cobra Acquisitions, which was hired to repair power lines but has scarce experience in disaster cleanup."[25] Additional questioning concerning the contracting review process, including the exact involvement of FEMA in contracts paid out with its funds, is also part of federal inquiries.

"PREPA has defended the Whitefish Energy contract by noting that this company was the only bidder that didn't require a down payment, and would handle its own logistics. PREPA is bankrupt and $9 billion in debt, and other better-established companies required significant down payments in order to offset the risk that PREPA might not be able to pay off contract work. While federal entities have yet to come to conclusions in their inquiries into Whitefish's involvement in rebuilding Puerto

Rico's grid, the probe has already begun to broaden."[26] The federally-mandated oversight board has also launched its own inquiry into the Whitefish deal, and has used the fallout as a reason for installing an emergency manager for PREPA.[27]

Congress and President Trump approved a $4.7 billion Community Disaster Loan for Puerto Rico in November 2017 that included money for the central government, its authorities, and its municipalities. More than five months after Maria Puerto Rico has received none of this money; critics state that the Whitefish Cobra scandal stalled channeling of federal funds toward the Island; while Roselló seeks help from Congressional leaders to deal with the U.S. Treasury, which he says is blocking a hurricane disaster loan.[28]

Puerto Rico's economy faces a hard road ahead. "The latest indicators suggest the decline in real gross national product (GNP) for 2017-18 could be close to double digits. The government's most recent revised fiscal plan painted a bleak picture of Puerto Rico struggling to jumpstart an ailing economy that was wounded further still after suffering one of its worst natural disasters in a century. Puerto Rico has requested $94.4 billion in Federal Disaster Relief Assistance, but its projections assume the island will get $35.3 billion. While the previous 10-year fiscal plan, issued in March of last year, set aside some $3.9 billion to pay the island's creditors across five years, or an average of about $787 million annually, the new plan, revised after the hurricane, contains no funds to pay creditors. Now, Gov. Ricardo Roselló is saying the government will wait for the bankruptcy proceedings enabled by the Puerto Rico Oversight, Management & Economic Stability Act (Promesa) to be completed to determine debt repayment. In addition to disaster relief assistance, Puerto Rico requires external liquidity support to finance the gap until fiscal measures are fully implemented, according to fiscal plan numbers."[29]

Post-Hurricane Conditions and Social Consequences

Post-hurricane social conditions and consequences have proved difficult. Among these, migration and food insecurity are emphasized.

Migration has served as an "escape valve" and a "revolving door" since the 1950s.

Hurricane Maria made a bad situation intolerable.

The Center for Puerto Rican Studies at Hunter

College has estimated that between 2017 and 2019, Puerto Rico could lose up to 470,335 residents, or 14% of its population. These projections were quickly superseded as over 300,000 Puerto Ricans landed in Florida after the hurricane— over twice the number of Cubans who arrived in Florida during the Mariel boatlift in 1980. The out-migration totals since Hurricane Maria exceed the number that left the island during the entire previous decade of economic stagnation and recession.[30]

Puerto Rico imports 85% of its daily food consumption due to neglect of the island's farm sector and increased urban development.[31]

As of mid-October, with continuing shortages of clean water, food, power, and electricity in the aftermath of the hurricanes, Bread for the World Institute believes that about 80 percent of the population, regardless of income, suffers from food insecurity. Aid delivery has been slow so far. One reason is that, because of the Jones Act, supplies imported by sea must originate from or be shipped through the continental United States. This lengthens the time it takes for supplies to arrive and increases prices. But in an emergency such as this, there is simply not enough time or money to comply with such restrictions. More flexibility is essential in order to spare people from hunger and other needless suffering. Hurricane Irma (and Maria) destroyed the Island's agriculture and disrupted food supply chains. Moreover, for some weeks, sea transportation was paralyzed and docks were unable to distribute much need supplies. Water, gas and food were scarce. As the communications and electrical system also collapsed, chaos ensued to obtain basic goods and services. Water system recovered faster, although there are areas still without water supply.[32]

In the United States, and also in Puerto Rico, the government's response to address food insecurity is articulated through the fifteen programs administered by the Food and Nutrition Services Program of the United States Department of Agriculture. Among these programs, the largest are the Nutrition Assistance Program (PAN), the School Lunch Program, and the Special Nutritional Supplement Program for Women, Infants and Children (WIC), which stands for Women, Infants and Children). The help provided by these programs does not free households from food insecurity. In Puerto Rico there is a Food Safety Law (Act No. 133 of 2008) and it recognizes as a matter of food security the promotion, development, promotion and subsistence of the agriculture of the country, in all its meanings. Yet, it has not been possible to prove that specific measures have been implemented to comply with the law.

The U.S. Department of Agriculture (USDA) has made efforts to address the nutrition needs of Puerto Rican residents affected by Hurricanes Irma and Maria. As of September 29th, 40,296 cases of USDA Food have been used by volunteer organizations to feed residents in Puerto Rico congregated settings and shelters. Puerto Rico has also been approved to operate the Disaster Household Distribution program; and the Federal Emergency Management Agency (FEMA) has provided millions of meals and millions of liters of water to the people of Puerto Rico. Additional meals and water continue to arrive to the islands regularly via air and sea. Since day one, USDA has worked hand in hand with FEMA and will continue to support emergency feeding centers.[33] However, some of the criticisms have been directed at FEMA especially regarding the distribution of roof toldos which it has taken months to make available to the population.

How Proposed Alternatives Face Systematic Rejection

A matter of consensus in the United States and the island is that Puerto Rico lacks a development strategy and without it, the exit from the crisis is unfeasible. In Puerto Rico, alternatives have been proposed yet these are ignored by mainstream political actors and institutions. Important components of an alternative and sustainable development model are food, energy and financial sovereignty.[34] By way of conclusion, some initiatives and suggestions are outlined.

Among these, Casa Pueblo must be emphasized. Casa Pueblo

originated as a cultural project against proposed open mining in Adjuntas and grew to become a natural reserve, Bosque Modelo, that encompasses an extension of 390,000 cuerdas[35] throughout 31 municipalities. Engineer and founder Alexis Massol is a winner of the Goldman Award (also known as the Environmental Nobel Prize). In the post-María context, Casa Pueblo has led a solar energy campaign installing solar energy in homes (in coordination with the diaspora and several foundations) and acquiring and distributing solar bulbs and refrigerators. Calling for a solar revolution, their campaign is a real alternative for people most affected by the hurricane and unattended by the government. But the pro-statehood government, instead of helping promote solar energy as an alternative and recognizing Casa Pueblo's excellent initiative, has announced as of March 5, 2018, that it is considering the imposition of yet another tax, this time on solar energy on those who opt out of PREPA's inefficient and expensive service. This is an inept abuse of power that fails to address people's suffering due to lack of access to electricity.

Another important component is the role that the University of Puerto Rico could play in an alternative development strategy. This strategy and not the lack of this strategy is the only element that still distinguishes Puerto Rico from the other countries of the region—not tourism, nor finance, or ports. While Puerto Rico only looked north or was forced to, the countries of the Greater Caribbean successfully developed all these alternatives.

What privileges the uniqueness of the UPR are three main characteristics: a good ranking in the region thanks to the peer-reviewed publications of its professors; its status as a Hispanic Serving Institution (HSI) within the US (those that serve the Hispanic population); and its low tuition costs that reflect its mission to provide an accessible education to society. The universities of Latin America and the Caribbean located above the UPR in the ranking (especially those of Brazil and Mexico) do not qualify as HSI. Those that qualify as HSI in the US do not have a fully bilingual faculty with PhDs and enough academic publications that make it possible for them to take up large-scale teaching in Spanish. This classification as HSI qualifies the UPR for a number of federal grant opportunities. In recent years, the UPR has managed to significantly increase the amount of money it receives in external funds. In addition, the lower credit costs position the institution to attract students from the United States, as well as from other parts of the world; and these students can also study online. Additional budget cuts will ruin an important competitive advantage that Puerto Rico still has, as a world class university at affordable prices. Why launch such an attack at the only public investment that is not in crisis, and by virtue of its exceptionality, should be the axis of regional socioeconomic development alternatives?[36]

Food sovereignty and agroecology have flourished in recent years, with some very important and interesting projects led by young farmers, some linked to the University of Puerto Rico. Among them we find social comedores ("social lunchrooms"); agroecological projects; and initiatives that seek to promote agricultural exports and farmers' markets.

In the area of financial sovereignty or a movement against the debt, an important alternative stands out. In September 2016, the Citizen Front for Auditing the Debt was created. This initiative also proposed creating a Citizen Observatory on Public Debt, and initiating an educational campaign through social networks. But as mentioned above, the earlier Commission for Comprehensive Audit of Public Credit faced government dismissal of its members and budgetary cuts.

At this historical juncture, Puerto Rico shares many of the region's problems. Hopefully this writing serves to denounce what we endure here in the Caribbean and to build bridges of solidarity to develop comparative studies that shed light on alternatives.

In sum, the components to build an alternative development model are present in Puerto Rico with many people contributing sustainable options. What we lack is a government commited to people's well being that is willing to construct alternatives from below.

ENDNOTES

1   Aponte-García, Maribel, "Las Consecuencias Sociales de los Desastres Naturales en el Caribe. Reflexiones desde Puerto Rico." *Megafon la batalla de las ideas* No. 18/2 (octubre 2017): 1.

2   Aponte-García, Maribel, "Las Consecuencias Sociales de los Desastres Naturales en el Caribe. Reflexiones desde Puerto Rico." *Megafon la batalla de las ideas* No. 18/2 (octubre 2017): 2.

3   Aponte-García, "Las Consecuencias Sociales".

4   Aponte-García, "Las Consecuencias Sociales".

5   Aponte-García, "Las Consecuencias Sociales".

6   Aponte-García, "Las Consecuencias Sociales".

7   "Fifth Amendment – Double Jeopardy – Dual-Sovereignty Doctrine- Puerto

Rico v. Sanchez Valle." Harvard Law Review, (accessed March 3, 2017), http:// harvardlawreview.org/wp-content/uploads/2016/11/347-356_Online.pdf.

8   In the face of the crisis, we must: learn from Cuba the system of handling post-hurricane situations, a system that they have come to study in the US after Katrina; and take up the regional policy options for environmental governance and cooperation suggested by regional organizations and institutions.

9   See also Emilio Pantojas-García's work on this subject.

10   Aponte-García Maribel and Orengo-Serra, Karen, "Puerto Rico: Building a Strategic Trade and Industrial Policy," Latin American Perspectives (2018): 16.

11   Aponte-García, Maribel, "New Strategic Regionalism. The First Ten Years of the Bolivarian Alliance. Critical Thought Award Collection", Latin American Social Science Research Council (CLACSO)-Asdi and Social Science Research Center (2014): 52.

12   Aponte-García, El Nuevo Regionalismo Estratégico, 52.

13   Santos, Héctor I. "Cabotage Laws: A Colonial Anachronism", Revista de Derecho Puertorriqueño, no. 36 (1997): 5.

14   Aponte-García, El Nuevo Regionalismo Estratégico, 52.

15   Aponte-García, El Nuevo Regionalismo Estratégico, 52.

16   Redacción Aristegui Noticias, Quiere Trump que 50% de los contenidos de vehículos en el TLC sean hechos en EU, Aristegui Noticias, 14 de octubre de 2017, "US wants to increase the local content requirement for trucks, automobiles and large engines to 85 percent (from 62.5 percent); and insists that 50 percent of the content must be manufactured in that country. In addition, Trump argues that the current content rules are too lax and have allowed the automakers to bring too many cheap parts from China and other Asian countries, resulting in a flight of jobs south of the border," https://aristeguinoticias.com/1410/ mexico/quiere-trump-que-50-de-los-contenidos-de-vehiculos-en-el-tlc-sean-hechos-en-eu/, accessed January 20, 2018.

17   Belgum, Deborah, "The U.S. Free-Trade Agreement with Central America Is Next in Line for a Makeover," Import/Export, October 12, 2017, https://www. apparelnews.net/news/2017/oct/12/us-free-trade-agreement-central-america-next-line-/.

18   This section based on Aponte-García, "Puerto Rico: Los Fondos Buitres en un Contexto Colonial," first published by Grupo de Trabajo, Latin American Social Science Research Council (CLACSO). Crisis y Economía Mundial, Nuestra América XXI, Desafíos y Alternativas, in Spanish and translated and reproduced with their permission, https://www.academia.edu/31788295/ Bolet%C3%ADn_Nuestra_América_XXI_5, 6-7.

19   http://www2.pr.gov/presupuestos/BUDGET20112012/BudgetSummary/ Debt%20Service.pdf, p. 6.

20   Nathan Bomey, "John Roberts appoints New York judge to oversee Puerto Rico bankruptcy," USA TODAY, accessed February 10, 2018, https://www.usatoday. com/story/money/.../puerto-rico...laura-taylor-swain/101329204.

21   Ibid

22   Eva Lloréns Vélez, "Judge Swain rejects $1 billion loan to Prepa" Caribbean Business, February 15, 2018, http://caribbeanbusiness.com/judge-swain-re-

jects-1-billion-loan-to-prepa/.

23 "Akon Says US Government Stopped Him from Restoring Power to Puerto Rico, Facebook Twitter Google", The Black Loop, accessed February 28, 2018, https://www.theblackloop.com/akon-puerto-rico/.

24 Vann R. Newkirk II, "The Puerto Rico Power Scandal Expands," The Atlantic, accessed January 15, 2018, https://www.theatlantic.com/politics/archive/2017/11/puerto-rico-whitefish-cobra-fema-contracts/544892/).

25 Vann R. Newkirk II, "The Puerto Rico Power Scandal Expands," The Atlantic, accessed January 15, 2018, https://www.theatlantic.com/politics/archive/2017/11/puerto-rico-whitefish-cobra-fema-contracts/544892/).

26 Vann R. Newkirk II, "The Puerto Rico Power Scandal Expands," The Atlantic, accessed January 15, 2018, https://www.theatlantic.com/politics/archive/2017/11/puerto-rico-whitefish-cobra-fema-contracts/544892/).

27 Vann R. Newkirk II, "The Puerto Rico Power Scandal Expands," The Atlantic, accessed January 15, 2018, https://www.theatlantic.com/politics/archive/2017/11/puerto-rico-whitefish-cobra-fema-contracts/544892/).

28 Robert Slavin, "Puerto Rico governor complains U.S. Treasury is blocking emergency loan," The Bond Buyer, accessed March 2, 2018, https://www.bondbuyer.com/news/puerto-rico-governor-complains-us-treasury-is-blocking-emergency-loan.

29 Eva Lloréns Vélez, "Puerto Rico Economic Outlook 2018: The Climb Begins," Caribbean Business, accessed February 25, 2018, http://caribbeanbusiness.com/puerto-rico-economic-outlook-2018-the-climb-begins/.

30 Pedro Cabán, "Puerto Rico's Forever Exodus." NACLA, accessed February 28, 2018, https://nacla.org/news/2018/02/22/puerto-rico's-forever-exodus.

31 Puerto Rico Agriculture, "Puerto Rico Agriculture: Lack of food security in Puerto Rico." Caliricans. The California Puerto Rican Connection, accessed January 10, 2018, http://www.caliricans.com/2014/09/agriculture-experts-warn-lack-food-security-puerto-rico/.

32 Marlysa D. Gamblin, "Food Insecurity Food Insecurity in Puerto Rico: The aftermath of the hurricanes," Bread for the World, October 20,2017, http://www.bread.org/blog/food-insecurity-puerto-rico-aftermath-hurricanes.

33 "USDA Continues Disaster Assistance in Puerto Rico, Release No. 0130.17, accessed February 12, 2018, https://www.fns.usda.gov/pressrelease/2017/013017.

34 Aponte-García, Maribel. "Joya para el desarrollo socio económico regional," El Nuevo Día, March 8, 2017, https://www.elnuevodia.com/opinion/columnas/joyaparaeldesarrollosocioeconomicoregio al-columna-2298501html.

35 In Puerto Rico, a cuerda is a traditional unit of land area nearly equivalent to 3,930 square meters,[1][2] or 4,700 square yards, 0.971 acre, or 0.393 hectare (ha).

36 Aponte-García, Maribel. "Joya para el desarrollo socio económico regional."

WHY GETTING THE TRUTH OUT IS SO DIFFICULT

RWANDA AND THE DEMOCRATIC REPUBLIC OF CONGO IN THE PROPAGANDA SYSTEM

David Peterson and Edward S. Herman*

Elsewhere we have written that the breakup of Yugoslavia "may have been the most misrepresented series of major events over the past twenty years."[1] But the far bloodier and more destructive invasions, insurgencies, and civil wars that have ravaged several countries in the Great Lakes region of Central Africa over the same years may have been subjected to even greater misrepresentation.

To a remarkable degree, all major sectors of the Western establishment swallowed a propaganda line on Rwanda that turned perpetrator and victim upside-down. In the much-cited 1999 study, *"Leave None to Tell the Story": Genocide in Rwanda*, on behalf of Human Rights Watch and the International Federation of Human Rights in Paris, Alison Des Forges writes that "By late March 1994, Hutu Power leaders were determined to slaughter massive numbers of Tutsi and Hutu opposed to [Hutu President Juvénal] Habyarimana," and that on April 6, 1994, with the assassination of Habyarimana, "[a] small group of his close associates...decided to execute the planned extermination."

* This article is taken from Herman and Peterson's book, *The Politics of Genocide*, (Monthly Review Press, 2009)

Although "responsibility for killing Habyarimana is a serious issue," writes Des Forges, it pales in comparison to "responsibility for the genocide. We know little about who assassinated Habyarimana." This is a false statement, as we show in detail below. "We know more about who used the assassination as the pretext to begin a slaughter that had been planned for months" is true enough, but in exactly the opposite sense reported by Des Forges.[2]

During testimony at a major trial of four Hutu former military officers before the International Criminal Tribunal for Rwanda (ICTR), Des Forges acknowledged that by April 1992 (i.e., a full twenty-four months before "The Genocide" is alleged to have been perpetrated), the "government in charge of Rwanda [had become] a multiparty government, including Tutsi representatives, and it is for that reason alone that it is impossible to conclude that there was planning of a genocide by that government."[3]

Although Des Forges tried to salvage the Hutu conspiracy model, alleging plans by individual Hutu members of the coalition government to use their "official powers" to carry out a preplanned genocide, this model disintegrated on cross-examination.[4] Des Forges could not explain how Hutu "individuals" used these "powers" without the knowledge of their Tutsi and Rwandan Patriotic Front (RPF) associates. Furthermore, she was forced to admit that pro-RPF ministers were in cahoots with the RPF and its plans for war (which we describe below), and that after the Habyarimana assassination, the RPF did not simply respond in self-defense to a Hutu-organized killing spree, but initiated its own killing spree. In other words, while the Hutu members of Rwanda's power-sharing government would have had great difficulty organizing a genocide against the Tutsi, the Tutsi-led RPF was well-positioned to paralyze any government response to plans it had developed—and that were implemented—to avoid the threat of a free election the RPF was destined to lose, to assassinate the Hutu president, and to take over the country by military force. Yet Des Forges's dramatic concessions before the ICTR never turned up in the Western media, and in her public statements thereafter she continued to repeat the official propaganda line about a Hutu conspiracy to commit genocide, right up to the very end.[5]

To accept the standard model of "The Genocide," one must ignore the large-scale killing and ethnic cleansing of Hutus by the RPF long before the April-July 1994 period, which began when Ugandan forces invaded Rwanda under President (and dictator) Yoweri Museveni on October 1, 1990. At its inception, the RPF was a wing of the Ugandan army, the RPF's leader, Paul Kagame, having served as director of Ugandan military intelligence in the 1980s. The Ugandan invasion and resultant combat were not a "civil war," but rather a clear case of *aggression*. However, the invasion led to no reprimand or cessation of support by the United States or Britain—and, in contrast to Iraq's invasion of Kuwait just two months before, which was countered in the Security Council by a same-day demand that Iraq withdraw its forces immediately—the Council took no action on the Ugandan invasion of Rwanda until March 1993. It did not even authorize an observer mission (UNOMUR) until late June 1993, the RPF by then having occupied much of northern Rwanda and driven out several hundred thousand Hutu farmers.[6]

It is clear that Museveni and the RPF were perceived as serving U.S. interests, and that the government of President Habyarimana was targeted for ouster.[7] UN Security Council inaction flowed from this political bias. In his assessment of the years he spent representing U.S. interests in Africa, former Assistant Secretary of State Herman Cohen raised the question of why, as of October 1, 1990, the "first day of the crisis," as he calls it, "did [the United States] automatically exclude the policy option of informing Ugandan President Museveni that the invasion of Rwanda by uniformed members of the Ugandan army was totally unacceptable, and that the continuation of good relations between the United States and Uganda would depend on his getting the RPF back across the border?"[8] This question is naïve but revealing—the answer, like that to the question of why the United States lobbied for the withdrawal of UN forces from Rwanda as "The Genocide" was getting under way in April 1994, is that the Ugandan army and RPF were doing what the United States wanted done in Rwanda.

The United States and its allies worked hard in the early 1990s to weaken the Rwandan government, forcing the abandonment of many of the economic and social gains from the social revolution of 1959, thereby making the Habyarimana government less popular, and helping to reinforce the Tutsi minority's economic power.[9] Eventually, the RPF was able to achieve a legal military presence inside Rwanda, thanks to a series of ceasefires and other agreements. These agreements led to the Arusha Peace Accords of August 1993, pressed upon the Rwandan government by the United States and its allies, called for the "integration" of the armed forces of Rwanda and the RPF, and for a "transitional," power-sharing government until national elections could be held in 1995.[10]

These Peace Accords positioned the RPF for its bloody overthrow of a relatively democratic coalition government, and the takeover of the Rwandan state by a minority dictatorship.

As we have already suggested, the established perpetrator-victim line requires suppression of the crucial fact that the April 6 shooting-down of the government jet returning Rwanda President Juvénal Habyarimana and Burundi President Cyprian Ntaryamira to Kigali, that killed everyone onboard, was carried out by RPF commandos (as discussed below), and had been regarded by RPF planners as an essential first strike in its final assault on the government. Although the mass killings *followed* this assassination, with the RPF rapidly defeating any military resistance by the successor to Habyarimana's coalition government and establishing its rule in Rwanda, these prime *génocidaires* were, and still are today, portrayed as heroic defenders of Rwanda's national unity against Hutu "extremists" and the *Interahamwe* militia, who were the RPF's actual victims.

Acceptance of this line also requires the suppression of a key verdict in a December 2008 Judgment by the ICTR.[11] This seven-and-a-half year trial of four former high-ranking Hutu members of the Rwanda military produced an acquittal of all four defendants on the Tribunal's most serious charge: participation in a conspiracy to commit genocide against the country's Tutsi minority. To the contrary, the court ruled unanimously that the evidence was "consistent with preparations for a political or military power struggle and measures adopted in the context of an on-going war with the RPF that were used for other purposes from 6 April 1994."[12]

Of course, it was the RPF that had been organized to carry out a "military power struggle" against Rwanda's Hutu majority for several years prior to April 1994; and with its Tutsi base a numerical minority in the country (at most 15 percent overall), the RPF recognized that they would suffer an almost certain defeat in the free elections called for by the Arusha Accords. But the fact that the RPF itself conspired to assassinate Habyarimana and to carry out subsequent mass killings remains entirely beyond the grasp of the ICTR. Although it has failed to convict a single Hutu of conspiracy to commit genocide, the ICTR has never once entertained the question of an *RPF conspiracy*—despite the RPF's rapid overthrow of the Hutu government and capture of the Rwandan state. This, we believe, flows from U.S. and allied support of the RPF, reflected in media coverage, humanitarian intellectuals' and NGO activism, as well as the ICTR's jurisprudence. Like the International Criminal Tribunal for the Former Yugoslavia (ICTY), the ICTR was a creation of the Security Council.[13] Both have served Western, and notably U.S., purposes throughout their remit, but the ICTR has acted far more uncompromisingly than the ICTY—which makes this particular Judgment even more striking and important.[14]

Paul Kagame and the RPF were creatures of U.S. power from their origins in Uganda in the 1980s. Allan Stam, a Rwanda scholar who once served with the U.S. Army Special Forces, notes that Kagame "had spent some time at Fort Leavenworth...not too far before the 1994 genocide." Fort Leavenworth is the U.S. Army's "commander general staff college...where rising stars of the U.S. military and other places go to get training as they are on track to become generals. The training that they get there is on planning large scale operations. It's not planning small-scale logistic things. It's not tactics. It's about how do you plan an invasion. And apparently [Kagame] did very well."

By 1994, Kagame's RPF possessed, in addition to the necessary manpower and material, a sophisticated plan for seizing power in Rwanda that, in its final execution, Stam says, "looks staggeringly like the United States' invasion of Iraq in 1991." Stam adds that the RPF launched its final assault on the Rwandan government almost immediately after the assassination of Habyarimana, within 60 to 120 minutes of the shooting-down of his jet, with "50,000 [RPF] soldiers mov[ing] into action on two fronts, in a coordinated fashion"—clearly "a plan that was not worked out on the back of an envelope."[15]

So the Hutu conspiracy model, still at the center of establishment belief even if implicitly rejected by the ICTR, suffers from the RPF-Kagame locus of responsibility for the triggering event (the shoot-down of Habyarimana's jet during its approach to Kigali airport) and the incredible speed and coordinated nature of the RPF's military response, which again suggest detailed planning, and a different set of conspirators.

But there is also the fact that the alleged Hutu perpetrators of "The Genocide" were the ones *driven from power*, with several million Hutus sent fleeing from Rwanda by July 4, the date by which the RPF had taken Kigali. We also see that, before the end of July, Washington withdrew diplomatic recognition from the ousted government and awarded it to the RPF—the "entity that exercises effective control in Rwanda," a State Department spokesman explained. And we see that, at the same time, Washington began dispatching U.S. troops and large-scale aid to Kigali,[16] after having lobbied and voted at the Security Council on April 21 for a withdrawal of virtually all UN troops, over the objections of Rwanda's ambassador,[17] positively facilitating both the slaughters and the RPF's conquest of power. If the established narrative about "who used the assassination as a pretext" were true, then Rwanda would be the first case in history in which a minority population, suffering destruction at the hands of its tormentors, drove its tormentors from power and assumed control of a country, all in the span of less than one hundred days. We find this incredible in the extreme.

So does a body of important but suppressed research. An investigation in July and August 1994, sponsored by the UN High Commissioner for Refugees (UNHCR) to document Hutu massacres of Tutsis, found instead massacres of Hutu civilians in RPF-controlled areas of Rwanda on the order of 25,000-45,000. This finding led the UNHCR to take the extraordinary step of blocking Hutu refugees from returning to Rwanda in order to protect them. Prepared by Robert Gersony, the report, covered in the *New York Times*, "concluded that there was 'an unmistakable pattern of killings and persecutions' by soldiers of the [RPF]...'aimed at Hutu populations.'" But the Gersony report "set off a bitter dispute within the world organization and led the Secretary General to demand that the United Nations officials refrain from discussing it," in an effort to placate the RPF and, more importantly, its Western sponsors.[18] Officially, the report "does not exist" at the United Nations,[19] and Gersony was instructed never to discuss his findings (a ban he has largely respected).[20]

A memorandum drafted in September 1994 for the eyes of Secretary of State Warren Christopher reported that the UNHCR team "concluded that a pattern of killing had emerged" in Rwanda, the "[RPF] and Tutsi civilian surrogates [killing] 10,000 or more Hutu civilians per month, with the [RPF] accounting for 95% of the killing." This memorandum added that "the UNHR team speculated that the purpose of the killing was a campaign of ethnic cleansing intended to clear certain areas in the south of Rwanda for Tutsi habitation. The killings also served to reduce the population of Hutu males and discouraged refugees from returning to claim their lands."[21] The added significance of this campaign was that the south of Rwanda shares a border with northern Burundi, where a majority Tutsi population long has dwelled.

Separately, U.S. academics Christian Davenport and Allan

Stam estimated that more than one million deaths occurred in Rwanda from April through July 1994,[22] concluding that the "majority of victims were likely Hutu and not Tutsi." Initially sponsored by the ICTR, but later dropped by it, the Davenport-Stam work shows convincingly that the theaters where the killing was greatest correlated with spikes in RPF activity (i.e., with RFP "surges," in their terminology), as a series of RPF advances, particularly in the month of April 1994, created roving patterns of killing. In fact, they describe at least seven distinct "surges" by the RFP (e.g., "they surged forward from the North downward into the Northwest and middle-eastern part of the country"), and every time, an RPF "surge" was accompanied by serious local bloodbaths.[23] Then, in late 2009, Davenport-Stam reported what they called the "most shocking result" of their research to date: "The killings in the zone controlled by the FAR [i.e., the Hutu-controlled Armed Forces of Rwanda] seemed to escalate as the RPF moved into the country and acquired more territory. When the RPF advanced, large-scale killings escalated. When the RPF stopped, large-scale killings largely decreased."[24]

With these facts, Davenport-Stam appeared to link the mass killings of 1994 to RPF actions. This work also suggests that the mass killings were not directed against the Tutsi population. Moreover, a number of observers, as well as participants in the events of 1994, claim that the great majority of deaths were Hutu, with some estimates as high as two million.[25]

Yet Davenport-Stam shy away from asserting the most important lesson of their work: not only that the majority of killings took place in those theaters where the RPF "surged," but also that the RPF was the only well-organized killing force within Rwanda in 1994, and the only one that planned a major military offensive.[26] Clearly, the chief responsibility for Rwandan political violence belonged to the RPF, and not to the ousted coalition government, the FAR, or any Hutu-related group. But Davenport-Stam are inconsistent on the question of likely perpetrators, with their evidence of probable RPF responsibility contradicted by assertions of primary responsibility on the part of the FAR.[27]

In short, their work does not break away from the mainstream camp, overall. However, they do acknowledge that forms of political violence took place, other than a straightforward Hutu "genocide" against the minority Tutsi—in itself, a rarity in Western circles. As with the suppressed Gersony report, the Davenport-Stam findings caused great dismay at the United Nations, not to mention in Washington and Kigali.

Davenport and Stam themselves have been under attack and in retreat since they were expelled from Rwanda in November 2003, upon first reporting that the "majority of the victims of 1994 were of the same ethnicity as the government in power" and have been barred from entering the country ever since.[28] The established narrative's 800,000 or more largely Tutsi deaths resulting from a "preprogrammed genocide" committed by "Hutu Power" appears to have no basis in any facts, beyond the early claims by Kagame's RPF and its politically motivated Western sponsors and propagandists.

We also know a lot more about "who assassinated Habyarimana." In one of the most important, and also suppressed, stories about "The Genocide," former ICTR investigator Michael Hourigan developed evidence as far back as 1996-1997, based on the testimony of three RPF informants who claimed "direct involvement in the 1994 fatal rocket attack upon the President's aircraft," and "specifically implicated the direct involvement of [Kagame]" and other members of the RPF. But in early 1997, when Hourigan hand-delivered his evidence to the ICTR's chief prosecutor Louise Arbour, the latter was "aggressive" and "hostile," Hourigan recounts in a 2006 affidavit,[29] and advised him that the "investigation was at an end because in her view it was not in [the ICTR's] mandate." This decision, which "astounded" Hourigan, was rejected by former ICTR chief prosecutor Richard Goldstone, who told a Danish newspaper that the assassination was "clearly related to the genocide," as it was the "trigger that started the genocide."[30]

Suppressing evidence of the assassination's perpetrator has been crucial in the West, as it seems awkward that the "trigger" for "The Genocide" was ultimately pulled, not by the officially designated Hutu villains, but by the Tutsi victors in this conflict, the RPF, long-supported by the United States and by its close allies (who very possibly aided the assassins in the shoot-down).[31] It has also been important to suppress the fact that the first Hutu president of Burundi, Melchior Ndadaye, had been assassinated by Tutsi officers in his army in October 1993, an action celebrated by the RPF and arousing fears among Rwanda's Hutu.

A far more comprehensive eight-year investigation by the French magistrate Jean-Louis Bruguière, who had been asked to rule on the deaths of the three French nationals operating the government jet that was shot down in April 1994, concluded that the assassination followed from Kagame's rejection of the Arusha power-sharing accords of August 1993, and that for Kagame, the "physical elimination" of Habyarimana was therefore essential to achieving the goal of an RPF-takeover in Rwanda.[32] Bruguière issued nine arrest warrants for high-ranking RPF members close to Kagame, and requested that the ICTR itself take up Kagame's prosecution, as under French law, Bruguière could not issue an arrest warrant for a head of state.[33]

As best we can tell, the existence of Hourigan's evidence has been reported only once in two U.S. newspapers (the *Los Angeles Times* and *Seattle Times*), and never in the *New York Times*, *Washington Post*, or *Wall Street Journal*; Bruguière's findings were mentioned in several U.S. newspapers (sixteen that we have found), including three short items in the *Washington Post*, a major report in the *Los Angeles Times* (reprinted in the *Seattle Times*), and one blurb apiece in the *New York Times* and *Wall Street Journal*, which totaled ninety-four words.[34] Interestingly, the U.S. media have reported fairly often on Bruguière's work as a "counterterrorism" specialist in France, including several dozen items in the *New York Times*, *Washington Post*, and *Wall Street Journal*. But when we checked the U.S. media for Bruguière's eight-year inquiry into mass killings in Rwanda—a case where his focus was on a U.S. client-agent as the primary villain—their interest declines to almost zero.[35] The propaganda system works.

The invasions, assassinations, and mass slaughters by which the RPF shot its way to power in Kigali advanced many objectives, and their support by the "enlightened" states are regarded by many of the defense teams that practice before the ICTR as reflecting a *quid pro quo* between Washington and the RPF: Washington gains a strong military presence in Central Africa, a diminution of its European rivals' influence, proxy armies to serve its interests, and access to the raw material-rich Democratic Republic of Congo (DRC, known as Zaire into 1997); while the RPF renews Tutsi-minority control of Rwanda, and gains a free hand to kill any perceived internal rivals, along with a client state's usual immunities, money, weapons, foreign investment, and a great deal of international prestige.

One year after ICTY and ICTR chief prosecutor Carla Del Ponte (successor to Louise Arbour) opened what she called the "Special Investigation" of the RPF in 2002, she was terminated as chief prosecutor at the ICTR, despite taking her plea directly to Secretary-General Kofi Annan, whom Del Ponte called "inflexible" on the question. In her memoirs, Del Ponte recounts a June 2002 meeting with Kagame at his presidential abode in Kigali, during which Kagame, "fuming," told her:

"If you investigate [the RPF], people will believe there were two geno-cides....All we did was liberate Rwanda." This was followed by a May 2003 meeting with Pierre-Richard Prosper, the Bush administration's ambassador-at-large for war crimes, who, in Del Ponte's words, "backed the Rwandans," and "suggested that [she] surrender responsibility for in-vestigating and prosecuting the alleged crimes of the RPF." By the time Del Ponte was able to meet with Annan in New York in late July 2003, she told Annan, "This will be the end of the Special Investigation," to which Annan replied: "Yes. I know."[36]

"It is clear that it all started when we embarked on these Special Investigations," Del Ponte told an interviewer after her position with the ICTR ended, "pressure from Rwanda contributed to the non-renewal of my mandate."[37] Doubtless, pressure from other sources with a lot more clout with the Security Council played an even greater role. Former ICTR (and ICTY) spokesperson Florence Hartmann also recounts ex-tensive interference by the United States, Britain, and Kagame's RPF in every effort by the Office of the Prosecutor to investigate RPF crimes.[38] Hassan Jallow, Del Ponte's successor at the ICTR, has stated on the re-cord that he does not believe the assassination of Habyarimana belongs within the ICTR's mandate. Under his charge (from September 2003 on), the Office of the Prosecutor systematically dragged its feet when it came to the crimes of the RPF, always pleading a need to carry out "ad-ditional inquiries," without ever bringing a single indictment.[39] Through the end of 2008, 100 percent of the ICTR's indictments for "serious vio-lations of international humanitarian law" committed during 1994 have been brought against Hutu members of the former government and eth-nic Hutus more generally, and none against members of the RPF, despite the ICTR's Statute, making no distinctions on the basis of ethnicity or political allegiance.[40] Neither the RPF's violent takeover of Rwanda, its massacre of "10,000 or more Hutu civilians" per month in 1994, nor any of its other numerous postwar slaughters, have ever once been disturbed by criminal charges at the ICTR.

Very big lies about Rwanda are now institutionalized and are part of the common (mis)understanding in the West. In reality, Rwanda's Paul Kagame is one of the great mass murderers of our time, far surpass-ing Uganda's former dictator Idi Amin.[41] Yet, thanks to the remarkable myth structure that surrounds him, he enjoys immense popularity with his chief patron in Washington, his image of big-time killer transmuted into that of an honored savior, deserving strong Western support. Philip

Gourevitch, one of Kagame's prime apologists for many years, portrays him as an emancipator, a "man of action with an acute human and political intelligence," who "made things happen." He also compares Kagame to "another famously tall and skinny civil warrior, Abraham Lincoln."[42] A more recent hagiography by Stephen Kinzer portrays Kagame as the founding father of a New Africa, "one of the most amazing untold stories of the modern history of revolution," as Kinzer explains it, because Kagame overthrew a dictatorship, stopped a genocide, and turned Rwanda into "one of the great stars" of the continent, with Western investment and favorable PR flowing.[43] In fact, what Kagame overthrew was a multiethnic, power-sharing, coalition government; what Kagame imposed was a Tutsi-dominated dictatorship; and what Kagame turned Rwanda and the whole of Central Africa into was a rolling genocide that is ongoing. But it is true that he is a shining "star" in the Western firmament and its propaganda system.

According to this same myth structure, "The United States did almost nothing to try to stop [the Hutu genocide]," in Samantha Power's view, but instead "stood on the sidelines" as "bystanders to genocide."[44] But this is doubly false. What the United States and its Western allies (Britain, Canada, and Belgium) really did was to sponsor the U.S.-trained Kagame; support his invasion of Rwanda from Uganda and the massive ethnic cleansing prior to April 1994; weaken the Rwandan state by forcing an economic recession and the RPF's penetration of the government and throughout the country; and then press for the complete removal of UN troops. They did this because they didn't want UN troops to stand in the way of Kagame's conquest of the country, even though Rwanda's Hutu authorities were urging the dispatch of *more* UN troops.[45]

Former UN Secretary-General Boutros Boutros-Ghali also wanted to increase UN troop strength,[46] and complained bitterly in his memoirs about the "obstruction" caused by the Clinton administration: "The U.S. effort to prevent the effective deployment of a UN force for Rwanda succeeded, with the strong support of Britain," he wrote; the Security Council "meekly followed the United States' lead."[47] (We may recall that Samantha Power also claimed that the United States "looked away" when Indonesia invaded East Timor in 1975, when in fact the United States gave Indonesia the go-ahead, the arms to carry out the invasion, and diplomatic protection in the United Nations. Whenever the United States colludes in a genocidal process, Power pretends that U.S. guilt, at worst, comes from remaining a mere "bystander"; never from acting as an accomplice, let alone a perpetrator.)

In the Rwanda "genocide" case, the "human rights" community played an unusually active role in supporting the real aggressors and killers, in close parallel with their own governments' perspectives and policies. As in the case of the Western aggressions against Yugoslavia (1999) and Iraq (2003), Human Rights Watch and other nongovernmental organizations simply ignored the "supreme international crime" (or "act of aggression by Uganda," in Herman Cohen's phrase), while conveniently, and in hugely biased fashion, paying attention to lesser human rights violations.[48] They downplayed or ignored entirely the refugee crisis created by the Ugandan-RPF invasion and occupation of northern Rwanda and the armed penetration and *de facto* subversion of the rest of the country by the RPF. Every response to these by the Habyarimana government, from October 1990 on, was scrutinized for "human rights" violations and framed as evidence of unlawful state repression. The NGOs systematically evaded the massive evidence of RPF responsibility for the April 6, 1994, shoot-down, surely because the finding conflicts with their deep commitment to the model of a preplanned Hutu genocide and the RPF's self-defensive rescue of Rwanda—the twin components of the established perpetrator-victim line. We believe that their biases played an important role in supporting the RPF's aggression, its penetration of the country, and the execution of its final assault on power. Above all, we believe that their biases and propaganda contributed substantially to the mass killings that followed—all in accord with the needs of actual U.S. policy.

On March 8, 1993, just days before the Security Council took up the situation in Rwanda for the first time, a consortium of four human rights organizations led by Human Rights Watch and calling itself the International Commission of Inquiry into Human Rights Abuses in Rwanda issued its Report.[49] The Commission concluded that, rather than Rwanda's having suffered an invasion by Uganda, from which the Habyarimana government had yet to liberate its country, the Habyarimana government was instead guilty of something very close to a genocidal rampage against the country's Tutsi minority, with 2,000 dead since October 1990, "systematic killings," widespread rape, and a "climate of terror."[50] Alison Des Forges, one of the Commission's co-chairs, later commented that this report "put Rwandan human rights abuses squarely before the international community."[51] But it was only the Habyarimana government's alleged abuses on which the Commission focused.

The Commission produced its report after its members spent no more than two weeks on the ground in Rwanda in January of that year, and only two hours in territory controlled by the RPF. The Commission itself had close ties to the RPF, its sponsors "either directly funded by the RPF or infiltrated by it," Robin Philpot reports.[52] Prior to her work on this Commission, Des Forges had worked for the U.S. Department of State and National Security Council.

William Schabas, a Canadian member of the Commission, issued a press release at the time the full report was released that bore the title "Genocide and War Crimes in Rwanda"[53]—drawing attention to a category of crime that not even the establishment narrative alleges was to begin for another thirteen months. Stressing that, in the work of the Commission the "word genocide has been mentioned on a number of occasions," Daniel Jacoby, the president of the International Federation of Human Rights League, stated that the situation in Rwanda "is not simply an ethnic confrontation. It goes beyond that. Responsibility for the killings can be placed extremely high."[54] Human Rights Watch's annual *World Report* covering 1993 noted that, when the RPF launched its major offensive that year, "it justified the offensive in part by the need to counter human rights abuses of the Rwanda government" such as those put squarely before the world by the Commission's report. In short, with the brunt of its findings coming down against the Habyarimana government, the Commission's work served to delegitimize the government of Rwanda and enhance the legitimacy of the armed forces of the RPF. As the RPF quickly used the Commission's claims to justify a new killing spree, we believe the case can be made that the overall impact of this report—and of the work of HRW and its allies with respect to Rwanda over the past two decades—was to underwrite the mass killings to follow, including the vast numbers in the DRC, regularly explained as carried out by the benevolent RPF and Uganda in search of Hutu "*génocidaires*."

In a study we conducted for *The Politics of Genocide*, we found that the 1994 mass killings in Rwanda were referred to as "genocide" more frequently than in any other theater of atrocities—i.e., 3,199, or nearly triple the number for Darfur.[55] This, we believe, follows from the successful framing of the Hutus as the villains, executing a preplanned "genocide" against the Tutsis (a nefarious and mythical bloodbath at one and the same time) and Kagame's RPF as the defender-savior of the Tutsis and of Rwanda and Central Africa as a whole, with the RPF unexpectedly finding itself one day the new power in the country. But it also cleared the ground for Kagame and Uganda's Yoweri Museveni—

Kagame's ally and the two staunchest U.S. clients in the region—to invade and occupy the DRC and beyond periodically, without opposition from the "international community."

The Pentagon has very actively supported these invasions of the DRC, even more heavily than it supported the RPF's drive to take Kigali. This support led to the killing of many thousands of Hutu refugees in a series of mass slaughters (ca. 1994-1997), and also provided cover for a greater series of Kagame-Museveni assaults on the DRC that have destabilized life in this large country of perhaps sixty million people, with millions perishing in the process.[56] In his letter of resignation to Chief Prosecutor Hassan Jallow, Filip Rentjens, a Dutch academic and one-time expert witness before the ICTR, took issue with the "impunity" that protects the RPF leadership from prosecution. "[RPF] crimes fall squarely within the mandate of the ICTR," he wrote. "[T]hey are well documented, testimonial and material proof is available, and the identity of the RPF suspects is known....It is precisely because the regime in Kigali has been given a sense of impunity that, during the years following 1994, it has committed massive internationally recognized crimes in both Rwanda and the DRC."[57]

This again has been compatible with Western interests and policy, as it contributed to the replacement of Mobutu with the more amenable Laurent Kabila (and later his son Joseph), and the opening up of the DRC to a new surge of ruthless exploitation of precious gems, rare industrial minerals, and timber by Western companies in a different kind of "resource war"—a fine illustration of "shock therapy" with murderous human consequences for the Congolese people. This plunder is the equivalent of "one tsunami every six months" for more than a decade,[58] but with large gains for a small business and military elite. In a series of UN reports, which coined the phrase "elite networks" to denote the "politically and economically powerful groups involved in the exploitation activities" that lie at the heart of the DRC genocide, we read that "The war economy controlled by the three elite networks [Kinshasa, Kigali, and Kampala] operating in the Democratic Republic of the Congo dominates the economic activities of much of the Great Lakes region....Years of lawlessness and a Government incapable of protecting its citizens have allowed the armed groups to loot and plunder the country's resources with impunity....They have built up a self-financing war economy centered on mineral exploitation"—and sales to the transnationals that manufacture the personal computers and cell phones of our everyday lives.[59]

The U.S.-supported leaders Paul Kagame and Yoweri Museveni have undeniably been key actors in the terrible bloodbaths of the DRC. Considering their U.S. support, these were benign bloodbaths, in contrast with killings in Darfur or Kosovo. In research for our book, we found that in only seventeen items in the large number of newspapers we surveyed did someone refer to deaths in the DRC as "genocide." This amounted to one "genocide" reference for every 317,647 deaths (based on an estimated 5,400,000 deaths for the period under consideration). When we contrast this with how the same newspapers treated, say, the nefarious bloodbath of the Kosovo Albanians that was attributable to an official enemy, where only twelve deaths were necessary to receive one "genocide" reference,[60] the basic outline of the politics of genocide could not be made more stark or clear.

ENDNOTES

1   Edward S. Herman and David Peterson, "The Dismantling of Yugoslavia," *Monthly Review* 59, no. 5 (October 2007), 1.

2   Allison Des Forges, *"Leave None to Tell the Story": Genocide in Rwanda* (New York: Human Rights Watch, 1999), 5-6, 185.

3   See *Prosecutor v. Augustin Ndindiliyimana* (or *Military II*) (ICTR-00-56-I), Transcript, September 19, 2006, 4, lines 13-22. Here we note that, in contrast to the trials and related courtroom activity before the International Criminal Tribunal for the Former Yugoslavia (ICTY), which transcribes and archives to its official website virtually everything (except for redacted materials), virtually none of the trial and related courtroom activity before the International Criminal Tribunal for Rwanda (ICTR) is archived on the ICTR's official website. In consequence, we are unable to provide Web links to much of the ICTR's material.

4   For the extended testimony of Prosecution witness Alison Des Forges, see *Prosecutor v. Augustin Ndindiliyimana*, September 18, 2006, through October 16, 2006, which produced a total of seventeen days of testimony. Given that Rwanda's civilian intelligence services were in the hands of a pro-Rwandan Patriotic Front minister, three consecutive prime ministers under a power-sharing accord had been either pro- or subsidized by the RPF, and Rwanda's "integrated" military then combined the armed forces of the Tutsi-led RPF that was seeking the overthrow of the government alongside the government's regular army, the cross-examination of Des Forges from September 21 on shows her failing to support the standard model of the "Rwandan genocide."

5   Alison Des Forges died in a commuter plane crash on February 12, 2009, while returning to her home in Buffalo, New York. An obituary written by Human

Rights Watch Executive Director Kenneth Roth praised his longtime colleague for "her central role in the prosecution of the Hutus" ("A Heroine for Human Rights," *Huffington Post*, February 15, 2009). It is true that Des Forges acted energetically on behalf of the Prosecution at the ICTR and in similar venues against the Hutu in general, but the perception of her "expertise" flowed less from her knowledge of Rwanda, than her tirelessness as an advocate for the standard model of the "Rwandan genocide," and the thoroughness with which this model has been institutionalized in the United States and Britain. In 1991, Des Forges went to Rwanda on behalf of the U.S. government, and in her own words, "attempted to put my knowledge into a policy-oriented framework." "What was new was the relationship to the United States government," she explained. Later, "I went to Rwanda in July of '92 as a consultant to the United States government, again for the same democracy project. Then I went back in the first part of January '93 as the co-chair of an international commission to investigate human rights abuses in Rwanda." (Here quoting Des Forges's testimony in *Prosecutor of the Tribunal Against Jean Paul Akayasu* (ICTR-96-4), Transcript, February 12, 1997, 112-14.) As the real policy of the U.S. government from at least 1990 on was regime-change in Rwanda, namely, the ouster of the Hutu government by the RPF, as well as the ouster of France from the region (France had backed the Hutu government), we can easily see how Des Forges's work beginning in 1991 helped provide cover for the U.S. takeover of as many as four countries via its proxies in Uganda and the RPF in Rwanda. In short, Alison Des Forges's career is best understood in terms of the services she performed on behalf of U.S. power-projection in Central Africa, with this policy-oriented work couched in the rhetoric of "human rights." In the process, Des Forges badly misinformed a whole generation of scholars, activists, and the cause of peace and justice.

6   See Jonathan Clayton, "Rwanda to appeal to UN Security Council on rebel invasion," Reuters, October 15, 1990; UN Security Council Resolution 812 (S/RES/812), March 12, 1993; and UN Security Council Resolution 846 (S/RES/846), June 22, 1993.

7   For compelling evidence on this point, see Robin Philpot, *Rwanda 1994: Colonialism Dies Hard* (E-Text as posted to the Taylor Report Website, 2004), esp. Chap. 1-7.

8   Herman J. Cohen, *Intervening in Africa: Superpower Peacemaking in a Troubled Continent* (New York: St. Martin's Press, 2000), 177-78.

9   See Philpot, *Rwanda 1994*, esp. the Conclusion.

10   See the Peace Agreement between the Government of the Republic of Rwanda and the Rwandese Patriotic Front, signed at Arusha on 4 August 1993 (A/48/824-S/26915) U.N. General Assembly, December 23, 1993. A total of seven documents were gathered together as the "Arusha Peace Accords," the earliest the N'Sele Cease-fire Agreement dating from 1991.

11   See *Judgment*, The Prosecutor v. Théoneste Bagosora et al. (ICTR-98-41-T), International Criminal Tribunal for Rwanda, December 18, 2008. The four defendants in this case were "Colonel Théoneste Bagosora, the directeur de cabinet of the Ministry of Defence, General Gratien Kabiligi, the head of the

operations bureau (G-3) of the army general staff, Major Aloys Ntabakuze, the commander of the elite Para Commando Battalion, and Colonel Anatole Nsengiyumva, the commander of the Gisenyi operational sector" (para. 1).

12   Ibid., para. 13, quoting from the Oral Summary of the case read in court the day the verdict was delivered. For the *Judgment*'s full discussion of the acquittal on this charge, see Sect. 2.1, "Conspiracy to Commit Genocide," para. 2084-2112.

13   See UN Security Council Resolution 827 (S/RES/827), May 25, 1993, which established the ICTY to "prosecut[e] persons responsible for serious violations of international humanitarian law committed in the territory of the former Yugoslavia between 1 January 1991 and a date to be determined by the Security Council upon the restoration of peace." (para. 2); and see UN Security Council Resolution 955 (S/RES/955), November 8, 1994, which established the ICTR to "prosecut[e] persons responsible for genocide and other serious violations of international humanitarian law committed in the territory of Rwanda and Rwandan citizens responsible for genocide and other such violations committed in the territory of neighbouring States, between 1 January 1994 and 31 December 1994" (para. 1).

14   For criticisms of the ICTY, see Michael Mandel, *How America Gets Away with Murder: Illegal Wars, Collateral Damage, and Crimes Against Humanity* (Ann Arbor, MI: Pluto Press, 2004); and John Laughland Travesty: *The Trial of Slobodan Milosevic and the Corruption of International Justice* (New York: Pluto Press, 2007). For criticisms of the ICTR, see Hans Köchler, *Global Justice or Global Revenge: International Criminal Justice at the Crossroads* (New York: Springer-Verlag Wien, 2003); and Charles Onana, *Les Secrets de la Justice Internationale: Enquêtes truquées sur le génocide rwandais* (Paris: Editions Duboiris, 2005).

15   Allan C. Stam, "Coming to a New Understanding of the Rwanda Genocide," a lecture before the Gerald R. Ford School of Public Policy, University of Michigan, February 18, 2009, our transcription.

16   "Rwandan embassy closed, U.S. seeks to remove Rwanda from UN Council," Agence France Presse, July 15, 1994; "Clinton Orders Nonstop Aid Flights for Rwandan Victims," Associated Press, July 22, 1994; "U.S. recognizes new government in Rwanda," Reuters, July 29, 1994; "200 U.S. troops going into Kigali to open airport," Reuters, July 29, 1994.

17   See UN Security Council Resolution 912 (S/RES/912), April 21, 1994, para. 8. The force levels of the UN Assistance Mission in Rwanda were reduced to a target of 270 infantry, down from 1515 on April 20, and 2,165 as of April 6. In the words of Rwandan UN Ambassador Jean-Damascène Bizimana: "[T]he international community does not seem to have acted in an appropriate manner to reply to the anguished appeal of the people of Rwanda. This question has often been examined from the point of view of the ways and means to withdraw [UNAMIR], without seeking to give the appropriate weight to the concern of those who have always believed, rightly, that, in view of the security situation now prevailing in Rwanda, UNAMIR's members should be increased to enable it to contribute to the re-establishment of the cease-fire and to assist in the establishment of security conditions that could bring an end to the violence....The

option chosen by the Council, reducing the number of troops in UNAMIR...is not a proper response to this crisis." "The situation concerning Rwanda," UN Security Council (S/PV.3368), April 21, 1994, 6.

18 Raymond Bonner, "U.N. Stops Returning Rwandan Refugees," *New York Times*, September 18, 1994. Also see Chris McGreal and Edward Luce, "Death Threats Force Out Aid Workers," *The Guardian*, October 3, 1994; Jean-Michel Stoullig, "UN spotlights claims of summary Rwandan reprisal killings," Agence France Presse, October 4, 1994.

19 See the treatment of the Gersony Report in Des Forges, *"Leave None to Tell the Story,"* specifically "The Gersony Mission," 726-732, which reproduces the UNHCR letter stating that the Gersony Report "does not exist" (727).

20 See the recollection of a meeting with Robert Gersony in Gérard Prunier, *Africa's World War: Congo, the Rwandan Genocide, and the Making of a Continental Catastrophe* (New York: Oxford University Press, 2009), 15-16; and n.59-62, 373. As Prunier describes it: "Gersony's conclusion was that between early April and mid-September 1994 the RPF had killed between 25,000 and 45,000 people, including Tutsis. The UNHCR, which had commissioned the study for quite a different purpose, was appalled" (16).

21 George E. Moose, "Human Rights Abuses in Rwanda," Information Memorandum to The Secretary, U.S. Department of State, undated though clearly drafted between September 17 and 20, 1994. This document was called to our attention by Peter Erlinder, the director of the Rwanda Documents Project at William Mitchell College of Law, St. Paul, Minnesota, ICTR Military-1 Exhibit, DNT 264.

22 Christian Davenport and Allan Stam, *Rwandan Political Violence in Space and Time*, unpublished manuscript, 2004 (available at Christian Davenport's personal website, "Project Writings"). For all of Rwanda from April through July 1994, these authors report a total of 1,063,336 deaths (28), based on their analysis of a minimum of eight different mortality estimates for the relevant period.

23 Ibid., see esp. 30-33.

24 Christian Davenport and Allan C. Stam, "What Really Happened in Rwanda?" *Miller-McCune*, October 6, 2009.

25 In 1999, former RPF military officer Christophe Hakizimana submitted a letter to the UN Commission of Inquiry into the Actions of the United Nations during the 1994 Genocide in Rwanda (S/1999/1257). In his letter, which detailed the RPF's military strategy from 1990 on, Hakizimana claimed that the RPF was responsible for killing as many as two million Hutu in Rwanda and the Democratic Republic of Congo, and he informed the Commission that by indicting Hutu, the ICTR was focusing on the wrong side in the conflict. We base this on personal communications with the international criminal lawyer Christopher Black of Toronto, who, since 2000, has served as defense counsel before the ICTR on behalf of the Hutu General Augustin Nindiliyimana, a former Chief of Staff of the Rwanda Gendarmerie (or National Police).

26 For a more critical discussion of these issues, see Stam, "Coming to a New Understanding of the Rwanda Genocide," and our discussion of this above.

27 See Davenport and Stam, *Rwandan Political Violence in Space and Time*, 2004.

Davenport-Stam organize their work according to three "jurisdictions" that we find deeply flawed: Namely, territory controlled by the Rwandan government and army, by the Rwandan Patriotic Front, and territory that falls along the lines of battle between the two. They write that "the actor with the greatest monopoly of coercion within a specific locale is generally held to be responsible for violent behavior in that locale" (25). (Also see Figure 1, "1994 Rwandan Political Violence: Total Deaths by Troop Control," 29.) On the basis of this problematic assumption, Davenport-Stam contend that as "the majority of deaths took place within areas under the control of [the Rwandan government and army]—totaling 891, 295," the government and army are responsible for these deaths, which "could be classified" as genocide, among other possible crimes (28). But as the RPF in fact moved rapidly and decisively from battlefield success to battlefield success to control of the entire country, it is frankly counterintuitive to treat the badly out-gunned, out-maneuvered, and ultimately routed government forces as in control of anything. On the contrary, the chief responsibility for Rwandan political violence in 1994 lay with the RPF and its project of driving the coalition government from power and seizing the Rwandan state.

28   Davenport and Stam, "What Really Happened in Rwanda?"

29   Affidavit of Michael Andrew Hourigan, International Criminal Tribunal for Rwanda, November 27, 2006. For other sources that discuss the suppression of the Hourigan memorandum, see Philpot, *Rwanda 1994*, esp. Chap. 6, "It shall be called a plan crash"; Mark Colvin, "Questions unanswered 10 years after Rwandan genocide," PM, Australian Broadcasting Corporation, March 30, 2004; Mark Doyle, "Rwanda 'plane crash probe halted'," BBC News, February 9, 2007; and Nick McKenzie, "UN 'shut down' Rwanda probe," The Age, February 10, 2007.

30   Richard Goldstone's remarks were reported by the Danish newspaper *Berlingske Tidende*. We are taking them from "ICTR/Attack—April 6th 1994 Attack Fits the ICTR's Mandate (Goldstone)," Hirondelle News Agency, December 13, 2006.

31   See Philpot, *Rwanda 1994*, Chap. 6, "It shall be called a plane crash."

32   See Jean-Louis Bruguière, Request for the Issuance of International Arrest Warrants, Tribunal de Grande Instance, Paris, France, November 21, 2006, 15-16 (para. 100-103).

33   Andrew England, "Rwanda president faces arrest," *Financial Times*, November 22, 2006; Chris McGreal, "French judge accuses Rwandan President of assassination," *The Guardian*, November 22, 2006; Fergal Keane, "Will we ever learn the truth about this genocide?" *The Independent*, November 22, 2006.

34   Findings based on both Factiva (*tnwp*) and NewsBank searches from January 1, 2000 through December 31, 2008. The sole truly serious effort in a U.S. newspaper to report and analyze both Michael Hourigan's and Judge Bruguière's work was Sebastian Rotella, "French Magistrate Posits Theory on Rwandan Assassination," *Los Angeles Times*, February 17, 2007 (later reprinted in the *Seattle Times*).

35   Findings based on both Factiva (*tnwp*) and NewsBank searches from January 1, 2000 through December 31, 2008. Using the Factiva database to search the

New York Times, Wall Street Journal, and *Washington Post* for mentions of the name "Bruguière," we found approximately 100 items; but when we narrowed this search down to Bruguière's work in relation to Rwanda, we found only five items in all. Likewise with the NewsBank database for all U.S. newspapers: Bruguière's work was reported in well over 400 items, but his work in relation to Rwanda in only 17.

36   Carla Del Ponte, with Chuck Sudetic, *Madame Prosecutor: Confrontations with Humanity's Worst Criminals and the Culture of Impunity: A Memoir* (New York: Other Press, 2009), esp. Chap. 9, "Confronting Kigali: 2002 and 2003," 223-241. Also see Steven Edwards, "Del Ponte says UN caved to Rwandan pressure," National Post, September 17, 2003.

37   "Interview with Carla Del Ponte—'If I Had Had the Choice, I Would Have Remained Prosecutor of the ICTR'," Hirondelle News Agency, September 16, 2003.

38   See Florence Hartmann, *Paix et Chatiment: Les Guerres Secretes de la Politique et de la Justice Internationales* (Paris: Flammarion, 2007), 261-75.

39   "ICTR/Military I—Dallaire Wanted Americans to Investigate on Presidential Plane Crash," Hirondelle News Agency, February 9, 2004. In one illustration of Jallow's foot-dragging, he told the UN Security Council in December 2005 that the "allegations made against the Rwandan Patriotic Front have also been under consideration. Following the evaluation of the results of earlier investigations, it has become necessary to carry out additional inquiries into these allegations." (UN Security Council (S/PV.5328), December 15, 2005, 14.) But Jallow's "additional inquiries" were strictly *pro forma,* and the same delaying tactics served him through the end of 2008, at which date, no member of the RPF had ever been indicted by the ICTR, notwithstanding the chief prosecutor's "additional inquiries."

40   For the ICTR's founding Statute, see the Annex to UN Security Council Resolution 955 (S/RES/955), November 8, 1994. For a complete list of every case ever to have been indicted by the ICTR, see "Status of Cases."

41   Conservative estimates of the number of Ugandans killed under the Idi Amin dictatorship (1971-1979) are 100,000 victims, with high-end estimates of some 300,000. See Richard H. Ulmann, "Human Rights and Economic Power: The United States Versus Idi Amin," *Foreign Affairs,* April, 1978. As Ulmann noted at the time, "In any contemporary lexicon of horror, Uganda is synonymous with state-become-slaughterhouse." This is manifestly not true of Rwanda or the Democratic Republic of Congo in the areas under Kagame-RPF control: No matter how many lives Kagame and the RFP have taken, and these number many times the Idi Amin toll, their reign of terror has never entered the contemporary lexicon of horror.

42   Philip Gourevitch, *We wish to inform you that tomorrow we will be killed with our families: Stories from Rwanda* (New York: Picador, 1998), 225. Gourevitch concludes: "Kagame had proven himself quite effective at getting what he wanted, and if Kagame truly wanted to find an original response to his original circumstances, the only course open to him was emancipation. That was certainly how he presented it, and I didn't doubt that that was what he wanted."

226.

43 Stephen Kinzer, *A Thousand Hills: Rwanda's Rebirth and the Man Who Dreamed It* (Hoboken, NJ: John Wiley & Sons, 2008). Here we are quoting Kinzer's own words from a two-minute promotional video that his publisher circulated in 2008. (See "Kinzer speaks about the President Kagame," as posted to *YouTube*.) At the hagiographic extreme for the literature on Paul Kagame and Rwanda, every chapter of Kinzer's book is introduced by quotes from Kagame ("For me, human rights is about everything" (Chap. 18)). "Kagame is the man of the hour in modern Africa," Kinzer writes. "The eyes of all who hope for a better Africa are upon him. No other leader has made so much out of so little, and none offers such encouraging hope for the continent's future." 337.

44 Samantha Power, *"A Problem from Hell": America and the Age of Genocide* (New York: Harper Perennial, 2002), 334-335. Also see Power, "Bystanders to Genocide," *The Atlantic*, September, 2001.

45 See the statement by the Rwandan UN Ambassador Jean-Damascène Bizimana at n.17, above.

46 See *Special Report of the Secretary-General on the United Nations Assistance Mission for Rwanda* (S/1994/470), April 20, 1994, specifically "Alternative 1," para. 13-14, which Boutros-Ghali himself endorsed.

47 Boutros Boutros-Ghali, *Unvanquished: A U.S.-U.N. Saga* (New York: Random House, 1999), 129-41; here 138, 135. According to Robin Philpot, Boutros-Ghali told him on the record that "The genocide in Rwanda was 100 percent the responsibility of the Americans!" See the Introduction to Philpot, *Rwanda 1994*.

48 See Edward S. Herman, David Peterson, and George Szamuely, "Human Rights Watch in Service to the War Party," *Electric Politics*, February 26, 2007.

49 See *Report of the International Commission of Inquiry into human rights violations in Rwanda since October 1, 1990* (New York, March, 1993). Besides Africa Watch (Human Rights Watch, USA), the other NGOs behind this Commission were the International Federation of Human Rights Leagues (France), the Inter-African Union for Human Rights and the Rights of Peoples, and the International Center for Human Rights and Democratic Development (Canada).

50 Ibid. In a section titled "The Question of Genocide," after laying out Article II of the Genocide Convention, the Commission concluded that "many Rwandans have been killed for the sole reason that they were Tutsi," although it added that "casualty figures…may be below the threshold required to establish genocide," 29. Besides Africa Watch (Human Rights Watch, USA), the other NGOs behind this Commission were the International Federation of Human Rights Leagues (France), the Inter-African Union for Human Rights and the Rights of Peoples, and the International Center for Human Rights and Democratic Development (Canada).

51 Des Forges, *"Leave None to Tell the Story,"* 93.

52 Philpot, *Rwanda 1994*, Chap. 4, "Scouts at Her Majesty's Service."

53 Linda Melvern, *A People Betrayed: The Role of the West in Rwanda's Genocide* (New York: Zed Books, 2000), 56.

54   "Rwanda: Report blames government for mass slayings," Inter Press Service, March 8, 1993.

55   See Edward S. Herman and David Peterson, *The Politics of Genocide* (New York: Monthly Review Press, 2010), Table 1: "Differential attributions of 'genocide' to different theaters of atrocities," 35.

56   See Benjamin Coghlan et al., *Mortality in the Democratic Republic of Congo: An Ongoing Crisis, International Rescue Committee-Burnet Institute*, January, 2008, ii. Also see the accompanying Press Release, January 22, 2008.

57   Filip Reyntjens' January 11, 2005 letter of resignation to Hassan Jallow is quoted in John Laughland, *A History of Political Trials: From Charles I to Saddam Hussein* (New York: Peter Lang Ltd., 2008), 211. The Reyntjens letter continued: "Article 6(2) of the [ICTR's] Statute explicitly rules out immunity, including for Heads of state or government or for responsible government officials. This principle is contravened when, as is currently the case, a message is sent out that those in power need not fear prosecution," 211-12.

58   The phrase "one tsunami every six months" was used in reference to the eastern Congo by then-head of the UN Office for the Coordination of Humanitarian Affairs Jan Egeland, based on the belief at the time that the December 26, 2004 tsunami in the Indian Ocean had taken 300,000 lives. Hence, in Egeland's words: "In terms of the human lives lost…this is the greatest humanitarian crisis in the world today and it is beyond belief that the world is not paying more attention." In Peter Daou, "Congo Crisis: 'One Tsunami Every Six Months,'" AlertNet, March 17, 2005.

59   See the final two reports by Mahmoud Kassem et al. of the UN Panel of Experts on the Illegal Exploitation of Natural Resources and Other Forms of Wealth of the Democratic Republic of the Congo: S/2002/1146, October 8, 2002 (para. 152-153, 12); and S/2003/1027, October 15, 2003. Also see Björn Aust and Willem Jaspers, *From Resource War to "Violent Peace": Transition in the Democratic Republic of Congo*, Bonn International Center for Conversion, Paper No. 50, 2006. These authors note that approximately one-third of the earth's known cobalt deposits, and two-thirds of its known columbo tantalite (coltan) deposits, are to be found in the DRC (Appendix 2, 149).

60   Based on an estimated 4,000 deaths for the period under consideration.

WESTERN IMPERIALISM AND THE USE OF PROPAGANDA

Christopher Black

The US-NATO military alliance is a world-encompassing threat. It is now conducting various forms of hybrid warfare against Russia, China, Iran, North Korea, Venezuela, Syria, Iraq, Afghanistan, and most of Africa. They have destroyed directly or are largely responsible for the destruction of the socialist nations of the USSR, Yugoslavia, Afghanistan, Iraq, Libya, Syria and too many to name in Latin America, Africa and Asia. Destruction is the fate that each nation on earth can expect unless it pays homage and obeisance to these neo-feudal overlords who promise protection in return for national servitude, in return for the complete surrender of their people and natural resources to increase the rate of profit for the capital that controls the NATO military machine. For NATO is first and foremost the armed fist not only of the United States and its allies as nations, but is the armed fist of the capitalists of those nations who are prepared to strike against any nation, capitalist or socialist, that stands in their way of obtaining profit.

The primary concern they have, in order to preserve their control, is for the preservation of the new feudal mythology that they have created: that the world is a dangerous place, that they are the protectors, that the danger is omnipresent, eternal, and omnidirectional, comes from without, and comes from within. The mythology is constructed and presented through all media; journals, films, television, radio, music, advertising, books, the internet in all its variety. All available information systems are used to create and maintain scenarios and dramas to convince the people that they, the protectors, are the good and all others are the bad.

We are bombarded with this message incessantly. They have succeeded in luring us into all their communication platforms, so that no one is able to ignore the constant flow of information into their consciousness and subconscious. They have us locked to our screens. The have our attention. They have us hypnotized and under this state of hypnosis we are fed so many images we cannot take in any of them and so we drown in the river of information washing over us, barely able to breathe, unable to think, blind from looking.

The techniques used to accomplish this fall under the term "propaganda," a word that in itself was neutral in meaning. There can be good and bad propaganda depending on who is putting it out, who the receiver is and the objectives they have. Socialists use propaganda. The capitalists have theirs. Socialist propaganda has the goal of educating working people about their power and ability to mold society to serve the interests of working people and to do that it has to be honest or be ignored. But here I am writing about the techniques used by the capitalist states to maintain their control of the citizens in order to advance their interests, for example creating acceptance for "austerity," that is, the lowering of living standards for working people in order to increase profits for those with capital, but I will focus on another example, war.

The use of propaganda in this sense, and by which I mean the use of fabrications, distortions and misrepresentations of reality and true facts in order to evoke an emotional response in the receiver of the desired type and the desired action to follow, is the backbone of the capitalist-imperialist mythology and system and the immediate means of its delivery is through the news media. Watching the political, national and world "news" on television is a surreal experience. You have a dissociative experience as the presenters present not "news" but carefully crafted scripts, inventing scenarios out of whole cloth that have nothing to do with what is really happening in any given situation. Even the weather "news" is crafted to keep mention of abrupt climate change to a minimum and sports "news" seems like a rehearsal for war news to come, laden with military analogies.

While "the first casualty of war is truth" is a truism, even "truth" can be twisted to their ends. The use of information to mold the minds of people is as old as recorded history but technological innovations in the nineteenth and twentieth centuries have created means of distribution of information and mass communication that are much more efficient and powerful than in the past and in fact modern propaganda could not exist without these technological means. Marshal McLuhan enigmatically said "the medium is the message" but in a lecture he gave in New York City in 1966 he changed it to "the medium is the massage, not the message, it really works us over, it really takes hold and massages the population in a savage way."

The French philosopher, Jacques Ellul, in his famous book *Propaganda; The Formation of Men's Attitudes*, wrote that most people are easy prey for propaganda because of their firm but erroneous conviction that it is composed only of lies and "tall stories" and that, conversely, what is true cannot be propaganda. But modern propaganda relies not just on the ridiculous lies of past, outmoded forms of propaganda. It operates instead with many different kinds of truth; half-truth, limited truth, truth out of context. Even Joseph Goebbels, the Nazi Minister of Propaganda, always insisted that German Army communiqués be as accurate as possible.

A second basic misconception that makes people vulnerable to propaganda is the notion that it serves only to change opinions when that is only its first and subordinate function. The most important function of propaganda is to lead people to action, to support the policy of the government creating the propaganda, or, where they fear opposition to those policies, to non-action. There are two types of propaganda. Agitation propaganda—agitprop—is aimed at leading people to take action in a desired direction. The second technique is integration propaganda, the most dominant type used internally in modern society that is designed to make citizens adjust to required patterns of belief.

All of this relies on the citizen's own need to make sense of events and circumstances, and their shared illusion that when so doing, they are "judging for themselves." Most people's need for help in order to get a grip on what is right, accepted and expected, linking us to others like ourselves, is one of the keys to propaganda's success as a tool. The modern citizen is no longer in touch with their family, village, and the other social groups that held society together before industrialization and modern communications left us ever more isolated. Now each citizen is a atomized being thrown into a mass society with only their own feeble resources to rely on, facing their isolation, loneliness and irrelevancy except as consumers of a culture whose enablers are bent on getting free labour power from them to create profit for the rich and extracting from their pockets the pitiful wages they are allotted. People feed on propaganda to draw from it their reason for being, a feeling of personal involvement in events, as an outlet for repressed instincts, for anger and depression and their encouraged sense of self-righteousness. McLuhan states that the citizens become part of the propaganda machine not just by absorbing the information fed to them but by then diffusing it to others in their social networks. We become part of the machine.

In another classic work, *Propaganda*, Edward Bernays describes the "invisible government" that "molds" our minds, "informs" our tastes and "suggests" our ideas. Bernays was a public relations advisor of the US government during WWI, and since he was the nephew of Sigmund Freud, was aware of the importance of psychological techniques to analyze and mold behavior. His experience in the war led him to characterize propaganda in neutral terms, as the "conscious and intelligent manipulation of the organized habits and opinions of the masses" and as, "a logical result of the way in which our democratic society is organized." Similarly, Walter Lippmann, in his book *Public Opinion*, describes as one of the main goals of governance in a democracy the "manufacture of consent," a phrase picked up by Edward Herman and Noam Chomsky in their great book on the use of propaganda by the American government during the Vietnam War, *Manufacturing Consent*. Lippmann refers to three elements that are important to the success of these techniques, "a causal fact, the creative imagination, the will to believe," out of which people create the very fictions they then respond to. We see this with the bizarre situation in the USA since Donald Trump was elected President where Russian involvement in US elections is invented out of whole cloth by powerful factions opposed to his faction, repeated by the media, echoed back into the media by the people reacting to it, reinforced by the very people that put it out in a rapidly expanding spiral of fiction that becomes, by infinite repetition, a "truth" that must be dealt with.

The news media, often referred to as the "Fourth Estate," an allusion to the idea of the separation of powers in government as well with the role of journalism as a kind of corrective force against the abuses of power, shows in that situation that there is in fact no separation of powers between the ruling classes who have charge of the machinery of the state and the news media; that the very idea of a fourth estate is one of the illusions of democracy.

Karl Marx was never more right when he wrote in "The German Ideology" that,

> The ideas of the ruling class are in every epoch the ruling ideas, i.e. the class which is the ruling material force of society, is at the same time its ruling intellectual force. The class, which has the means of material production at its disposal, has control at the same time over the means of mental production, so that thereby, generally speaking, the ideas of those who lack the means of mental production are subject to it. The ruling ideas are nothing more than the ideal expression of the dominant material relationships, the dominant material relationships grasped as ideas.

The media then serve this relationship by setting up the means by which the dominant ideology is spread among the people. The medium in this sense then is the message; once immersed in it, the medium of information distribution and exchange becomes itself the message of the dominant class.

A basic democratic principle or belief is that with power comes responsibility, especially a responsibility to prevent the abuse of that power. The citizen is taught that one of the duties of the media is to examine the use and abuse of power and to inform the people about it. Since most people are also taught to accept the authority and good intentions of the government and the media, they are easily persuaded that what is told to them must be the truth. Critical thinking is not a subject taught in most schools nowadays and in any case takes too much work and time for the average citizen to apply. Everything is filtered through dark glasses.

How then can governments and the media be made to act responsibly in providing citizens with the information they need to contribute to a stable society on the one hand, and to the goal of "speaking truth to power" on the other when the majority of the media is owned and controlled by the very economic and political forces that control the state that they should be watching?

We have seen in the past, how quickly a "free press" can be

transformed into a machine to support a war that serves the interests of a few while damaging the interests of the many. We saw how the mass media were harnessed in this way in the two world wars. Every government waging war relies on this control, when all we demand, as John Lennon did, is that they "Just give us some truth."

The so-called "War on Terror" is a prime example of this. We are told, the world over, by every government, that we are in a "war against terrorism." But terrorism is an action, a tactic, a strategy. It's a method, not a person, a group, a country. How can there be a war against a method of war? But they want us to fight a method and never ask the why or the who, suggesting that that doesn't matter anymore. They tell us not to be concerned with why something happens, only how it happens.

Let's face it: Americans, with all the creative skills of Madison Avenue, have got the entire world to use a phrase that George Bush first used in 2001 after the strange event in New York that has all the indicia of a state attack on its own people to justify the invasions of Afghanistan and then Iraq. It has become a euphemism and a justification for all the wars they have waged since. The people don't need to know why "terrorists" exist, or who they are and what motivates them, or even whether they really exist, for they are just "terrorists."

Sometimes the war is against a "regime" that is "terrorizing" its own people according to the "responsibility to protect" mafia that act as the chorus to the principal players in this theatre, as was done to Yugoslavia and Libya; or a regime that "terrorizes the world," as we saw with Iraq. Sometimes the war is a phony war against "terrorists" who are really mercenary forces fighting for the USA and its allies. We see this in Syria. We have seen it used against Russia. The result is the same.

When the Americans say they are fighting "terrorists" in Iraq, they really mean they are fighting the resistance to their invasion and occupation. When they same the same thing in Afghanistan, the same holds true, they are fighting a national resistance. The Russians, when they say they are fighting "terrorism" in Syria, know that in fact they are fighting the United States and its allies and proxy forces.

The bombings and shootings in Europe, Asia, the US, and Russia are all connected to the real war that is being conducted by the United States against the world it wants to control, and, in fact, can better be described as a war of terror being waged against the rest of us by the United States and its vassal states.

The War On Terror is in fact The American War Against The

World. For isn't that what we are dealing with from the United States itself to Latin America, to Africa, from Europe to Asia—non-stop wars since World War II ended? You can even say that World War II never did really end. It just went through different stages, from the defeat of the German and Japanese empires in 1945 to the war by the American corporate state first against all socialist and worker oriented governments worldwide, then afterwards against any country, even of a capitalist orientation, that demanded or demands a fair price for its resources or that won't obey orders from Washington.

The acts of terrorism by US proxy elements and forces in Syria and Ukraine, for example, are a type of hybrid warfare, used both against the targeted country—Syria and Russia—and against the American people and the peoples of its allies in order to create the propaganda necessary to obtain their support for the very wars in which they are the first victims. In other words, they get the people to cut their own throats.

For the result is the same: new oppressive security laws and surveillance, more calls for war on the middle east, and the use of emergency laws, as we see in France, being used to terrorize working people with the threat of harsher working conditions for less pay in order to give industrialists more profit. Is that not a form of terrorism, class terrorism?

The NATO build-up of forces in Eastern Europe threatening Russia, is that not an attempt to terrorize the Russian people? The American buildup of forces around China, is that not an attempt to terrorize the Chinese people with the threat of war unless they kowtow to the American president?

The American renewal of its nuclear arsenal, making the use of nuclear weapons even more likely, the British promise to do the same, the constant threats of world war coming from NATO leaders, the lies and distortion propagated by the western mass media directed against their own peoples to make them fear even their own shadows, are these not acts of terrorism against the peoples of the entire world?

The word "terrorism" conveys nothing. It contains no useful information that can lead to an understanding of events and circumstances. It is a word used to dope the mind, paralyze thought, sap the will. Language is an important tool of control of the people. To accept such terms of propaganda used by the powers that want to control us is to surrender to them completely because once we do that, we lose the ability think rationally, to analyze, to question, to think for ourselves.

Describing the reality of the manipulating and manipulated

western media in his last book, *Numero Zero*, Umberto Eco has a newspaper editor say, "let's just stick to spreading suspicion. Someone is involved in fishy business, and though we don't know who it is, we can give him a scare. That's enough for our purposes. Then we'll cash in, our proprietor can cash in, when the time is right."

A prime example of that is the Panama Papers scandal that rocked the world media for weeks in the spring and summer of 2016. On Sunday, April 3, 2016 a story detailing the illicit sequestering of wealth offshore with a Panamanian law firm, possibly indicating an attempt at fraud, or tax or sanctions evasion, appeared simultaneously in all the world's major media. Attributed to a shadowy organization called the International Coalition of Investigative Journalists (ICIJ), it had all the hallmarks of an operation by western secret services to attempt to subvert targeted governments. The primary target was President Putin in order to influence the elections in Russia and to further attempt to portray him as a criminal in the eyes of the peoples of the west.

But the targets also include FIFA directors, continuing the harassment of FIFA by the United States government, in order to keep Russia out of the next world cup football games, also Lionel Messi one of the world's best football players, perhaps because he refused a request by President Obama's daughters to meet him when Obama visited Argentina, Jackie Chan, no doubt punishment for supporting the Communist Party of China, and various people blacklisted by the United States for dealing with North Korea, Iran, Hezbollah, Syria and other American designated enemies.

The immediate positioning of President Putin as the principal target of this story, despite the fact he is not mentioned in the documents, coupled with the timing of the story make a reasonable observer conclude that this information was not released just to inform the public but to subvert and discredit chosen governments, that is, it was a propaganda operation, using the kind of information that will get the attention of the masses. The rich hiding their money is always a good way to generate anger among the people and to provoke unrest in order to destabilize governments, as subsequently happened in Iceland. It does not matter whether the information in the story is true or not; those victimized will have little chance or media space to present any rebuttal. The story is given center stage, and that's all that most people see.

This conclusion is the more inescapable when the true nature of the ICIJ is revealed. For to understand what this story is about it is important to know who put it out, with whom they are connected and who provides the money.

The key is found in the list of the members of the Advisory Board, the Board of Directors and the funders of its parent organization, the Centre For Public Integrity (CFPI). The ICIJ states on its website that it is a non-profit organizsation. That technically may be true but they failed to add that they act for the profit of the people who fund them and who control their operations. Funders of the CFPI include the Democracy Fund, the Carnegie Foundation, the Ford Foundation, the MacArthur Foundation, the Open Society Foundations of George Soros, the Rockefeller Brothers Fund, the Rockefeller Family Fund and many others of the same pedigree. Individual donors include such people as Paul Volcker, former chairman of the US Federal Reserve and many others of the powerful US corporate and financial elite.

Its Advisory Board includes Geoffrey Cowan, who was appointed Director of Voice of America by President Clinton in 1994 and was in 1994-96 associate director of the United States Information Agency. He is now president of the Annenberg Foundation which has hosted US presidents at its retreat in California, dubbed Camp David West, including President Obama. He is also a member of the Council on Foreign Relations which is the American think tank whose membership includes several former heads of the CIA, several US Secretaries of State, and connected media figures and which has the role of promoting globalization, free trade and other economic and foreign policies for the benefit of the rich and powerful in America.

The Advisory Board also includes Hodding Carter III, former assistant secretary of state under President Carter and later a journalist for major western media such as BBC, ABC, CBC, CNN, NBC, PBS, *Wall Street Journal*, and now President of the Knight Foundation. Also included: Edith Everett, President of Gruntal and Company, one of the oldest and biggest investment banks in New York City; Herbert Hafif, connected establishment lawyer; Kathleen Hill Jamieson, Dean of the Annenberg School for Communication, an expert on the use of the media for political purposes including how to influence political campaigns and elections; Sonia Jarvis, a lawyer who once worked with President Clinton; Harold Hongji Koh who was a legal adviser at the US Department of State from 2009 to 2013, nominated by President Obama, who in March 2010 gave a speech supporting the legality of drone assassinations; Charles Ogletree, Harvard law professor and a close friend of President Obama; Allen Pusey, publisher and editor of the American Bar Association Journal; Ben Sherwood, co-chair of Disney

Media, former president of ABC News and also a member of the Council on Foreign Relations. Paul Volcker not only is an individual financial supporter but is also on the Board. Aside from his position as a former chairman of the Federal Reserve (1979-1987) he was also chair of the US Economic Advisory Board, appointed by President Obama (2009-2011) a former chair of the Trilateral Commission, worked for the Chase Manhattan Bank and is very close to the Rockefeller family.

It also includes Harold Williams, former Chair of the US Securities and Exchange Commission (1977-1981) and member of board of directors of dozens of companies; William Julius Wilson, professor of sociology at Harvard; and last but not least, Christiane Amanpour, chief war propagandist for CNN, who just a few days after the story came out, appeared on CNN acting out a charade in which she interviewed a staffer from the ICIJ about the Panama Papers while pretending not to know anything about them. She was in fact interviewing a member of her own organization but she never informed her viewers of this.

Here's the point. This is not some independent, disinterested muckraking group dedicated to truth and democracy, nor indeed a research-based institute. This is an elite group lending their prestigious names and titles to shore up the credibility of what are otherwise simply functioning propagandists who, under the cloak of journalism, practice the art of deception on behalf of the American government and secret services. Indeed in the annual report, they even quote President Obama approving their work. In January 2017 this same group launched an attack on the government of China with another story of "leaked" financial documents implicating the Chinese leadership and have done it again in this new story, no doubt part of the "pivot to China." They released more information late in 2017.

The role of the western media is not to inform the public but, as Umberto Eco says, "to teach people how to think," to manipulate opinion and action. Their suppression of critical information is a lie and as that other great writer, Jose Saramago, wrote, they use "the lie as a weapon, the lie as the advance guard of tanks and cannons, the lie told over the ruins, over the corpses, over humanity's wretched and perpetually frustrated hopes."

It is time for these people to be exposed for what they are and called to account for their deception of the people they claim to serve.

For whatever form the propaganda takes it is a crime against the people, a crime against the republic, and a crime against democracy. Not only that: it is a part of the hybrid warfare campaign being conducted and because it is used to provoke a large and aggressive general war, it is a war crime.

It is a crime against the people because the people are in essence the nation. The leaders of our nations are merely our state representatives placed in positions of power through various more or less "democratic" mechanisms to act on our behalf for our benefit. But when these leaders instead represent secret cabals of financiers and industrialists who want to use the government machinery for their private benefit against the interests of their people then they have betrayed them. If their wars were just they would not need to use propaganda. But their wars are not just, they are the actions of gangsters writ large and so to get the people to go along, to fool them, they, by necessity, have to lie to the people.

It is a crime against democracy for the same reason, for democracy means that representatives of the people put in positions of power have a duty to inform the people honestly on all issues, to present all the facts and arguments, and most importantly, fulfil their duty to preserve the peace and to seek peaceful resolutions of differences between nations. But again, their wars for the profit of a few are always against the interests of the people and so the lies become entrenched in the historical record and further the system of control; with each lie the grave of democracy is dug deeper as the public's ability to perceive truth recedes.

It is a war crime because the propaganda is used to provoke war, to sustain war, to turn other people, declared to be the enemy, into beings that need to be killed. It robs them of their humanity, of their kinship with us, their desires and dreams, and makes them into vermin to be destroyed with ease and even joy in the killing. It turns us into salivating monsters calling for death of the other and cheering when the bombs explode; turns us all into the Hillary Clinton lunatic who cackled like some satanic demon as she claimed credit for a great man being cut to pieces before her eyes.

I could give dozens, hundreds, thousands of examples of how the propaganda is being used. As an international lawyer, my own experience at the ad hoc war crimes tribunals taught me that their primary function was not criminal justice but to put out propaganda about the western version of the wars concerned, to cover up the role of the west in those wars and to justify future wars.

The New York Times, BBC, CNN, CBC and the rest of the western media are full of it every day, with every day worse than the day before, against Russia, China, North Korea, Iran, Syria Venezuela, all the present targets. We all sense that the intensity if it is increasing, the vitriol is becoming more hysterical and absurd with every headline.

The journalists who write these propaganda pieces and the presenters who read them on television are among the worst of criminals as they sit there looking attractive, with their fake smiles and fake concern, while taking lots of money to lie to our faces every day. It takes a very low person to sit there and lie to their fellow citizens so easily. It takes someone who has no sense of morality whatsoever. One could say, and some do, that they are sociopaths. At minimum they are criminals, and they deserve to be in the dock with the leaders that hand them the scripts they read so willingly. Some have called for a new code of ethics for journalists and media but teaching ethics to such as these would surely be futile. What is required is a change in control of the media so that it serves the interests of the people and that cannot be achieved so long as capital rules.

It is not only necessary to eliminate nuclear weapons and downgrade militaries, it is also necessary to eliminate the psychological weapons that are used to justify, provoke and prolong war. Lenin once said that "disarmament is an ideal of socialism" and it was, we must not forget, the USSR that developed the ideals of international peace and responsibility for wars of aggression. The successor state of Russia still advances these principles. On the second day of the creation of Soviet power the Decree on Peace was issued that made it a matter of state policy that aggressive war is a crime. Up until then it was assumed that nation states had an inherent right to go to war for their own interests.

War propaganda is a way of preparing for aggressive war and consequently is a war crime. This was confirmed at the Nuremberg Tribunal in 1946.

This was echoed in the Resolution of the General Assembly of the United Nations of November 3, 1947 that denounced war propaganda;

> The General Assembly condemns all forms of propaganda, in whatsoever country conducted, which is either designed or likely to provoke or encourage any threat to the peace, breach of the peace, or act of aggression.

A Soviet draft definition of aggression presented to the General

Assembly in 1957 defined war propaganda as ideological aggression. Their draft stated that a state has committed ideological aggression when it "encourages war propaganda, encourages propaganda for the use of atomic or other weapons of mass extermination and stimulates Nazi-fascist views, racial or national superiority, or hatred and disdain for other peoples."

But before that the Supreme Soviet on March 12, 1950 had passed a domestic law on the defense of peace that stated:

> The Supreme Soviet of the USSR is guided by the high principles of the Soviet peace policy, which seeks to strengthen peace and friendly relations between the peoples, recognises that human conscience and the concept of right of the peoples, who, during one generation suffered the calamities of two wars, cannot accept that the conduct of war propaganda remain unpunished, and approves the proclamation of the Second World Congress of the Partisans of Peace, who expressed the will of the entire progressive mankind concerning the prohibition and condemnation of criminal war propaganda.
> The Supreme Soviet decrees,
>
> > *1. To recognise that war propaganda under whatever form it is made, undermines the cause of peace, creates the threat of new war and is the graves crime against humanity.*
> >
> > *2. To bring to court person guilty of war propaganda and to try them as having committed a most grave criminal offense.*

The Western powers blocked that 1957 Russian UN resolution to denounce war propaganda even though it was in accord with the principles of the United Nations Charter, which makes it a duty of all member states to preserve the peace. The West relied on arguments of "free speech," arguments that do not hold water since war propaganda is not designed to enlighten people but to twist their minds into thoughts of war, and is the equivalent of hate speech.

The Rome Statute of the International Criminal Court today contains a clause that arguably encompasses these principles in Article 5, dealing with aggression, though this clause is not yet in effect. It is one of the grave problems with the ICC, that aside from being controlled effectively by the US and European Union for their purposes, its statute does not include a specific section on war propaganda. But then the United States and its allies prevented the inclusion of such a clause just as they had prevented the adoption of the 1957 Soviet resolution at the UN so that they could continue using war propaganda as part of their arsenal for world control.

One day we can hope that those responsible for the war propaganda will face the peoples' justice but in the meantime we must be aware that every time we are confronted with it—when we open a newspaper, turn on the television, or radio, click that link on the internet—we are the victims of a war crime. The use of war propaganda is an integral part of the crime of aggression, and it is being committed against each and every one of us. And if that does not make you angry then what hope is there for peace in this world?

'CRUISE MISSILE LEFT' COMPLICIT IN AMERICAN ESCALATION TOWARD WORLD WAR III

Danny Haiphong

*Both Amy Goodman and Glenn Greenwald
joined the imperial chorus that the Syrian government
bore responsibility for an attack that had
yet to be proven even happened.*

*Cruise missile liberals, meet your brethren—
the cruise missile pinkos*

The US-led alliance of imperial nations has waged war on Syria for eight years with the hopes of overthrowing the independent Arab nationalist state led by President Bashar Al-Assad. Syria was believed to be another domino destined to fall in imperialism's great power game to contain any international threat to its rule. Former NATO general Wesley Clark revealed US plans in 2007 to use the September 11th attacks to justify the overthrow of seven countries in five years: Iraq, Iran, Libya, Lebanon, Somalia, Sudan, and Syria. Most of these countries have since been thrown into chaos by way of US imperial expansion in the Middle East and North Africa. Clark's admission should be enough to clarify the Trump Administration's most recent airstrikes on Syria as punishment for Syria's purported use of chemical weapons against its own citizens as an escalation of the broader war for US hegemony in the region and the world—not so much as it concerns the military significance of the strikes, but rather in driving home the symbolic implication by the very flimsiness of their pretext: the US will do what it wants, and who is going to stop us?

Yet many who reside in the United States view the war on Syria through the lens of the US empire. This lens is articulated by both US political parties, their foreign partners, and their faithful corporate media servants. These expert liars claim that Assad is a butcher and the Syrian government a brutal "regime." They don't talk about how the US military occupies a large portion of Syria, coincidently in the country's most resource rich region.[1] Also ignored is the fact that US allies such as Saudi Arabia and Turkey have loathed the Syrian government for its decision in 2009 to construct an independent pipeline[2] with Iran and Iraq to transport precious gas and oil resources to European markets. They pay no mind to the fact that the US, Saudi Arabia, Qatar, Turkey, and Israel, to name a few, have funded and armed hundreds of thousands of jihadist mercenaries for seven years in hopes that they would be rid of "the butcher" Assad and his nationalist policies. Imperialism wants Assad out because he stands in the way of US goals to dominate the region and keep Iran, Russia and China's rise to global prominence at bay.

Syria is presently the number one target of US imperialism. The ongoing war there has the potential to spark the kind of confrontation between great powers unforeseen in human history. In many ways, this confrontation has already begun. Russian forces in Syria have daily confronted US-backed jihadists armed with American-made weapons. US coalition strikes have killed Russian military personnel.[3] Just prior to Trump's airstrikes, seven Iranians were murdered in Syria by Israeli fighter jets.[4] Russia has spent years enhancing its military capabilities in order to address the US threat, whether in Syria or at its own borders with NATO.

Yet when the US, UK, and France launched over a hundred strikes on Syrian territory on April 14th, few in the US and West expressed any public outrage. Anti-war groups like the United National Anti-war Coalition (UNAC) mobilized around the country, but that was about it. Americans were once again immobilized for the usual reasons. Wall to wall pro-war corporate media coverage blaming Assad for what was billed as retribution effectively drowned out any anti-war analysis from reaching the ears of most Americans. Perhaps the most important factor in the lack of outrage was the scant possibility that American troops were going to be sacrificed during the escalation. No Russians were hit by the strikes, so a larger military confrontation was unlikely. And the US military showed how weak it has become as the Syrian government was able to shoot down a majority of the strikes with decades-old Soviet technology.[5]

Americans usually care about American troops dying but have a difficult time developing class-based solidarity with people around the world. The Black radical tradition has historically been the force that counters white supremacist chauvinism and pro-war sentiments in the US. But eight years of Obama effectively shifted the Black polity so far right that polls showed Black Americans possessing a more favorable view of Obama's declaration of war against Syria in 2013 than whites and Latinos. Neoliberal identity politics and the two-party duopoly system has for now swallowed the left whole. The Democratic Party wing of imperialism has dug deep into Wall Street coffers to disguise itself as the anti-Trump "resistance" that will bring stability back to the empire, i.e. will enforce it.

The Democrats and their Republican allies seek a more stable Administration in Washington to properly manage the affairs of the ruling class. Those affairs mainly deal with the questions of austerity and war. Trump has been deemed "morally unfit" for the Presidency by the likes of James Comey because his unpredictable and egoist tendencies make him less interested in the preservation of empire and more interested in the preservation of the voting bloc and conditions that made his Presidency possible. We largely have the "cruise missile left" to thank for the lack of an alternative to the crisis of US imperialism. This cruise missile left has aligned with the Democratic Party and the intelligence agencies against Trump and has dropped any anti-war, anti-imperialist, and anti-capitalist tendencies in the process.

Nowhere is this clearer than in its position on Syria. The cruise missile left is best represented by the likes of *Democracy Now!* and *The Intercept.* Both sources have worked together to subtly forward the agenda of US imperialism. Since 2011, Amy Goodman has never strayed from the NATO line on countries such as Libya, Syria, and Russia. Like the corporate media, Goodman and her staff at *Democracy Now!* have provided positive coverage of so-called humanitarian groups like the White Helmets[6] which have long been proven to work directly with

NATO-armed jihadist mercenaries ravaging Syria.[7] *The Intercept* and *Democracy Now!* have refused to invite any guests on their media that deviate from the NATO line on Syria.

These alternative news sources have benefited from the corporate takeover of the US media. *Democracy Now!* and *The Intercept act* as an escape valve from corporate media lies, which make them more difficult to criticize on those occasions when they serve the same interests as the corporate media outlets that spurred their formation. In their coverage of the alleged chemical attack in Douma, both Amy Goodman and Glenn Greenwald joined the imperial chorus that the Syrian government bore responsibility for an attack that had yet to be proven had even happened. Even Secretary of Defense James "Mad Dog" Mattis admitted that the US lacked evidence[8] backing up their claims against Assad. *The Intercept* and *Democracy Now!* staked their firm position against the Syrian government despite the overwhelming evidence that Syria had destroyed its chemical weapons in the OPCW brokered deal between Russia and the US in 2013—in fact, had turned these over to the US itself for destruction[9]—and that Syria, Russia, and their allies are the only parties interested in coming to a peaceful resolution to the war.

Cruise missile leftists thus bear much of the responsibility for the US, UK, and French airstrikes conducted against Syria on April 14th. After the strikes, Amy Goodman invited Chelsea Manning and so-called activist Rahmah Kudaimi to her show. Manning was given little time to speak while over seventy percent of the joint interview was taken up by Kudaimi's assertions that US airstrikes "enable" the Syrian " regime. " Kudaimi practically begged the US to conduct the airstrikes correctly and fulfill the legitimate demand of the Syrian people to overthrow the Syrian government. Nowhere did Amy Goodman challenge such blatant support of US imperial objectives in Syria and beyond.

Democracy Now! and *The Intercept* are more interested in facilitating the overthrow of the Syrian government than in examining their own government's role in the region. Neither source gives any coverage to the influx of head-chopping jihadist mercenaries whose roots lie in the CIA-sponsored war in Afghanistan in 1979. Neither mentions how numerous primary sources, such as the leaked 2012 Defense Intelligence Agency[10] document, pin US, Turkish, and Saudi support for "Salafists" in Syria for the rise of ISIS. Responsibility for the millions of displaced and hundreds of thousands of dead Syrians falls at the feet of US imperialism. And the cruise missile left would rather the world become engulfed in the flames of World War III than admit this fact.

The US government is the most murderous entity the world has ever known yet the focus of the cruise missile left maintains the chauvinistic and racist depictions of the Syrian government. These depictions have been proven to be outright lies time and time again. The Syrian government is the rightfully elected government of the Syrian people. President Bashar Al-Assad was reelected to office in 2014 by a large majority. Cruise missile leftists on *Democracy Now!* or *The Intercept* never bother to ask how a nation attacked by imperialist forces would advance its struggle against them by murdering its own citizens, or could survive long if there were indeed a legitimate rebellion of its people.

The imperial war on Syria is legitimate to the cruise missile left because it allows the Anglo-Zionist empire to express its intervention as humanitarian, similar to the US-NATO R2P (Responsibility to Protect) invasion of Libya. Gaddafi was painted by the cruise missile left as a barbaric and despotic dictator who was ludicrously claimed to have armed his Black mercenary army with Viagra to rape women and children. Assad has faced the same treatment as Gaddafi. The political legitimacy that collaboration with imperialism affords means much more to the cruise missile left than solidarity with oppressed people. That won't get you lucrative partnerships with foundations like First Look Media, the primary conduit for billionaire Pierre Omidyar's support for *The Intercept* or the Open Society, a conduit for billionaire George Soros' heavy support for Democracy Now![11]

Democracy Now! and *The Intercept* not only betray the people of Syria and Russia when they peddle pro-war narratives, but also poor and working-class people here in the United States. Neither the terror of police occupation and mass incarceration in the Black community nor the poverty being enforced across the boards by the US austerity regime will become any less ruthless should US imperialism spark a nuclear conflict in Syria.

ENDNOTES

1   https://www.mintpressnews.com/how-the-us-occupied-the-30-of-syria-con-

taining-most-of-its-oil-water-and-gas/240601/

2   https://www.counterpunch.org/2016/09/15/assads-death-warrant/

3   http://www.newsweek.com/us-military-kills-russians-syria-airstrikes-against-assad-supporters-reports-803949

4   https://www.haaretz.com/middle-east-news/russia-outs-israel-two-israeli-fighter-jets-struck-iranian-base-in-syria-1.5979943

5   https://www.theguardian.com/world/2018/apr/14/russia-claims-syria-air-defences-shot-down-majority-missiles

6   https://www.alternet.org/grayzone-project/how-white-helmets-became-international-heroes-while-pushing-us-military

7   http://21stcenturywire.com/2017/11/28/vanessa-beeley-presents-new-white-helmets-expose-to-swiss-press-club-geneva/

8   https://www.rt.com/usa/423961-mattis-syria-chemical-evidence/

9   https://www.washingtonpost.com/world/national-security/2014/06/29/3f6b6a88-fe1f-11e3-8176-f2c941cf35f1_story.html?utm_term=.007ac161e720

10 https://www.rt.com/usa/312050-dia-flynn-islamic-state/

11 http://www.boilingfrogspost.com/2013/10/18/bfp-expose-cia-obama-george-soros-coordinated-misinformation-campaign-targets-russia/

THE UNITED STATES AS A "SH*THOLE" COUNTRY

THE SH*THOLE PHENOMENON AT HOME AND ABROAD

Richard Falk

Disguising the Sh*thole Mission

Ever since the decline and fall of European colonialism the U.S. foreign policy has generally done its best to control the economic, political, and social development of countries in Africa, Asia, and the Middle East. Earlier it had dominated the Western Hemisphere, and at the end of 19th century, by recourse to warfare, the country acquired the colonial possessions of Spain (Hawaii, Cuba, Philippines, Puerto Rico). American leaders reconciled this outright imperial venture with maintaining national pride associated with breaking away from the British Empire in the Revolutionary War. The rationalization for acquiring Spain's colonial possessions was to provide these subjugated peoples with the blessings of supposedly benign American control. As any halfway honest student of history knows American control turned out to be no less cruel or exploitative than Spanish colonial rule. It was colonialism under a different flag, and as abusive of the native population.

Stripping away the ideology of U.S. expansionism exposes a set of realities devoted to squeezing wealth from Third World societies, confiscating or unjustly appropriating their resources, and as a result producing sh*thole conditions of impoverishment, corrupted elites, oppressive government, as well as a mixture of nationalist resistance and the collective loss of self-esteem. It is no wonder that persons so subjugated would seek to escape to countries where their life prospects would improve. Hence, migration and immigration was often facilitated by the greedy efforts of the American labor market to import cheap labor, especially after overt slavery was ended by the American Civil War.

What motivated the political leadership of the United States to engage in this kind of predatory behavior around the world? It was, at first, materialist greed, civilizational arrogance, and the need for export markets and sources of raw materials to satisfy the compulsions of nineteenth century industrial capitalism, essentially maximizing profits while ignoring massive poverty.

With the advent of Marxism, climaxing with the Cold War, came the American effort to protect capitalism against the appeals of socialism. Throughout the Cold War, as soon as the label of "Marxist" was pinned on a natural and nationally beneficial turn toward economic nationalism, the United States intervened as necessary to keep foreign governments from meeting the needs and attaining the aspirations of their own peoples. Iran (1953), Guatemala (1954), Chile (1973), and Nicaragua (1980s) are the most notable illustrations of Washington's inclination to seize a variety of excuses to engage in both covert and armed interventions to overthrow *democratically elected* governments. In some respect these governments shared the fatal mistake of seeking to gain control of their own national economic policy framework at the expense of foreign investors who had often been milking their economy by reaping excess profits while avoiding paying reasonable taxes. Early in revolutionary Cuba, Castro embarrassed the U.S. government by agreeing to compensate foreign investors on the basis of their assessed value as declared to the pre-revolutionary Batista government for purposes of taxation.

The several decades of Cold War were followed by 20 years of relative calm. Then came the 9/11 attacks providing a major excuse to carry American military power to the four corners of the earth, supposedly to achieve security in the face of terrorist threats. Yet this was never the whole story, and may not have been the main motivating explanation. 9/11 afforded an opportunity, seized by the neocon leadership, to pursue a far more ambitious geopolitical agenda. The Democratic opposition and the public sheepishly followed this militarist path without even posing serious questions.

While there is no doubt that the 9/11 attacks were a crime, was it reasonable and prudent that they were treated as an "act of war," the occasion for launching major wars against the distant countries of Afghanistan and Iraq, whose governments were never even seriously accused of complicity in the attacks? These aggressive policies produced a new wave of a sh*thole experiences for foreign societies, and for the United States they gave rise to blowback retaliations. Those resisting the American global security system with its globalizing neoliberal economic dimensions struck back with low technology tactics and weapons wherever an opening existed. The most significant blowbacks led to the growth of hyper-nationalist politics that clamped down on freedoms and minorities at home as well as gave a blank check to police and military spending. Combined with neoliberal finance capitalism, this meant a declining standard of living for 80% of Americans and a political reflex that blamed such a downturn in material expectations on immigrants, Muslims, and foreign adversaries.

Alongside these cause-and-effect explanations, preferred in our scientifically oriented civilization, is a less discernible collective narcissism: we Americans proclaim ourselves to be the best and certainly believe we know what is best for others. Our early national voices of vanity pretentiously projected their new country as "the city on the hill" that foreign societies should be encouraged to look up to, or as "the new Jerusalem" where a spiritualized politics was being constructed before the admiring eyes of the world. This kind of nationalist pride covered up and blindsided crimes of the greatest severity that were being committed from the time of the earliest settlements: genocide against native Americans, reliance on the barbarism of slavery to facilitate profitable cotton production and the supposedly genteel life style of the Southern plantations. This unflattering national picture should be enlarged to include the exploitation of the resources and good will of peoples throughout Latin America, who, once freed from Spanish colonial rule, quickly found themselves victimized by American gunboat diplomacy that paved the way for American investors or joined in crushing those bold and brave enough to engage in national resistance against the abuse of their homelands.

We as a country have never truly acknowledged the full extent of these crimes or the degree to which treating others so wretchedly deforms the national character of the perpetrator, contributing to elaborate rituals of denial so as to avoid confronting unpleasant realities embedded in an accurate rendering of the national narrative. We employ a variety of euphemisms and prohibitions designed to cover depraved behavior with a thick veil of ignorance and deception. Even 50 years after atomic bombs were dropped on Hiroshima and Nagasaki, a political backlash by "patriotic" groups forced the cancellation of an exhibition at the Smithsonian Institution in Washington that was planned to convey the extent of devastation and civilian tragedy endured by the population of these two Japanese cities. Instead of the politics of truth we have lived these many decades under the cloud of the fake cover story that dropping those bombs on these cities saved the lives of one million American soldiers that would have been killed in a land invasion of Japan. Such a tale overlooks Japan's diplomatic overtures seeking the war's end on terms favorable to the United States, and the degree to which the main motivations for dropping these bombs of mass destruction was to avenge the Japanese attack on Pearl Harbor and, more so, to send a signal to Moscow that the U.S. now possessed this super-weapon that could be used against Soviet cities, should the Kremlin dare to challenge the West.

In contemporary reality, the wellbeing of all but a tiny elite minority among the American people has long been subordinated to the vagaries of capital accumulation now globalized while the American people as a whole, especially minorities and the poor, were being ever more rendered almost superfluous and marginalized, necessarily sacrificed for the benefit of neoliberal versions of capitalism. National and global economic policy was being guided more consciously by the efficiencies of globalized finance capitalism and the promises of automation as the preferred alternative to organized labor. "Make way for the robots!" was the secret wish of the private sector, eager to supplant workers with machines. The labor force of the country was becoming an impediment to the efficient conduct of the financialization of capitalism. Robots were unlikely to complain about, let alone revolt due to the misallocation of public resources or grotesque disparities in wealth and income.

The wellbeing of the citizenry was reduced to an empty political slogan. The Occupation Movement and then Bernie Sanders made many of us realize that while 1% was prospering, 99% were languishing. Acute national inequalities were creating a deteriorating standard of living for most Americans, especially reflected in escalating costs and the declining quality of health, education, and housing. The proper reaction to such a crisis of gross inequality should have been at the very least a new, "new deal" that achieved a massive progressive redistribution of wealth and income that corrected current imbalances, and was designed to favor the 99%. As well, restoring the country's infrastructure should have begun to be treated as the number one priority of the deceptively wealthiest member of the sh*thole club of sovereign states.

This didn't happen at the last presidential election in 2016. Instead the sociopathology of Trumpism happened. The sh*thole world out there is being blamed for the diverse torments suffered by Americans, but instead of fixing the problems and situating responsibility where it belongs, Trump and his Republican allies have actually aggravated the causes of distress throughout the country, punishing those who are most vulnerable among us with crude threats and vindictive policies, producing panic and pain. In essence, the wider Trump phenomenon, incidentally not confined to the U.S., blames the victims at home and abroad, whether they be African Americans who have been scorched by police brutality or undocumented Hispanics trembling at the prospect of deportation and family breakup. Checking on the internationalization of Trumpism I recently asked a friend who had just returned from her native city of Calcutta whether she preferred Modi to Trump, and she responded with a resounding laugh that conveyed the sense that even posing such a choice was itself a travesty.

The Making of a Sh*thole America

If we try to identify the harm done to the American people, to the ideals of American constitutionalism, to America's global leadership role, and to the promise of democracy, we begin to appreciate the extent to which the wrongs done to others create intense blowback effects that are doing severe harm in the U.S. To be clear and honest, the wrongs of Trumpism are not unique to Trump. As the introductory overview suggests, the roots and deeds can be traced back historically to the earliest days of the American republic when genocide and slavery were the bedrock hidden foundations of the American political, social, and economic edifice. In this sense, although there were always "better angels" present and active within the political culture, it is important to acknowledge that the United States was a sh*thole country long before Trump's vulgar audacity went viral.

True, demonizing the whole continent of Africa, while seeming to celebrate the United States as the promised land for the whole world, did project an unusually tasteless image of what might be called white supremacist geopolitics. Characteristically, Trump denied his own disgraceful words uttered in the presence of reliable witnesses, but the PR damage had been done, and the frantic efforts by White House spin masters to reel back the language seemed artless and unconvincing, especially in view of Trump's campaign racism and his notorious comment ("there are fine people on both sides") reacting to violent encounters between anti-racists and neo-fascist demonstrators in Charlottesville.

What may be most at issue is whether it is reasonable to treat the United States as a sh*thole country as of the early twenty-first century. And if so, is such a dark indictment limited to the activities of Trump and his accomplices, or does it stretch back, winding its way through the history of the country, with various moral ups and downs along the way? I think that Trump has trumped his predecessors by departing from the public ideals of the country as authoritatively set forth in the Declaration of Independence and the first ten amendments of the Constitution, and solemnly invoked by leaders of all political persuasion on ritual occasion, which while hypocritical at least challenged the country to live up to standards of decency and fairness.

Even George W. Bush, despite a lawless and reactionary foreign policy that inflicted massive damage on foreign societies, made it a point to affirm American ideals of equality and non-discrimination based on race and class.

After 9/11 Bush made a concerted effort to distinguish between the perpetrators of the attacks and Islam as a religion and the Muslim minority in America. And Barack Obama, while not departing from the essentials of Bush's war against terror, mostly did his best to reclaim this image of gradually achieved decency in relation to American society, and its continued struggle to achieve a fairer, more just, society in all its aspects. Nonetheless, Obama, like Bush, was a creature of the system and performed in a manner that departed from these ideals, with deportations and punitive reactions to patriotic disclosures of crimes of war by Chelsea Manning and of anti-democratic surveillance and meta-data collections by Edward Snowden.

In effect, thinking more specifically about the derogatory labeling of the United States, it seems helpful to draw some distinctions. We are a sh*thole country to the extent that our leaders and citizenry accept extreme poverty, police brutality, environmental degradation, and global warming as non-issues while scapegoating Muslims, Hispanics, non-white immigrants, and refugees while projecting a world of drug addicts and Islamic radicals posing dire threats to the future. Such an inversion of societal realities and challenges does warrant the sh*thole labeling in the spirit of honest disclosure.

Beyond this, when our leaders portray America as doing good for others and itself without connecting the dots between intervention abroad and terrorism at home, it represents a combination of bad faith and faulty analysis. After World War II we insisted that Germany and Japan be exposed to their own criminality and depraved political behavior before they could be allowed to reclaim normalcy as a sovereign state entitled to full membership and participation in international society. Without the humiliation of defeat and occupation it is likely that these countries would have also avoided accountability for the sh*thole experiences of their past. Can the American people learn what it is to be a sh*thole country without undergoing such a traumatic pedagogy as lost wars and foreign occupation?

Part of such a learning process would relate to the whole current debate about immigration, legal and illegal, and refugees. We deform the economies and political realities facing people in foreign countries living in the corrupted aftermath of colonialism and capitalism, and then wonder why we should treat those that seek a better life as other than criminals and drug dealers. We forget the close interplay between our interventions, their civil strife, and the transnational migrations of desperate people in search of safety and security.

Europe is proving as unwilling to accept responsibility for giving rise to such desperate human behavior as is the United States. Instead of addressing the causes of refugee flows and transnational migration, walls are built, families broken, and immigrants are blamed for bringing crime and lawlessness wherever they go.

There is actually a double lesson to be learned. First of all, do not be so arrogant as to condemn other countries for failures that were brought about by our own efforts to exploit and dominate them. Do not condemn Africa without holding the institutions of slavery, colonialism, and capitalism significantly responsible. Without self-scrutiny there will be no learning, only recrimination, cycles of violence, endless repetition.

And even more centrally, don't look at the shortcomings of foreign societies without noticing those at home, especially in the ways vulnerable human beings are treated and the wealth of the society is distributed. Gross inequality is directly contrary to the claims of being a democratic society. As distinguished thinkers such as Tocqueville and Montesquieu long ago appreciated, democracies are much more fundamentally sustained by "the spirit of equality" than by periodic elections. To the extent that the American political system has become what John Dewey and Fred Dallmayr call "a money culture" we have forfeited and denigrated our democratic credentials. And if we lose those credentials, then judging ourselves by the standards Trump uses to judge others, we will indeed remain a sh*thole country.

A Concluding Remark

The American narrative continues to unfold, and it is far from over. The Trump rise represents the dramatic reemergence of the long repressed and supposedly renounced, yet obviously not extinguished, fascist virus that was always present, but mostly dormant and closeted, in the American body politic.

The challenge facing the American people is whether the relation of forces in the citizenry can be sufficiently altered so that those elements committed to a post-racist and materially equitable America can regain the initiative in the unfinished moral/political/economic/cultural struggle. If not, then the sh*thole unfolding will become more and more painful to experience for ourselves and for others.

More than gestures of reform are necessary. The Democratic Party, as now constituted, is too entangled with Wall Street and the workings of neoliberal globalization to offer the American people a benevolent alternative future that depends on the outcome of a struggle against the misallocation of resources in both public and private sectors. There needs to be a demilitarization of foreign policy and a reallocation of public resources to ensure that all of the people will have their needs met when it comes to diet, health, education, and shelter, as well as enjoying the restoration of infrastructure and the benefits of environmental protection.

Private sector radical reform would involve the establishment of a genuinely progressive tax on income and wealth so as to correct recent trends toward grotesque levels of inequality. Such patterns of economic reform would also need to be coupled with enhanced international regulation so that trade, investment, and finance served the needs and goals of *people* rather than satisfied the greed and ambition of those that focus on the efficiencies of *capital.*

In other words, reclaiming the mantle of a legitimate sovereign state requires more than getting rid of Trump and Trumpism, although that is the immediate priority. It is such a high priority because the relations between the state and the people are moving rapidly into that most dangerous of political territory—the terrain of pre-fascism, with truth mangled and trust betrayed. Beyond the menace of Trump and Trumpism lie the challenges associated with creating a social, economic, and cultural order that connects the quality of democracy with an ethos of equality or the lesser and more attainable goal of equity or fairness. Such an outlook requires a new understanding of citizen engagement, vital for a true democracy, that is aware that only transformative politics, guided by a commitment to justice for all, can have any hope of meeting the daunting political, social, economic, and ecological challenges confronting not only the American people, but humanity as a whole. As the lead international actor for the past century the United States needs to accept some responsibility for making foreign societies so unlivable that people flee elsewhere in desperation, and take steps to improve the situation.

To avoid and repudiate sh*thole status in the 21st century also requires a new *global* outlook as well as a transformed *national* outlook. The human species is challenged as a species by global warming and by the threats of nuclear weaponry. Our ability to meet such a challenge depends on leadership that is attuned to this wider reality and a peace and equity pedagogy that infuses education with a commitment to equality, equity, and a celebration of differences across such boundaries as ethnicity, race, religion, gender, nationality, class, and health without disrupting the specifics of identity that give meaning to our lives.

THE COSTS OF AMERICAN NARCISSISM

Kevin Barrett

Donald Trump, the 45th president of the United States, is widely reviled as a fool and a madman. And it isn't just adversaries like Kim Jong Un who have questioned the "dotard" president's intellect and stability. If Wolff's *Fire and Fury* is even 50 percent accurate, most of the people around Trump tend to agree with Kim.

Twenty-seven mental health professionals write in *The Dangerous Case of Donald Trump: 27 Psychiatrists and Mental Health Experts Assess a President* that Trump's narcissism seems extreme if not downright pathological. One of the authors, Bandy Lee, an assistant clinical professor of psychiatry at the Yale School of Medicine, has briefed Democratic lawmakers on the president's mental state. Though professional psychiatric associations discourage diagnoses-at-a-distance, seventy thousand self-described mental health professionals have signed a Change.org petition entitled "Trump is mentally ill and must be removed."

One possibility that mainstream liberal-left orthodoxy rarely considers is that Trump's psychological issues may reflect deeper personality disorders in the American character. US Americans are known globally for their narcissistic approach to world politics. Few know much about what is going on outside their borders, and even fewer really care. The YouTube comedy classic *Americans Are Not Stupid* has a bit of fun with the paradoxical fact that voters in the supposedly democratic nation that dominates the globe know virtually nothing, and care less, about the world they are running.[1]

But it isn't just the ordinary folks who display narcissistic ignorance. Daniel Ellsberg's book *The Doomsday Machine: Confessions of a Nuclear War Planner* shows that the brilliant, highly-educated architects of our nuclear war fighting plans and command and control systems have difficulty grasping the viewpoints of others (for instance, how nuclear first-strike plans look to the people being targeted) as well as the likely consequences of their blindly self-centered actions.[2]

People who pump up their own egos and lash out at others often wind up harming themselves, having denigrated their victims to such an extent that it impairs their ability to imagine retaliation. Donald Trump, whose Twitter war on the world is undermining his presidency, is an extreme example. In hopes of learning something about a larger American pattern, not just Trump's individual idiosyncrasies, I propose to psychoanalyze the 45th president's infamous remark about "sh*thole countries."

Trump's scatological insult to Caribbean and African nations (and brown-skinned peoples in general) is a not-atypical example of the president's habit of badmouthing the world. The *New York Times* has documented 425 of Trump's Twitter insults, which exemplify a pattern of behavior that might be charitably described as juvenile.[3] When schoolboys talk like that, we tell them to grow up. If they persist in their antisocial verbal behavior, they might be sent to a psychoanalyst who would diagnose their arrested development: The foul-mouthed bad boy's personality has somehow gotten stuck at what Freud called the anal sadistic stage of psychosexual development. This is the phase characteristic of two-year-olds. Its highlights include intermittent sadism, excessive interest in feces, and extravagant assertions of ego.

Why do sadism, scatology, and egomania coincide? Because the two-year-old's ego is learning to see itself as separate from the mother's body and the larger world. Feces represent the self (matter from inside the body) that is forcibly expelled into the not-self outside the body—a process emblematic of the child's newfound power and control. At the same phase of development, the mother's breast, the site where any incipient self/non-self distinction has always most blissfully dissolved, is suddenly seen as not-self: something that the child can bite without feeling the pain. Sadistic behavior toward the non-self becomes a way of affirming and aggrandizing the newly-developing self.

Trump tweets like a two-year-old, and the liberal establishment is horrified. But the president's sadistic, scatological egomania is all too American. For the United States, like the anal-sadistic child, is insecure about its newly-developing identity. It views the self (USA! USA! USA!) as the site of all goodness and power, and the Other, the non-American, as a constellation of sh*tholes fit to be bullied, bombed, exploited, starved, and generally mistreated with an intensity often corresponding to the darkness of skin in the local inhabitants.

The USA's sadistic aggression against un-American "sh*thole countries" symbolically equates to the throwing of feces, a common form of warfare among primates. But unlike the many species of monkeys who, when collectively angered, fling turds at neighboring tribes, the USA shits on its enemies by dropping bombs, dumping garbage, offloading unwanted goods at below-market prices that bankrupt indigenous industries, and looting everything of value. It is this process of sadistic exploitation that turns potentially viable nations with promising human and natural resources into hyper-exploited "sh*thole countries" exporting impoverished surplus populations as desperate refugees and emigrants.

The imperial colonizer's view of the Other nation as a place to devour value and offload waste is satirized in Swift's *Gulliver's Travels*.[4] Trump/America, like Gulliver, seems to imagine that the proper role for little brown people is to provide him a place to take a humungous dump, dutifully cart it offstage in a wheelbarrow, and then exhaust and bankrupt themselves striving to feed his gargantuan appetite. Like the Lilliputans who consider saving themselves from Gulliver-induced famine by starving him or shooting him with poisoned arrows, but hold back for fear of catching diseases from the gigantic rotting corpse, the world, tempted to kill the US empire by collapsing the dollar, holds back for fear of the lethal putridity that a suddenly dead (as opposed to slowly dying) American leviathan might emit.

The sado-masochism inherent in the relationship between the imperial hegemon and "sh*thole" client regimes is exemplified by the empire's widespread offloading of torture. It is widely accepted, and not entirely untrue, that, as Barack Obama famously said, the USA normally does not torture people—at least not openly, directly, legally, as a matter of public policy within the nation's borders. Instead, it offloads the horrors of torture by delegating the dirty work to its clients, whose professional sadists are trained by CIA specialists.[5]

This convenient arrangement, which offers the US government plausible deniability, was disrupted after 9/11 when neoconservatives—whose first loyalty is to Israel, the only nation that openly vaunts its practice of legalized torture—tried to "Israelify" America by fully legalizing and normalizing the torture of Arabs and Muslims, while disguising said torture with such euphemisms as "enhanced interrogation." Obama subsequently tried to roll back the Bush-Cheney regime's normalization of torture. But by refusing to prosecute the torturers, he left the door open for Trump, who has embraced sadism with a vengeance under the slogan "torture works!" and placed a known torturer, Gina Haspel, at the head of the CIA.

The 9/11 false flag operation was designed in part to pump up America's national sadism, weaponize it, and deploy it against Israel's enemies.[6] By generating a fabricated American revenge motif, 9/11 legitimized the torture, murder, and looting of the people of Afghanistan, Iraq, and other countries by linking them to the imaginary TV spectacle of September 11, 2001. The sadistic basis of the post-9/11 "crusade" (as Bush revealingly called it) was put on display with the release of the notorious Abu Ghraib photos, along with other revelations about America's worldwide torture gulag of "black sites" where suspected al-Qaeda operatives and innocent taxi drivers alike were swept up and abused. Estimates of the number of victims of this extrajudicial kidnapping and torture machine are well into the six figures; more than one hundred thousand people in Iraq alone were illegally imprisoned during the US war of aggression against Iraq between 2003 and 2009.[7] A total of around thirty-two million people have been murdered—up to five million directly, and twenty-seven million by indirect effects—in the 9/11 wars, according to Australian mass mortality expert Dr. Gideon Polya.[8] Afghanistan, Iraq, Libya, Syria, Somalia, and Sudan have been destroyed or degraded into "sh*thole countries" emitting a rising flood of desperate refugees, whose skin pigmentation and religious background apparently terrify Trump and much of his base.

This largely phantasmagoric fear of hordes of brown people overflowing from "sh*thole countries" upon which America has been dumping its bombs evokes a racist fear of *contamination*. The immigrants are seen as literal and figurative disease vectors. Such exotic tropical illnesses as Zika and Ebola (which pose statistically insignificant threats) stimulate mass panics, as fear of tropical diseases blends with the fear of the brown-skinned people among whom they occur. Ebola, with its colorfully horrific digestive-tract symptoms including explosive diarrhea and vomiting, is an especially apt representation of the fear of death/feces/brown people in the white American collective unconscious.

Alongside this biological contamination panic is a closely linked fear of social and behavioral contamination. Darker-skinned men have long been viewed by white communities as a sexual threat, as exemplified by the lynch mobs of the early twentieth century (a forerunner of the current epidemic of police executions of black men). Since 9/11, this fear of sexual potency signified by skin pigmentation has expanded to include a fear of immigrant and especially Muslim fertility. As European and European-American populations contract toward their pre-imperialist share of global population, the demographic expansion of Muslims and brown people is envisioned as a threat to the power and purity of white nations and communities. Muslims in particular—the main targets of the 9/11 public relations stunt[9]—are feared and hated due to their predilection for the "traditional family values" whose abandonment is the main cause of white demographic collapse. Such Muslim traditionalism is equated with sexism and patriarchy in the imagination of the Left, and with hordes of invading rapists in the imagination of the Right. These fears offer dreamlike images that disguise the reality that gave rise to them: Muslim sexuality, due to the widely respected institution of marriage, is both slightly more fertile, and significantly more restrained than non-Muslim sexuality, resulting in a modest relative increase in Muslim populations (as well as significantly lower rates of violent crime, suicide, divorce, single-parent families, drug and alcohol addiction, STDs, and other negative social indicators in Muslim communities).[10] Though the 9/11-instigated murder of millions of Muslims has marginally impacted Islam's demographic rise, even as the ideological war on Islam undermines the religiously-driven family values responsible for Muslims' higher birthrates and relatively healthy families and communities, overall trends still favor the continued expansion and social health advantages of the global Muslim *ummah*. Likewise, Islam's religious rituals and ideologies have survived the onslaught of secular modernity, and offer plausible alternatives to the dominant manifestations of hegemonic secular humanism—which include nationalism, capitalism, Marxism, and the current ultra-hegemon, neoliberalism.[11] This is the actual "Muslim threat" whose dream disguises terrorize the West.

Although Muslim immigration is having a real demographic impact on Europe, where birthrates have collapsed far below replacement level, it is in fact a negligible factor in the United States. Instead, it is immigration from Latin America, and modest but significant discrepancies between white and nonwhite birthrates, that promise (or threaten) to make whites just another American minority by 2050. Trump's animus against Mexicans, against whom his "Great Wall of America" project is directed, reflects white demographic fears, and leads many to wonder whether the Trump voter's real but dream-disguised wish is actually to "make America white again."

Though the president's remark about "sh*thole countries" ostensibly targeted the Caribbean and Africa, he would undoubtedly include Mexico and other Latin American nations (as well as Islamic countries) under that description, which evokes the stereotypically dirty public toilets of neo-colonized lands. Indeed, the expression "sh*thole country" uses metonymy to identify entire nations with their supposedly dirty public toilets; like such toilets, the nations so depicted are envisioned as run-down, poorly-maintained, generally filthy sites emblematic of low social status. Mexico and its southern neighbors, like its Caribbean neighbors to the east, are obviously key targets of the Trumpian imagination, as well as prime sources of "contaminating" brown-skinned immigration.

Indeed, "fecal contamination" and "Mexico" are linked in the white American collective unconscious. Americans visit Mexico far more than any other developing country, and regularly contact *turista* during their visits. Indeed, many a gringo has spent an inordinate amount of time unpleasantly experiencing the "sh*tholes" of Mexico. Such experiences undoubtedly inform the unconscious fears that put wall-building Trump in the White House—a victory achieved by targeting neurotic voters in swing states with messages that appealed to their neuroses, thereby manipulating their voting behavior below the level of consciousness.[12]

Fear of "Sh*thole Countries": An American Projection

Sigmund Freud popularized the notion of projection: the mechanism by which individuals protect themselves from recognizing their own unacceptable impulses and accompanying anxieties by attributing them to others. This psychological mechanism undoubtedly plays a role in xenophobia in general, and that of Donald Trump and many of his supporters in particular. Working class Americans have lost ground economically, and white American workers especially seem to have suffered psychologically from perceived loss of status. Sociologist James Petras estimates that about "500,000 mostly white working class victims" have died from narcotics overdoses and interactions between 1996 and 2016, a phenomenon he calls "genocide by prescription."[13] The collapse of white working class life expectancy, driven by exploding mortality among individuals in their prime years of adulthood, has been so pronounced as to push US life expectancy downward for the first time in recorded history, despite advances in longevity for every other group.[14] As Petras argues herein, this mass die-off has been consciously engineered:

> Since the advent of major political-economic changes induced by neoliberalism, America's oligarchic class confronts the problem of a large and potentially restive population of millions of marginalized workers and downwardly mobile members of the middle class made redundant by "globalization" and an armed rural poor sinking ever deeper into squalor. In other words, when finance capital and elite ruling bodies view an increasing "useless" population of white workers, employees and the poor in this geographic context, what "peaceful" measures can be taken to ease and encourage their "natural decline"?[15]

Trump voters, many of whom have experienced a decline in living standards from the middle class American norm to what were once considered Third World conditions, have good reason to fear the US becoming a "sh*thole country" (meaning a poorer country that would be less likely to offer well-maintained public toilets and other amenities such as good schools, libraries, culture and esthetics, transportation, health, recreation, and infrastructure). They have good reason to think that, barring drastic changes, America's greatness is behind it. But if they believe that contamination from brown-skinned countries is the problem, they are projecting. And if they embrace Trump's "solution" to that ostensible problem—building walls, cutting or stopping immigration, gutting the public sector, showering money on the rich, throwing away soft power and diplomacy, turning Mideast policy over to Kushner's Israeli and Saudi associates, and pumping up America's already bloated military in preparation for further adventures—they will, far from making America great again, greatly accelerate America's decline into something resembling a stereotypical sh*thole country. Why? The single biggest reason the USA is falling apart is military spending, which is greater than that of the next eight biggest-spending countries combined.[16]

In his new book *In the Shadows of American Empire*, Alfred McCoy endorses the prediction of the National Intelligence Council that US hegemony will end by 2030.[17] Imperial collapse will bring a major crash in American living standards and an accompanying decline toward "sh*thole country" status. Among the many causes of US imperial decline, McCoy singles out the coming decline and fall of the dollar as the world's reserve currency due to its massive debt (currently at over $20 trillion) which gives the US a debt-to-GDP ratio of over 100 percent. And the single biggest factor driving that debt is the bloated military budget, which Trump is massively inflating by a historic 10 percent in 2019.[18]

Yet such figures actually underestimate the real cost of military spending and war. Interest on the national debt, lost productivity (due to the diversion and waste of limited human and natural resources away from the productive economy), and increases in the many negative social indicators such as violent crime, suicide, and drug addiction that are tightly correlated with military spending are some of the reasons why feeding the Pentagon starves the domestic real economy and kills social capital.[19] Yet Trump imagines that throwing even more money at the military will somehow "make America great again." In making that mistake, he seems to be narcissistically preoccupied with projecting an image of strength, manliness, and homicidal virility ("my button is bigger than his button, and mine works!") while ignoring the reality on the ground: America is in decline primarily and precisely due to its misallocation of resources in favor of the military-industrial complex.

Trump's obsession with image over reality is often construed as pathological. Indeed, one of the key signs of serious mental disorders is a breakdown in reality testing, that is, the inability to distinguish the external world from one's own emotional reactions to it. But American exceptionalism—which Trump, to his credit, has questioned— exemplifies the same pathology. American exceptionalists, who dominate the US policy-making elite, narcissistically imagine that their own nation is somehow radically different from, and better than, other nations. Like the Israelis with their "chosenness" syndrome, Americans invoke this narcissistic ideology to systematically claim prerogatives for themselves that they deny others. When Americans meddle in other nations' elections, that's okay, because "we are the good guys"; but when Russians are accused of playing small-time games in American politics via Facebook ads, the end of the world is nigh. Like the Israelis, American exceptionalist imperialists are courting their own demise by exhibiting willful blindness to the viewpoint of the Other.

Sh*thole America and Its Toilet Paper Dollar

No psychoanalysis of Trump's "sh*thole countries" gaffe would be complete without the mention of money, which Freud famously held to be the symbolic equivalent of feces. A person overly fond of "piling up" money, in Freud's view, is a symbolic collector of excrement. The perverse connection between matter that symbolizes the highest possible value (gold) and the lowest possible value (shit) is illustrated in the famous folktale, cited by Freud, in which the devil offers piles of gold that turn to piles of shit when he leaves.

The modern real-world equivalent of the devil in Freud's folktale is the economic hit man (EHM). John Perkins describes in *Confessions of an Economic Hit Man* how, when working for a firm that fronted for an NSA-World Bank-USAID consortium, he strong-armed leaders of developing countries into accepting huge loans encumbered by unrepayable interest. The pile of gold dumped on the corrupt elites of those countries would quickly turn into a pile of shit from which the country would never be able to dig itself out. Instead, it would have to turn over its real assets—minerals, forests, water, roadways, and future productivity—to the international usury cartel. Perkins' account memorably describes how developing nations are turned into "sh*thole countries" by the predatory international bankers (and the US-based institutions they dominate). These same globalist financiers, of course, are also turning the US into a "sh*thole country" by orchestrating wars and other excuses for big military budgets, which are always borrowed from private bankers at unpayable compound interest.

The Freudian gold-vs.-lead opposition (with gold symbolizing value/life/fantasy and lead symbolizing shit/death/reality) is famously depicted in the climactic scene of Shakespeare's *The Merchant of Venice*, which outranks Ezra Pound's Canto XLV as the greatest Western literary work on usury. It reappears, more or less, in John Perkins' account of the EHM with "gold" (or its Federal Reserve equivalent) in one hand and "lead" (a bullet) in the other:

> "Congratulations Mr. President," Mr. Perkins says, assuming the role of the businessman, or economic hit man, as he likes to call his previous profession. "I just want you to know that in this hand I have a couple of hundred million dollars for you and your family if you play the game our way." With the practiced timing of an expert storyteller, Mr. Perkins pauses. "And in this hand I have a gun with a bullet in case you decide to keep your campaign promises."[20]

Perkins references *The Merchant of Venice* in his description of the first empire built primarily by usury: "Thus, we make loans to countries like Ecuador with the full knowledge that they will never repay them; in fact, we do not want them to honor their debts, since the nonpayment is what gives us our leverage, our pound of flesh."[21] The whole racket, Perkins explains, rests on the empire's ability to create as much fiat currency as it wishes, so that non-repayment by debtor nations isn't a problem. But the petrodollar— so named because Saudi Arabia has propped up the otherwise overvalued greenback by refusing to sell oil in any other currency—will almost certainly lose its status as de facto global reserve currency during the coming decade. As in Freud's favorite folktale, the devil, that head usurer of the empire of usury, will suddenly vanish from our shores, and Americans will discover that his gold has turned to shit. The resulting crisis in the US domestic economy will likely push the erstwhile world hegemon further down the road toward sh*thole nation status, giving Americans a noxious taste of the foul medicine their leaders have been foisting on the world.

This will mark the end of the "American century"—the roughly one hundred years during which the US profited, at least relative to the rest of the world, from the international usury cartel's depredations. The two-phase World War of the first half of the twentieth century benefitted the US economically by destroying its global competition. By midcentury the US had half the world's manufacturing capacity, a third of global GDP, and most of Europe's former colonies in its orbit. By sucking resources from the Third World to the imperial center, the US economy maintained its globally dominant position.

But despite the economic boom, the world wars and the changes they brought to the US arguably nudged the nation toward sh*thole status in ways few Americans realized at the time. In *The Geography of Nowhere: The Rise and Decline of America's Man Made Landscape*, James Kunstler explores the qualitative collapse of America's built environment during the course of the twentieth century.[22] In almost all ways, America was a vastly higher-quality place (in terms of architecture, design, materials, urban layout, public spaces, and so on) in 1900 than it was in 1950, and it has been getting worse rather than better ever since. Though Kunstler's primary villain is the automobile, he also suggests that American men who fought in the two-phased World War suffered from a war-induced spiritual malaise that contributed to the degradation.

One possible link between the spiritual and material destruction of the wars, and the domestic quality-collapse described by Kunstler, is the twentieth century triumph of usury, enshrined in America by the rise of the Federal Reserve banking cartel. Colonel House, the eminence grise behind President Woodrow Wilson, acted as the representative of the world's biggest banking families when he created the Fed in 1913 by pushing the requisite legislation through Congress.[23] Perhaps not coincidentally, House was also the individual most responsible for orchestrating the US entry into World War I in a Rothschild quid-pro-quo delivered to Britain in return for Palestine.[24] The 1913 takeover of America by the international usury cartel, which proceeded to drown the world in debt thanks to the world wars it orchestrated and guided, may have helped nudge the US toward the spiritual-material crisis described by Kunstler. For alongside war's pernicious effect on the human spirit we must consider the impact of an increasingly debt-based economy on human decision-making. Economic actors struggling with debt may turn toward ever-more-rapid production and distribution at the expense of quality and durability. Under debt-based currency systems like those that dominate today's global economy, explosive but superficial "growth" masks qualitative decline. The illusion of endless exponential growth promised by usury glitters like gold, but the reality is that everything turns to shit.

Conclusion

I have diagnosed Trump's "sh*thole countries" gaffe as a case of projection and scapegoating. A real effort to "make America great again" would mobilize not against Muslims, Mexicans, and brown-skinned immigrants, but against the two biggest enemies of both the United States and the rest of humanity: militarism and usury. America's infrastructure could be rebuilt, and the nation qualitatively upgraded beyond our wildest utopian imaginings, if we summoned the political will to disempower the international banking cartel, seize its wealth, devote that wealth to public spending, implement a global debt jubilee, institute a transparent public banking system, and slash military spending to the bone. The subsequent global rollback of military spending, accompanied by the universal triumph of public currency over privately issued usury money, could usher in a new golden age—one in which not only America, but also the former victims of its empire, could achieve greatness.

ENDNOTES

1   *Americans Are Not Stupid*, https://www.youtube.com/watch?v=fJuNgBkloFE.

2   Daniel Ellsberg, *The Doomsday Machine: Confessions of a Nuclear War Planner*, NY, Bloomsbury, 2017.

3   Jasmine C. Lee and Kevin Quealy, "The 425 People, Places and Things Donald Trump Has Insulted on Twitter: A Complete List," *New York Times*, January 3, 2018. (https://www.nytimes.com/interactive/2016/01/28/upshot/donald-trump-twitter-insults.html).

4   Jonathan Swift, *Gulliver's Travels*, Part One, Chapter 2, http://www.literature-project.com/gulliver-travel/gulliver_2.htm.

5   Alfred McCoy, *A Question of Torture: CIA Interrogation, From the Cold War to the War on Terror*, NY, Holt, 2006.

6   Christopher Bollyn, *Solving 9-11: The Deception That Changed the World*, Christopher Bollyn, 2012, http://www.bollyn.com/solving-9-11-the-book.

7   Michael Christie, "US Military Shuts Largest Detainee Camp in Iraq," Reuters, September 17, 2009.

8   Gideon Polya on real cost of 9/11 wars," http://noliesradio.org/archives/135624.

9   "The 9/11 tragedy is the most successful and most perverse publicity stunt in the history of public relations." Lynn Margulis, statement to PatriotsQuestion911.com website, August 27, 2007. http://patriotsquestion911.com/professors.html#Margulis

10 Javed Jamil, *Muslims Most Civilized, But Not Enough*, Mission Publications, 2013.

11 Murad Hoffman, *Islam: The Alternative*; Wendy Brown, *Undoing the Demos: Neoliberalism's Stealth Revolution*, NY, Zone, 2015.

12 *Trumping Democracy*, http://cinemalibrestudio.com/clsblog/2017/11/ 15/ trumpingdemocracy/). See also Nicholas Confessore and Danny Hakim, "Data Firm Says 'Secret Sauce' Aided Trump; Many Scoff," *New York Times*, March

6, 2017, https://www.nytimes.com/2017/03/06/us/politics/cambridge-analytica.html.

13   James Petras and Robin Eastman-Abaya, "Genocide by Prescription: The 'Natural History' of the Declining White Working Class in America," https://petras.lahaine.org/genocide-by-prescription-the-natural-history/.

14   World Socialist Web Site, "Life expectancy declines for white Americans." https://www.wsws.org/en/articles/2016/04/21/pers-a21.html.

15   Petras.

16   Peter G. Peterson Foundation, "U.S. Defense Spending Compared to Other Countries," https://www.pgpf.org/chart-archive/0053_defense-comparison.

17   Alfred McCoy, *In the Shadows of American Empire*, Chicago, Haymarket, 2017.

18   David S. Cloud, "Trump proposes huge increase in military spending," *Los Angeles Times*, February 12, 2018.

19   Robert Reuschlein, "Empire Economics," https://www.academia.edu/4044446/EMPIRE_ECONOMICS_Peer_Review_AWARD_12ppt.4p_13-14.

20   Landon Thomas, Jr. "Confessing to the Converted," *New York Times*, February 19, 2006, http://www.nytimes.com/2006/02/19/business/yourmoney/confessing-to-the-converted.html.

21   John Perkins, *Confessions of an Economic Hit Man*, p.250, NY: Penguin, 2006.

22   James Kunstler, *The Geography of Nowhere: The Rise and Decline of America's Man Made Landscape*, NY, Simon and Schuster, 1994.

23   Laurent Guyénot, *From Yahweh to Zion: Jealous God, Chosen People, Promised Land...Clash of Civilizations*, p.226, Sifting and Winnowing, 2018.

24   Guyénot, 221-228.

US CAPITALISM AND THE OPIOID EPIDEMIC

Robin Eastman Abaya

Introduction

The link between capitalism and opium reaches back to the middle of the 19th century, when the British empire forcibly promoted opium consumption and induced and addicted millions of Chinese people to become opium addicts. In order to undermine resistance and conquer and exploit China.

In the 21st century, a similar process, dubbed the "opioid epidemic," is ravaging American workers, families, neighborhoods, communities, cities and states—the entire fabric of US society.

Official government investigators identify 500,000 opioid killings, based on the understated medical accounts. Most likely many millions of additional opioid deaths were attributed to heart failure and other causes derived from opioids.

It's the opioid epidemic that accounts for the "declining labor force participants among prime age workers" per Federal Reserve head Janet Yellen's testimony to the US Senate.

For over a decade the opioid deaths were ignored by both political parties, by writers and academics of the left and right, and by doctors and hospital administrators. But more important the Federal Drug Administration (FDA) approved the manufacture, marketing and sale of billions of opioid-addicting drugs to tens of millions of US citizens. Between 1999-2014 opioid drug corporations earned $10 billion dollars annually.

In the following section, we will discuss the larger picture, the powerful socio-economic and political forces who have benefited and profited from the addiction and killing of millions of Americans – past and present.

The Addiction Power Elite

Today there is a rush among government officials, to hold hearings and consider legislation to "alleviate" or "treat" the opioid crises.

Of late a few leftist journalists have attacked the pharmaceutical industry, and others have cited the "negligence" of the FDA.

While hundreds of thousands of Americans have been murdered by opioids and thousands more are dying every day, the Left and the Democratic Party demand equal access to toilets for transgenderites and investigations of fake Russian plots as the route to seize control of the electoral machinery.

The "drug epidemic" is about the structure of power and social relations. At its roots, American capitalism has degraded, impoverished and exploited US workers and employees with increasing intensity over the past two decades. Workers have lost collective workplace and political influence. Working conditions have deteriorated—capitalists can hire and fire at their will; salaries, pensions and death benefits have declined.

The decline of working conditions has led to a deterioration of social conditions: family, neighborhood and community life has been torn asunder. Anxiety and insecurity is rampant among workers and employees everywhere.

Income inequalities have widened, health and educational inequalities have deepened. Children of the upper 20% have privileged access to elite universities based on family and ethnic ties; elite families have the most thorough and advanced medical care.

Working people are treated in a cursory and inadequate way by physician assistants and subject to long-waiting emergency rooms. Instead of being given appropriate health care they are prescribed pain killers—opioids, approved by the FDA and manufactured and marketed by billionaire pharmaceutical corporations.

The opioid killing fields have their origins and logic in the convergence of several inter-related features of US capitalism.

- The capitalist class increases profits by lowering the cost of production by reducing health costs for labor. This leads to workers' dependence on relatively cheap and available opioids, which lead to addiction and death.
- Capitalists dismiss workers who suffer from workplace injuries—which forces workers to avoid sick leave and to rely on opioids to get them through. The manufacturers falsely claim the opiods are not addictive.
- Capitalists profit from the premature death by addiction of older workers thereby lowering pension and health payments.
- Capitalists hire younger workers (eighteen to thirty years old) at lower tier pay and benefits scales. They are subject to the insecurities of contingent employment, as part of the "gig economy" (outsourcing to "self-employed" workers and employees). They are forced to rely on opioids to overcome physical and mental disabilities. This accounts for the "mystery" of declining levels of young workers' labor participation despite relatively high employment.

In sum, the structure and relations of contemporary US capitalism is the general cause of the opioid epidemic. None of the current programs to alleviate addiction call into question the systemic causes—because they operate under the rules and dominance of their paymasters.

Big Pharma Drives the Opioid Epidemic

Billion dollar pharmaceutical corporations produce, manufacture, manipulate and market the killer opioids.

The leading opioid patron is the Sackler family, founded and directed by the recently deceased Raymond Sackler and his family. Born to a Jewish eastern European family the Sacklers rose from producing laxatives and ear wax to devising the highly addictive "pain killers" (sic) oxycontin in the 1990s.

The Sacklers established a large-scale sales force to bribe, convince and deceive doctors that Oxy was not addictive and harmful.

Doctors were enticed with all expenses conferences on pain killers or paid lucrative fees to promote the benefits of Oxy to their colleagues.

The Sacklers net worth rose to $14 billion dollars per the *Forbes* billionaires listing. Murder by opioid addiction multiplied by the tens of thousands.

The Sacklers became patrons of the arts and sciences in New York, London, and Tel Aviv. New York glitterati swooned, Queen Elizabeth awarded Sackler a knighthood, as a multitude of American Oxy addicts were killed a year.

Under Sackler's lead other pharma billionaires joined the slaughter; the killing rate multiplied.

The killing fields finally led to the Sacklers being fined a token $634.5 million dollars in 2007 for fraudulently downplaying the abuse and addiction of Oxy—little more than the cost of doing business. The power of the Sacklers assured they would never be accused of any "misconduct"—or murder—in any court case, which might lead to personal punishment!

Medical Practitioners, Hospitals and Government Are Complicit

Oxy and other addictive drugs are still mass produced, killing over 50,000 people each year. The chain of causation goes from systemic capitalist profiteering by billionaire pharmaceutical corporations to hospital corporate enterprises to doctors and their staff. And the government has done little to stop it.

Bear in mind: these are prescription drugs, prescribed by medical professionals. Thousands of doctors, whether by bribes or ignorance, are implicated in the promotion of the addiction. This malpractice is so well-known it even became the subject of a CNN Exclusive titled "The more opiods doctors prescribe, the more money they make". Many doctors are employed by corporate hospitals who want patients. Many employ physician assistants who order the addictive pain killers for their patients.

Not just doctors but hospitals prescribe the drugs; per the results of a National Library of Medicine/National Institutes of Health study, "Among 623,957 hospitalizations, 92 882 (14.9%) were associated with a new opioid claim."

The principal political accomplice of death by addiction is the federal government.

The President and Congress, Democrats and Republicans, ignored the epidemic in large part because they were bought off by big pharma. As the British newspaper, the *Guardian,* noted, "Drugmakers have poured close to $2.5bn into lobbying and funding members of Congress over the past decade."

The Federal Drug Administration has ignored and thereby culpably approved the opiod killing fields. Even today, despite the widespread recognition of opiod effects, as above indicated, and even as the toll has surpassed 500,000 victims, death by addiction is still FDA approved.

Only after two decades did a few governors see a source of revenue via lawsuits against big pharma. Senate sponsored investigations have added up the death toll but no laws terminating the sale of opioids and prosecuting the pharma killers is on the agenda.

What is to be Done?

The drug addiction epidemic is a million-person killing field. The victims and their effective executioners, the merchants of death, have a name and location in the capitalist system.

The vast majority of victims are working class: the low paid, young and old, the insecure and under employed, and especially those without adequate health care.

Over 5 million are afflicted: a truly American Holocaust leaving family survivors in the multi-millions.

The executioners and their accomplices are rich, college-educated patrons of the arts, who receive excellent health care, and are politically well connected. To date, they have been enjoying immunity from conviction.

The addiction crises reflects a class struggle of the upper class against the middle and lower classes, of which opioids are only one instance. But therein lies the basis to approach a solution.

There are historical precedents for successfully eliminating drug traffickers, beginning with the case of China. A century of British-sponsored opium deaths ended with the Chinese revolution of 1949, whose leadership proceeded to arrest, prosecute and execute the opium "entrepreneurs," followed by the rehabilitation of addicts, and their incorporation into the workforce.

Likewise, in Cuba, the revolutionary government smashed the

drug and brothel centers run by Meyer Lansky and the Mafia, and forced them to flee to Miami, Palermo and Tel Aviv.

The first step in a drug war in the US requires the organization of mass movements, anti-drug lawyers, doctors and community organizers.

The second step involves a program to outlaw addictive drug sales and the prosecution, arrest and jailing of the manufacturers, distributors and salespersons of addictive drugs.

This process requires attacking and transforming the economic roots of drug addiction—the capitalist system, which induces the pain and suffering, the corporations which produce and distribute the toxic pain/killer, and the private medical system which prescribes the drugs —all for private profit.

Successful local struggles can build the political power base that moves "studies" and "critiques" to direct action and electoral changes.

Outlawing the source of profit can weaken the power of the billionaire drug dealers and their political allies that have noxious effects other than medical ones.

Millions of lives are at stake, people have their survival to win.

ENDNOTES

1 https://www.bloomberg.com/news/articles/2017-07-13/yellen-says-opioid-use-is-tied-to-declining-labor-participation.

2 https://www.cnn.com/2018/03/11/health/prescription-opioid-payments-eprise/.

3 "Hospital Prescribing of Opioids to Medicare Beneficiaries." https://www.ncbi.nlm.nih.gov/pmc/articles/PMC4955877/.

4 Chris McGreal, "How big phrama's money – and its politicians – feed the opiod crisis," The Guardian, October 19, 2017. https://www.theguardian.com/us-news/2017/oct/19/big-pharma-money-lobbying-us-opioid-crisis.

REPORT OF THE SPECIAL RAPPORTEUR ON EXTREME POVERTY AND HUMAN RIGHTS ON HIS MISSION TO THE UNITED STATES OF AMERICA[*]

Philip Alston

Human Rights Council
Thirty-eighth session
18 June–6 July 2018
Agenda item 3

I. Introduction

1. The Special Rapporteur on extreme poverty and human rights visited the United States of America from 1 to 15 December 2017, in accordance with Human Rights Council resolution 35/19. The purpose of the visit

[*] UN Doc A/HRC/38/33/Add.1, 4 May 2018, see https://undocs.org/A/HRC/38/33/ADD.1.

was to report to the Council on the extent to which the Government's policies and programmes relating to extreme poverty are consistent with its human rights obligations and to offer constructive recommendations to the Government and other stakeholders. The Special Rapporteur is grateful to the Government for inviting him, for facilitating his visit and for continuing its cooperation with the Council's accountability mechanisms that apply to all States.[1]

2. During his visit, the Special Rapporteur met with government officials at the federal, state, county and city levels, members of Congress, representatives of civil society, academics and people living in poverty. He also received more than 40 detailed written submissions in advance of his visit.[2] He visited California (Los Angeles and San Francisco), Alabama (Lowndes County and Montgomery), Georgia (Atlanta), Puerto Rico (San Juan, Guayama and Salinas), West Virginia (Charleston) and Washington, D.C. He is deeply grateful to all those who organized community consultations for him in these locations, and to the US Human Rights Network, which devoted a full day of its 2017 national convening in Atlanta to his country visit.

3. The strict word limit for this report makes it impossible to delve deeply into even the key issues. Fortunately, there is already much excellent scholarship and many civil society analyses of the challenges of poverty in the United States.[3] In the present report, the Special Rapporteur aims to bring together some of those analyses, identify the key poverty-related problems and explain the relevance of the international human rights obligations of the United States in this context. As with all such country visits, the consideration of the report by the Human Rights Council will enable other States to examine the extent to which the United States is living up to its international obligations.

II. Overview

4. The United States is a land of stark contrasts. It is one of the world's wealthiest societies, a global leader in many areas, and a land of unsurpassed technological and other forms of innovation. Its corporations are global trendsetters, its civil society is vibrant and sophisticated and its higher education system leads the world. But its immense wealth and expertise stand in shocking contrast with the conditions in which vast numbers of its citizens live. About 40 million live in poverty,

18.5 million in extreme poverty, and 5.3 million live in Third World conditions of absolute poverty[4] It has the highest youth poverty rate in the Organization for Economic Cooperation and Development (OECD), and the highest infant mortality rates among comparable OECD States. Its citizens live shorter and sicker lives compared to those living in all other rich democracies, eradicable tropical diseases are increasingly prevalent, and it has the world's highest incarceration rate, one of the lowest levels of voter registrations in among OECD countries and the highest obesity levels in the developed world.

5. The United States has the highest rate of income inequality among Western countries.[5] The $1.5 trillion in tax cuts in December 2017 overwhelmingly benefited the wealthy and worsened inequality. The consequences of neglecting poverty and promoting inequality are clear. The United States has one of the highest poverty and inequality levels among the OECD countries, and the Stanford Center on Inequality and Poverty ranks it 18th out of 21 wealthy countries in terms of labour markets, poverty rates, safety nets, wealth inequality and economic mobility. But in 2018 the United States had over 25 percent of the world's 2,208 billionaires.[6] There is thus a dramatic contrast between the immense wealth of the few and the squalor and deprivation in which vast numbers of Americans exist. For almost five decades the overall policy response has been neglectful at best, but the policies pursued over the past year seem deliberately designed to remove basic protections from the poorest, punish those who are not in employment and make even basic health care into a privilege to be earned rather than a right of citizenship.

6. The visit of the Special Rapporteur coincided with the dramatic change of direction in relevant United States policies. The new policies: (a) provide unprecedentedly high tax breaks and financial windfalls to the very wealthy and the largest corporations; (b) pay for these partly by reducing welfare benefits for the poor; (c) undertake a radical programme of financial, environmental, health and safety deregulation that eliminates protections mainly benefiting the middle classes and the poor; (d) seek to add over 20 million poor and middle class persons to the ranks of those without health insurance; (e) restrict eligibility for many welfare benefits while increasing the obstacles required to be overcome by those eligible; (f) dramatically increase spending on defence, while rejecting requested improvements in key veterans' benefits; (g) do not

provide adequate additional funding to address an opioid crisis that is decimating parts of the country; and (h) make no effort to tackle the structural racism that keeps a large percentage of non-Whites[7] in poverty and near poverty.

7. In a 2017 report, the International Monetary Fund (IMF) captured the situation even before the impact of these aggressively regressive redistributive policies had been felt, stating that the United States economy "is delivering better living standards for only the few", and that "household incomes are stagnating for a large share of the population, job opportunities are deteriorating, prospects for upward mobility are waning, and economic gains are increasingly accruing to those that are already wealthy".[8]

8. The share of the top 1 per cent of the population in the United States has grown steadily in recent years. In 2016 they owned 38.6 per cent of total wealth. In relation to both wealth and income the share of the bottom 90 per cent has fallen in most of the past 25 years.[9] The tax reform will worsen this situation and ensure that the United States remains the most unequal society in the developed world. The planned dramatic cuts in welfare will essentially shred crucial dimensions of a safety net that is already full of holes. Since economic and political power reinforce one another, the political system will be even more vulnerable to capture by wealthy elites.

9. This situation bodes ill not only for the poor and middle class in America, but for society as a whole, with high poverty levels "creating disparities in the education system, hampering human capital formation and eating into future productivity."[10] There are also global consequences. The tax cuts will fuel a global race to the bottom, thus further reducing the revenues needed by Governments to ensure basic social protection and meet their human rights obligations. And the United States remains a model whose policies other countries seek to emulate.

10. Defenders of the status quo point to the United States as the land of opportunity and the place where the American dream can come true because the poorest can aspire to the ranks of the richest. But today's reality is very different. The United States now has one of the lowest rates of intergenerational social mobility of any of the rich countries.[11] Zip codes, which are usually reliable proxies for race and wealth,

are tragically reliable predictors of a child's future employment and income prospects. High child and youth poverty rates perpetuate the intergenerational transmission of poverty very effectively, and ensure that the American dream is rapidly becoming the American illusion. The equality of opportunity, which is so prized in theory, is in practice a myth, especially for minorities and women, but also for many middle-class White workers.

11. New technologies now play a central role in either exacerbating or reducing poverty levels in the United States. Some commentators are singularly optimistic in this regard and highlight the many potential benefits of new technologies, including those based on artificial intelligence, for poverty reduction efforts in fields as diverse as health care, transportation, the environment, criminal justice, and economic inclusion.[12] Others acknowledge the downsides, and especially the potential negative effects of automation and robotization on future employment levels and job security.[13] But remarkably little attention has been given to the specific impact of these new technologies on the lives of the poor in American society today.[14] Such inquiries have significance well beyond that pertaining to the poor, since experience shows that those in poverty are often a testing ground for practices and policies subsequently applied more broadly. In the present report, the Special Rapporteur seeks to stimulate deeper reflection on the impact of new technologies on the human rights of the poorest.

III. Human rights dimension

12. Successive administrations, including the current one, have determinedly rejected the idea that economic and social rights are full-fledged human rights, despite their clear recognition not only in key treaties that the United States has ratified, such as the Convention on the Elimination of All Forms of Racial Discrimination, but also in the Universal Declaration of Human Rights, which the United States has long insisted other countries must respect. But denial does not eliminate responsibility, nor does it negate obligations. International human rights law recognizes a right to education, a right to health care, a right to social protection for those in need and a right to an adequate standard of living. In practice, the United States is alone among developed countries in insisting that, while human rights are of fundamental importance, they do not include rights that guard against dying of hunger, dying from a

lack of access to affordable health care or growing up in a context of total deprivation. Since the United States has refused to accord domestic recognition to the economic and social rights agreed by most other States in the International Covenant on Economic, Social and Cultural Rights and other treaties,[15] except for the recognition of some social rights, and especially the right to education, in state constitutions, the primary focus of the present report is on those civil and political rights reflected in the United States Bill of Rights and in the International Covenant on Civil and Political Rights, which the United States has ratified.

IV. Who are "the poor"?

13. In thinking about poverty, it is striking how much weight is given to caricatured narratives about the purported innate differences between rich and poor that are consistently peddled by some politicians and media. The rich are industrious, entrepreneurial, patriotic and the drivers of economic success. The poor are wasters, losers and scammers. As a result, money spent on welfare is money down the drain. If the poor really want to make it in the United States, they can easily do so: they really can achieve the American dream if only they work hard enough. The reality, however, is very different. Many of the wealthiest citizens do not pay taxes at the rates that others do, hoard much of their wealth offshore and often make their profits purely from speculation rather than contributing to the overall wealth of the American community.

14. In imagining the poor, racist stereotypes are usually not far beneath the surface. The poor are overwhelmingly assumed to be people of colour, whether African Americans or Hispanic "immigrants". The reality is that there are 8 million more poor Whites than there are poor Blacks.[16] The face of poverty in America is not only Black or Hispanic, but also White, Asian and many other backgrounds.

15. Similarly, large numbers of welfare recipients are assumed to be living high on "the dole". Some politicians and political appointees with whom the Special Rapporteur spoke were completely sold on the narrative of such scammers sitting on comfortable sofas, watching cable television or spending their days on their smartphones, all paid for by welfare. The Special Rapporteur wonders how many of those politicians have ever visited poor areas, let alone spoken to those who dwell there. There are anecdotes aplenty, but little evidence. In every society, there

are those who abuse the system, as much in the upper income levels as in the lower. But in reality, the poor are overwhelmingly those born into poverty, or those thrust there by circumstances largely beyond their control, such as physical or mental disabilities, divorce, family breakdown, illness, old age, unliveable wages or discrimination in the job market.

V. Current extent of poverty in the United States of America

16. There is considerable debate over the extent of poverty in the United States, but the present report relies principally upon official government statistics, especially from the United States Census Bureau. It defines and quantifies poverty in America based on "poverty thresholds" or official poverty measures, updated each year. These thresholds have been used since President Lyndon B. Johnson's war on poverty in the 1960s and use a set of dollar value thresholds that vary by family size and composition to determine who is in poverty.[17] Following much criticism of the official poverty measures, the Census Bureau developed a supplemental poverty measure, which is preferred by many experts.[18] According to the official poverty measures, in 2016, 12.7 per cent of Americans were living in poverty;[19] according to the supplemental poverty measure, the figure was 14 per cent.[20]

VI. Problems with existing governmental policies

17. There is no magic recipe for eliminating extreme poverty, and each level of government must make its own good-faith decisions. At the end of the day, however, particularly in a rich country like the United States, the persistence of extreme poverty is a political choice made by those in power. With political will, it could readily be eliminated. What is known, from long experience and in the light of the Government's human rights obligations, is that there are indispensable ingredients for a set of policies designed to eliminate poverty. They include: democratic decision-making, full employment policies, social protection for the vulnerable, a fair and effective justice system, gender and racial equality, respect for human dignity, responsible fiscal policies and environmental justice.

As shown below, the United States falls well short on each of these measures.

A. Undermining of democracy

18. The cornerstone of American society is democracy, but it is being steadily undermined, and with it the human right to political participation protected in article 25 of the International Covenant on Civil and Political Rights. The principle of one person, one vote applies in theory, but is increasingly far from the reality.

19. In a democracy, the task of government should be to facilitate political participation by ensuring that all citizens can vote and that their votes will count equally. However, in the United States there is overt disenfranchisement of more than 6 million felons and ex-felons,[21] which predominantly affects Black citizens since they are the ones whose conduct is often specifically targeted for criminalization. In addition, nine states currently condition the restoration of the right to vote after prison on the payment of outstanding fines and fees. A typical outcome is that seen in Alabama, where a majority of all ex-felons cannot vote.[22]

20. Then there is covert disenfranchisement, which includes the dramatic gerrymandering of electoral districts to privilege particular groups of voters, the imposition of artificial and unnecessary voter identification requirements, the blatant manipulation of polling station locations, the relocation of Departments of Motor Vehicles' offices to make it more difficult for certain groups to obtain identification, and the general ramping up of obstacles to voting, especially for those without resources. The net result is that people living in poverty, minorities and other disfavoured groups are being systematically deprived of their right to vote.

21. It is thus unsurprising that the United States has one of the lowest turnout rates in elections among developed countries, with only 55.7 per cent of the voting-age population casting ballots in the 2016 presidential election.[23] Registered voters represent a much smaller share of potential voters in the United States than in just about any other OECD country. Only about 64 per cent of the United States voting-age population was registered in 2016, compared with 91 per cent in Canada and the United Kingdom of Great Britain and Northern Ireland, 96 per cent in Sweden and nearly 99 per cent in Japan. Low turnouts are also explained by the perception that election outcomes will have no impact on the lives of poor people. One politician remarked to the Special Rapporteur on

how few campaign appearances most politicians bother to make in overwhelmingly poor districts, which reflects the broader absence of party representation for low-income and working-class voters.[24]

22. The link between poverty and the absence of political rights is perfectly illustrated by Puerto Rico. If it were a state, it would be the poorest in the Union. But it is not a state, it is a mere "territory". Puerto Ricans who live on the island have no representative with full voting rights in Congress and cannot vote in presidential elections, although they can vote in Presidential primaries. In a country that likes to see itself as the oldest democracy in the world and a staunch defender of political rights on the international stage, more than 3 million people who live on the island have no real power in their own capital.

23. Puerto Rico has a fiscal deficit and a political rights deficit, and the two are not easily disentangled. The Special Rapporteur met with the Executive Director of the Financial Oversight and Management Board that was imposed by Congress in 2016 on Puerto Rico as part of the Puerto Rico Oversight, Management, and Economic Stability Act. There is little indication that social protection concerns feature in a meaningful way in the Board's analyses. At a time when even the IMF is insisting that social protection should be explicitly factored into prescriptions for fiscal adjustment (i.e., austerity), the Board should take account of human rights and social protection concerns as it contemplates far-reaching decisions on welfare reform, minimum wage and labour market deregulation.

24. It is not for the Special Rapporteur to suggest any resolution to the hotly contested issue of the constitutional status of Puerto Rico. Many interlocutors, however, made clear the widespread feeling that Puerto Ricans consider their territory to be colonized and that the United States Congress is happy to leave them in a limbo in which they have neither meaningful Congressional representation nor the ability to govern themselves. In the light of recent Supreme Court jurisprudence and Congress's adoption of the Puerto Rico Oversight, Management, and Economic Stability Act there seems to be good reason for the Special Political and Decolonization Committee of the United Nations to conclude that the island is no longer a self-governing territory.

B. Shortcomings in basic social protection

25. It is sometimes argued that President Johnson's war on poverty has failed miserably because, despite the "trillions of taxpayer dollars" spent on welfare programmes over the past five decades, the official poverty rate has remained largely unchanged.[25] The proposed solution then is to downsize the safety net by making it more "efficient", "targeted" and "evidence-based," while underlining the need to move "from welfare to work."[26]

26. These ideas underpin both Speaker Paul Ryan's blueprint for welfare reform[27] and the budget proposed by President Donald Trump for the fiscal year 2019, which decries "stubbornly high" enrolment in welfare programmes, and describes millions of Americans as being "in a tragic state of dependency on a welfare system that does not reward work, and in many cases, pays people not to work".[28]

27. The available evidence, however, points in a very different direction. A 2014 White House report concluded that the war on poverty had been highly successful.[29] Based on the supplemental poverty measure, poverty rates in the United States fell from 26 per cent in 1967 to 16 per cent in 2012 —a decline of nearly 40 per cent.[30] The Census Bureau calculates that programmes such as Social Security, refundable tax credits (earned income tax credit), the Supplemental Nutrition Assistance Program, the Supplemental Security Income programme and housing subsidies collectively prevented about 44 million Americans from falling into poverty in 2016.[31]

28. The following sections address shortcomings in both the existing social protection system for the poorest Americans and in the assumptions underlying the administration's policy responses.

An illusory emphasis on employment

29. Proposals to slash the meagre welfare arrangements that currently exist are now sought to be justified primarily on the basis that the poor need to leave welfare and go to work. The assumption, especially in a thriving economy, is that there are a great many jobs out there waiting to be filled by individuals with low educational qualifications, often with disabilities of one kind or another, sometimes burdened with a criminal

record (often poverty related), without meaningful access to health care, and with no training or effective assistance to obtain employment. It also assumes that the jobs they could get will make them independent of state assistance.

30. In reality, the job market for such people is extraordinarily limited, and even more so for those without basic forms of social protection and support. The case of Walmart, the largest employer in the United States, is instructive. Many of its workers cannot survive on a full-time wage in the absence of food stamps. This fits in a broader trend: the share of households that, while having earnings, also receive nutrition assistance rose from 19.6 percent in 1989 to 31.8 percent in 2015.[32] Up to $6 billion annually goes from the Supplemental Nutrition Assistance Program and other public assistance programmes to support workers in firms like Walmart, providing a huge indirect subsidy to the relevant corporations.[33] Walmart lobbied heavily for tax reform,[34] from which it will save billions, and then announced it would spend an additional $700 million in increasing employee wages and benefits for its workers.[35]

But the resulting rise in the debt of the United States, due in part to the tax reform,[36] has then been used to justify a proposed 30 per cent cut in Supplemental Nutrition Assistance Program funding over a decade.[37]

31. In terms of job availability, the reality is very different from that portrayed by the welfare-to-work proponents. Despite the strong economy, there has been a long-term decline in employment rates; by 2017, only 89 per cent of males aged 25 to 54 were employed.[38] While "supply" factors such as growing rates of disability, increasing geographic immobility and higher incarceration rates are relevant, a 2016 White House report concluded that reductions in labour supply were far less important than reductions in labour demand in accounting for the long-run trend.[39] In the future, new technologies, such as self-driving cars, 3D printers and robot-staffed factories and warehouses, may lead to a continuing decline in demand for low-skilled labour. Leading poverty experts have concluded that, because of this rising joblessness, the poverty population in the United States "is becoming a more deprived and destitute class, one that's disconnected from the economy and unable to meet basic needs".[40]

32. Earlier experiments with welfare reform, particularly the Clinton-era replacement of Aid to Families with Dependent Children with the Temporary Assistance for Needy Families programme, should caution present-day proponents of "welfare to work". The impact of the 1996 welfare reform on poor, single mothers has been especially dramatic. Many took low-wage jobs after the reform and "the increase in their earnings was often cancelled out by their loss of welfare benefits, leaving their overall income relatively unchanged."[41] The situation of single mothers who could not find work deteriorated.[42] As a result, there was a 748(!) per cent increase in the number of children of single-mother families experiencing annual $2-a-day poverty between 1995 and 2012.[43]

Use of fraud as a smokescreen

33. Calls for welfare reform take place against a constant drumbeat of allegations of widespread fraud in the system. Government officials warned the Special Rapporteur that individuals are constantly coming up with new schemes to live high on the welfare hog, and that individual states are gaming the welfare system to cheat the federal Government. The contrast with tax reform is instructive. In the tax context, immense faith is placed in the goodwill and altruism of the corporate beneficiaries, while with welfare reform the opposite assumptions apply. The reality, of course, is that there are good and bad corporate actors and there are good and bad welfare claimants. But while funding for the Internal Revenue Service to audit wealthy taxpayers has been reduced, efforts to identify welfare fraud are being greatly intensified.[44] Revelations of widespread tax avoidance by companies and high-wealth individuals draw no rebuke, only acquiescence and the maintenance of the loopholes and other arrangements designed to facilitate such arrangements. But revelations of food stamps being used for purposes other than staying alive draw howls of outrage from government officials and their media supporters.

34. Yet, despite repeated requests to officials for statistics on welfare fraud, the Special Rapporteur has received little convincing evidence. The Government collects data on "improper payments" made by federal departments and agencies, but this is a much broader concept than fraud. A 2016 Government Accountability Office report showed an error rate in 2015 of 3.66 per cent for the Supplemental Nutrition Assistance

Program and 4.01 per cent for public housing and rental assistance. By contrast, the error rate for travel pay by the Department of Defense was 8 percent.[45]

35. The percentage of Supplemental Nutrition Assistance Program benefit dollars issued to ineligible households or to eligible households in excessive amounts was as low as 2.96 per cent in 2014.[46]According to the Center on Budget and Policy Priorities, the overwhelming majority of those errors result from mistakes by different parties, rather than from dishonesty or fraud by recipients.[47]Almost 60 per cent of the dollar value of overpayments by states resulted from mistakes by the government, rather than recipients.[48] In 2015, 55 per cent of 723,111 investigations found no fraud.[49]

36. Fraud rhetoric is commonly used against persons with disabilities, large numbers of whom allegedly receive disability allowances when they could actually be working full time. When the Special Rapporteur probed into the reasons for the very high rates of persons with disabilities in West Virginia receiving benefits, government officials explained that most recipients had attained low levels of education, worked in demanding manual labour jobs and were often exposed to risks that employers were not required to guard against.

Social protection for children

37. Appropriate cognitive and socio-emotional stimulation, adequate nutrition and health care, and stable and secure environments early in life are all essential ingredients in maximizing children's potential and achieving optimal life outcomes. Empirical evidence suggests strong correlations between early childhood poverty and adverse life outcomes, particularly those related to achievement skills and cognitive development.

38. From this perspective, the shockingly high number of children living in poverty in the United States demands urgent attention. In 2016, 18 percent of children (13.3 million) were living in poverty, and children comprised 32.6 per cent of all people in poverty.[50]About 20 per cent of children live in relative income poverty, compared to the OECD average of 13 per cent.[51] Contrary to stereotypical assumptions, 31 per cent of poor children are White, 24 per cent are Black, 36 per cent are Hispanic

and 1 per cent are indigenous.[52] This is consistent with the fact that the United States ranks 25th out of 29 industrialized nations in investing in early childhood education.[53]

39. Poor children are also significantly affected by the country's crises regarding affordable and adequate housing. On a given night in 2017, about 21 per cent (or 114,829) of homeless individuals were children.[54] But this official figure may be a severe underestimate, since homeless children temporarily staying with friends, family or in motels are excluded from the point-in-time count.[55] According to the Department of Education, the number of homeless students identified as experiencing homelessness at some point during the 2015/16 school year was 1,304,803.[56]

40. The infant mortality rate, at 5.8 deaths per 1,000 live births, is almost 50 per cent higher than the OECD average of 3.9.[57] On a positive note, the United States has increased health insurance coverage for children through the expansion of Medicaid and the Children's Health Insurance Program, bringing child health insurance rates to a historic high of 95 per cent.[58] These achievements are, however, under threat, as discussed below.

41. In addition, the Supplemental Nutrition Assistance Program kept 3.8 million children out of poverty in 2015,[59] and in 2016, the earned income tax credit and the child tax credit lifted a further 4.7 million children out of poverty.[60] By contrast, the reach and impact of the Temporary Assistance for Needy Families programme has been very limited. In 2016, only 23 per cent of families in poverty received cash assistance from that programme, and the figure is less than 10 per cent in a growing number of states.[61]

Adult dental care

42. The Affordable Care Act greatly expanded the availability of dental care to children, but not for adults. Some 49 million Americans live in federally designated "dental professional shortage areas" and Medicare (the programme for the aged and those with disabilities) does not cover routine dental care.[62] The only access to dental care for the uninsured is through the emergency room, where excruciating pain can lead to an extraction. Even for those with coverage, access is not guaranteed, as

only a minority of dentists see Medicaid patients.[63] Poor oral hygiene and disfiguring dental profiles lead to unemployability in many jobs, being shunned in the community and being left unable to function effectively. Yet there is no universal programme to address those issues, which fundamentally affect the human dignity and ultimately the civil rights of the persons concerned.

C. Reliance on criminalization to conceal the underlying poverty problem

Criminalization of the homeless

43. The official point-in-time estimates of homelessness in 2017 show a nationwide figure of 553,742, including 76,501 in New York, 55,188 in Los Angeles and 6,858 in San Francisco.[64] There is ample evidence that these figures significantly underestimate the actual scale of the problem.

44. In many cities, homeless persons are effectively criminalized for the situation in which they find themselves. Sleeping rough, sitting in public places, panhandling, public urination and myriad other offences have been devised to attack the "blight" of homelessness. The criminalization of homeless individuals in cities that provide almost zero public toilets seems particularly callous. In June 2017, it was reported that the approximately 1,800 homeless individuals on Skid Row in Los Angeles had access to only nine public toilets.[65] Los Angeles failed to meet even the minimum standards the United Nations High Commissioner for Refugees sets for refugee camps in the Syrian Arab Republic and other emergency situations.[66]

45. Ever more demanding and intrusive regulations lead to infraction notices for the homeless, which rapidly turn into misdemeanours, leading to warrants, incarceration, unpayable fines and the stigma of a criminal conviction that in turn virtually prevents subsequent employment and access to most housing. Yet the authorities in cities such as Los Angeles and San Francisco often encourage this vicious circle. On Skid Row in Los Angeles, 14,000 homeless persons were arrested in 2016 alone, an increase of 31 per cent over 2011, while overall arrests in the city decreased by 15 per cent.[67] Citizens and local authorities, rather than treating homeless persons as affronts to their sensibilities and neighbourhoods, should see in their presence a tragic

indictment of community and government policies. Homelessness on this scale is far from inevitable and reflects political choices to see the solution as law enforcement rather than adequate and accessible low-cost housing, medical treatment, psychological counselling and job training.[68] The Right to Rest Act introduced in California, Colorado and Oregon is an example of the type of legislative approach needed to shift from the criminal justice response to a human rights-centred response to homelessness.

46. As the Special Rapporteur explained in more detail in his 15 December 2017 statement,[69] coordinated entry systems to match housing supply for the homeless to demand have been introduced in Los Angeles, San Francisco and elsewhere. These are premised partly on the idea that homelessness is a data problem and that new information technologies are key to solving it.[70] But despite the good intentions behind them, including the reduction of duplication and fragmentation in service delivery, coordinated entry systems simply replicate many problems associated with existing policy responses. They contribute to the process of criminalization by requiring the homeless to take part in an intrusive survey that makes many feel they "are giving up their human right to privacy in return for their human right to housing."[71] Many participants fear that police forces have access to data collected from the homeless; it could be concluded from conversations between the Special Rapporteur and officials and experts that this fear may well be justified. The introduction of coordinated entry systems has also been criticized for being costly and diverting resources and attention away from the key problem, which is the lack of available housing for those in need.[72] New information technology-based solutions, such as coordinated entry systems, might bring improved reliability and objectivity, but the vulnerability scores they produce have been challenged for their randomness.[73]

Treatment of the poor in the criminal justice system

47. In many cities and counties, the criminal justice system is effectively a system for keeping the poor in poverty while generating revenue to fund not only the justice system but many other programmes. The use of the legal system to raise revenue, not to promote justice, as was documented so powerfully in a 2015 report on Ferguson, Missouri by the Department of Justice[74] is pervasive around the country.

48. So-called fines and fees are piled up so that low level infractions become immensely burdensome, a process that affects only the poorest members of society, who pay the vast majority of such penalties. Driving licences are also commonly suspended for a wide range of non-driving related offences, such as a failure to pay fines.[75] This is a perfect way to ensure that the poor, living in communities that have steadfastly refused to invest in serious public transport systems, are unable to earn a living that might have helped to pay the outstanding debt. Two paths are open: penury, or driving illegally, thus risking even more serious and counterproductive criminalization.

49. Another practice that affects the poor almost exclusively is that of setting large bail bonds for a defendant who seeks to go free pending trial. Some 11 million people are admitted to local jails annually, and on any given day more than 730,000 people are being held, of whom almost two thirds are awaiting trial, and thus presumed to be innocent. Yet judges have increasingly set large bail amounts, which means that wealthy defendants can secure their freedom while poor defendants are likely to stay in jail, with severe consequences such as loss of jobs, disruption of childcare, inability to pay rent and deeper destitution.

50. A major movement to eliminate bail bonds is gathering steam across the United States, and needs to be embraced by anyone concerned about the utterly disproportionate negative impact of the justice system upon the poor. The purpose of the reform is to link pretrial detention to risk rather than wealth. A growing number of jurisdictions are adopting risk assessment tools to assist in pretrial release and custody decisions. This is a positive development, but the widespread use of risk assessment tools also raises human rights concerns.

51. The fear is that highly political questions about the level of risk that society considers acceptable are hidden behind the veneer of technical design choices, that obscure algorithms disproportionally identify poor defendants as "high risk" by replicating the biased assumptions of previous human decision makers,[76] and that private contractors who develop risk assessment tools will refuse to divulge their content on the grounds that the information is proprietary, which leads to serious due process concerns affecting the civil rights of the poor in the criminal justice system.[77]

52. Solutions to major social challenges in the United States are increasingly seen to lie with privatization, especially in the criminal justice system. Bail bond corporations, which exist in only one other country in the world, precisely because they distort justice, encourage excessive and often unnecessary levels of bail, and lobby for the maintenance of a system that by definition penalizes the middle class and the poor.[78]

53. In some states, minor offences are routinely punished by placing the offender on probation, overseen by a for-profit corporation, entirely at the expense of the usually poor offender. Those who cannot pay are subject to additional fees, supervision and testing.[79] Similarly, in 26 states judges issue arrest warrants for alleged debtors at the request of private debt collectors, thus violating the law and human rights standards. The practice affects primarily the poor by subjecting them to court appearances, arrest warrants that appear on background checks, and jail time, which interfere with their wages, their jobs, their ability to find housing and more.[80]

D. Persistent discrimination and poverty

Race

54. The United States remains a chronically segregated society. Blacks are 2.5 times more likely than Whites to be living in poverty, their infant mortality rate is 2.3 times that of Whites, their unemployment rate is more than double that for Whites, they typically earn only 82.5 cents for every dollar earned by a White counterpart, their household earnings are on average well under two thirds of those of their White equivalents, and their incarceration rates are 6.4 times higher than those of Whites.[81] These shameful statistics can only be explained by long-standing structural discrimination on the basis of race, reflecting the enduring legacy of slavery.[82]

55. Ironically, politicians and mainstream media portrayals distort this situation in order to suggest that poverty in America is overwhelmingly Black, thereby triggering a range of racist responses and encouraging Whites to see poverty as a question of race. Too often the loaded and inaccurate message that parts of the media want to convey is "lazy Blacks sponge off hard-working Whites."

Gender

56. Women often experience the burdens of poverty in particularly harsh ways. Poor pregnant women who seek Medicaid prenatal care are subjected to interrogations of a highly sensitive and personal nature, effectively surrendering their privacy rights.[83] Low-income women who would like to exercise their constitutional, privacy-derived right to access abortion services face legal and practical obstacles, such as mandatory waiting periods and long driving distances to clinics. This lack of access to abortion services traps many women in cycles of poverty.[84] When a child is born to a woman living in poverty, that woman is more likely to be investigated by the child welfare system and have her child taken away from her.[85] Poverty is frequently treated as a form of "child neglect" and thus as cause to remove a child from the home,[86] a risk exacerbated by the fact that some states do not provide legal aid in child welfare proceedings.[87]

57. Racial discrimination makes matters even worse for many poor women. Black women with cervical cancer—a disease that can easily be prevented or cured—have lower survival rates than White women, due to later diagnosis and treatment differences,[88] owing to a lack of health insurance and regular access to health care. The United States has the highest maternal mortality ratio among wealthy countries, and black women are three to four times more likely to die than White women. In one city, the rate for Blacks was 12 times higher than that for Whites.[89]

58. In rural areas, women face significantly higher poverty rates, as well as related child poverty.[90] In economically depressed areas of the Midwest, rural Appalachia and the deep south unemployment is high and essential services, such as childcare, health care and grocery stores, are unavailable or difficult to access.[91] A lack of adequate public transport means that families are unable to access decent supermarkets and instead rely predominantly on expensive and poorly stocked local stores. In general, poor women and their children are more likely to be obese and suffer serious health issues and non-communicable diseases that hinder them for the rest of their lives.[92]

59. Female immigrants, who often suffer racial discrimination from employers and find it more difficult to get jobs, experience higher poverty rates and have much less access to social protection benefits than other

women.[93] Undocumented women live a kind of half-life, in which they experience exploitation, abuse and wage theft, and are refused access to utilities such as water, but are unable to seek assistance or protection for fear of deportation.[94] While their undocumented status raises difficult legal and policy questions, their shadow existence as mothers of United States citizens and as domestic, sex or other workers undermines their ability to live a life in dignity. Even many permanent residents who have lived in the United States for less than five years are excluded from coverage under the Affordable Care Act[95] and assistance such as the Supplemental Nutrition Assistance Program, the Temporary Assistance for Needy Families programme and housing benefits.[96]

60. Lack of Internet connectivity in rural impoverished communities negatively affects access to social protection benefits, other government services and even employment.[97] In West Virginia, where an estimated 30 per cent of the population lack access to high speed broadband (compared to 10 percent nationally) and 48 percent of rural West Virginians lack such access (compared to 39 percent of the rural population nationally),[98] the government has no serious plans to improve access.

Indigenous peoples

61. The Special Rapporteur heard testimonies from Chiefs and representatives of federally recognized and non-recognized tribes on widespread extreme poverty in their communities. Indigenous peoples, as a group, suffer disproportionately from multidimensional poverty and social exclusion. The 2016 poverty rate among American Indian and Alaska Native peoples was 26.2 per cent, the highest among all ethnic groups.[99] Indigenous peoples also have the highest unemployment rate of any ethnic group: 12 per cent in 2016, compared to the national average of 5.8 percent.[100] One in four indigenous young people aged 16 to 24 are neither enrolled in school nor working.[101]

62. Disparities between indigenous and non-indigenous health status have long been recognized but not effectively addressed. American Indians and Alaska Natives face almost a 50 per cent higher death rate than do non-Hispanic White people, due to illnesses such as heart disease, cancer, chronic liver disease and diabetes.[102] Poverty, unemployment, social exclusion and loss of cultural identity also have significant mental health ramifications and often lead to a higher prevalence of substance

abuse, domestic violence and alarmingly high suicide rates in indigenous communities, particularly among young people. Suicide is the second leading cause of death among American Indians and Alaska Natives aged between 10 and 34.[103]

63. In entering a "trust relationship" with the recognized tribes, the Government assumed duties to provide for economic and social programmes to ensure the welfare of the relevant indigenous groups.[104] But their very high poverty rates attest to the Government's failure in this respect. Chronic underfunding of the relevant federal government departments is a significant part of the problem.[105] The situation has also been compounded by paternalistic attitudes,[106] which run directly counter to the approach reflected in international human rights law and standards, particularly the United Nations Declaration on the Rights of Indigenous Peoples, which the Government endorsed in 2010.

64. The situation of non-federally recognized tribes is even more desperate, for they are not eligible to benefit from federally funded programmes. While 567 tribes are federally recognized, some 400 are not.[107] The latter exist in a context in which their way of life is not legally sanctioned, they are disempowered and their culture is threatened. Failure to collect disaggregated data for those tribes also hinders the development of evidence-based policies to address their situation.

E. Confused and counterproductive drug policies

65. The opioid crisis has devastated many communities, and the addiction to pain-control opioids often leads to heroin, methamphetamine and other substance abuse. Instead of responding with increased funding and improved access to vital care and support, the federal Government and many state governments have instead mounted concerted campaigns to reduce and restrict access to health care by the poorer members of the population.[108]

66. In terms of welfare, the main responses have been punitive. States increasingly seek to impose drug tests on recipients of welfare benefits, with programmes that lead to expulsion from the programme for repeat offenders. Others have introduced severe punishments for pregnant women who abuse drugs. Medical professionals recognize that such policies are counterproductive, highly intrusive and misplaced. The urge

to punish rather than assist the poor often also has racial undertones, as in the contrast between the huge sentences handed down to those using drugs such as crack cocaine (predominantly Black) and those using opioids (overwhelmingly White).

F. Environmental pollution

67. Poor rural communities throughout the United States are often located close to polluting industries that pose an imminent and persistent threat to their human right to health.[109] At the same time, poor communities benefit very little from these industries, which they effectively subsidize because of the low tax rates offered by local governments to the relevant corporations.

68. Poor communities suffer especially from the effects of exposure to coal ash, which is the toxic remains of coal burned in power plants. It contains chemicals that cause cancer, developmental disorders and reproductive problems,[110] and is reportedly dumped in about 1,400 sites around the United States—70 per cent of which are situated in low-income communities.[111] In Puerto Rico, the Special Rapporteur visited Guayama, where poor communities live close to a plant owned by Applied Energy Systems (AES) that produces coal ash. Community members noted severe negative impacts on their health and economic activities; neither federal nor local authorities had taken action. In March 2018 the Environmental Protection Agency proposed a new rule that would significantly undermine existing inadequate protections against coal ash disposal.

69. In Alabama and West Virginia, a high proportion of the population is not served by public sewerage and water supply services. Contrary to the assumption in most developed countries that such services should be extended by the government systematically and eventually comprehensively to all areas, neither state was able to provide figures as to the magnitude of the challenge or details of any planned government response.

VII. Conclusions and recommendations

70. The following analysis focuses primarily on the federal level. It is nonetheless ironic that those who fight hardest to uphold state rights also fight hard to deny city and county rights. If the rhetoric about encouraging

laboratories of innovation is to be meaningful, the freedom to innovate cannot be restricted to state politicians alone.

1. Decriminalize being poor

71. Punishing and imprisoning the poor is the distinctively American response to poverty in the twenty-first century. Workers who cannot pay their debts, those who cannot afford private probation services, minorities targeted for traffic infractions, the homeless, the mentally ill, fathers who cannot pay child support and many others are all locked up. Mass incarceration is used to make social problems temporarily invisible and to create the mirage of something having been done.

72. It is difficult to imagine a more self-defeating strategy. Federal, state, county and city governments incur vast costs in running jails and prisons. Sometimes these costs are "recovered" from the prisoners, thus fuelling the latter's cycle of poverty and desperation. The criminal records attached to the poor through imprisonment make it even harder for them to find jobs, housing, stability and self-sufficiency. Families are destroyed, children are left parentless and the burden on governments mounts. But because little is done to address the underlying causes of the original problem, it continues to fester. Even when imprisonment is not the preferred option, the standard response to those facing economic hardship is to adopt policies explicitly designed to make access to health care, sick leave and welfare and child benefits more difficult to access and the receipt of benefits more stigmatizing.

73. A cheaper and more humane option is to provide proper social protection and facilitate the return to the workforce of those who are able. In the United States, it is poverty that needs to be arrested, not the poor simply for being poor. Acknowledge the plight of the middle class.

74. Only 36 percent of Republican voters consider that the federal Government should do more to help poor people, and 33 per cent believe that it already does too much.[112] The paradox is that the proposed slashing of social protection benefits will affect the middle classes every bit as much as the poor. Almost a quarter of full-time workers, and three quarters of part-time workers, receive no paid sick leave. Absence from work due to illness thus poses a risk of economic disaster. About 44 per cent of adults either could not cover an emergency expense costing $400

or would need to sell something or borrow money to do it. Over a quarter of all adults are classified as having no access or inadequate access to banking facilities.[113] The impacts of automation, artificial intelligence and the increasing fluidity of work arrangements mean that employer-provided social protection will likely disappear for the middle classes in the years ahead. If this coincides with dramatic cutbacks in government benefits, the middle classes will suffer an ever more precarious economic existence, with major negative implications for the economy as a whole, for levels of popular discontent and for political stability.

3. Acknowledge the damaging consequences of extreme inequality

75. The United States already leads the developed world in income and wealth inequality, and it is now moving full steam ahead to make itself even more unequal. But this is a race that no one else would want to win, since almost all other nations, and all the major international institutions, such as OECD, the World Bank and IMF, have recognized that extreme inequalities are economically inefficient and socially damaging. The trajectory of the United States since 1980 is shocking. In both Europe and the United States, the richest 1 per cent earned around 10 per cent of national income in 1980. By 2017 that had risen slightly in Europe to 12 per cent, but massively in the United States, to 20 per cent. Since 1980 annual income earnings for the top 1 per cent in the United States have risen 205 per cent, while for the top 0.001 per cent the figure is 636 per cent. By comparison, the average annual wage of the bottom 50 per cent has stagnated since 1980.[114]

76. The problem is that "inequality" lacks salience with the general public, who have long been encouraged to admire the conspicuous, and often obscene, consumption of billionaires and celebrities. What extreme inequality actually signifies is the transfer of economic and political power to a handful of elites who inevitably use it to further their own self-interest, as demonstrated by the situation in various countries around the world. While the poor suffer, so too do the middle class, and so does the economy as a whole. High inequality undermines sustained economic growth. It manifests itself in poor education levels, in adequate health care and the absence of social protection for the middle class and the poor, which in turn limits their economic opportunities and inhibits overall growth.

77. Extreme inequality often leads to the capture of the powers of the State by a small group of economic elites. The combined wealth of the United States Cabinet is around $4.3 billion. As noted by Forbes: "America's first billionaire president has remained devoted to the goal of placing his wealthy friends in his Cabinet, a top campaign promise."[115] And many regulatory agencies are now staffed by "political appointees with deep industry ties and potential conflicts".[116] Extreme inequality thus poses a threat not just to economic efficiency but to the well-being of American democracy.

4. Recognize a right to health care

78. Health care is, in fact, a human right. The civil and political rights of the middle class and the poor are fundamentally undermined if they are unable to function effectively, which includes working, because of a lack of the access to health care that every human being needs. The Affordable Care Act was a good start, although it was limited and flawed from the outset. Undermining it by stealth is not just inhumane and a violation of human rights, but an economically and socially destructive policy aimed at the poor and the middle class.

5. Get real about taxes

79. At the state level, the demonizing of taxation means that legislatures effectively refuse to levy taxes even when there is a desperate need. Instead they impose fees and fines through the back door, some of which fund the justice system and others of which go to fund the pet projects of legislators. This sleight-of-hand technique is a winner, in the sense that the politically powerful rich get to pay low taxes, while the politically marginalized poor bear the burden but can do nothing about it. There is a real need for the realization to sink in among the majority of the American population that taxes are not only in their interest, but also perfectly reconcilable with a growth agenda. A much-cited IMF paper concluded that redistribution could be good for growth, stating: "The combined direct and indirect effects of redistribution—including the growth effects of the resulting lower inequality—are on average pro-growth."[117]

ENDNOTES

1   The Special Rapporteur is grateful for the superb research and analysis undertaken by Christiaan van Veen, Anna Bulman, Ria Singh Sawhney and staff of the United Nations Office of the High Commissioner for Human Rights.

2   Submissions available at www.ohchr.org/EN/Issues/Poverty/Pages/Callforinput.aspx.

3   See, for example: Kathryn J. Edin and H. Luke Shaefer, *$2.00 a Day: Living on Almost Nothing in America* (New York, Mariner Books, 2016); Matthew Desmond, *Evicted: Poverty and Profit in the American City* (New York, Crown Publishers, 2016); Sasha Abramsky, *The American Way of Poverty: How the Other Half Still Lives* (New York, Nation Books, 2013); and Peter Edelman, *Not a Crime to Be Poor: The Criminalization of Poverty in America* (The New Press, New York, 2017).

4   Jessica L. Semega, Kayla R. Fontenot and Melissa A. Kollar, Income and Poverty in the United States: 2016—Current Population Reports (United States Census Bureau, September 2017), pp. 12 and 17. Available at www.census.gov/content/dam/Census/library/publications/2017/demo/P60-259.pdf. See also Angus Deaton, "The U.S. can no longer hide from its deep poverty problem", *New York Times*, 24 January 2018.

5   World Income Inequality Database, available at www.wider.unu.edu/project/wiid-world-income-inequality-database.

6   See www.forbes.com/sites/forbespr/2018/03/06/forbes-32nd-annual-worlds-billionaires-issue/#43e9e95a10e0.

7   In the present report, references to race or ethnicity include the following classifications used by the United States Census Bureau: American Indian or Alaska Native, Asian, Black and White (see www.census.gov/topics/population/race/about.html).

8   IMF, "United States: staff report for the 2017 Article IV Consultation", para. 14.

9   Jesse Bricker and others, "Changes in U.S. family finances from 2013 to 2016: evidence from the Survey of Consumer Finances", Federal Reserve Bulletin (September 2017), vol. 103, No. 3, p. 10.

10   IMF, "United States: staff report", para. 18

11   Raj Chetty and others, "The fading American dream: trends in absolute income mobility since 1940", National Bureau of Economic Research Working Paper 22910 (December 2016), p. 2. See also Jonathan Davis and Bhashkar Mazumder, "The decline in intergenerational mobility after 1980", Opportunity & Inclusive Growth Institute working paper (29 March 2017), available at www.minneapolisfed.org/institute/working-papers/17-21.pdf.

12   Executive Office of the President, National Science and Technology Council Committee on Technology, "Preparing for the future of artificial intelligence"(October 2016), p. 1. See also Elisabeth A. Mason, "A.I. and big data could power a new war on poverty", *New York Times*, 1 January 2018.

13   Charles Varner, Marybeth Mattingly and David Grusky, "The facts behind the visions", Pathways (Spring 2017), p. 4.

14   Cathy O'Neil, "The ivory tower can't keep ignoring tech", *New York Times*, 14

November 2017

15 The United States is the only country in the world that has not ratified the Convention on the Rights of the Child, which protects the economic and social rights of children.

16 Semega, Fontenot and Kollar, Income and Poverty, p. 12.

17 Ibid., p. 43.

18 Written submission by the Georgetown Center on Poverty and Inequality, 4 October 2017, p. 2.

19 Semega, Fontenot and Kollar, Income and Poverty, p. 12.

20 Liana Fox, "The supplemental poverty measure" (September 2017), p. 1. Available at www.census.gov/content/dam/Census/library/publications/2017/demo/p60-261.pdf.

21 The Sentencing Project, "6 million lost voters: state-level estimates of felony disenfranchisement, 2016".

22 Marc Meredith and Michael Morse, "Discretionary disenfranchisement: the case of legal financial obligations" (January 2017). Available at www.sas.upenn.edu/~marcmere/workingpapers/DiscretionaryLFOs.pdf.

23 Pew Research Center, "U.S. trails most developed countries in voter turnout" (15 May 2017).

24 See also Karen Long Jusko, *Who Speaks for the Poor? Electoral Geography, Party Entry, and Representation* (Cambridge University Press, 2017).

25 See, for example, Task Force on Poverty, Opportunity, and Upward Mobility, A Better Way: Our Vision for a Confident America (June, 2016).

26 Ibid.

27 David Morgan, "Speaker Ryan pledges to work with Trump on bold agenda", Reuters, 9 November 2016.

28 Office of Management and Budget, Efficient, Effective, Accountable: An American Budget (2018), p. 3.

29 Council of Economic Advisors, The War on Poverty 50 Years Later: A Progress Report (2014), p. 45.

30 Christopher T. Wimer and others, "Trends in poverty with an anchored supplemental poverty measure", Colombia Population Research Center working paper (2013

31 Fox, "The Supplemental Poverty Measure", p. 10.

32 See www.ers.usda.gov/data-products/chart-gallery/gallery/chart-detail/?chartId=82672.

33 Clare O'Connor, "Report: Walmart workers cost taxpayers $6.2 billion in public assistance", *Forbes*, 15 April 2014.

34 Center for Responsive Politics, reporting on lobbying activity on tax issues in 2017. Available at www.opensecrets.org/lobby/issuesum.php?id=TAX&year=2017.

35 Michael Corkery, "Walmart's bumpy day: from wage increase to store closings", *New York Times*, 11 January 2018.

36 "Growing the deficit: the Senate passes a tax bill", *Economist*, 2 December 2017.

37 Julie Hirschfeld Davis, "White House proposes $4.4 trillion budget that adds $7

trillion to deficits," *New York Times*, 12 February 2018.

38   Varner, Mattingly and Grusky, "The facts", p. 4.

39   Council of Economic Advisers, "The long-term decline in prime-age male labor force participation" (2016).

40   Varner, Mattingly and Grusky, "The facts", p. 4.

41   Robert A. Moffitt and Stephanie Garlow, "Did welfare reform increase employment and reduce poverty?" *Pathways* (Winter, 2018), p. 19.

42   Ibid.

43   H. Luke Shaefer and Kathryn Edin, "Welfare reform and the families it left behind", *Pathways* (Winter, 2018), p. 24.

44   Arthur Delaney, "Rich fraud, poor fraud: the GOP's double standard on tax mistakes", *Huffington Post*, 14 December 2017.

45   United States Government Accountability Office, report to Congressional committees on improper payments (June 2016), appendix III.

46   See https://fns-prod.azureedge.net/sites/default/files/snap/2014-rates.pdf. See also Center on Budget and Policy Priorities, "SNAP: combating fraud and improving program integrity without weakening success", 9 June 2016, p. 10. Available at www.cbpp.org/sites/default/files/atoms/files/6-9-16fa-testimony. pdf.

47   Center on Budget and Policy Priorities, "SNAP: combating fraud", p. 11.

48   Ibid.

49   See https://fns-prod.azureedge.net/sites/default/files/snap/2015-State-Activity-Report.pdf.

50   Semega, Fontenot and Kollar, Income and Poverty, p. 14.

51   OECD, "How does United States compare on child well-being?"(November 2017).

52   Heather Koball and Yang Jiang, "Basic facts about low-income children: children under 18 years, 2016"(National Center for Children in Poverty, January 2018).

53   Robert Wood Johnston Foundation, "Can early childhood interventions improve health and well-being?"(March 2016).

54   United States, Department of Housing and Urban Development, The 2017 Annual Homeless Assessment Report (AHAR) to Congress, Part 1: Point-in-time estimates of Homelessness, p. 8.

55   Madeline Daniels, "Housing Department's count of homeless children and youth problematic", 19 November 2015. Available from https://campaignfor-children.org/news/press-release/housing-departth-problematic/.

56   National Center for Homeless Education, Federal Data Summary: School Years 2013–14 to 2015–16, p.iii.

57   OECD, "How does United States compare".

58   Joan Alker and Alisa Chester, "Children's health coverage rate now at historic high of 95 percent" (Georgetown University Health Policy Institute, October 2016).

59   Centeron Budget and Policy Priorities, "Policy basics: the Supplemental Nutrition Assistance Program (SNAP)" (February 2018).

60   Center on Budget and Policy Priorities, "Policy basics: the child tax credit"

(October 2017).

61   Center on Budget and Policy Priorities, "TANF reaching few poor families" (December 2017).

62   Mary Otto, *Teeth: The Story of Beauty, Inequality, and the Struggle for Oral Health in America* (New York, The New Press, 2017), p. vii.

63   Ibid., pp. 37, 120 and 171.

64   United States, Department of Housing and Urban Development, The 2017 Annual Homeless Assessment Report.

65   Alastair Gee, "At night on Skid Row, nearly 2,000 homeless people share just nine toilets", *The Guardian*, 30 June 2017.

66   See https://emergency.unhcr.org/entry/33015/emergency-sanitation-standard.

67   Gale Holland and Christine Zhang, "Huge increase in arrests of homeless in L.A. –but mostly for minor offenses", *Los Angeles Times*, 4 February 2018.

68   See, for example, Gary Blasi and Phillip Mangano, "Stop punishing and start helping L.A.'s homeless", *Los Angeles Times*, 30 June 2015.

69   See paras. 54–61. Available at www.ohchr.org/EN/NewsEvents/Pages/DisplayNews.aspx?NewsID=22533&LangID=E.

70   See, for example, City of Los Angeles, Comprehensive Homeless Strategy (2016), p. 49.

71   Statement made during a civil society consultation, San Francisco, 6 December 2017.

72   A recent publication estimated that in Los Angeles alone the coordinated entry system had cost about $11 million since its introduction, including only the cost of technical resources, software and extra personnel, not the cost of providing actual housing or services. (Virginia Eubanks, *Automating Inequality* (New York, St. Martin's Press, 2018), p. 113.

73   Ibid., chap. 3.

74   See   www.justice.gov/sites/default/files/opa/press-releases/attachments/2015/03/04/ferguson_police_department_report.pdf.

75   See, for example, Lawyers'Committee for Civil Rights of the San Francisco Bay Area and others, "Not just a Ferguson problem: how traffic courts drive inequality in California"(2015)

76   Written submission to the Special Rapporteur from Edward W. Felten and Bendert Zevenbergen, Princeton University.77AI Now, "AI Now 2017 report".

78   See, for example, www.hrw.org/report/2018/02/20/set-fail/impact-offender-funded-private-probation-poor.

79   Human Rights Watch, "Set up to Fail": The Impact of Offender-Funded Private Probation on the Poor (2018).

80   American Civil Liberties Union, "First-ever national report on widespread court practices that coerce payments from people in debt without due process", February 2018. See also American Civil Liberties Union, *A Pound of Flesh: The Criminalization of Private Debt* (2018).

81   Economic Policy Institute, "50 years after the Kerner Commission" (26 February 2018). See also Fred Harris and Alan Curtis (eds.), *Healing Our Divided Society* (Temple University Press, 2018).

82   Center for American Progress, "Systematic inequality: how America's structur-

al racism helped create the black-white wealth gap" (2018). See also Tommie Shelby, *Dark Ghettos: Injustice, Dissent and Reform* (Belknap Press, 2016).

83 Khiara M. Bridges, *The Poverty of Privacy Rights* (Stanford University Press, 2017).

84 Diana Greene Foster and others, "Socioeconomic outcomes of women who receive and women who are denied wanted abortions in the United States", *American Journal of Public Health*, vol. 108, No. 3 (March 2018), p. 407.

85 Written submissions to the Special Rapporteur from National Advocates for Pregnant Women and the Center for Reproductive Rights.

86 Maren K. Dale, "Addressing the underlying issue of poverty in child-neglect cases" (10 April 2014). Available at www.americanbar.org/aba.html.

87 Written submission to the Special Rapporteur from National Advocates for Pregnant Women.

88 Wonsuk Yoo and others, "Recent trends in racial and regional disparities in cervical cancer incidence and mortality in United States", *PLOS ONE*, vol.12, No. 2 (February 2017).

89 New York City Department of Health and Mental Hygiene, Pregnancy-Associated Mortality: New York City, 2006–2010. Available from www1.nyc.gov/assets/doh/downloads/pdf/ms/pregnancy-associated-mortality-report.pdf.

90 See, for example, Southern Rural Black Women's Initiative for Economic and Social Justice, Unequal Lives: The State of Black Women and Families in the Rural South, p. 6.

91 Lisa R. Pruitt and Janet L. Wallace, "Judging parents, judging place: poverty, rurality and termination of parental rights", Missouri Law Review, vol. 77 (2011),p. 117.

92 See, for example, Southern Rural Black Women's Initiative for Economic and Social Justice, Unequal Lives.

93 See www.migrationpolicy.org/article/immigrant-women-united-states#Poverty.

94 Written submission to the Special Rapporteur from the Miami Workers Center and others on the feminization of poverty in Miami; Azadeh Shahshahani and Kathryn Madison, "No papers? You can't have water: a critique of localities' denial of utilities to undocumented immigrants", *Emory International Law Review*, vol. 31, No. 4(2017),

95 Samantha Artiga and Anthony Damico, Health Coverage and Care for Immigrants, issue brief (The Henry J. Kaiser Family Foundation, 2017).

9 6See, for example, the submission from the Miami Workers Center and others, and Shahshahani and Madison, "No papers?".

97 See, for example, the written submission to the Special Rapporteur from Access Now. Broadband access is also seriously lacking in the South (Southern Rural Black Women's Initiative for Economic and Social Justice, Unequal Lives, p. 16).

98 West Virginia Center on Budget and Policy and American Friends Service Committee, 2016 State of Working West Virginia: Why is West Virginia so Poor?, p. 55.

99 United States Census Bureau, "American Indian and Alaska Native Heritage — Month: November 2017". Available at www.census.gov/content/dam/Census/

newsroom/facts-for-features/2017/cb17-ff20.pdf.

100   The Aspen Institute, 2017 State of Native Youth Report: Our Identities as Civic Power, p. 33.

101   Ibid., p. 37.

102   David Espey and others, "Leading causes of death and all-cause mortality in American Indians and Alaska Natives", American Journal of Public Health (June 2014), vol. 104, No. S3.

103   Centers for Disease Control and Prevention, Leading Causes of Death Reports, 1981–2016.

104   See www.acf.hhs.gov/ana/resource/american-indians-and-alaska-natives-the-trust-responsibility.

105   See, for example, United States Government Accountability Office, Progress on Many High-Risk Areas, While Substantial Efforts Needed on Others, report to congressional committees (February 2017). Available at https://www.gao.gov/assets/690/682765.pdf.

106   See A/HRC/21/47/Add.1, para. 15.

107   United States Government Accountability Office, Federal Funding for Non-Federally Recognized Tribes (April 2012). Available at www.gao.gov/assets/600/590102.pdf.

108   See, for example, Debra E. Houry, Tamara M. Haegerich and Alana Vivolo-Kantor, "Opportunities for prevention and intervention of opioid overdose in the emergency department", Annals of Emergency Medicine (2018)

109   Bill Chameides, "A look at environmental justice in the United States today,"Huffington Post Blog, 20 January 2014. Available at www.huffingtonpost.com/bill-chameides/a-look-at-environmental-j_b_4633223.html.

110   Earthjustice, "Fighting for protections from coal ash". Available at https://earthjustice.org/our_work/cases/2012/legal-fight-for-long-overdue-coal-ash-protections.

111   Oliver Milman, "A civil rights 'emergency': justice, clean air and water in the age of Trump", *The Guardian*, 20 November 2017

112   Pew Research Center, "Majorities say Government does too little for older people, the poor and the middle class"(2018). Available at http://assets.pewresearch.org/wp-content/uploads/sites/5/2018/01/30104502/01-30-18-groups-release.pdf.

113   Board of Governors of the Federal Reserve System, Report on the Economic Well-Being of U.S. Households in 2016 (May 2017).

114   Facundo Alvaredo and others, coordinators, World Inequality Report 2018, (World Inequality Lab).

115   Chase Peterson-Withorn, "The $4.3 billion Cabinet: see what each top Trump advisor is worth," *Forbes*, 5 July 2017.

116   D. Ivory and R. Faturechi, "The deep industry ties of Trump's deregulation teams", *New York Times*, 11 July 2017.

CONTRIBUTORS

Sami Al-Arian is a Palestinian-American civil rights activist who was a computer engineering professor and a tenured academic at the University of South Florida receiving several teaching awards and grants. During his four decades in the US (1975-2015), Dr. Al-Arian founded numerous institutions and publications in the fields of education, research, religion and interfaith, as well as civil and human rights. He was a prolific speaker across many US campuses, especially on Palestine, Islam and the West, and Civil Rights. After a contentious interview on FOX News following the September 11 attacks, Dr. Al-Arian's tenure came under attack and his professorship became the most significant academic freedom case since Angela Davis. In 2001, he was named by *Newsweek* the "premiere civil rights activist" in the US for his efforts to repeal the use of Secret Evidence in US immigration courts. He spent over 11 years in prison and under house arrest (2003-2014) before the government had to drop all of the charges. His US story was featured in the 2007 award-winning documentary "USA vs. Al-Arian," and in the 2016 book *Being Palestinian: Personal Reflections on Palestinian Identity in the Diaspora*. Dr. Al-Arian has written dozens of articles that were translated to many languages focusing on US foreign policy, Palestine, and the Arab Spring phenomena. Dr. Al-Arian is currently the director of the Center for Islam and Global Affairs (CIGA) and public affairs professor at Istanbul Zaim University in Turkey.

Baffour Ankomah, former Editor of the London-based *New African* magazine, is a pan-African writer and editor who hails from Ghana but has lived in the Diaspora (principally in the UK and Zimbabwe) for the past 33 years. In 38 years of his journalism career, Africa and its many causes have been his passion. As Editor of New African from 1999 to 2014, he turned the magazine into a veritable mouthpiece of the African continent, a voice which was respected worldwide. His personal column, Baffour's Beefs, which has been running in *New African* since 1987, is a big hit and a must-read for the magazine's worldwide readers. Now based in Zimbabwe, he and his wife Elizabeth run their own media consultancy and fashion house called African Interest which trades under the trademark 'I am African'.

Maribel Aponte-García is Full professor and researcher at the Graduate School of Business and the Social Science Research Center, University of Puerto Rico, Río Piedras Campus; and Caribbean Region Representative, Directing Committee, Latin American Social Science Research Council (CLACSO). She holds a PhD in Economics from the University of Massachusetts at Amherst; and has authored numerous refereed articles on regionalism, value chains and enterprises; one video collection on Cuba; and four books on regionalism and Latin American and Caribbean development. Her most recent works are on Cuba; the Bolivarian Alliance for the Americas; Geopolitics, regionalism, natural resources and chain mapping, for which she was awarded the Ruy Mauro Marini Prize by CLACSO; and food sustainability and trade regimes in Bolivia.

Kevin Barrett, an American Muslim and PhD Islamic Studies scholar, is one of America's best-known critics of the War on Terror. He is the translator and publsher; of *Laurent Guyénot's From Yahweh to Zion* (2018) and has authored and edited several books, including *Orlando False Flag* (2016), *ANOTHER French False Flag* (2016) and *We Are NOT Charlie Hebdo* (2015). Dr. Barrett has appeared many times on Fox, CNN, PBS and other broadcast outlets, and has inspired feature stories and op-eds in the New York Times, the Christian Science Monitor, the Chicago Tribune, and other mainstream publications. A former teacher at colleges and universities in Paris, the San Francisco Bay Area, and Wisconsin, he currently works as author, talk radio host, False Flag Weekly News host, editor at Veterans Today, and TV pundit. His website is TruthJihad. com.

Christopher Black is an international criminal lawyer based in Toronto, Ontario, Canada where he defended accused in a wide variety of criminal offences, including acting as counsel in several murder trials. He was appointed amicus curiae in the Kuldip Singh Samra case in 1993 (the Osgoode Hall shootings) by Mr. Justice John O'Driscoll. He has been involved in high-profile cases involving human rights and war crimes and has defended those accused of these crimes in Rwanda (see Rwandan Genocide) and the former Yugoslavia and is on the list of counsel at the International Criminal Court.

Alba Carosio is professor, doctorate tutor and senior researcher of Postgraduate Studies at the Women´s Studies Center, Central University of Venezuela, so as Senior Researcher at the Rómulo Gallegos Center of Latin American Studies and at the Internacional Center Miranda. In charge of the Venezuelan Review for Women's Studies since 2007, and Venezuelan Representative at Directing Committee, Latin American Social Science Research Council (CLACSO). She holds a PhD in Social Sciences from Central University of Venezuela, and has authored numerous refereed articles on Ethics, Politics, Latin American issues, and Feminist/Gender Studies. Her most recents works are on challenges of Social Sciences and Humanities in Latin America and the Caribbean, contributions of feminist thought and movement and Chavism as movement and political thought.

Thomas Cox is a U.S. citizen who lives in Asia. In December 2015, he conducted an interview of a Viet Nam family, residents of Phong Nha Town in Quang Binh Province, who had been bombarded by Monsanto's Agent Orange being sprayed on them by U.S. planes.

Robin Eastman-Abaya is a Physician, educated in the Philippines at the University of the Philippines during the Marcos Dictatorship. 30 years experience as senior consultant pathologist diagnosing and documenting the overdose and premature death crisis among rural and small town citizens—covering a geographic range of around 13 impoverished and devastated counties in upstate New York. Her interests are documenting the health consequences of social and political decisions in a specific geographic context.

Richard Falk is an American professor emeritus of international law at Princeton University. He is the author or co-author of 30 books and the editor or co-editor of another 30 volumes, In 2008, the United Nations Human Rights Council (UNHRC) appointed Falk to a six-year term as a United Nations Special Rapporteur on "the situation of human rights in the Palestinian territories occupied since 1967." In 2017 UN ESCWA published his report, co-authored with Virginia Tilley, on Israel as an Apartheid State. His most recent books are *Power Shift: On the New Global Order* (2016) and *Revisiting the Vietnam War: Views of Richard Falk* (2017), edited by Stefan Andersson.

Mike Gravel is an American politician who was a Democratic United States Senator from Alaska from 1969 to 1981 and a candidate in the 2008 U.S. presidential election. As a Senator, Gravel became nationally known for his forceful but unsuccessful attempts to end the draft during the War in Vietnam and for putting the Pentagon Papers into the public record in 1971 at some risk to himself.

Danny Haiphong is an anti-imperialist activist and journalist in the NYC area. He is a contributing columnist for Black Agenda Report since 2013. The focus of his work has been on the endless war conducted by US imperialism. Danny sees such war as an extension of the broader class war on the poor and oppressed both in the US and around the world. His articles have been republished in independent outlets such as TruthOut, CounterPunch, and MintPressNews. Danny has also frequently been a guest in CPRnews with Don Debar and Black Agenda Radio with Glen Ford and Nellie Bailey. At the moment, Danny is collaborating on a book tentatively titled *American exceptionalism and American innocence: The Fake News of US Empire* with Professor Roberto Sirvent.

Edward S. Herman, professor emeritus of finance at the Wharton School, University of Pennsylvania, has written extensively on economics, political economy, and the media. Among his books are *Corporate Control, Corporate Power* (1981), *The Real Terror Network* (1982), and, with Noam Chomsky, *The Political Economy of Human Rights* (1979) and *Manufacturing Consent* (2002). Deceased.

Wayne Madsen is an investigative journalist, author and newspaper columnist. He has been a frequent political and national security commentator on television and radio networks. He has some forty years of experience in national security issues, including as a U.S. Naval officer and stints with the National Security Agency, State Department, and Defense Department contractor corporations. He is the author of 15 books on various topics, including data privacy, political corruption, intelligence matters, and genocide.

Charles Onana is a journalist of investigation and essayist Franco-Cameroonian, who is best known for his writings on the genocide in Rwanda, including his 2018 Ph.D. dissertation on the topic. He is also known for his pioneering work on the history of the skirmishes between Africans in the French army during the Second world War. He led the Pan-African Organization of Independent Journalists.

David Peterson is an independent journalist and researcher based in Chicago. He is coauthor, with Edward Herman, of "The Dismantling of Yugoslavia," *Monthly Review* (October 2007).

James Petras is Bartle Professor (Emeritus) of Sociology at Binghamton University in Binghamton, New York and adjunct professor at Saint Mary's University, Halifax, Nova Scotia, Canada who has published on Latin American and Middle Eastern political issues. He is the author of more than 62 books published in 29 languages, and over 600 articles in professional journals, including the *American Sociological Review, British Journal of Sociology, Social Research*, and *Journal of Peasant Studies.*

Alberto Robillato is a Canadian journalist, and former correspondent for Canadian Press, Latin America and Notimex.

Dr. Paul Craig Roberts is a former Assistant Secretary of the US Treasury, member of the US Congressional staff, associate editor and columnist for the Wall Street Journal, and columnist for Business Week, the Scripps Howard News Service, and Creators Syndicate. He has held academic appointments in six universities, including the William E. Simon Chair in Political Economy, Center for

Strategic and International Studies, Georgetown. He has testified before committees of Congress on 30 occasions. He is author or coauthor of twelve books and numerous articles in scholarly journals. Dr. Roberts was awarded the US Treasury's Meritorious Service Award for "outstanding contributions to the formulation of US economic policy," and France's Legion of Honor as "the artisan of a renewal in economic science and policy after half a century of state interventionism" by the government of Francois Mitterrand. His website is www.paulcraigroberts.org.

The Saker was born in a military family of "White" Russian refugees in western Europe where he lived most of his life. After completing two college degrees in the USA, he returned to Europe were he worked as a military analyst until he lost his career due to his vocal opposition to the western-sponsored wars in Chechnia, Croatia, Bosnia and Kosovo. After re-training as a software engineer, he moved to the Florida where he now lives. The Saker is the founder of the Saker Community of Blogs,which now features: 7 blogs (Main, French, Russian, Oceanian, Latin American, Italian, Serbian) written in 7 languages.. The main blog alone gets two to three million page views per month. The international Saker community is composed of about 100 volunteers including professional translators. Articles from the Saker blog are picked up by Russia Insider, the Asia Times, Information Clearing House and many others news sources and our work has been quoted by Paul Craig Roberts, Sheikh Imran Hosein, Pepe Escobar and many others.

Mark Schuller is Associate Professor of Anthropology and Nonprofit and NGO Studies at Northern Illinois University and affiliate at the Faculté d'Ethnologie, l'Université d'État d'Haïti. Schuller's research on NGOs, globalization, disasters, and gender in Haiti has been published in over three dozen book chapters and peer-reviewed articles as well as public media, including a column in *Huffington Post*. He is the author of two monographs, including *Humanitarian Aftershocks in Haiti (Rutgers, 2016)* and co-editor of five volumes, including Tectonic Shifts: Haiti since the Earthquake (Kumarian Press, 2012). He is co-director/co-producer of the documentary Poto Mitan: Haitian Women, Pillars of the Global Economy (2009). Schuller is co-editor of Berghahn Books' *Catastrophes in Context* and University of Alabama Press' *NGOgraphies: a Series of Ethnographic Reflections of NGOs*. Recipient of the Margaret Mead Award and the Anthropology in Media Award, he is active in several solidarity efforts.

Jose Maria Sison is a Filipino patriot, a proletarian revolutionary, professor, and internationalist. He is a Filipino statesman, known for his experience in and knowledge of the people's democratic government and revolutionary forces in the Philippines. He is sometimes consulted by high officials of foreign governments and by presidents, senators, congressmen and local officials of the Philippine reactionary government concerning peace negotiations with the National Democratic Front of the Philippines (NDFP) and related matters. He is recognized as the the foremost thinker and leader of the Filipino people's movement for national liberation and democracy in the last 50 years. Prof. Sison is the Chairperson of the International Coordinating Committee, International League of Peoples' Struggle.

Keith Harmon Snow is the 2009 Regent's Lecturer in Law & Society at the University of California, Santa Barbara, recognized for over a decade of work on war crimes, crimes against humanity and genocide. A photojournalist and war correspondent, he is a three time Project Censored award-winner; the author of the recently published book, *The Worst Interests of the Child*; and his photography is spotlighted on the Social Documentary Network. A presenter at the 65th Annual Conference on World Affairs, he is also a Grof-certified facilitator of Holotropic Breathwork, a Motivational Speaker, and a professional tree climbing instructor. His TED-talk is titled What Are You Waiting For? and his web sites are Conscious Being Alliance and All Things Pass.

S. Brian Willson commanded a United States Air Force combat security unit in Viet Nam. As a lawyer he critiques the US INjustice system and its equally criminal foreign policies. He is the author of *On Third World Legs* and *Blood On the Tracks,* and is featured in two documentaries, The Healing of Brian Willson, and Paying the Price for Peace. He is the recipient of numerous awards for his peace and justice activities, and in addition to his J.D., holds two honorary degrees. While peaceably blocking US munitions destined for Central America, he lost both legs and now walks on prostheses. His essays can be found at brianwillson. com. His book *Don't Thank Me For My Service: My Viet Nam Awakening to the Long History of US Lies* is forthcoming from Clarity Press.

INDEX